[redacted]

The PC System Architecture Series

by MindShare, Inc.

PCI System Architecture
Third Edition

PCMCIA System Architecture
16-Bit PC Cards
Second Edition

CardBus System Architecture

ISA System Architecture
Third Edition

Pentium™ Processor System Architecture
Second Edition

PowerPC™ System Architecture

Plug and Play System Architecture

80486 System Architecture
Third Edition

EISA System Architecture
Second Edition

CARDBUS SYSTEM ARCHITECTURE

MINDSHARE, INC.

Don Anderson
&
Tom Shanley

Addison-Wesley Publishing Company

Reading, Massachusetts • Menlo Park, California • New York
Don Mills, Ontario • Wokingham, England • Amsterdam
Bonn • Sydney • Singapore • Tokyo • Madrid • San Juan
Paris • Seoul • Milan • Mexico City • Taipei

For my wife Sheryl, in appreciation for her friendship, convictions, and support.

Library of Congress Cataloging-in-Publication Data

ISBN: 0-201-40997-6

Sponsoring Editor: Kathleen Tibbetts
Production Coordinator: Ellen Savett
Cover design: Barbara T. Atkinson
Set in 10-point Palatino by MindShare, Inc.

1 2 3 4 5 6 7 8 9 -MA- 99989796
First Printing, December 1995

Contents

About This Book

Part One—Introduction to CardBus

Chapter 1: Overview

Chapter 2: 16-Bit PC Cards— A Review

Contents

Chapter 6: CardBus Signal Interface

Part Three—CardBus Transaction Protocols

Chapter 7: Arbitration

Chapter 8: Intro to CardBus Transfers

Chapter 9: Memory Transfers

Contents

Chapter 17: CardBus Bridge Configuration Registers

Contents

Part Seven—The TI PCI1130 CardBus Bridge Chip

Chapter 23: The TI PCI 1130

Appendix A—CardBus Signaling Environment

Appendix B—PCI & CardBus Differences

Appendix C—References

Appendix D—Glossary

Figures

Figures

Tables

Tables

Acknowledgements

My thanks to those at Motorola GSTD in Scottsdale and National Semiconductor in South Portland, Maine for providing an audience for the first CardBus pilot classes and their thoughtful input regarding the organization and content of this book. Special thanks to Dave Dickens, et al, at Texas Instruments for providing information on their CardBus bridge, for providing many useful suggestions regarding the organization of this book, and for answering many implementation questions. Finally, thanks to John Odendahl of Dell Computer for reviewing key portions of this book.

About This Book

The MindShare Architecture Series

The MindShare Architecture book series includes: *ISA System Architecture, EISA System Architecture, 80486 System Architecture, PCI System Architecture, Pentium System Architecture, PCMCIA System Architecture, PowerPC System Architecture, Plug-and-Play System Architecture,* and *CardBus System Architecture.*

Rather than duplicating common information in each book, the series uses the building-block approach. *ISA System Architecture* is the core book upon which the others build. The figure below illustrates the relationship of the books to each other.

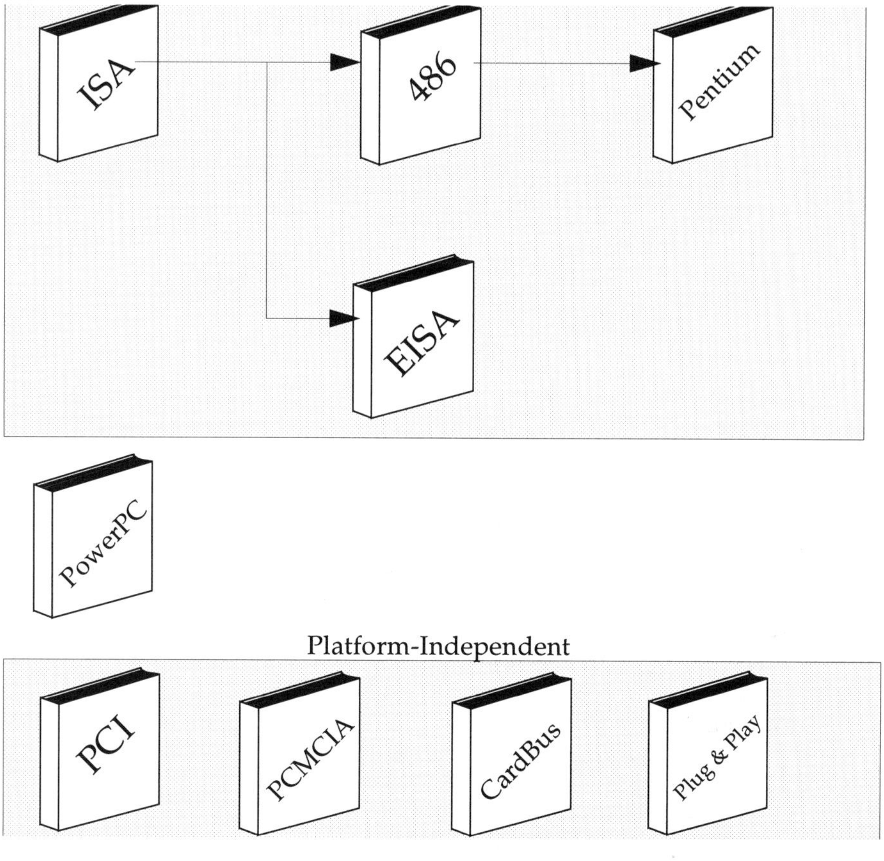

Cautionary Note

The reader should keep in mind that MindShare's book series often deals with rapidly-evolving technologies. This being the case, it should be recognized that the book is a "snapshot" of the state of the targeted technology at the time that the book was completed. We attempt to update each book on a timely basis to reflect changes in the targeted technology, but, due to various factors (waiting for the next version of the spec to be "frozen," the time necessary to make the changes, and the time to produce the books and get them out to the distribution channels), there will always be a delay.

Organization of This Book

CardBus System Architecture extends MindShare's coverage of the PCMCIA environment. The book is divided into seven parts and contains the chapters listed below:

Part I: Introduction to CardBus. Provides PCI and PCMCIA backgrounders and an introduction to CardBus.

Part II: The CardBus Socket Interface. Describes PC Card detection and powerup, as well as an introduction to the CardBus socket signal groups.

Part III: CardBus Transaction Protocols. Covers the following:

- Bus arbitration
- An introduction to CardBus transfers
- Detailed descriptions of memory transfers
- Detailed description of IO transfers
- Locked transfers
- Error handling

Part IV: CardBus Interrupts. Provides a detailed discussion of interrupt implementation for both the CardBus bridge and cards.

Part V: Configuration. Provides detailed descriptions of:

- The configuration process
- Configuration transactions
- CardBus bridge configuration registers
- CardBus card configuration registers
- CardBus card information structure (CIS)

Part VI: CardBus Software. Provides a description of Socket Services (SS), Card Services (CS), and Client Drivers (Enablers).

Part VII: The TI PCI1130 CardBus Bridge Chip. Provides an overview of the Texas Instruments PCI1130 CardBus Bridge.

Appendices. Describe the CardBus electrical signaling environment, the differences between PCI and CardBus, a list of suggested reference material, and a glossary of terms.

Who this Book is For

This book is intended for use by hardware and software design and support personnel. Due to the clear, concise explanatory methods used to describe each subject, personnel outside of the design field may also find the text useful.

Prerequisite Knowledge

It is highly recommended that the reader have a good knowledge of PC and processor bus architecture prior to reading this book, along with a sound knowledge of the 16-Bit PC Card implementations. It is important to note that CardBus technology is heavily-based on PCI and PCMCIA technology. Rather than duplicating a vast amount of information regarding these two foundation technologies in this book, it provides a basic backgrounder on them. The main focus is on the operation of the CardBus bridge and cards and how they differ from their parent technologies. Detailed descriptions of PCI and PCMCIA (now known as PC Card) are available in our books entitled *PCMCIA System Architecture* and *PCI System Architecture.*

Documentation Conventions

This document contains conventions for numeric values as follows.

Hexadecimal Notation

This section defines the typographical convention used throughout this book. Hex Notation All hex numbers are followed by an "h." Examples:

```
9A4Eh
0100h
```

Binary Notation

All binary numbers are followed by a "b." Examples:

```
0001 0101b
01b
```

Decimal Notation

Numbers without any suffix are decimal. When required for clarity, decimal numbers are followed by a "d." The following examples each represent a decimal number:

```
16
255
256d
128d
```

Signal Name Representation

Each signal that assumes the logic low state when asserted is followed by a pound sign (#). As an example, the CTRDY# signal is asserted low when the target is ready to complete a data transfer.

Signals that are not followed by a pound sign are asserted when they assume the logic high state. As an example, STSCHG is asserted high to indicate that a CardBus card function has encountered a status change event.

Identification of Bit Fields (logical groups of bits or signals)

All bit fields are designated in little-endian bit ordering as follows:

[X:Y],

where "X" is the most-significant bit and "Y" is the least-significant bit of the field. As an example, the CardBus address/data bus consists of CAD[31:0], where CAD31 is the most-significant and CAD0 the least-significant bit of the field.

Visit Our Web Page

Our current plans target January 1996 to bring our Web page online at:

www.mindshare.com

This date may slip a little due to our multitasking multiple projects simultaneously. As of this writing, we are currently defining content. As with anyone's web page, the content and therefore its value to you will increase over time.

We Want Your Feedback

MindShare values your comments and suggestions. You can contact us via mail, phone, fax or internet email.

Phone: (214) 231-2216, and, in the U.S., (800) 633-1440

Fax: (214) 783-4715

E-mail: mindshar@interserv.com

To request information on MindShare seminars, email your request to: mindshar@interserv.com.

Mailing Address

MindShare, Inc.
2202 Buttercup Drive
Richardson, Texas 75082

Part One

Introduction to CardBus

1 Overview

This Chapter

This chapter introduces background information regarding the emergence and design of the CardBus specification. CardBus implementations provide compatibility with 16-bit PC Cards and extend performance and functionality by adding 32-bit data transfers, and by employing PCI (Peripheral Component Interconnect) concepts.

The Next Chapter

The next chapter reviews PCMCIA's 16-Bit PC Card solution as background information that is important in understanding the CardBus implementation. Furthermore, CardBus provides backward compatibility to 16-bit PC Cards. This chapter discusses the major concepts and key features employed by 16-bit PC Cards. Key terms are also defined and sample transfers highlight the performance typically achieved with ISA-based 16-bit PC Card implementations.

Reminder

As stated in the About This Book chapter, it is strongly recommended that the reader have a good foundation in both PCI and PCMCIA before studying CardBus. This background may be obtained by reading the MindShare books entitled *PCMCIA System Architecture* and *PCI System Architecture* (all of our books are published by Addison-Wesley).

High Performance Mobile Computing

Continuing growth in the mobile computing environment has led to the need for higher performance systems to support popular graphics-based software. Associated with system performance is the need for high-speed peripheral devices that are small, lightweight, and energy efficient. The following types of peripheral devices have high throughput requirements:

- Graphics video adapters.
- Full-motion video adapters.
- SCSI host bus adapters.
- High speed network adapters.

Graphics Interface Performance Requirements

The Windows, OS/2 and Unix X-Windows user interfaces require extremely fast updates of the graphics image in order to move, resize and update multiple windows without imposing discernible delays on the end-user. Since the screen image is stored in video RAM, this means that the processor must be able to update and/or move large blocks of data within video memory very fast. The same is true for the updating of full-motion video in video ram.

SCSI Performance Requirements

The SCSI interface is used to move large blocks of data between target I/O devices and system memory. Mass storage devices such as hard disk drives, CD-ROM drives and tape backup subsystems typically reside on the SCSI bus. The time required to read or write files on hard drives or tape, or to read files from CD-ROM can impose delays on the end-user. Anything that can be done to speed up these block data transfers has a significant effect on overall system performance.

Network Adapter Performance Requirements

When a network adapter is used to transfer entire files of information to or from a server (a print or file server), the rate at which the information can be transferred between system memory and the network adapter detracts from or contributes to overall system performance.

Teleconferencing Performance Requirements

Figure 1-1 on page 11 illustrates three PCs linked via a telecommunications network. Each of the three units has the capability to simultaneously merge multiple graphics and video sources onto the screen in real-time. Figure 1-2 on page 12 illustrates the contents of each screen.

The large portion of the screen (devoted to a graphics image) is utilized to display the document under discussion. In order to successfully emulate an actual face-to-face conferencing situation, the system must be capable of updating this image fast enough to simulate flipping through the pages of a document at the rate of ten pages (or frames) per second. With an image resolution of 1280 x 1024 pixels and color resolution of 16 million colors (three bytes per pixel), the amount of video memory required to store one image is 3.93216Mbytes. To alter the graphics display at the rate of ten frames per second would require a video memory update rate of 39.3216Mbytes per second.

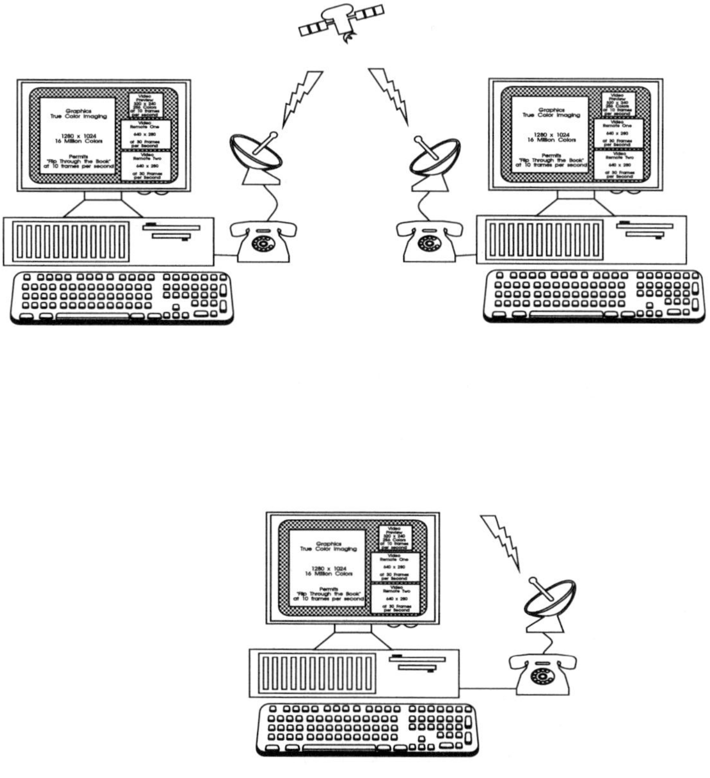

Figure 1-1: Video Teleconferencing

The video preview portion of the screen is used to display a real-time video image of a video source local to the unit. This image has a resolution of 320 x 240 pixels and a color resolution of 256 colors (one byte per pixel). In order to provide full-motion video, the image must be updated at the rate of thirty frames per second. The amount of video memory required to store one image would be 76.8Kbytes. To alter the graphics display at the rate of thirty frames per second would require a video memory update rate of 2.3Mbytes per second.

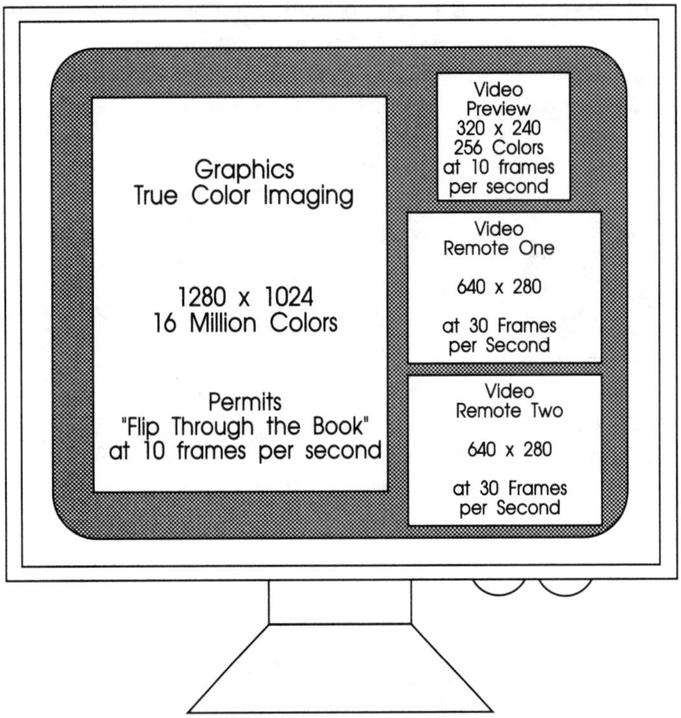

Figure 1-2: Screen Areas in a Typical Teleconferencing Environment

Each of the two video remote screen areas is used to display a full-motion video image from one of the other two participants. These images each have a resolution of 640 x 480 pixels and a color resolution of 256 colors (one byte per pixel). In order to provide full-motion video, each image must be updated at the rate of thirty frames per second. The amount of video memory required to store one image would be 307.2Kbytes. To alter each of the video remote windows at the rate of thirty frames per second would require a video memory update rate of 9.2Mbytes per second.

Each of the three video images would be transmitted in compressed video image format at the rate of 200Kbytes per second per video stream.

In summary, each host system must supply sufficient bus bandwidth to support the combined transfer rates required to update the images presented in the graphics, preview, remote one and remote two windows, as well as the three 200Kbyte per second compressed video streams. The bus structure must support the simultaneous transfer rates listed in table 1-1. ISA (8.33Mbytes per second) and the current version of EISA (33Mbytes per second) will not support the combined bandwidth requirement of 60.516Mbytes per second. The Micro Channel (40Mbytes per second) does not currently support the required rate, but the 64-bit Streaming Data Procedures (these were not supported on the PS/2 product line) are able to achieve transfer rates of 80 to 160Mbytes per second. As described later in this document, a 33MHz PCI bus currently supports a transfer rate of 132Mbytes per second. If the 64-bit PCI extension is implemented, a transfer rate of 264Mbytes per second can be achieved. PCI also supports a 66MHz PCI clock that can increase the maximum transfer rate to 528Mbytes per second, when using 64-bit devices. Table 1-2 lists the transfer rates for the video and other subsystems.

Table 1-1: Teleconferencing Transfer Rate Requirements

Screen Element	Transfer Rate (Mbytes/second)
Graphics Window	39.216
Preview Window	2.3
Video Remote One	9.2
Video Remote Two	9.2
Preview Compressed Video Stream	.2
Video Remote One Compressed Video Stream	.2
Video Remote Two Compressed Video Stream	.2
Total transfer rate required to support teleconferencing	60.516

Table 1-2: Required Subsystem Transfer Rates

Subsystem	(Mbytes per second)
Graphics	30 to 40
Full-Motion Video	2 to 9 per window
LAN	15 for FDDI (Fiber Distributed Data Interface)
	3 for Token Ring
	2 for Ethernet
Hard Disk	5 to 20 using SCSI
CD-ROM	2 using SCSI
Audio	1 for CD quality output

Mixing Portability with High Performance

The increased performance required in today's operating environments is being fueled by the need to transfer large blocks of data in an extremely short duration. This is especially true in relation to the multimedia, high-speed networking, and video teleconferencing environments, which are rapidly moving to the mobile computing environment.

16-Bit PC Cards

The 16-bit PCMCIA cards (aka 16-bit PC Cards) are used primarily in ISA-based portable systems. The performance of these PC Cards are constrained by the ISA bus, which provides a maximum data throughput of approximately 8MB/second; whereas, the theoretical maximum throughput of 16-bit PC Cards is 20MB/second. Major advantages of PC Cards are their small form-factor, low power consumption and hot insertion support.

PCI Devices

The need for higher performance expansion devices has been satisfied in the desktop environment with the Peripheral Component Interconnect bus (aka, PCI bus), which, at a bus speed of 33MHz, provides a theoretical maximum throughput of 132MB/second during burst transfers using a 32-bit wide data path. Many manufacturers are incorporating the PCI bus in their portable computers, providing the additional performance needed. These devices are typically embedded on the system board, since PCI expansion connectors and boards are relatively large and not well suited to portable computers.

CardBus Cards

CardBus combines the low-power, small form-factor, hot insertion capability, and light weight of PC Cards with the high-performance of PCI. CardBus PC Cards have a maximum theoretical throughput of 132MB/second by using the PCI transfer protocol. CardBus cards, when inserted into a 68-pin CardBus socket, are automatically detected and configured by PCMCIA-specific software.

2 16-Bit PC Cards—A Review

The Previous Chapter

The previous chapter introduced the need for CardBus and described the origins of CardBus technology.

This Chapter

This chapter reviews PC Card implementation. It reviews the relationships between the various hardware and software elements employed in a typical PC Card environment. The elements discussed include: the PCMCIA Host Bus Adapter (HBA); the PC Card socket; the PC Card; socket services; card services; and enablers.

The Next Chapter

The next chapter discusses the PCI concepts upon which CardBus transactions are based, including a review of key PCI features.

16-Bit PC Card Overview

PCMCIA's 16-bit PC Cards were introduced primarily for the mobile computing environment to provide a small form-factor, low-power alternative to the much larger and power hungry ISA peripheral devices employed in most PCs. Memory card support was defined first, followed by IO cards. PC Card peripherals, like most of their ISA cousins, are implemented as target-only devices.

PC Cards come in a wide range of memory and IO devices. Memory devices include RAM, Flash memory and various types of ROM. IO devices include voice, data and FAX modems; network interface cards; wireless communications (such as Global Positioning Systems (GPS), pagers and networks); AT Attachment (ATA) Hard Drives (also called IDE drives); small computer system interface (SCSI) adapters; and many others.

Memory cards

Memory cards were introduced as an alternative to the mechanical floppy drive. In other words, memory cards are used to emulate the floppy drive subsystem. PCMCIA the defined hardware and software support necessary to implement a standardized method for supporting this disk drive emulation.

Memory cards implemented as virtual floppy disks must also have the ability to be inserted and removed from the system at any time (as with floppy disks). When a card is installed, software must be able to access the files stored on the memory card or write new files to it. This ability is accomplished through the PC Card's hot insertion capability. When a PC Card is inserted into a socket, PCMCIA-specific software recognizes the insertion and automatically configures and enables the memory card, preparing it to be immediately accessed as a floppy drive.

IO Cards

Support for IO cards was added by PCMCIA in release 2.0 of the specification, permitting IO peripheral devices to be implemented as small PC Cards. These PC Cards also retain the hot insertion capability of memory card designs.

16-Bit PC Card Features

The key features of 16-bit PC Cards are listed in Table 2-1.

Table 2-1: PCMCIA Feature Summary

Feature	Description
Small Form-Factor: Three Physical Device Types Defined	PCMCIA cards have a standard length and width of 85.6mm (3.370″) X 54.0mm (2.126″). The card type determines the card's thickness. Type 1 = 3.3mm (0.130″); Type 2 = 5.0mm (0.197″); Type 3 = 10.5mm (0.413″).

Table 2-1: PCMCIA Feature Summary (Continued)

Feature	Description
Host Bus Independence	PCMCIA sockets can be connected to a wide variety of host buses. Sockets are connected to the host systems via host bus adapters designed for a particular bus interface.
Three Address Spaces	PCMCIA supports common memory address space (standard memory addresses), attribute memory space (for automatic configuration) and IO address space.
64 MB of Address Space	Twenty-six address lines provide address space of up to 64 MB for each address space.
16-bit Data Path	Sixteen data lines permit word transfers to/from PC Cards.
IO Device Support	IO devices as well as memory devices can be implemented in the credit card form-factor.
Direct Memory Access (DMA) Support	The PC Card standard incorporated DMA support so that standard PC expansion devices that use DMA can be supported in PC Card implementations and take advantage of the existing software.
Multifunction PC Cards Support	The PC Card standard directly supports PC Cards that include multiple memory or IO functions or both.
Automatic Configuration	When installed, PC Cards are configured automatically without the need for user intervention.
Software Transparency	Software written for standard host bus devices can be used when accessing the same device that is implemented in a PC Card. Once the PC Card is installed and configured it typically behaves like any other host device.
Easy to Implement Configuration Software	PCMCIA provides a standard software interface, simplifying the design and implementation of device-drivers required to configure PC Cards.

Table 2-1: PCMCIA Feature Summary (Continued)

Feature	Description
Low-voltage support	The PC Card standard supports 5 volt, 3.3 volt and what PCMCIA refers to as X.X voltage (an arbitrary low voltage to be specified sometime in the future).
Support for several different file systems on a single card	PC Cards provide a means for specifying support for a variety of different data-recording formats and data organizations.
Execution of code directly from memory card	PCMCIA memory cards, typically implemented as virtual disks, can be accessed directly to fetch code, without first copying it to main memory. This support requires a software protocol called XIP (execute-in-place).

16-Bit PC Card Performance

The maximum throughput associated with 16-bit PC Card transfers is 20MB/second. Most systems that employ 16-bit PC Cards interface the card sockets to the ISA bus. As a result, PC Card performance is governed by the ISA bus which has a maximum theoretical throughput of 8MB/second.

Figure 2-1 on page 21 illustrates a typical 16-Bit memory transfer via the ISA bus. Note that the total cycle time (setup, command, and recovery time) of 270ns equates to a one wait state ISA default transfer, which required 375ns to complete. This yields a transfer rate of 5.33 Mbytes per second. The fastest transfer supported over the ISA bus requires 250ns and governs the maximum performance that is achievable with 16-bit memory cards.

The maximum throughput that can be obtained by PC Cards is based on a minimum cycle time of 100ns defined by the PC Card standard for memory transfers. A maximum of two bytes can be transferred every 100ns for a maximum transfer rate of 20Mbytes per second. IO transfers have a minimum cycle time of 255ns, yielding a maximum transfer rate of 7.8Mbytes per second. Since a cycle time of 255ns exceeds a zero wait state ISA transfer, PC Card IO transfers have a maximum transfer rate of 5.33Mbytes per second.

Figure 2-1: 16-Bit PC Card Memory Transfer

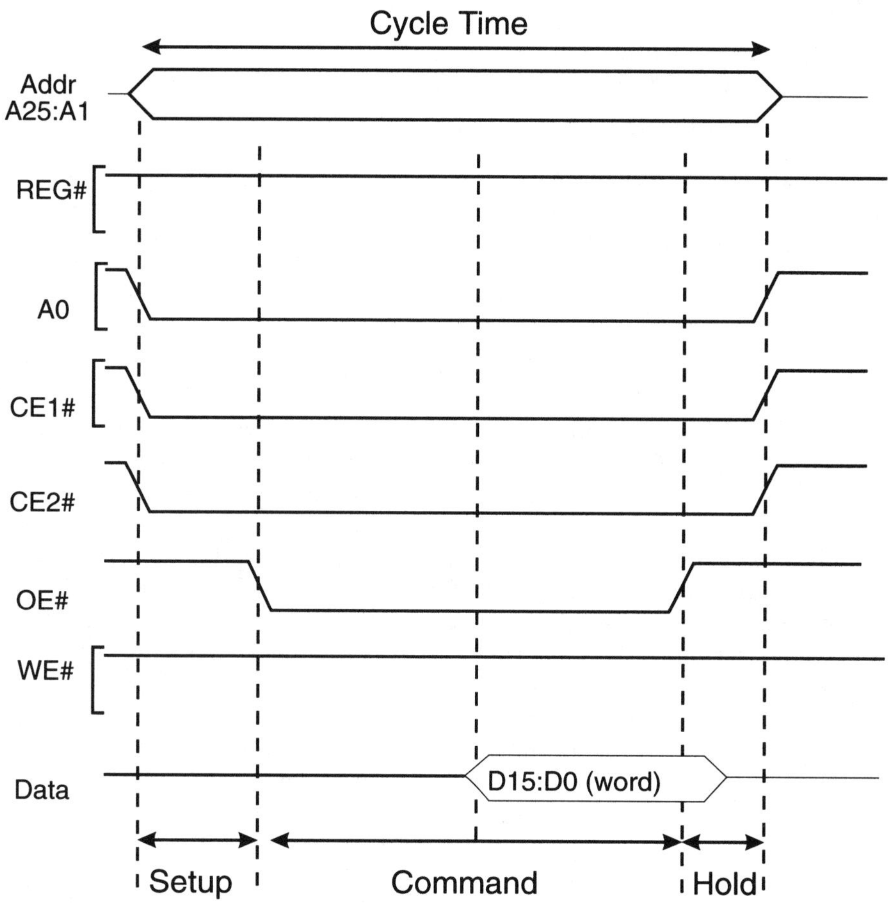

Review of 16-Bit PC Card Operation

The following discussion introduces the hardware and software elements that comprise a typical PC-Card solution. The purpose of each element is defined and its role in PC Card operation and the hot insertion capability is described.

The 16-bit PC Card solution typically consists of:

Hardware

- The 16-Bit PC Card
- PCMCIA Socket
- The PCMCIA Host Bus Adapter (HBA)

Software

- Socket Services
- Card Services
- PC Card Enablers

The host bus adapter (HBA) bridges the host expansion bus (e.g. ISA, EISA, Micro Channel, or PCI) to the PC Card socket or sockets. The PCMCIA software architecture consists primarily of a PC Card's enablers, card services and socket services. These software layers exist to support PCMCIA's automatic configuration and "hot insertion" capability. The term hot insertion is frequently used to refer to the ability of PC Cards to be inserted into a socket when power is applied to the PC. The system automatically detects and configures the PC Card allowing the system to treat it as a floppy disk. That is, once a PC memory card is inserted into a socket, the user can read files or write files just as if a floppy disk had been inserted into a floppy drive. From the user's perspective, the ability to format the memory card (virtual disk), perform chkdsk commands and read and write files is the same as with a floppy drive. The only perceptible difference is the lightning speed at which these operations occur when compared to the speed of the same operations performed with a floppy drive. This is due to the much faster access to solid state media.

Figure 2-2 on page 23 illustrates the relationships between each of the hardware and software elements that comprise a PCMCIA solution, and identifies the typical supplier of each element. The definition and need for each element is described in the following sections. A wide variety of hardware applications can be implemented using PC Cards. Many PC Cards consist of memory devices used to emulate floppy or hard drives. These virtual drives provide very fast access and provide a data transfer medium much less susceptible to harsh environmental conditions when compared to magnetic media (such as diskettes and magnetic tape). If these devices are to be used as replaceable media, the system must be able to recognize when a card is inserted or removed and provide the ability to access the card as if it were a floppy disk.

PCMCIA also supports IO devices such as modems, IDE (ATA) hard drives and LAN controllers. Support also exists for multifunction devices (i.e., a PC Card that contains more than one logical device, or function). Regardless of the type of PC Card implemented (memory, IO, or multifunction), PCMCIA systems are designed to permit their automatic detection and configuration. The PCMCIA automatic configuration capability is in some ways similar to that employed by the Micro Channel and EISA system designs, but eliminates the user intervention required with these systems and permits insertion and configuration while power is applied to the system. In Micro Channel and EISA designs, the manufacturer of an adapter board must supply a configuration file that describes the possible configuration options for the board. The system manufacturer also supplies a configuration file describing the resources used by the basic system, along with a variety of configuration options. A configuration utility program must be run by the user to merge all the configuration information together (system and installed boards). The configuration software then determines an overall conflict-free configuration that satisfies the requirements of the system and all expansion boards.

Figure 2-2: Relationship of PCMCIA Software and Hardware

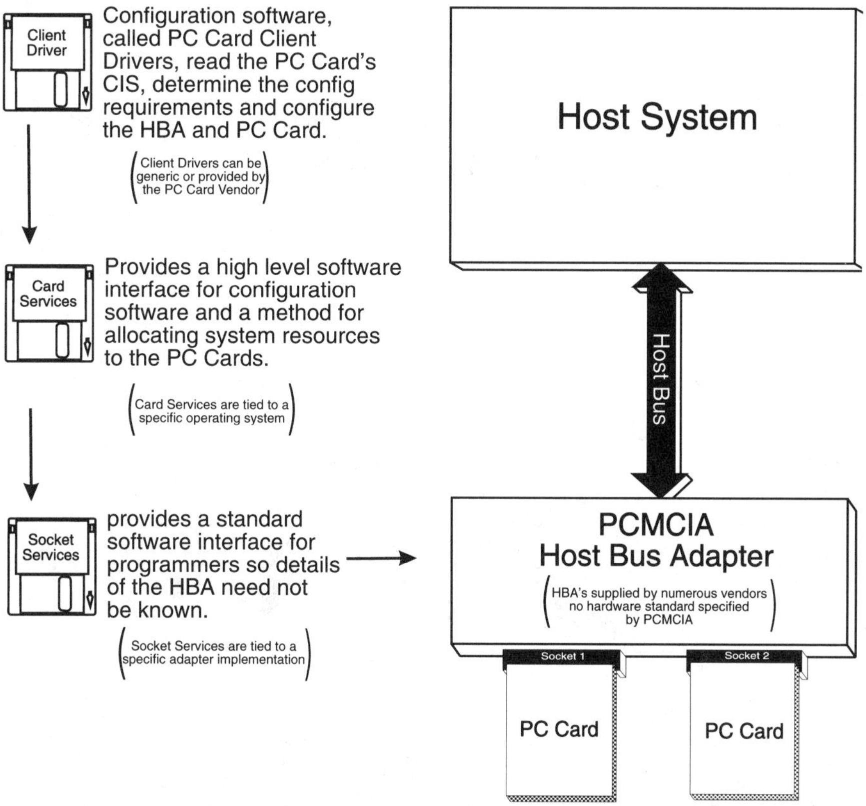

PC Cards incorporate configuration option information in non-volatile memory within the card itself, rather than requiring a companion diskette that contains the configuration option information. This configuration data is kept in an area within the card known as the card information structure (CIS). The CIS is mapped into the PC Card's attribute memory space. Refer to Figure 2-3 on page 24.

PC Card enabler software installs each time the system is powered up. This software checks for the presence of PC Cards that are installed. If a PC Card is detected, the software reads the contents of its CIS to determine the type of device, the system resources that it requires, and the configuration options that are possible. The enabler is then responsible for configuring the PC Card so it can be accessed. PC cards, unlike the Micro Channel and EISA boards, can be inserted either before or after the system is powered up. As a result, enablers must remain available for PC Cards in the event a card is installed following system power-up. Hardware notifies the software when a new card is installed, so that it can be properly configured into the system. When a card is removed, again hardware detects the card's removal and notifies software that the device is no longer installed.

Figure 2-3: The Card Information Structure Contains Configuration Options for the PC Card

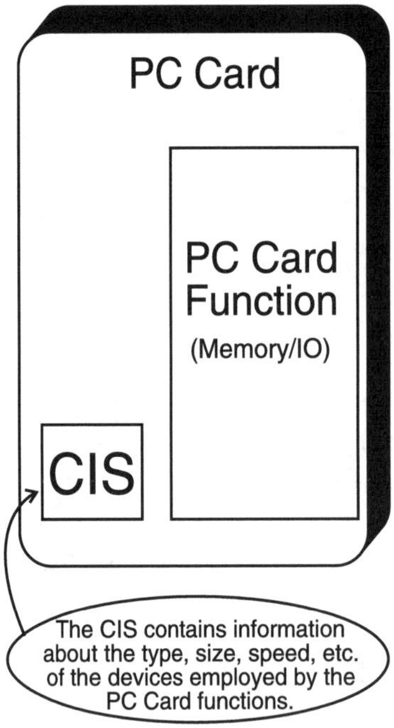

The PCMCIA configuration software consists of one or more PC Card enablers that recognize, enable, and configure the PC Card. This software sometimes comes with a particular PC Card (typically as part of a device driver) that the card manufacturer provides when the PC Card is purchased. This type of PC Card enabler is usually responsible for installing only the PC Card for which it was designed. Other PC Card enablers, sometimes called generic or super-enablers, are typically supplied by the system manufacturer. Generic enablers evaluate the configuration requirements of a card by scanning and evaluating (parsing) the CIS. If the generic enabler recognizes the card type, it will then attempt to configure the card itself or dynamically load the appropriate enabler from a library residing on disk. Ideally, a single PC Card super-enabler would be used to detect and configure all PC Cards. For a variety of reasons (to be discussed later), a single generic or super-enabler is not always possible today. In short, PCMCIA configuration software may consist of one or more PC Card enablers designed to identify and configure PC Cards.

PCMCIA Sockets and The PCMCIA Host Bus Adapter

PCMCIA sockets can be designed into a wide variety of PC bus architectures as well as non-PC designs, permitting interpretability of PC Cards. This connection between a given host bus (typically the ISA bus) and a PCMCIA socket is provided through a PCMCIA host bus adapter (HBA). The adapter acts as a bridge, passing host bus transactions to PC Cards installed in PCMCIA sockets. Refer to Figure 2-4 on page 26. Host bus adapters must be programmed by the system in order to gain access to PC Cards. The manner in which the host bus adapter is programmed is determined by the requirements of the PC Cards currently installed in the sockets it controls. Each PCMCIA socket has its own dedicated signal interface provided by the HBA. That is, signals are not bussed between sockets as in most expansion bus architectures. This of course means that the host bus adapter must have a separate interface to each socket along with a single interface to the host system. Access to each socket therefore is controlled through separate sets of socket interface circuitry, each of which must be initialized in order to gain access to a PC Card installed in a given socket.

Figure 2-4: Host Bus to PC Card Socket Adapter, or HBA

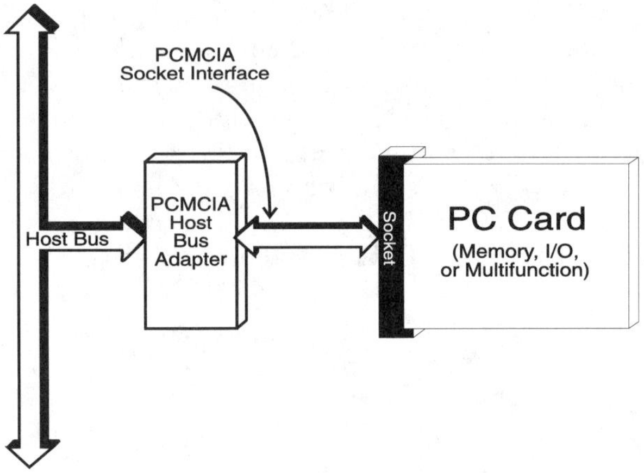

Initializing the Host Bus Adapter: Socket Services

Since host bus adapters (HBAs) must have a dual personality, (an interface to both the PCMCIA sockets and to the host system) the details of implementing an HBA has been left to the hardware developer and is not included within the PCMCIA specification. This means that a wide variety of HBA designs can (and do) exist for a given type of host interface.

Several chip manufacturers provide PCMCIA host bus adapter chips that system manufacturers can incorporate into their designs. For example, manufacturers of ISA to PCMCIA host bus adapters include: Cirrus Logic, DataBook, Intel, Texas Instruments, Vadem, VLSI Technology, and others. Each of these designs to some extent implement different registers and initialization algorithms. Differences between some HBAs are slight while differences between others are major. Software must initialize the HBA so that it can pass host expansion transactions to the PC card when it detects an address that resides within the range of addresses used by the PC Card. Since a variety of different HBAs can be used, programmers would have to write their software to interface to each type of host bus adapter in order to ensure proper operation in all system platforms. However, the PC Card specification provides a common software interface called socket services which hides the details of the hardware interface from the programmer. Socket services provides a low-level software interface that gives programmers access to a common set of functions that will permit initialization of any HBA. In IBM PC terminology, these functions can be thought of as merely extensions to the BIOS routines. Several software vendors have developed socket services for each of the major PCMCIA host adapters. These vendors include: American Megatrends, Award Software, Phoenix Technology, SystemSoft, Ventura Micro Inc., and others. Today most system designers license socket services from a software vendor, making it easier to implement PCMCIA solutions.

Configuring the Card: Card Services & Enablers

PC Cards require configuration software (enablers) that detect their presence, determine their configuration requirements and program them for operation within the system. This is true whether a card is already present when system power is applied or is installed after the system is powered up and fully operational. Configuration software for early PC Cards, designed before the introduction of socket services, had to program the host bus adapter to permit access to the card's memory address space. This required that the programmer of the configuration software know the details of the hardware interface and the protocol required to access and program the host bus adapter. Furthermore, these programmers had to poll status registers on the host bus adapter to detect when cards were inserted and removed, or when other status changes occurred at the socket (i.e., low-battery detection, write-protect switch position, or ready/busy indications). Since different host bus adapters have different hardware interfaces, programmers were required to provide a separate version of their software for each host bus adapter type. The introduction of socket services removed the burden of having to write card enablers to interface directly to the hardware.

In addition, the programmer must determine the system resources required by a PC Card and allocate them to the card. The resources that it assigns to its PC Card must not be already allocated to another device in the system. In the past, the programmer had to somehow determine what system resources were available to be allocated, or make an educated guess, hoping that the resources it was about to allocate were not already in use. These issues and others placed a heavy burden on the programmer to ensure that their cards worked in a given system. Fortunately, PCMCIA introduced another software layer called card services that lifts these burdens from the programmer.

Thanks to card services, the job of writing PC Card enablers is a much simpler task today, and far more reliable than was possible with early revisions of the specification. Card services provides a software layer consisting of high-level functions that programmers can call to gain access to a card, determine its configuration requirements, and request the system resources it requires. One of the primary functions that card services fulfills for enablers is system resource allocation. Card services maintains a database of system resources that are available for assignment to PC Cards. Once the enabler determines the configuration requirements of the card by reading the card's CIS, it requests that these resources be allocated to its card. If the resource is available, card services returns "success" to the enabler and the resource is then assigned. If the resource has already been used, then card services returns "failure" and another configuration option must be read from the CIS and tried. This process continues until one of the card's configuration options satisfies the request or until all options are exhausted, in which case the card cannot be configured. Card services also notifies enablers of card insertion and removal and other status change events. This eliminates the need for enablers to continually poll to determine if some status change has occurred.

Accessing PC Cards after Configuration

Once a PC Card has been detected and configured, it behaves like any other device that exists on the expansion (PCMCIA host) bus. This allows applications to access PC Cards directly through the normal methods used in a given operating environment. This access can be done without using the PCMCIA software interface (i.e. card and socket services). Figure 2-5 on page 29 illustrates the basic software flow during configuration and status reporting, versus run-time access (accesses made to a PC Card by application software once it has been configured). Each of the software components shown in Figure 2-5 are discussed in detail in later chapters and the relationships between them are further defined.

Figure 2-5: Configuration and Status Reporting Software Flow Versus Run Time Software Flow

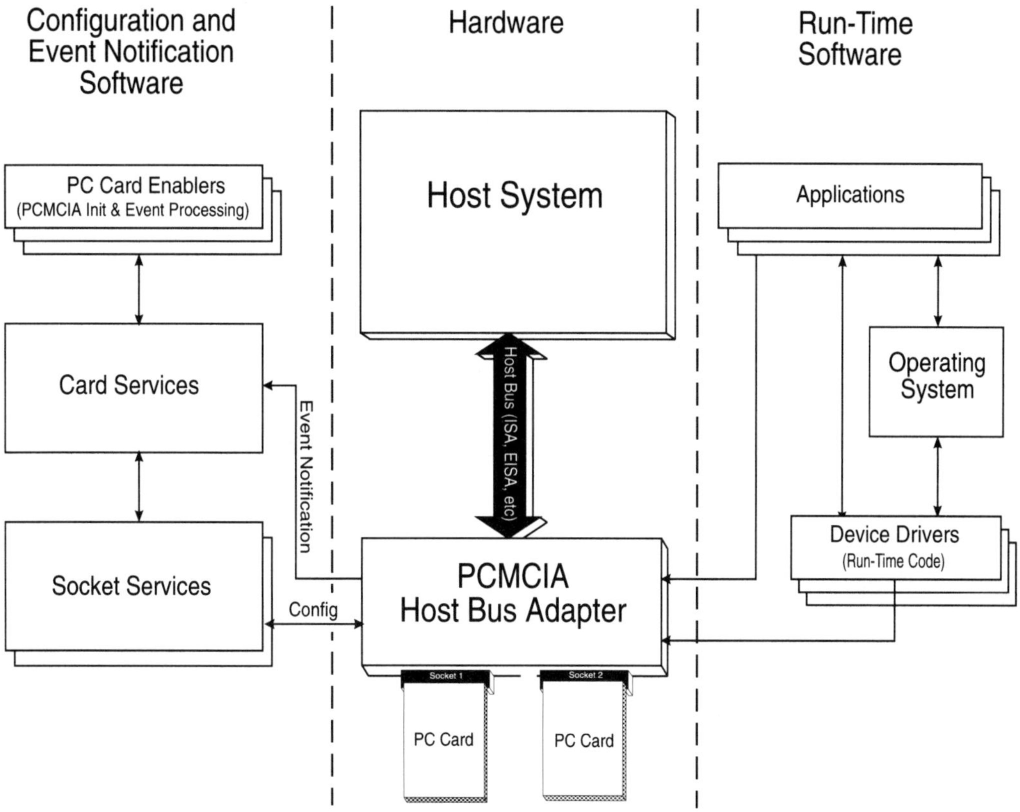

3 PCI—A Review

The Previous Chapter

The previous chapter provided a review of the PC Card implementation. It reviewed the relationships between the various hardware and software elements employed in a typical PC Card environment. The elements discussed included: the PCMCIA Host Bus Adapter (HBA); the PC Card socket; the PC Card; socket services; card services; and enablers.

This Chapter

This chapter reviews the PCI (Peripheral Component Interconnect) bus environment, including the key features and basics of PCI transfers.

The Next Chapter

The next chapter introduces the CardBus implementation.

PCI Overview

The PCI bus provides a high performance peripheral bus solution. The first release of the specification, version 1.0, became available on 6/22/92. Revision 2.0 became available in April of 1993. The current revision of the specification, 2.1, became available in June of 1995.

PCI stands for Peripheral Component Interconnect. The PCI bus can be populated with adapters requiring fast access to each other and/or system memory and that can be accessed by the host processor at speeds approaching that of the processor's full native bus speed. It is important to note that the PCI bus supports burst transfers. The length of the burst is negotiated between the initiator and target device and may be of any length. Table 3-1 on page 32 identifies some of PCI's major design goals. The following sections review the key PCI design issues.

Table 3-1: Major PCI Revision 2.1 Features Feature Description

Feature	Description
Processor Independence	Components designed for the PCI bus are PCI-specific, not processor-specific, thereby isolating device design from processor upgrade treadmill.
Support for up to 256 PCI functions per PCI bus	Although a typical PCI bus implementation supports approximately ten electrical loads, each PCI device package may contain up to eight separate PCI functions. The PCI bus logically supports up to 32 physical PCI device packages, for a total of 256 possible PCI functions per PCI bus.
Support for up to 256 PCI buses	The specification provides support for up to 256 PCI buses.
Low-power consumption	A major design goal of the PCI specification is the creation of a system design that draws as little current as possible.
Burst used for all read and write transfers	Supports 132Mbytes per second peak transfer rate for both read and write transfers. 264Mbytes per second peak transfer rate for 64-bit PCI transfers. Transfer rates of up to 528Mbytes per second are achievable on a 66MHz PCI bus.
Bus speed	Revision 2.0 spec supports PCI bus speeds up to 33MHz. Revision 2.1 adds support for 66MHz bus operation.
64-bit bus width	Full definition of a 64-bit extension.
Fast access	As fast as 60ns (at a bus speed of 33MHz) when an initiator parked on the PCI bus is writing to a PCI target.
Concurrent bus operation	High-end bridges support full bus concurrency with host bus, PCI bus, and the expansion bus simultaneously in use.

Table 3-1: Major PCI Revision 2.1 Features Feature Description (Continued)

Feature	Description
Bus master support	Full support of PCI bus initiators allows peer-to-peer PCI bus access, as well as access to main memory and expansion bus devices through PCI and expansion bus bridges. In addition, a PCI master can access a target that resides on another PCI bus in the bus hierarchy.
Hidden bus arbitration	Arbitration for the PCI bus can take place while another bus master is in possession of the PCI bus. This eliminates latency encountered during bus arbitration on buses other than PCI.
Low-pin count	Economical use of bus signals allows implementation of a functional PCI target with 47 pins and a functional PCI bus initiator with 49 pins.
Transaction integrity checking	Parity checking on the address, command and data.
Three address spaces	Memory, IO and configuration address space.
Auto-Configuration	Full, bit-level specification of the configuration registers necessary to support automatic peripheral detection and configuration.
Software Transparency	Software drivers utilize same command set and status definition when communicating with PCI device or its expansion bus-oriented cousin.
Expansion Cards	The specification includes a definition of PCI connectors and add-in cards.
Expansion Card Size	The specification defines three card sizes: long, short and variable-height short cards.

High Performance

Most PCI data transfers are accomplished using burst transfers. Most PCI bus masters and target devices are designed to support burst mode. It should be noted that a PCI target may be designed such that it can only handle single data phase transactions. When a bus master attempts to perform a burst transaction, the target terminates the transaction at the completion of the first data phase. This forces the master to re-arbitrate for the bus to attempt resumption of the burst with the next data item. The target terminates each burst transfer after the first data phase completes. This would yield very poor performance, but may be the correct approach for a device that doesn't require high throughput. Each burst transfer consists of the following basic components:

- The address and transfer type are output during the address phase.
- A data object (up to 32-bits in a 32-bit implementation or 64-bits in a 64-bit implementation) may then be transferred during each subsequent data phase.

Assuming that neither the initiator nor the target device inserts wait states in each data phase, a data object may be transferred on the rising-edge of each PCI clock cycle. At a PCI bus clock frequency of 33MHz, a transfer rate of 132Mbytes/second may be achieved. A transfer rate of 264Mbytes/second may be achieved in a 64-bit implementation when performing 64-bit transfers during each data phase. A 66MHz PCI bus implementation can achieve 264 or 524Mbytes/second transfer rates using 32 or 64-bit transfers. This chapter introduces the burst mechanism used in performing transfers over the PCI bus.

PCI Transfer Fundamentals

All PCI bus transactions consist of an address phase followed by one or more data phases. The exception is a transaction wherein the initiator uses a 64-bit address delivered in two address phases. An address phase is one PCI CLK in duration. The number of data phases depends on how many data transfers are to take place during the overall burst transfer. Each data phase has a minimum duration of one PCI CLK. Each wait state inserted in a data phase extends it by an additional PCI CLK.

Figure 3-1 on page 35 illustrates a PCI burst read transfer. In this example, a PCI initiator is performing three transfers within a single burst transaction. During burst transfers over a 32-bit PCI bus, four bytes can be transferred during each data phase. In this example, neither the initiator nor the target insert wait states (i.e. both are ready to make the transfer; IRDY# and TRDY# asserted), each data phase is one PCI clock cycle in duration. During the actual transfer the maximum transfer rate is 132Mbytes per second (4 bytes transferred during each consecutive 33Mhz clock).

The following sections discuss PCI transfers in more detail.

Figure 3-1: PCI Read Burst Transfer

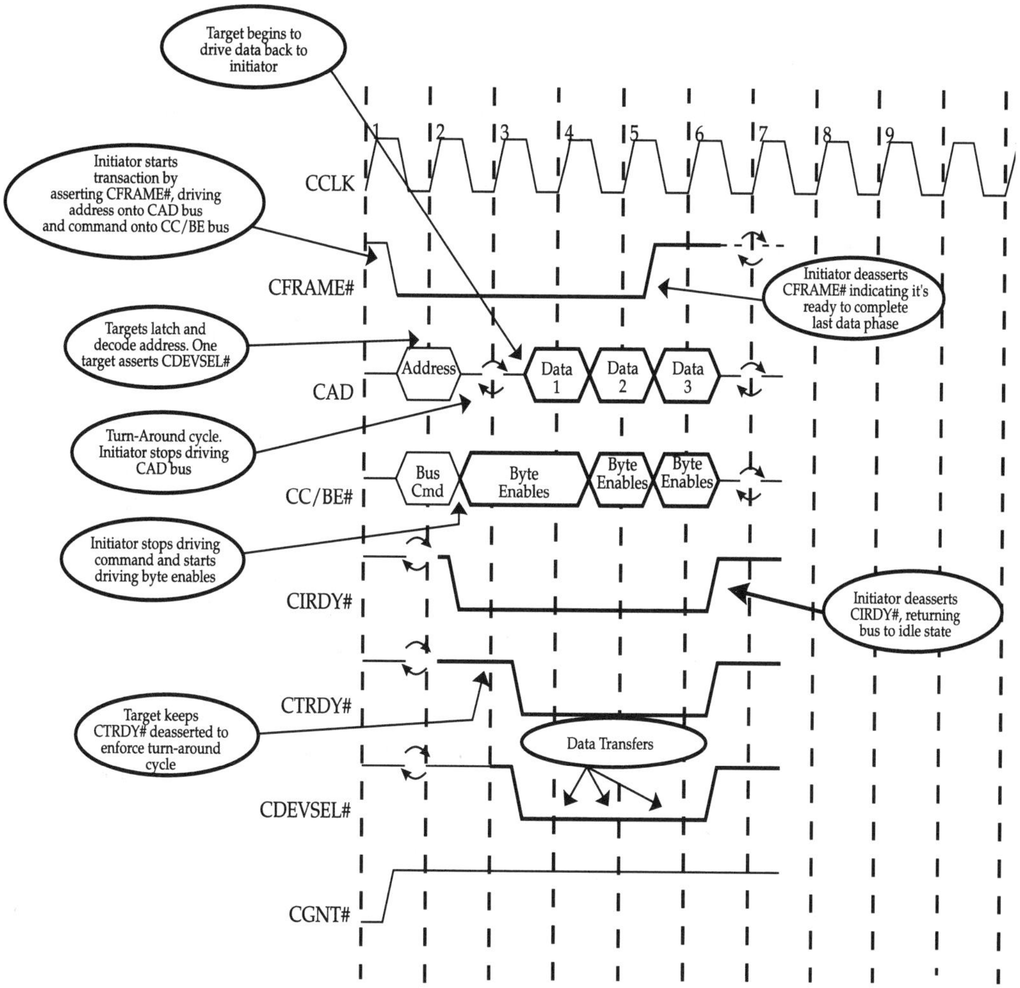

Synchronous Transactions

All actions on the PCI bus are synchronized to the PCI CLK signal. The frequency of the CLK signal may be anywhere from 0MHz to 33MHz. The revision 1.0 specification stated that all devices must support operation from 16 to 33MHz, while recommending support for operation down to 0MHz. The revision 2.x PCI specification indicates that **all** PCI devices **must** support PCI operation over the full 0 to 33MHz range. Support for operation down to 0MHz provides low-power and static debug capability. The PCI CLK frequency may be changed at any time and may be stopped (but only in the low state). Components integrated onto the system board may operate at a single frequency and may require a policy of no frequency change. Devices on add-in cards must support operation from 0 through 33MHz (because the card must operate in any platform that it may be installed in).

Address Phase

As stated earlier, every PCI transaction (with the exception of a transaction using 64-bit addressing) starts off with an address phase one PCI CLK period in duration. During the address phase, the initiator identifies the target device and the type of transaction. The target device is identified by driving a start address within its assigned range onto the PCI address/data bus. At the same time, the initiator identifies the type of transaction by driving the command type onto the PCI Command/Byte Enable bus. The initiator asserts the FRAME# signal to indicate the presence of a valid start address and transaction type on the bus. Since the initiator only presents the start address for one PCI clock cycle, it is the responsibility of every PCI target device to latch the address so that it may subsequently be decoded.

By decoding the address latched from the address bus and the command type latched from the Command/Byte Enable bus, a target device can determine if it is being addressed and the type of transaction in progress. It's important to note that the initiator only supplies a start address to the target (during the address phase). Upon completion of the address phase, the address/data bus is then used to transfer data in each of the data phases. Assuming that the target supports bursting, it is the responsibility of the target to latch the start address and to auto-increment it to point to the next doubleword during each subsequent data transfer.

Target Device Claims Transaction

When a PCI target determines that it is the target of a transaction, it must claim the transaction by asserting DEVSEL# (device select). If the initiator doesn't sample DEVSEL# asserted within a predetermined amount of time, it aborts the transaction.

Data Phase(s)

The data phase of a transaction is the period during which a data object is transferred between the initiator and the target. The data bytes to be transferred during a data phase is determined by the Command/Byte Enable signals asserted by the initiator during the data phase.

Both the initiator and the target must indicate that they are ready to complete a data phase, or the data phase is extended by a wait state one PCI CLK period in duration. The PCI bus defines individual ready signal lines for the initiator (IRDY#) and the target (TRDY#) for this purpose.

Transaction Termination

The initiator identifies the overall duration of a burst transfer with the FRAME# signal. FRAME# is asserted at the start of the address phase and remains asserted until the initiator is ready to complete the final data phase.

Bus Returns to Idle State

The initiator indicates that the last data transfer (of a burst transfer) is in progress by deasserting FRAME# and asserting IRDY#. When the last data transfer has been completed, the initiator returns the PCI bus to the idle state by deasserting its ready line (IRDY#).

If another bus master had previously been granted ownership of the bus by the PCI bus arbiter and were waiting for the current initiator to surrender the bus, it detects that the bus has returned to the idle state by sampling FRAME# and IRDY# both deasserted.

Low-Power Design

In keeping with the goal of low power consumption, the specification calls for low-power, CMOS output drivers and receivers to be used by PCI devices. The next chapter describes the reflected-wave switching used in the PCI bus environment to permit low-power, CMOS drivers to successfully drive the bus. If the address/data bus signals attached to the CMOS input receivers are permitted to float (around the switching region of the input buffers) for extended periods of time, the receiver inputs would oscillate and draw excessive current. To prevent this from happening, it is a rule in PCI that the address/data bus must not be permitted to float for extended periods of time. Since the bus is normally driven most of the time, it may be assumed that the pre-charged bus will retain its state while not being driven for brief periods of time during turnaround cycles.

Single vs. Multi-Function PCI Devices

A PCI physical device package may take the form a component integrated onto the system board or a PCI add-in card. Each PCI package may incorporate from one to eight separate functions. This is analogous to a multi-function card found in any ISA, EISA or Micro Channel machine. A package containing one function is referred to as a single-function PCI device, while a package containing two or more PCI functions is referred to as a multi-function device.

Plug and Play Support

PCI supports automatic detection and configuration of PCI devices each time the system boots. This is sometimes referred to as static configuration since it occurs only when the system is first powered up. In other words, PCI does not support hot insertion and dynamic configuration as PCMCIA does.

Configuration is performed by host software (contained within system ROM or the operating system) during system start-up. 256 bytes of configuration address space is provided for each PCI device. This configuration address space contains registers defined by the PCI specification that are encoded with the configuration requirements of the device. Configuration software reads these configuration registers to determine the system resources needed by the device (e.g., memory space, IO space, and interrupts). Configuration software then allocates system resources needed by the PCI device and assigns these resources to the devices by writing the selected values to the devices' configuration registers.

4 Intro to CardBus

The Previous Chapter

The previous chapter reviewed the characteristics of the PCI bus, it's performance and primary features.

This Chapter

This chapter introduces CardBus features and capabilities. It explains the fundamental concepts and terminology related to CardBus solutions.

The Next Chapter

The next chapter describes how the CardBus bridge detects that a PC Card is installed in a socket, differentiates between 16-bit PC Cards and CardBus cards, and determines the initial Vcc that should be applied to the socket.

CardBus: The Merging of Two Standards

CardBus combines the small form-factor, hot insertion capability, and low power designs available in the 16-bit PC Card environment with the power and performance of PCI cards. CardBus cards conform to PCMCIA's 16-bit PC Card form-factor and 68-pin connector, and include a high-speed signal interface based on the PCI bus.

CardBus systems maintain the 16-bit PC Card physical designs and provide backward compatibility with 16-bit PC Cards. CardBus bridges detect when a 16-bit PC Card is inserted into a card socket and configure the socket to provide compatibility with the 16-bit PC Card. When a CardBus card is inserted into the card socket, the system configures the interface to provide the same enhanced capabilities available to 32-bit PCI devices (including bus mastering). The CardBus solution provides a point-to-point connection between the card socket and CardBus bridge which permits a maximum theoretical throughput of 132MB/second.

Figure 4-1 illustrates the most likely implementation of a CardBus solution. Note that in this example, a PCI to CardBus bridge provides the connection between the PC Card socket and the PCI bus. The CardBus bridge illustrated in Figure 4-1 has two card sockets, one containing a CardBus Card and the other a 16-bit PC Card. This type of implementation provides users the ability to upgrade their portable systems with high performance small form-factor CardBus cards.

Figure 4-1: CardBus Bridge Incorporated into a PCI-Based System

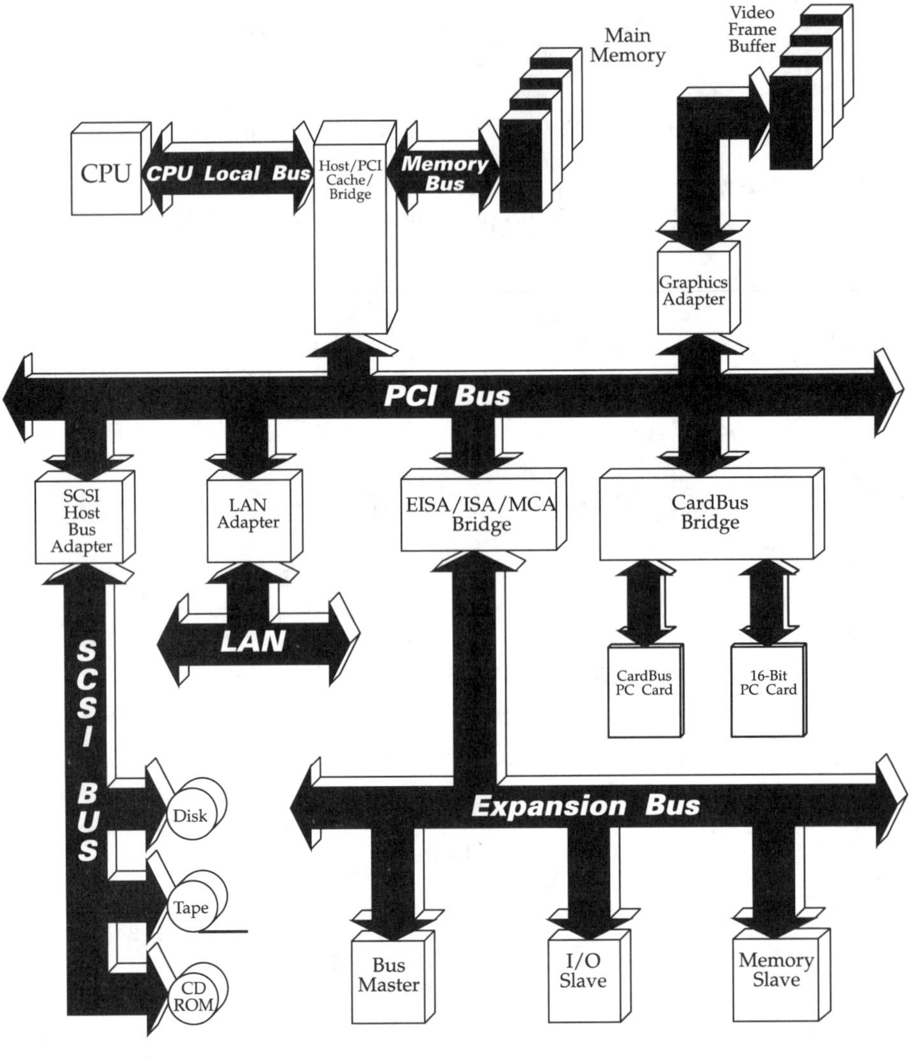

Another possible CardBus implementation is illustrated in Figure 4-2. In this example, the CardBus bridge connects the processor's bus directly to the card socket interface. The CardBus cards and the CPU share access to the host bus. This implementation permits CardBus access directly to the main system memory.

Figure 4-2: CardBus Bridge Interfacing Directly to Processor's Host Bus

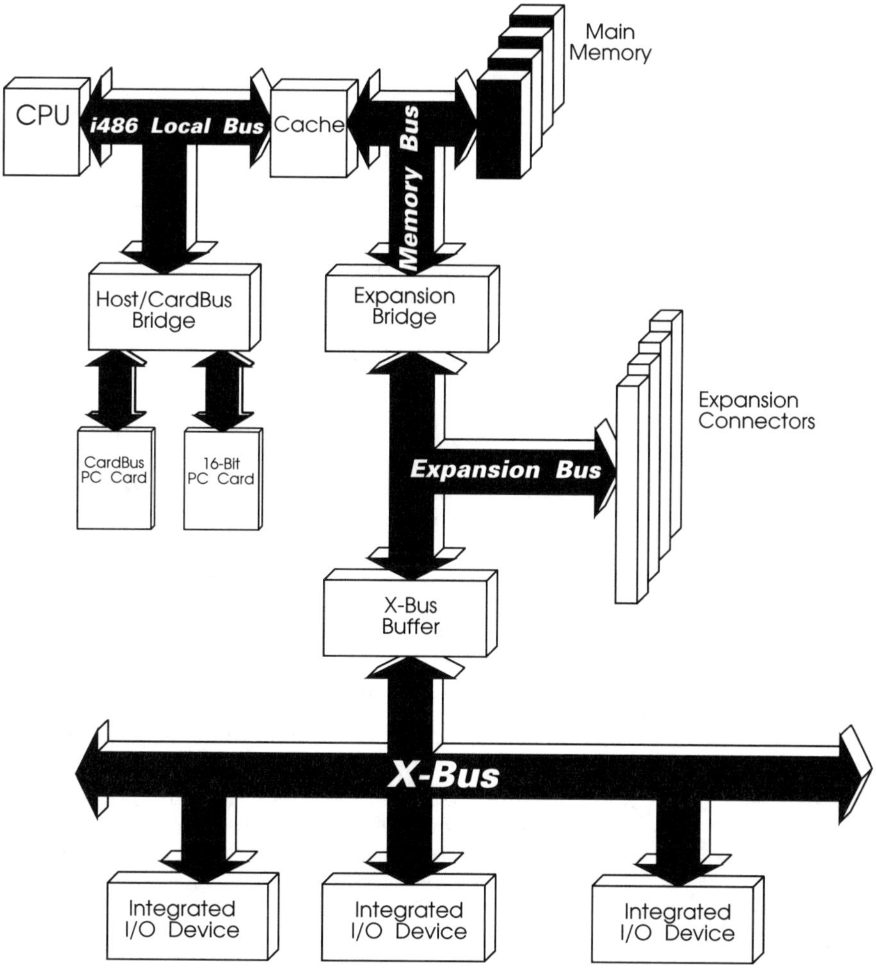

CardBus Features

Table 4-1 lists the key features associated with CardBus designs. These features include important characteristics of 16-bit PC Cards and PCI devices.

Table 4-1: Key CardBus Features

Feature	Description
Host Processor Independence	CardBus cards can be designed to interface to any host processor bus or to a PCI bus. In either case, the CardBus card designs are non-processor specific.
Low power consumption	A major design goal of CardBus is low power consumption. CardBus designs operate at 3.3vdc and lower voltages and use CMOS logic.
Burst transfers	Supports 132Mbytes per second peak transfer rate for both read and write transfers.
Bus speed	CardBus cards support a bus speed up to 33MHz.
Concurrent bus operation	Ability to support bus concurrency with host bus and/or PCI bus, and CardBus simultaneously in use.
Bus master support	CardBus devices implemented as bus masters (initiators), allow peer-to-peer CardBus access, as well as access to main memory and expansion bus devices through CardBus bridge and expansion bus bridges. In addition, a CardBus master can access a PC Card residing in another card socket or another target that resides on another PCI bus lower in the bus hierarchy.
Hidden bus arbitration	Arbitration for the PCI bus can take place while another bus master is currently performing a transaction. This eliminates latency that would otherwise be encountered during bus arbitration.
Low-pin count	Economical use of bus signals allows implementation of 32-bit address and data lines on CardBus implementations.

Table 4-1: Key CardBus Features (Continued)

Feature	Description
Transaction integrity checking	Parity checking on the address, command and data during each transaction.
Three address spaces	Memory, IO, and configuration address space.
Hot Insertion	Supports hot insertion and automatic configuration by using PCMCIA configuration software and PCI-like configuration registers.
Supports 16-Bit PC Cards and CardBus PC Cards	Uses 68-pin socket interface that can be configured for either 16-bit or CardBus cards.

CardBus Socket

CardBus uses the same 68-pin connector employed by 16-Bit PC Cards. The pin definition, however, is based on a combination of PCI signals for the transfer protocol, and PCMCIA signals to report hot insertion and socket status. PCI defines an expansion connector containing 108 pins versus the 68-pin connector defined for CardBus. The additional pins are due to the additional Vcc and ground pins available on the PCI connector, needed to reduce noise. CardBus designs employ a shrouded connector that provides additional grounding between the bridge and CardBus card.

Hot Insertion/Removal

CardBus provides the same hot insertion capability of 16-Bit PC Cards. CardBus cards employ the configuration address space common to PCI devices combined with the card information structure (CIS) used by 16-bit PC Cards. Support for dynamic configuration of CardBus cards is provided through PCMCIA configuration software (i.e. socket services, card services, and the CardBus client driver). Figure 4-3 on page 44 illustrates the software layers involved in the detection and configuration of CardBus cards.

Figure 4-3: PCMCIA Configuration Software Layers

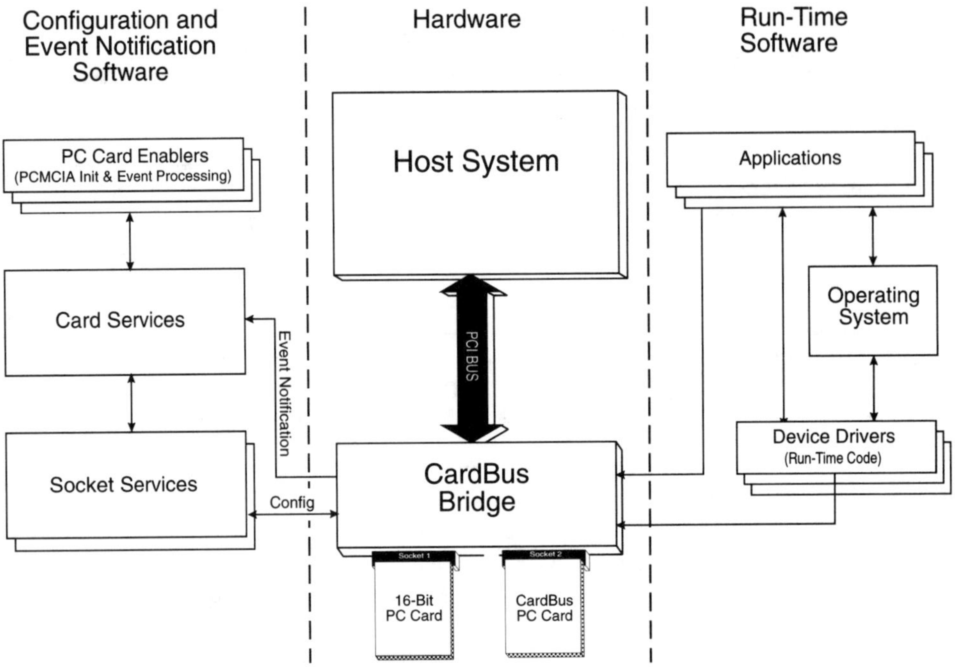

CardBus Transactions

CardBus devices use the PCI transaction protocol and signal definition. Figure 4-4 on page 45 illustrates a CardBus initiator performing a burst read transaction. Note that the signal names are the same as PCI except for the "C" prefix indicating CardBus. CardBus transactions and protocols are detailed in the following chapters.

Common Silicon

Since much of the CardBus functional design is based on the PCI bus protocol, some silicon vendors may choose to implement CardBus designs that can also be implemented directly on the PCI bus. However, many crucial differences exist between the two designs. Any differences between CardBus and PCI implementations are summarized at the end of each of the following chapters where relevant. The entire list of differences are included in "Appendix B—PCI & CardBus Differences" on page 383.

Figure 4-4: CardBus Burst Read Transfer

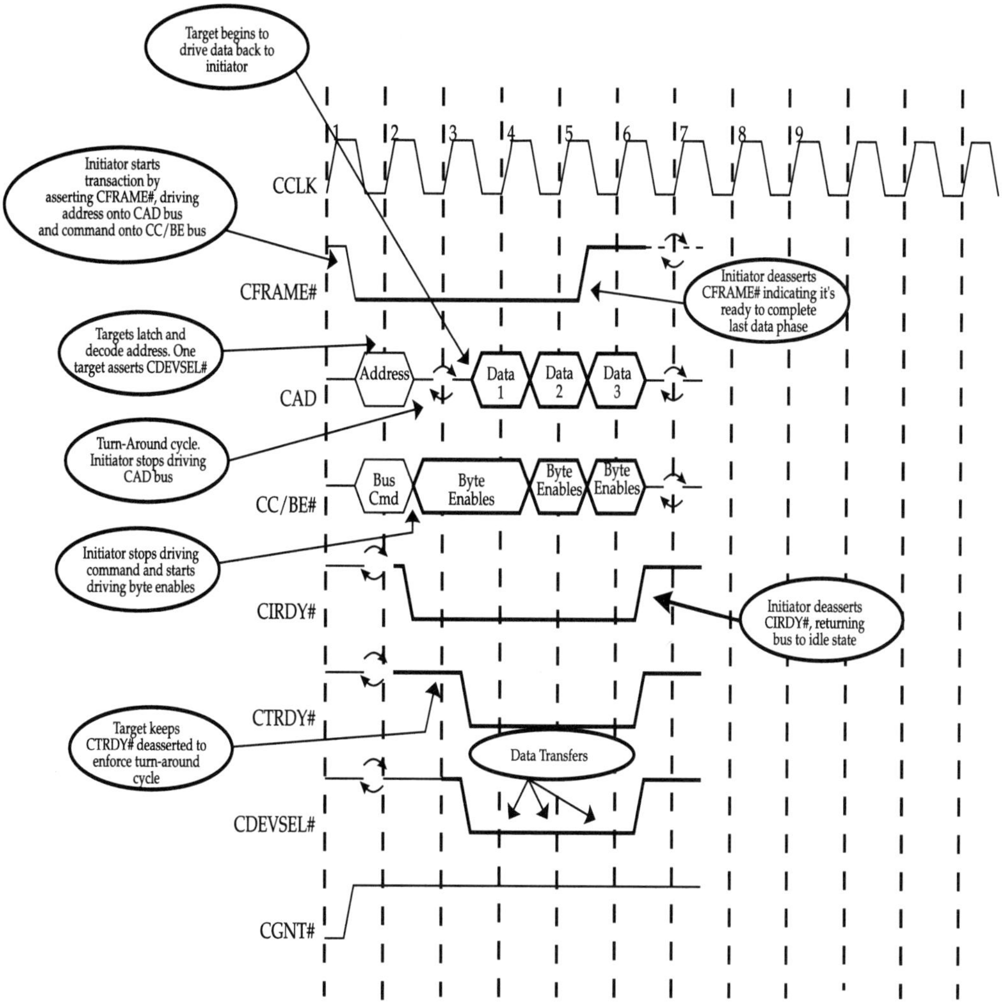

Part Two

The CardBus Socket Interface

5 PC Card Detection and Power-up

The Previous Chapter

The previous chapter introduced the capabilities of CardBus and defined the performance and features associated with CardBus cards.

This Chapter

This chapter describes the PC Card detection mechanism and defines how the CardBus bridge determines which Vcc should be initially supplied to the card socket.

The Next Chapter

The next chapter defines the CardBus signal interface. The purpose of each signal is discussed in relation to other signals and the system.

Introduction

Support of hot insertion requires that a CardBus bridge be able to detect the insertion of a PC Card, determine whether a CardBus or 16-bit PC Card has been installed, and apply the appropriate Vcc to the socket and PC Card. CardBus supports 16-bit PC Cards, including cards based on the PCMCIA release 2, or R2 cards, and cards based on the PC Card 95 standard. R2 cards require that 5vdc be initially applied to the socket, whereas, CardBus and 16-bit cards based on PC Card 95 specify the initial Vcc that they require via their voltage sense pins.

Detecting card insertion and determining card type and the initial Vcc to be applied to the socket is a two step process for the CardBus bridge. Card insertion is detected using the common card detect pins (named CD1# and CD2# for 16-bit PC Cards, and CCD1# and CCD2# for CardBus cards). Determining card type and the initial Vcc required the voltage sense pins (named VS1# and VS2# for 16-bit PC Cards and CVS1 and CVS2 for CardBus cards).

The Socket Interfaces

CardBus bridges maintain the socket interface signals in either a high impedance state or at zero volts when no PC Card is inserted into a card socket. Only the two Card Detect pins are pulled up to Vcc at the socket interface. The bridge recognizes that a PC Card has been inserted when both CD# pins are pulled to ground by the PC Card when it is inserted. The bridge must then determine which type of card has been installed, a 16-bit PC Card or a CardBus PC Card, determine the initial Vcc required, and configure the socket interface accordingly.

Figure 5-1 on page 51 illustrates the 68-pin connector and the pin definitions of the 16-bit PC Card socket and the CardBus socket. Several of the pins have the same basic function in both interfaces:

- Vcc
- VPP1
- VPP2
- Ground
- Card Detect pins (CD# and CCD#)
- Voltage Sense pins (VS# and CVS#)
- Reset (RESET and CRST)
- Status Change (STSCHG# and CSTSCHG)
- Audio (SPKR# and CAUDIO#)
- Interrupt (IREQ# and CINT#)

The CardBus bridge uses the voltage sense and card detect pins to determine the card type that has been inserted into the socket and to determine the initial Vcc voltage that should be applied to the PC Card installed.

Figure 5-1: CardBus Versus 16-Bit PC Card Socket Pinout

16-Bit	CardBus		Pin	Pin		CardBus	16-Bit
Ground	GND	→	35	1	←	GND	Ground
CD1#	CCD1#	←	36	2	↔	CAD0	Data 3
Data 11	CAD2	↔	37	3	↔	CAD14	Data 4
Data 12	CAD4	↔	38	4	↔	CAD3	Data 5
Data 13	CAD6	↔	39	5	↔	CAD5	Data 6
Data 14	RFU	↔	40	6	↔	CAD7	Data 7
Data 15	CAD8	↔	41	7	↔	CC/BE0#	CE1#
CE2#	CAD10	↔	42	8	↔	CAD9	Address 10
VS1# /Refresh*	CVS1	←	43	9	↔	CAD11	OE#
Reserved	CAD13	↔	44	10	↔	CAD12	Address 11
Reserved	CAD15	↔	45	11	↔	CAD14	Address 9
Address 17	CAD16	↔	46	12	↔	CC/BE1#	Address 8
Address 18	RFU	→	47	13	←	CPAR	Address 13
Address 19	CBLOCK#	→	48	14	←	CPERR#	Address 14
Address 20	CSTOP#	↔	49	15	←	CGNT#	WE#
Address 21	CDEVSEL#	↔	50	16	→	CINT#	READY
Vcc	Vcc	→	51	17	←	Vcc	Vcc
Vpp2	Vpp2	→	52	18	←	Vpp1	Vpp1
Address 22	CTRDY#	↔	53	19	←	CCLK	Address 16
Address 23	CFRAME#	↔	54	20	↔	CIRDY#	Address 15
Address 24	CAD17	↔	55	21	↔	CC/BE2#	Address 12
Address 25	CAD19	↔	56	22	↔	CAD18	Address 7
VS2# /Resrv	CVS2	←	57	23	↔	CAD20	Address 6
RESET	CRST	→	58	24	↔	CAD21	Address 5
WAIT#	CSERR#	←	59	25	↔	CAD22	Address 4
Reserved	CREQ#	—	60	26	↔	CAD23	Address 3
REG#	CC/BE3#	→	61	27	↔	CAD24	Address 2
BVD2	CAUDIO#	←	62	28	↔	CAD25	Address 1
BVD1	CSTSCHG	←	63	29	↔	CAD26	Address 0
Data 8	CAD28	↔	64	30	↔	CAD27	Data 0
Data 9	CAD30	↔	65	31	↔	CAD29	Data 1
Data 10	CAD31	↔	66	32	↔	RFU	Data 2
CD2#	CCD2#	←	67	33	↔	CCLKRUN#	WP
Ground	GND	→	68	34	←	GND	Ground

Detecting PC Card Insertion

The bridge monitors the state of the card detect pins to recognize that a PC Card has been inserted into a card socket. The card detect pins are pulled up to Vcc by the bridge and are both grounded when a PC Card is inserted. Figure 5-2 illustrates a 16-bit PC Card grounding the CD1# and CD2#, thereby indicating its presence in the socket. The PC Card simply provides a path to ground between the CD pins and the socket's ground pins. CardBus cards provide a path to ground between only one of their CCD# pins and ground, while the other CCD# pin is tied to either CVS1 or CVS2.

Figure 5-2: 16-Bit PC Card Presence Detection

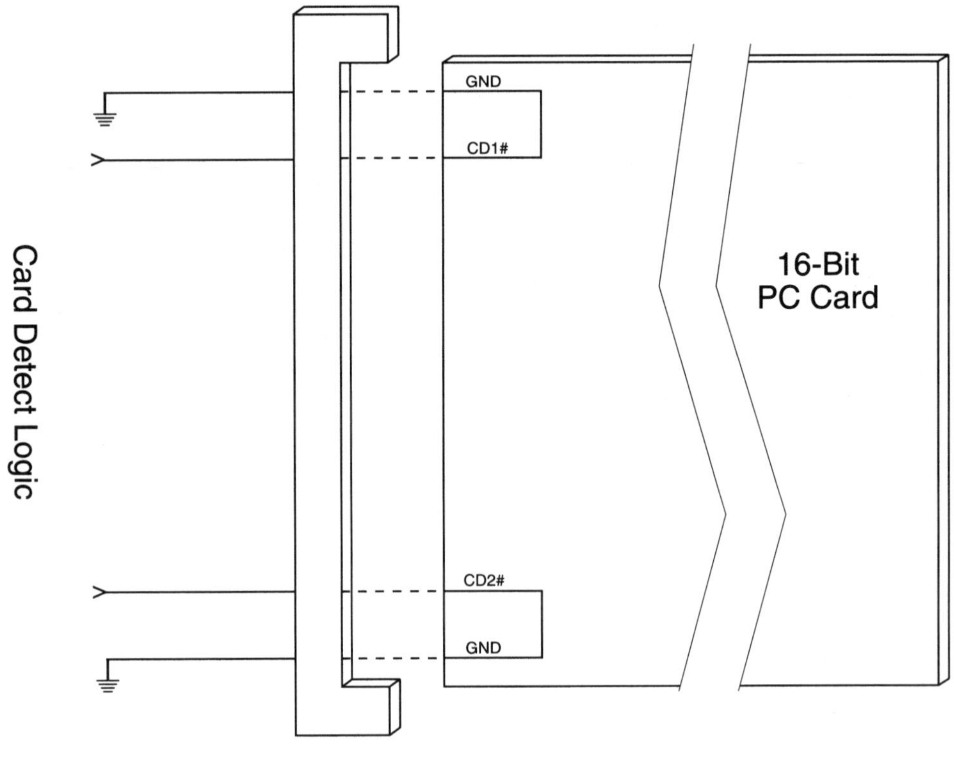

Figure 5-3 on page 53 illustrates a CardBus card designed for an initial Vcc of 3.3vdc. A CardBus card connects one of its CCD pins to one of its CVS pins to indicate the initial Vcc that it requires and to indicate it is a CardBus card (see the next section entitled, "Determining Card Type and Vcc"). Consequently, the

CardBus bridge must ground both CVS pins when a card is not present in a socket, thereby providing the ground path to the CCD pins and allowing card detection when a CardBus card is inserted.

Figure 5-3: CardBus PC Card Presence Detection

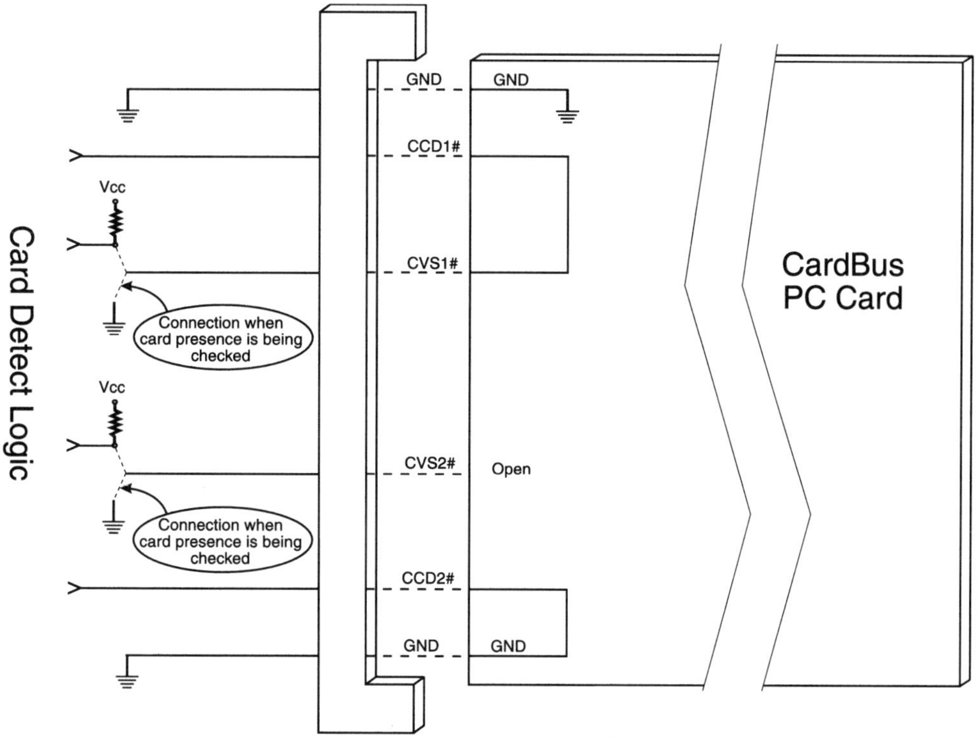

Determining Card Type and Vcc

Once the bridge has detected both card detect pins grounded, it must then perform an interrogation protocol using the card detect and voltage sense pins to determine the card type and the initial Vcc required by the PC Card. Table 5-1 on page 54 shows how a PC Card would connect its card detect and voltage sense pins to indicate card type and initial Vcc required.

Card Type

Card type is established by a PC Card's connection to its card detect pins, as shown in Table 5-1 on page 54:

- 16-bit cards: CD1# and CD2# tied to ground
- CardBus cards: one CCD# pin tied to ground; one CCD# tied to a CVS pin

To determine how the card detect lines are connected within the card the bridge performs an interrogation. Card type interrogation is performed by driving each voltage sense pin to Vcc and monitoring each card detect pin to check for continuity between one of the voltage sense pins and one of the card detect pins. When driving each voltage sense pin to Vcc, if both card detect lines remain at ground, the bridge recognizes that both card detect pins are tied to ground, and the card currently inserted into the socket is therefore a 16-bit PC Card. If either of the card detect pins are sampled at Vcc during the interrogation, the bridge recognizes that a CardBus card is installed. This indicates continuity between one of the voltage sense and card detect pins, thereby identifying the card as a CardBus card.

Table 5-1: PC Card's Card Detect and Voltage Sense Connections

CD1#/ CCD1#	CD2#/ CCD2#	VS1#/ CVS1	VS2#/ CVS2	Card Type	Initial Vcc
ground	ground	open	open	16-Bit	5 vdc
ground	ground	ground	open	16-Bit	3.3 vdc
ground	ground	open	ground	16-Bit	x.x vdc
ground	ground	ground	ground	16-Bit	3.3 & x.x vdc
CVS1	ground	CCD1#	open	CardBus	3.3 vdc
ground	CVS2	open	CCD2#	CardBus	x.x vdc
ground	CVS1	CCD2#	open	CardBus	y.y vdc
ground	CVS2	ground	CCD2#	CardBus	3.3 & x.x
CVS2	ground	open	CCD1#	CardBus	x.x & y.y
ground	CVS1	CCD2#	ground	CardBus	3.3, x.x & y.y

Initial Vcc

During the interrogation process, the bridge can also determine the Vcc that the card requires during its initial power-up sequence. How the PC Card connects its voltage sense pins determines its initial Vcc. For example, during card interrogation, the bridge pulls both voltage sense pins to Vcc. If the PC Card has both voltage sense pins tied to ground, the bridge would still detect ground at the CVS pins when it attempts to pull each line to Vcc. As shown in Table 5-1 on page 54, a PC Card having both CVS1 and CVS2 tied to ground indicates that it should be powered at 5vdc. Similarly, if the bridge determines that CVS1 is connected to CCD1# and that CVS2 is open (as illustrated in Figure 5-3 on page 53), then the CardBus card must be powered at 3.3vdc. Notice that Vcc for CardBus cards is a maximum of 3.3vdc.

Reporting Card Type and Vcc Requirements

Once the bridge has detected the type of PC Card installed in the socket and the initial Vcc required by the card, the bridge must set the appropriate bits in its Socket Event and Socket Present State registers. The bridge must set the appropriate bits in the Socket Present State register to indicate the card type and its initial Vcc requirement. Refer to Figure 5-4 on page 56. PCMCIA software reads the Socket Present State register to determine the card type (bits [5:4]) and the Vcc supported by the socket (bits 31:28) and PC Card (bits 13:10).

The Socket Event register pictured in Figure 5-5 on page 56, is set by the bridge to reflect a state change on both CCD1# and CCD2#. These bits, when set, signify a card insertion event at the socket. In response, the bridge generates a status change interrupt to notify PCMCIA software (card services) that an event has occurred. Note that an interrupt is only generated if the Socket Mask register has the CCD1# and CCD2# bits unmasked (bits [2:1] both set to one). The Socket Mask register is illustrated in Figure 5-6 on page 57.

For additional information regarding the socket status registers, refer to the Chapter entitled "Status Change Interrupts" on page 203.

Figure 5-4: Socket Present State Register

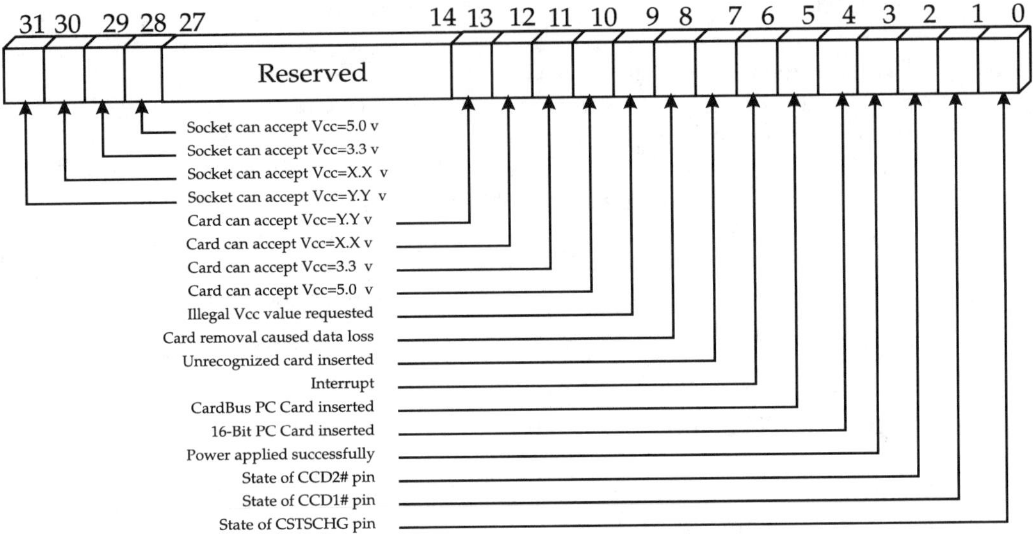

Figure 5-5: Socket Event Register

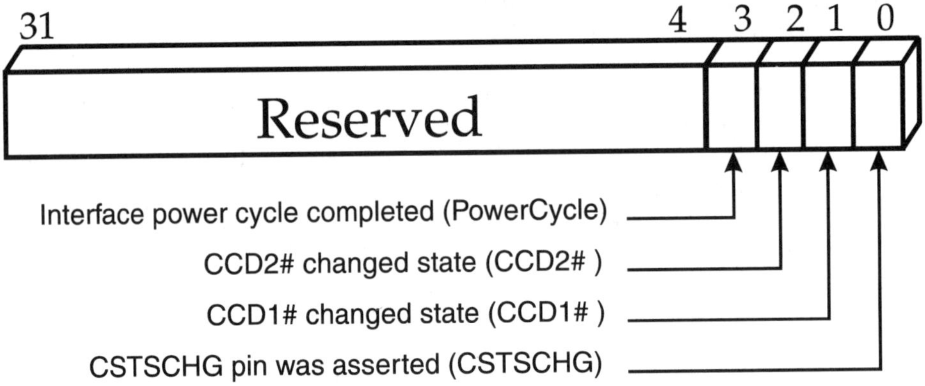

Figure 5-6: Socket Mask Register

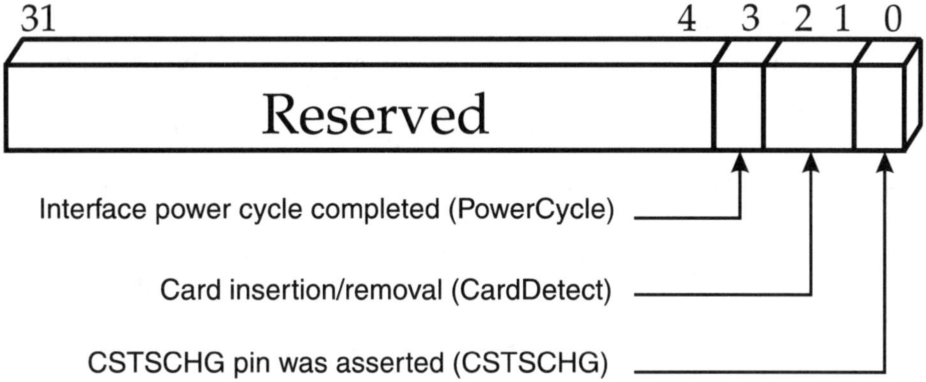

The Power-UP Sequence

The following steps summarize the actions taken by the system when a PC Card is inserted into a PC Card socket:

1. The CardBus bridge debounces CCD[2:1]# pins when it detects the signals in the low state (caused by the insertion of a PC Card).
2. The CardBus bridge interrogates the PC Card to detect card type (16-bit PC Card or CardBus card) and the initial voltage that should be applied to the socket. The bridge indicates the card type and initial Vcc requirements by setting the appropriate bits in the Socket Present State register.
3. The CardBus bridge then sets up the PC Card interface based on the card type detected. (i.e., the interface's socket interface is configured for a 16-bit memory-only interface or a CardBus interface.) In addition, the bridge must place all interface signals in a high impedance state or power them off. Note, however, that CVS[2:1]# must not be set to a high-Z state, to prevent CCD[2:1]# from indicating card removal. If the PC Card detected is a CardBus card, then CRST# must also be asserted.
4. A status change interrupt is generated by the CardBus bridge to notify card services (CS) of the event.
5. CS determines which socket experienced the status change and then reads the bridge's Socket Present State register (see Figure 5-4 on page 56) to determine the card type and Vcc requirements. Note that power must be applied via the software interface (not automatically by the hardware).
6. CS notifies socket services (SS) of the initial Vcc requirements. SS then loads

the appropriate register within the bridge, causing it to apply the specified Vcc and Vpp values. (Vcc, Vpp1, and Vpp2 must all be initially powered to the voltage specified by the CVS[2:1]# pins.

7. During power up the bridge must prevent glitches on the CSTSCHG pin from inadvertently causing a status change event. This is done by disabling the STSCHG field within the bridge's Socket Event register (see Figure 5-5 on page 56).
8. If the voltage requested by SS cannot be applied by the bridge, the bridge must set the BadVccReq field in its Socket Present State register. In this case, no power is applied to the socket.
9. When the bridge applies power to the socket, it also sets the PowerCycle bit in the Socket Event register. This causes another status change interrupt to inform CS that power has been successfully applied.
10. CS then causes CRST# to be deasserted. Note that only CS is allowed to control deassertion of CRST#, but it can be asserted by hardware. The card is now ready to be accessed and configured.

Note that during PC Card power-up, a significant amount of capacitance is instantaneously added to the power supply's load. This results in a large current draw (referred to as in-rush current). The system must ensure that the in-rush current does not allow Vcc to sag out of tolerance.

6 CardBus Signal Interface

The Previous Chapter

The previous chapter described the PC Card detection mechanism and defined how a CardBus bridge determines the type of PC Card installed in the socket and the Vcc that should initially be supplied to the card socket.

This Chapter

This chapter divides the PCI bus signals into functional groups and describes the function of each.

The Next Chapter

The next chapter describes the bus arbitration process, including the arbitration signaling protocol, the arbitration algorithm, and delayed transactions.

Introduction

This chapter introduces the signals employed by CardBus-compliant devices. Figure 6-1 on page 60 and Figure 6-2 on page 61 illustrate the signals used by CardBus cards when operating as a bus master (initiator) and when operating as a target, respectively. A CardBus device that can act as the initiator or target of a transaction would obviously have to incorporate both initiator and target-related signals. In actuality, there is no such thing as a device that is purely a bus master and never a target. At a minimum, a CardBus card must respond as the target during configuration reads and writes.

Each of the signal groupings are described in the following sections.

Figure 6-1: CardBus-Compliant Signals during Transactions in which PC Card is Bus Master

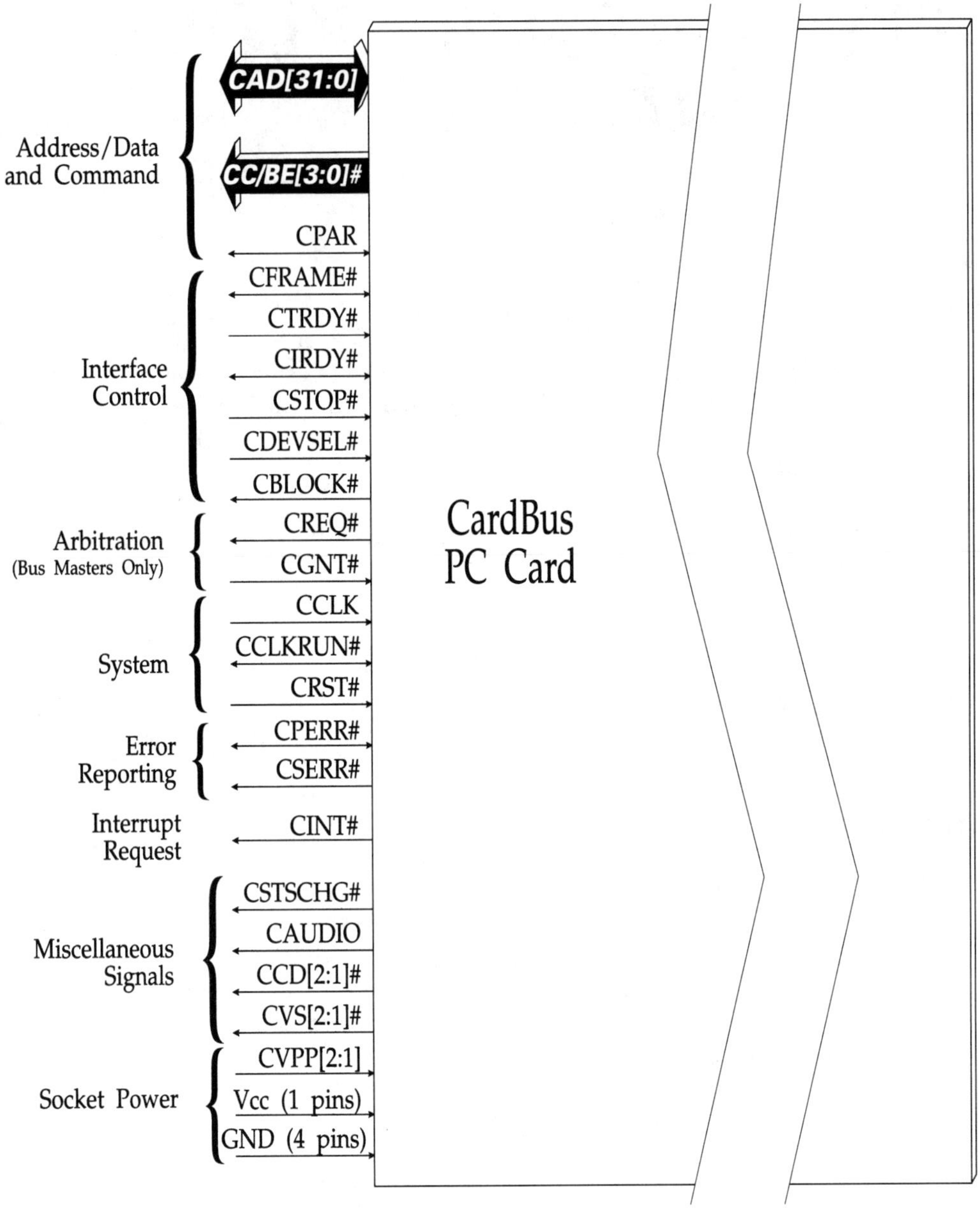

Figure 6-2: CardBus-Compliant Signals during Transactions in which PC Card is Target

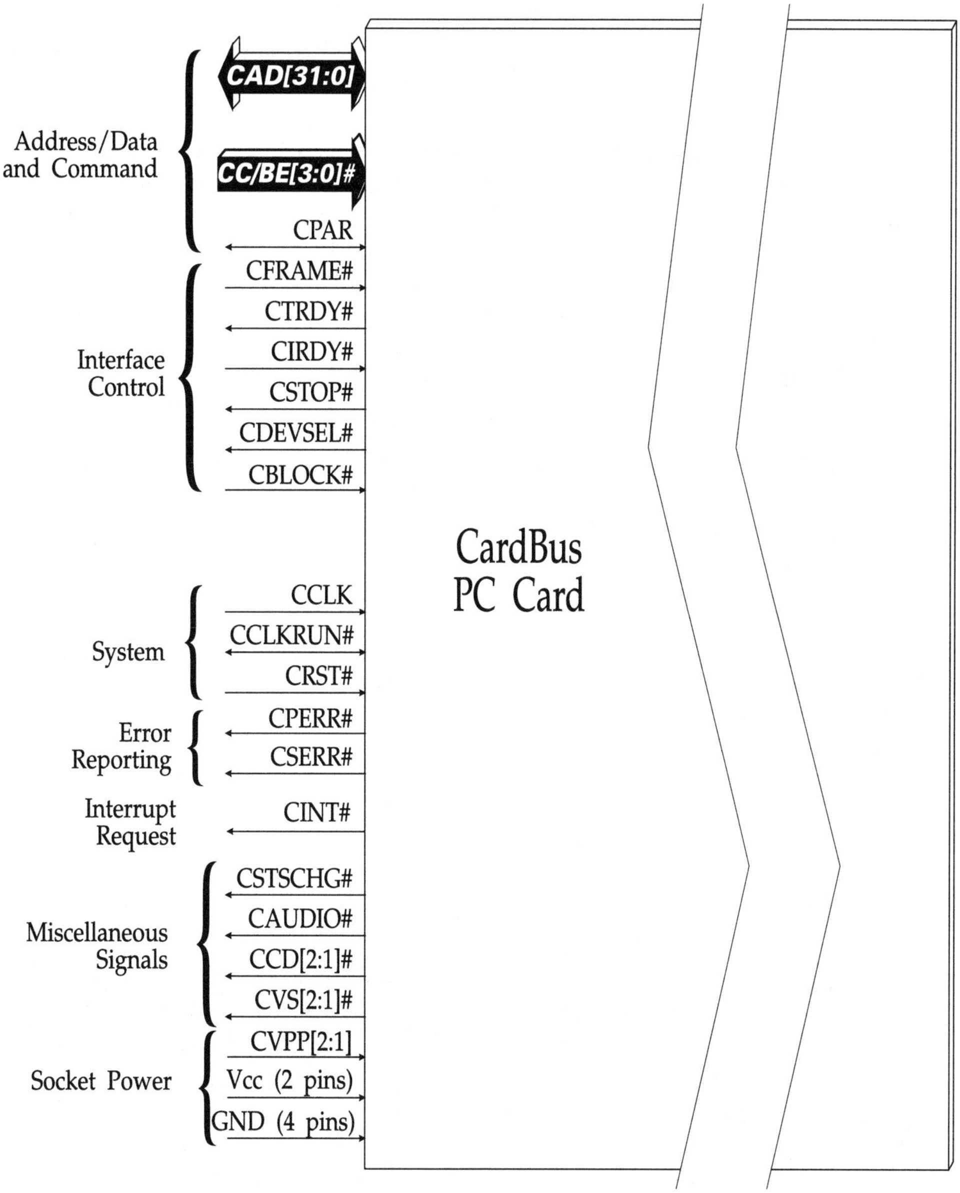

System Signals

CardBus Clock Signal (CCLK)

The CCLK signal is an input to a CardBus PC Card. It provides timing for all transactions, as well as bus arbitration. All inputs to CardBus devices are sampled on the rising edge of the CCLK signal, and are don't-care at all other times. All CardBus timing parameters are specified with respect to the rising-edge of the CCLK signal. All actions (with the exception of CINT#) on CardBus are synchronized to the CCLK signal. The frequency of the CCLK signal may be anywhere from 0MHz to 33MHz. The PC Card standard indicates that **all** CardBus devices **must** support CCLK operation within the 0MHz to 33MHz range. The clock frequency may be changed at any time as long as:

- The clock edges remain clean.
- The bus is idle.
- The minimum clock high and low times are not violated.
- There are no bus requests outstanding.
- CBLOCK# is not asserted.

The clock may only be stopped in a low state (to conserve power). As an exception, components designed to be integrated onto the system board may be designed to operate at a fixed frequency (of up to 33MHz) and may only operate at that frequency.

CCLKRUN# Signal

General

The CCLKRUN# signal is optional and is defined for the mobile (i.e., portable) environment. This section provides an introduction to this subject. Although the PC Card specification states that the clock may be stopped or its frequency changed, it does not define a method for determining when to stop (or slow down) the clock, or a method for determining when to restart the clock.

A portable system includes a central resource that includes the CardBus clock generation logic. With respect to the clock generation logic, the CCLKRUN# signal is a sustained tri-state input/output signal. The clock generation logic keeps CCLKRUN# asserted when the clock is running normally. During periods when the clock has been stopped (or slowed), the clock generation logic monitors CCLKRUN# to recognize requests from master and target devices for a change to be made in the state of the CardBus clock signal. The clock cannot be stopped if the bus is not idle. Before it stops (or slows down) the clock frequency, the clock generation logic deasserts CCLKRUN# for one clock to inform CardBus devices that the clock is about to stopped (or slowed). After driving CCLKRUN# high (deasserted) for one clock, the clock generation logic tri-states its CCLKRUN# output driver. The keeper resistor on CCLKRUN# then assumes responsibility for maintaining the deasserted state of CCLKRUN# while the clock is stopped (or slowed).

The clock continues to run unchanged for a minimum of four clocks after the clock generation logic deasserts CCLKRUN#. After deassertion of CCLKRUN#, the clock generation logic must monitor CCLKRUN# for two possible cases:

- After the clock has been stopped (or slowed), a master (or multiple masters) may require clock restart in order to request use of the bus. Prior to issuing the bus request, the master(s) must first request clock restart. This is accomplished by asserting CCLKRUN#. The master can assert CCLKRUN# after it has been deasserted for two successive CardBus clock cycles. When the clock generation logic detects the assertion of CCLKRUN# by another party, it turns on (or speeds up) the clock and enables its CCLKRUN# output driver to assert CCLKRUN#. When the requesting master detects that CCLKRUN# has been asserted for two successive rising-edges of the CardBus CLK signal, the master may then tri-state its CCLKRUN# output driver.
- When the clock generation logic has deasserted CCLKRUN#, indicating its intention to stop (or slow) the clock, the clock must continue to run for a minimum of four clocks. During this period of time, a target (or master) that requires continued clock operation (e.g., in order to perform internal housekeeping after the completion of a transaction) may reassert CCLKRUN# for two CardBus clock cycles to request continued generation of CCLK. When the clock generation logic samples CCLKRUN# reasserted, it continues to generate the clock (rather than stopping it or slowing it down). Devices are not permitted to pulse CCLKRUN# continuously to prevent the host system from stopping the clock. The specification doesn't define the period of time that the clock will continue to run after a request for continued operation. The author interprets this as implying that the period is system design-specific.

Reset Signal (CRST#)

When asserted, the reset signal forces all CardBus configuration registers, master and target state machines and output drivers to an initialized state. CRST# may be asserted asynchronously with respect to the CCLK edge, but must be deasserted synchronously with the clock edge. The system must assert CRST# during powerup, power down, or when power fails.

Address/Data Bus

The CardBus bus uses a time-multiplexed address/data bus. During the address phase of a transaction:

- The CAD bus, CAD[31:0], carries the start address. The resolution of this address is on a doubleword boundary (address divisible by four) during a memory or a configuration transaction, or a byte-specific address during an I/O read or write transaction. Additional information on memory and I/O addressing can be found in their respective chapters entitled "Memory Transfers" and I/O Transfers." For additional information on configuration addressing, See "Configuration Transfers" on page 237..
- The CardBus Command or Byte Enable bus, CC/BE[3:0]#, defines the type of transaction. The section entitled "Transaction Types" on page 99 defines the transaction types.
- The Parity signal, CPAR, is driven by the initiator one clock after completion of the address phase and one clock after the assertion of CIRDY# during each data phase of write transactions. It is driven by the currently-addressed target one clock after the assertion of CTRDY# during each data phase of read transactions.

One clock after completion of the address phase, the initiator drives CPAR either high or low to ensure even parity across the address bus, CAD[31:0], and the four Command/Byte Enable lines, CC/BE[3:0]#.

During each data phase:

- The data bus, CAD[31:0], is driven by the initiator (during a write) or the currently-addressed target (during a read).
- CPAR is driven by either the initiator (during a write) or the currently-addressed target (during a read) one clock after the assertion of CIRDY# (during a write) or CTRDY# (during a read) and ensures even parity across CAD[31:0] and CC/BE[3:0]#. If all four data paths are not being used dur-

ing a data phase, the agent driving the data bus (the master during a write or the target during a read) must ensure that a stable pattern is being driven onto all data paths (including those not being used to transfer data). This is necessary because CPAR must reflect even parity across the entire CAD and CC/BE buses.

- The Command/Byte Enable bus, CC/BE[3:0]#, is driven by the initiator to indicate the bytes to be transferred within the currently-addressed doubleword and the data paths to be used to transfer the data. Table 6-1 on page 65 indicates the mapping of the byte enable signals to the data paths and to the locations within the currently-addressed doubleword. Any combination of byte enables is considered valid and the byte enables may change from data phase to data phase.

Table 6-1: Byte Enable Mapping To Data Paths

Signal	Description
CC/BE3#	Data path 3, CAD[31:24], and the fourth location in the currently-addressed doubleword.
CC/BE2#	Data path 2, CAD[23:16], and the third location in the currently-addressed doubleword.
CC/BE1#	Data path 1, CAD[15:8], and the second location in the currently-addressed doubleword.
CC/BE0#	Data path 0, CAD[7:0], and the first location in the currently-addressed doubleword.

Preventing Excessive Current Drain

If the inputs to CMOS input receivers are permitted to float for long periods, the receivers tend to oscillate (the input transistors switch rapidly on and off), drawing excessive current. In order to prevent this phenomena and preserve the "green" nature of Cardbus, several rules are applied:

- When the bus is idle and no bus masters are requesting ownership, the CardBus bridge must enable its CAD, CC/BE and CPAR output drivers and drive a stable pattern onto these signal lines.
- During a data phase in a write transaction, the CardBus initiator must drive a stable pattern onto the CAD bus if it is not yet ready to deliver the next set of data bytes. During a data phase in a read transaction, the CardBus target

must drive a stable pattern onto the CAD bus if it is not yet ready to deliver the next set of data bytes.

Transaction Control Signals

Table 6-2 provides a brief description of each signal used to control a CardBus transfer.

Table 6-2: CardBus Interface Control Signals

Signal	Master	Target	Description
CFRAME#	In/Out	In	**Frame** is driven by the current initiator and indicates the start (when it's first asserted) and duration (the duration of its assertion) of a transaction. In order to determine that bus ownership has been acquired, the master must sample CFRAME# and CIRDY# both deasserted on the same rising-edge of the CardBus CCLK signal. A transaction may consist of one or more data transfers between the initiator and the currently-addressed target. CFRAME# is deasserted when the initiator is ready (i.e., has asserted CIRDY#) to complete the final data phase.
CTRDY#	In	Out	**Target Ready** is driven by the currently-addressed target. It is asserted when the target is ready to complete the current data phase (data transfer). A data phase is completed when the target is asserting CTRDY# and the initiator is asserting CIRDY# on the same rising-edge of the CCLK signal. During a read, CTRDY# asserted indicates that the target is driving valid data onto the data bus. During a write, CTRDY# asserted indicates that the target is ready to accept data from the master. Wait states are inserted in the current data phase until both CTDRY# and CIRDY# are sampled asserted.

Table 6-2: CardBus Interface Control Signals (Continued)

Signal	Master	Target	Description
CIRDY#	In/Out	In	**Initiator Ready** is driven by the current bus master (the initiator of the transaction). During a write, CIRDY# asserted indicates that the initiator is driving valid data onto the data bus. During a read, CIRDY# asserted indicates that the initiator is ready to accept data from the currently-addressed target. In order to determine that bus ownership has been acquired, the master must sample CFRAME# and CIRDY# both deasserted on the same rising-edge of the CardBus CLK signal. Also refer to the description of CTRDY# in this table.
CSTOP#	In	Out	The target asserts CSTOP# to indicate that it wishes the initiator to **stop** the transaction on the current data phase.
CBLOCK#	In/Out	In	Used by the initiator to **lock** the currently-addressed memory target during an atomic transaction series (e.g., during a semaphore read/modify/write operation). Refer to the description (in this chapter) under the heading "Resource Locking" on page 71 and to the chapter entitled "Locked Transfers" on page 157.
CDEVSEL#	In	Out	**Device Select** is asserted by a target when the target has successfully decoded the address and command. It acts as an input to the current initiator and the subtractive decoder (See "Data Phase(s)" on page 98.) in the expansion bus bridge. If a master initiates a transfer and does not detect CDEVSEL# active within six CCLK periods (from the assertion of CFRAME#), it must assume that the target cannot respond or that the address is unpopulated. A master-abort results.

Arbitration Signals

A CardBus card operating as an initiator has a pair of arbitration lines that connect it directly to the CardBus arbiter. When a CardBus master is ready to perform a transfer, it asserts its CREQ# line to the arbiter. When the arbiter has determined that the requesting master should be granted access to the bus, it asserts the master's CGNT# (grant) line. In the CardBus and PCI environments, bus arbitration can take place while another master is still performing a transfer. This is known as "hidden" arbitration. When a bus master receives grant from the arbiter, it must wait for the current initiator to complete its transfer before initiating its transaction. A CardBus bus master cannot assume ownership of the bus until CFRAME# is sampled deasserted (indicating the start of the last data phase by the current initiator) and CIRDY# is then sampled deasserted (indicating the completion of the last data phase). This indicates that the current transaction has been completed and the bus has been returned to the idle state. Bus arbitration is discussed in more detail in the chapter entitled "Arbitration" on page 81.

While CRST# is asserted, all masters must tri-state their CREQ# output drivers and must ignore their CGNT# inputs.

Interrupt Request Signal

CardBus cards that generate interrupts use a single interrupt request line (CINT#). Since CardBus supports up to eight functions within a single CardBus card, all functions that require use of an interrupt must share the single interrupt line. A detailed description of interrupts can be found in the chapter entitled "CardBus Function Interrupts" on page 193.

Error Reporting Signals

The sections that follow provide an introduction to the CPERR# and CSERR# signals. The chapter entitled "Error Handling" on page 171 provides a more detailed discussion of error detection and handling.

Data Parity Error

The **generation of parity** information is **mandatory** for all CardBus devices that drive address or data information onto the CAD bus. This is a requirement because the agent driving the CAD bus must assume that the agent receiving the data and parity will check the validity of the parity and may either flag an error or even fail the machine if incorrect parity is received.

The **detection and reporting of parity errors** by CardBus devices is **generally required**. The specification is written this way to indicate that, in some cases, the designer may choose to ignore parity errors. An example might be a video frame buffer. The designer may choose not to verify the correctness of the data being written into the video memory by the initiator. In the event that corrupted data is received and written into the frame memory, the only effect will be one or more corrupted video pixels displayed on the screen. Although this may have a deleterious effect on the end user's peace of mind, it will not corrupt programs or the data structures associated with programs.

Implementation of the CPERR# pin is required on all add-in CardBus cards (and is generally required on system board devices). The data parity error signal, CPERR#, may be pulsed by a CardBus device under the following circumstances:

- In the event of a data parity error detected by a CardBus target during a write data phase, the target must set the DETECTED PARITY ERROR bit in its CardBus configuration status register and must assert CPERR# (if the PARITY RESPONSE ENABLE bit in its configuration command register is set to one). It may then either continue the transaction or may assert CSTOP# to terminate the transaction prematurely. During a burst write, the initiator is responsible for monitoring the CPERR# signal to ensure that each data item is not corrupted in flight while being written to the target.
- In the event of a data parity error detected by the CardBus initiator during a read data phase, the initiator must set the DETECTED PARITY ERROR bit in its CardBus configuration status register and must assert CPERR# (if the PARITY RESPONSE ENABLE bit in its configuration command register is set to one).

The platform designer may include third-party logic that monitors CPERR# or may leave error reporting up to the initiator.

To ensure that correct parity is available to any CardBus devices that perform parity checking, all CardBus devices must generate even parity on CAD[31:0],

CC/BE[3:0]# and CPAR for the address and data phases. CPERR# is implemented as an output on targets and as both an input and an output on masters. The initiator of a transaction is responsible for reporting the detection of a data parity error to software. For this reason, it must monitor CPERR# during write data phases to determine if the target has detected a data parity error. The action taken by an initiator when a parity error is detected is design-dependent. It may perform retries with the target or may choose to terminate the transaction and generate an interrupt to invoke its device-specific interrupt handler. If the initiator reports the failure to software, it must also set the DATA PARITY DETECTED bit in its CardBus configuration status register. CPERR# is only driven by one device at time.

A detailed discussion of data parity error detection and handling may be found in the chapter entitled "Error Handling" on page 171.

System Error

The System Error signal, CSERR#, may be pulsed by any CardBus device to report address parity errors, data parity errors during a special cycle, and critical errors other than parity. CSERR# is required on all CardBus cards that perform address parity checking or report other serious errors using CSERR#. This signal is considered a "last-recourse" for reporting serious errors. Non-catastrophic and correctable errors should be signaled in some other way. In a PC-compatible machine, CSERR# typically causes an NMI to the system processor (although the designer is not constrained to have it generate an NMI). In a PowerPC, PREP-compliant platform, assertion of CSERR# is reported to the host processor via assertion of TEA# or MC# and causes a machine check interrupt. This is the functional equivalent of NMI in the Intel world. If the designer of a CardBus device does not want an NMI to be initiated, some means other than CSERR# should be used to flag an error condition (such as setting a bit in the device's status register and/or generating an interrupt request). CSERR# is an open-drain signal and may be driven by more than one CardBus agent at a time. When asserted, the device drives it low for one clock and then tri-states its output driver. The keeper resistor on CSERR# is responsible for returning it to the deasserted state.

A detailed discussion of system error detection and handling may be found in the chapter entitled "Error Detection and Handling."

Resource Locking

The CBLOCK# signal is an optional signal for CardBus initiators, but is mandatory on any device providing system memory (i.e., a device that implements executable memory or memory that contains system data (managed by the operating system).

An initiator requiring exclusive access to a target may use the CBLOCK# signal if it isn't currently being driven by another initiator. When the target device is addressed and CBLOCK# is deasserted by the initiator during the address phase and then asserted during the data phase, the target device is reserved (i.e., locked) for as long as the CBLOCK# signal remains asserted. If the target is subsequently addressed by another bus master while the lock is still in force, the target issues a retry to the initiator. While a target is locked, other bus masters (that don't require exclusive access to a target) are permitted to acquire the bus to access targets other than the locked target.

Miscellaneous Signals

Power

Vcc is specified at 3.3, x.x (< 3.3), or y.y (< x.x) vdc for CardBus cards. x.x and y.y vdc are to be defined in a future version of the PC Card Standard. The maximum current budget allowed is 1 amp, with a maximum of 70ma during configuration.

Card Detection

The card detection signals, CCD[2:1]# are used in conjunction with the CVS[2:1] signals to determine when a CardBus card is installed in a socket. Refer to the section entitled "Detecting PC Card Insertion" on page 52 for details regarding the detection of a CardBus card.

Audio

The audio signal, CAUDIO, is defined as either a single amplitude digital waveform, or it may carry pulse width modulated (PWM) audio information. The signal can be passed from the CardBus bridge to the system's speaker.

Status Change

The optional CardBus status change signal (CSTSCHG#) is asserted when a PCMCIA-defined event occurs within the card. The events that may be signaled include:

- Low-Battery Warning
- Dead Battery
- Write-Protect
- Ready or Busy

When one of these events occurs, the CardBus card asserts its CSTSCHG# pin to notify the CardBus bridge. The bridge in turn can generate an interrupt that invokes PCMCIA software to handle the event. Note that CSTSCHG# is asynchronous to CCLK.

Signal Types

The signals that comprise the CardBus interface are electrically defined in one of the following fashions:

- IN defines a signal as a standard input-only signal.
- OUT defines a signal as a standard output-only signal.
- I/O defines a signal as a standard input/output signal.
- T/S defines a signal as a bi-directional, tri-state input/output signal.
- T/S, OUT defines a signal as a tri-state output.
- S/T/S defines a signal as a sustained tri-state signal that is driven by only one owner at a time. An agent that drives an s/t/s pin low must actively drive it high for at least one clock before tri-stating it. A pullup resistor is required to sustain the inactive state until another agent takes ownership of and drives the signal. The resistor is supplied as a central resource in the system design. The next owner of the signal cannot start driving the s/t/s signal any sooner than one clock after it is released by the previous owner.

This is ensured by the bus protocol.
- O/D defines a signal as a bi-directional, open-drain signal. The signaling agent asserts the signal when needed, but returning the signal to the inactive state is accomplished by a weak pull-up resistor.
- O/D, OUT defines a signal as an open-drain output.

Table 6-3 on page 73 defines the CardBus card and socket signal types.

Table 6-3: Signal Types

Signals	Type	
	Card	Socket
CCLK	IN	OUT
CCLKRUN#	O/D	S/T/S
CRST#	IN	OUT
CAD[31:0]	T/S	T/S
CC/BE[3:0]#	T/S	T/S
CPAR	T/S	T/S
CFRAME#	S/T/S	S/T/S
CTRDY#	S/T/S	S/T/S
CIRDY#	S/T/S	S/T/S
CSTOP#	S/T/S	S/T/S
CBLOCK#	S/T/S	S/T/S
CDEVSEL#	S/T/S	S/T/S
CREQ#	T/S, OUT	IN
CGNT#	IN	T/S, OUT
CPERR#	S/T/S	S/T/S
CSERR#	O/D	IN
CINT#	O/D	IN
CSTSCHG#	T/S, OUT	IN

Table 6-3: Signal Types (Continued)

Signals	Type	
	Card	Socket
CAUDIO#	OUT	IN
CCD[2:1]#	OUT	IN
CVS[2:1]	I/O	I/O

Central Resources

Any CardBus bridge must provide several support functions necessary for the proper operation of CardBus devices. These support functions include:

- A CardBus arbiter to support CardBus masters. The PC Card Standard does not define the decision-making process utilized by the CardBus arbiter. The design of the arbiter is therefore bridge-specific.
- Pullup resistors on signals that are not always driven to a valid state. Refer to Table 6-4 on page 74.
- Default ownership of the socket interface.
- CardBus Clock control.

Table 6-4: Location of Resistors on Socket Interface Pins

Pin	R2 Name	CB Name	R2 Host	CB Host	R2 Card	CB Card
1	GND	GND				
2	D3	CAD0			pull-down	
3	D4	CAD1			pull-down	
4	D5	CAD3			pull-down	
5	D6	CAD5			pull-down	
6	D7	CAD7			pull-down	
7	CE1#	CC/BE0#			pull-up	
8	A10	CAD9			pull-down	
9	OE#	CAD11			pull-up	
10	A11	CAD12			pull-down	
11	A9	CAD14			pull-down	
12	A8	CC/BE1#			pull-down	
13	A13	CPAR			pull-down	

Table 6-4: Location of Resistors on Socket Interface Pins (Continued)

Pin	R2 Name	CB Name	R2 Host	CB Host	R2 Card	CB Card
14	A14	CPERR#		Note 2	pull-down	
15	WE#	CGNT#			pull-up	pull-up
16	IREQ#	CINT#	pull-up	pull-up		
17	Vcc	Vcc				
18	Vpp1	Vpp1				
19	A16	CCLK			pull-down	
20	A15	CIRDY#		Note 2	pull-down	
21	A12	CC/BE2#			pull-down	
22	A7	CAD18			pull-down	
23	A6	CAD20			pull-down	
24	A5	CAD21			pull-down	
25	A4	CAD22			pull-down	
26	A3	CAD23			pull-down	
27	A2	CAD24			pull-down	
28	A1	CAD25			pull-down	
29	A0	CAD26			pull-down	
30	D0	CAD27			pull-down	
31	D1	CAD29			pull-down	
32	D2	RESERVED			pull-down	
33	IOIS16#	CCLKRUN#		Note 2		
34	GND	GND				
35	GND	GND				
36	CD1#	CCD1#	pull-up	pull-up		
37	D11	CAD2			pull-down	
38	D12	CAD4			pull-down	
39	D13	CAD6			pull-down	
40	D14	RESERVED			pull-down	
41	D15	CAD8			pull-down	
42	CE2#	CAD10			pull-up	
43	VS1	CVS1#	Note 1	Note 1		
44	IORD#	CAD13			pull-up	
45	IOWR#	CAD15			pull-up	
46	A17	CAD16			pull-down	
47	A18	RESERVED			pull-down	

Table 6-4: Location of Resistors on Socket Interface Pins (Continued)

Pin	R2 Name	CB Name	R2 Host	CB Host	R2 Card	CB Card
48	A19	CBLOCK#		Note 2	pull-down	
49	A20	CSTOP#		Note 2	pull-down	
50	A21	CDEVSEL#		Note 2	pull-down	
51	Vcc	Vcc				
52	Vpp2	Vpp2				
53	A22	CTRDY#			pull-down	
54	A23	CFRAME#			pull-down	pull-up
55	A24	CAD17			pull-down	
56	A25	CAD19			pull-down	
57	VS2	CVS2#	Note 1	Note 1		
58	RESET	CRST#		Note 2	pull-up	
59	WAIT#	CSERR#	pull-up			
60	INPACK#	CREQ#	pull-up			
61	REG#	CC/BE3#			pull-up	
62	SPKR#	CAUDIO#	Note 3	pull-up		
63	STSCHG#	CSTSCHG#	pull-up	Note 2		
64	D8	CAD28			pull-down	
65	D9	CAD30			pull-down	
66	D10	CAD31			pull-down	
67	CD2#	CCD2#	pull-up	pull-up		
68	GND	GND				

Note 1. The pull-up can be integrated into the adapter's CVS output buffers.

Note 2. The pull-ups can be eliminated from the CardBus interface if specific conditions are met that ensure proper operation in some circumstances (See list below). The pull-ups on these pins are required for the 16-bit PC Card interface.

Note 3. 16-bit hosts must pull-up BVD2 to avoid sensing a battery-low condition when JEIDA memory cards are inserted.

If the associated condition is satisfied, pull-ups can be eliminated from the following pins:

1. **CRST#** — CardBus bridge guarantees the signal will not be in a high-Z state when a CardBus card is present.
2. **CSTSCHG#** — CardBus bridge ensures that remote wakeup isn't falsely

signaled when socket is empty.

3. **CCLKRUN#** — Clock stopping is not implemented and bridge never puts signal in a high-Z state.
4. **CIRDY#, CTRDY#, CDEVSEL#, CSTOP#** — Bridge ensures the signal is always driven when the bus is idle.
5. **CPERR#** — bridge ensures signal is always driven when bus is idle. Note that CPERR# lags the end of transfer by two clock cycles.
6. **CBLOCK#** — bridge ensures the signal is always driven when bus is idle.

Part Three

CardBus Transaction Protocols

7 Arbitration

The Previous Chapter

The previous chapter divided the PCI bus signals into functional groups and described the function of each group.

This Chapter

This chapter describes the bus arbitration process, including the arbitration signaling protocol and timing, and the concept of delayed transactions. The CardBus standard defines the timing of the request and grant handshaking, but not the procedure used to determine the winner of the arbitration. The algorithm used by the bus arbiter to decide which of the requesting bus masters will be granted use of the bus is system-specific and outside the scope of the specification.

The Next Chapter

The next chapter describes the types of transactions supported by CardBus. Command types are defined and protocol essentials are detailed.

The Arbitration Handshaking Protocol

At a given instant in time, one or more CardBus cards and/or PCI initiators may require use of the PCI bus to perform a data transfer. Each requesting initiator asserts its request output to inform the bus arbiter of its request for use of the bus. Each initiator connects to the arbiter via a separate pair of request/grant signals (CREQ#/CGNT# for CardBus and REQ#/GNT# for PCI). When a CardBus card needs the bus it asserts its CREQ# line and waits for its CGNT# line to be asserted by the arbitration logic. CardBus uses the same arbitration signaling protocol as PCI. This arbitration process is said to be hidden because the arbiter can determine which of the bus masters asserting request has the highest priority request pending, and can assert the winning bus master's CGNT# line, and do so while the current bus owner continues its burst transfer.

The arbiter asserts only one grant signal to indicate the bus master that gets to use the bus when the current initiator completes its transaction.

Request/Grant Timing

The signaling protocol used during bus arbitration is illustrated in Figure 7-1 on page 84 and summarized below. In the illustration, bus master A requires the bus to perform two transactions. The first consists of a three data phase write and the second transaction type is a single data phase write. Bus master B only requires the bus to execute a single transaction consisting of one data phase, and the arbiter recognizes that bus master B has a higher priority than bus master A.

1. An initiator needing use of the bus asserts its CREQ# pin, notifying the arbiter that it needs to perform a transaction. Note that on the rising edge of clock one, device **A**'s CREQ# line is sampled asserted by the arbiter.
2. The arbiter asserts the initiator's CGNT# signal, indicating that it is the winner of the arbitration and is granted use of the bus when the current transaction ends. Note that on the rising edge of clock two device **A** samples its CGNT# pin asserted.
3. Bus master **A** monitors the bus to detect the end of the current transaction. Note that the bus returns to the idle state at the end of each bus transaction. Bus master **A** watches for the bus idle state to detect the end of the transaction (i.e., both CFRAME# and CIRDY# deasserted). When initiator **A** samples CGNT# asserted on the rising edge of clock two, it also detects that the bus is idle. Note that although bus master **B** samples it CGNT# pin asserted in clock four, initiator **A** does not signal the idle state until clock seven.
4. The initiator starts its transfer in the clock cycle in which it detects that the bus has returned to the idle state (e.g., clock cycles two and ten for initiator **A** and clock cycle seven for initiator **B**).
5. If the initiator needs to perform only a single transaction, it must deassert its CREQ# line when beginning its transfer. This notifies the arbiter that the initiator does not need the bus after this transaction, allowing it to grant use of the bus to another initiator that has a need for the bus. The current owner however can complete its transfer, after which it will signal the bus idle condition. This behavior is illustrated by initiator **B** in clock seven when it starts its transaction by asserting CFRAME# and deasserts CREQ#.
6. If the initiator wishes to perform another transaction, it must keep its CREQ# line asserted when it asserts CFRAME#. If it's CGNT# line is still asserted when the first transaction completes (during the idle state), the initiator can start a second transfer. The arbiter will keep the initiator's CGNT# line asserted unless another bus master with a higher priority asserts its

request. Note that initiator **A** keeps its CREQ# signal asserted when it starts a transaction during clock two. However, since initiator **A**'s CGNT# line is sampled deasserted on the rising edge of clock seven, initiator **A** must relinquish control of the bus.

7. If, during a transfer, an initiator detects it's CGNT# line has been deasserted by the arbiter (because it has been preempted), it knows that another bus master has been granted use of the bus next. The bus master with a pending transfer must wait for the current initiator to end its transfer (indicated by the bus idle state) before beginning its transfer. This mechanism assumes that the current owner will relinquish control of the bus within a reasonable period of time. The amount of time that an initiator can retain the bus once it has been preempted is restricted by its master latency timer (see "Master Latency Timer" on page 90).

Figure 7-1: Sample Arbitration Between Two CardBus Initiators

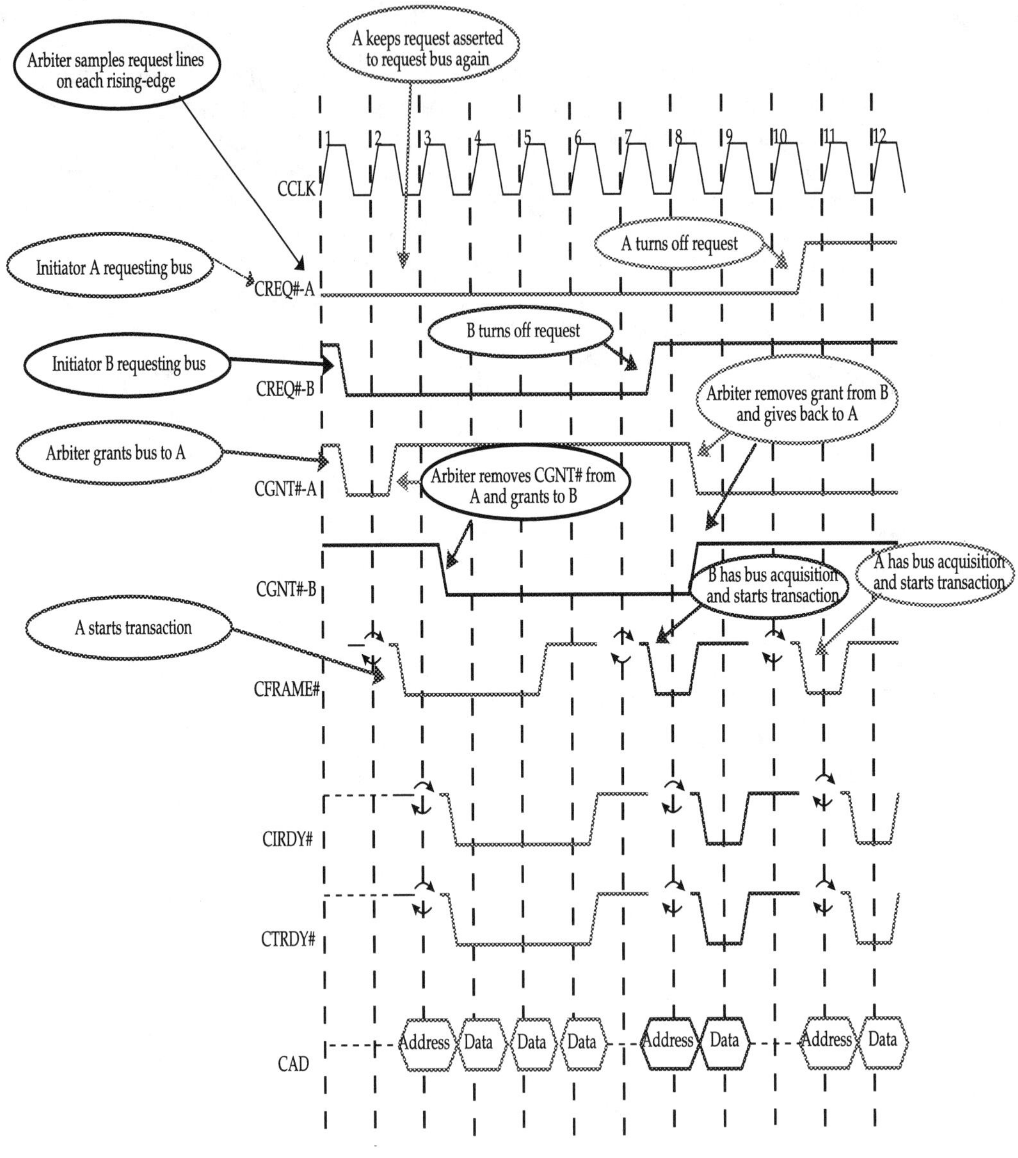

Arbitration with Single-Socket Bridge

The CardBus bridge plays a crucial role in the arbitration process. The bridge itself may or may not have it own arbiter depending on whether it controls a single CardBus socket or multiple sockets. Figure 7-2 on page 85 on illustrates a PCI/CardBus bridge with a single CardBus card socket. In this case, the bridge does not include an arbiter. When the CardBus card asserts its CREQ# line, the bridge forwards the CREQ# to the PCI arbiter by asserting its REQ# line. Similarly the GNT# line is passed to the CardBus card's CGNT# pin.

Figure 7-2: Arbitration Signaling with Single-Socket PCI/CardBus Bridge.

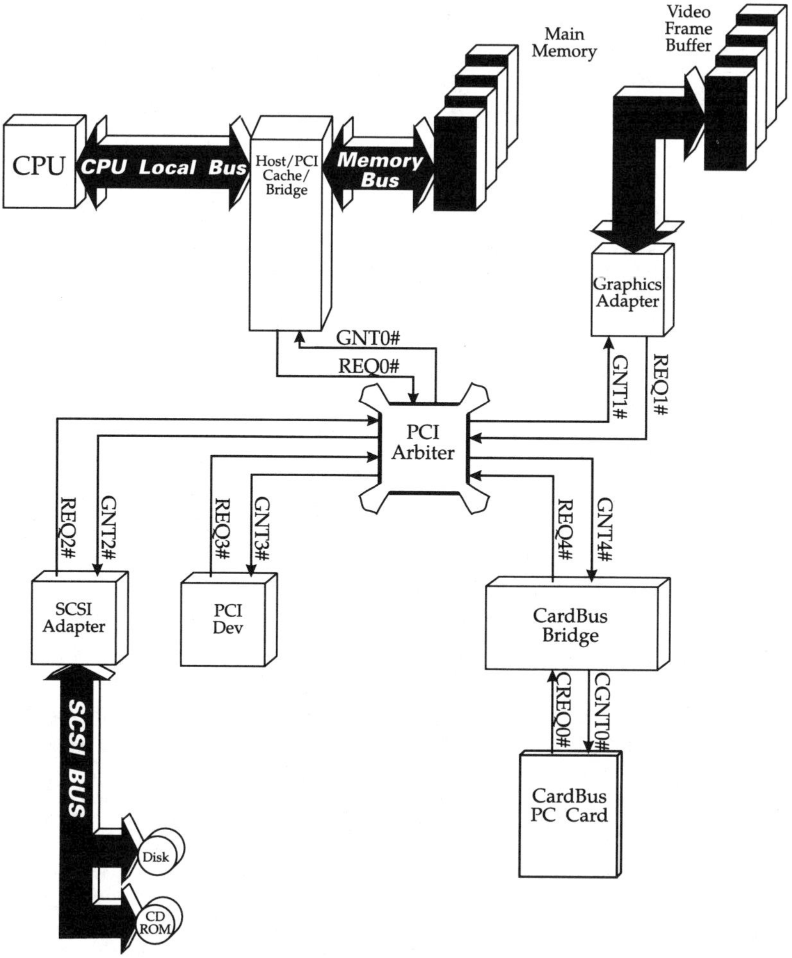

Arbitration with Multiple-Socket Bridge

When a CardBus bridge supports multiple CardBus cards, the bridge must also contain a arbiter. Refer to Figure 7-3 on page 87. The arbitration signal routing employed and the functionality of the bridge arbiter is implementation specific. Two primary mechanisms are likely to be employed:

- PCI-based Arbitration — Arbitration occurs within the PCI arbiter since all CardBus transactions use PCI bus.
- CardBus Bridge-based Arbitration/PCI-based Arbitration — Arbitration occurs locally within the CardBus bridge and the winning CardBus initiator performs a local transaction to determine if a PC Card is the target device. If a PC Card is not the target then the CardBus bridge must arbitrate for ownership of the PCI bus.

PCI-based Arbitration

The arbiter within the PCI/CardBus bridge may be designed to always obtain ownership of the PCI bus regardless of the target device location. In this case, the bridge must arbitrate between the CardBus initiators (CREQn# lines) to determine the highest priority CardBus card that has a request pending. The bridge then asserts its REQ# line to notify the central PCI arbiter that the CardBus bridge requires access to the PCI bus. Note that the arbiter does not directly assert the CGNTn# pin, but rather waits for GNT# from the PCI central arbiter before asserting CGNTn# to the card.

When CGNTn# is returned to the CardBus card, the bridge then passes the FRAME# and IRDY# from the PCI bus to the CardBus socket's CFRAME# and CIRDY# pins card so it can monitor the PCI bus and detect the PCI bus idle state before beginning its transaction. When the CardBus initiator detects the idle state, it begins its transaction by asserting CFRAME#. In response the CardBus bridge would assert its FRAME# signal to forward the CardBus transaction to the PCI bus.

In this implementation all CardBus transactions are propagated onto the PCI bus. If another PC Card is the target of the transaction, the bridge's input buffers will detect the PCI transaction being driven by the CardBus card and pass the transaction on to the target PC Card.

CardBus Bridge-based Arbitration/PCI-based Arbitration

The CardBus arbiter determines the highest priority CardBus card that has a request pending and immediately asserts its CGNTn# pin. When the CardBus card detects the bus idle condition, it begins its transaction. This permits the bridge to determine if the target device resides within a local PC Card and if so, completes the transaction without obtaining ownership of the PCI bus. If the target device is not a PC Card, then the CardBus bridge must assert its REQ# line to request ownership of the PCI bus.

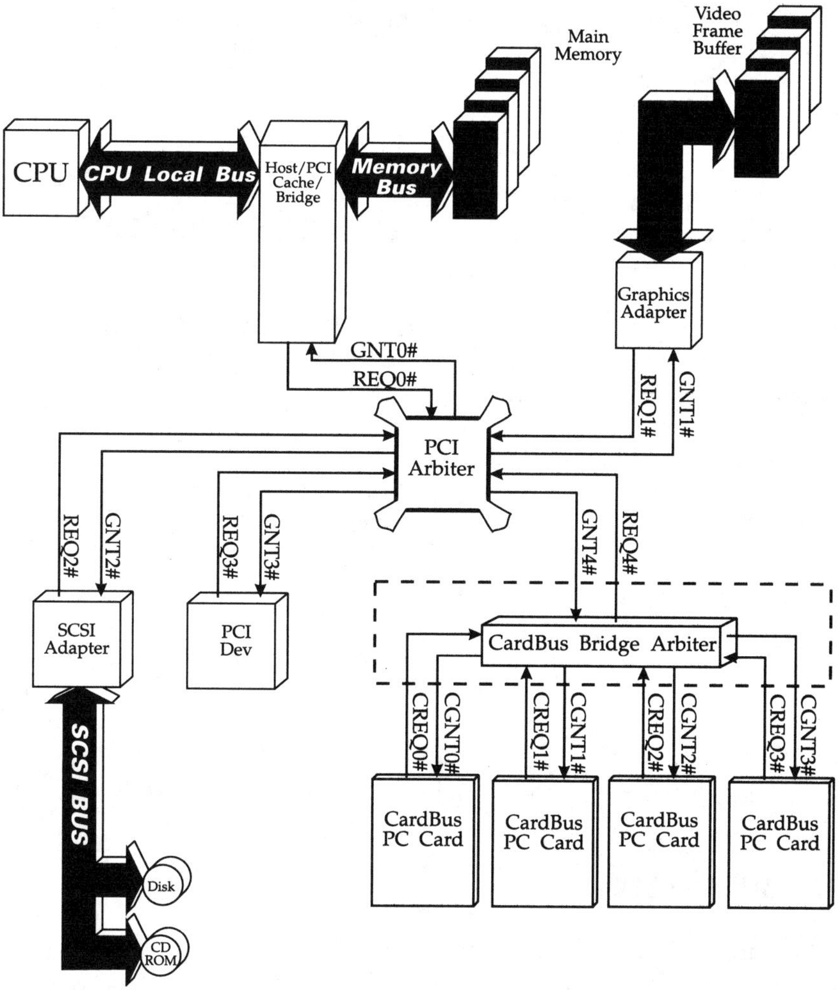

Figure 7-3: Arbitration Signaling with a Four Socket PCI/CardBus Bridge

Arbiter Behavior During Bus Idle

The CardBus bridge is responsible for keeping the CAD bus, CC/BE bus and CPAR from floating (to keep the CardBus CMOS input buffers on all devices from oscillating and drawing excessive current). The bridge must be designed to drive the CAD bus, CC/BE# lines and CPAR during periods when the bus is idle. However, the bridge need not turn on all of its output drivers in a single clock (it may take up to eight clocks, but two to three clocks is recommended). This procedure ensures that the bus doesn't float during bus idle periods. Table 7-1 defines the various states that the CardBus interface can be in at a given moment in time.

Table 7-1: Determining the Bus State

CFRAME#	CIRDY#	Description
deasserted	deasserted	Bus Idle.
deasserted	asserted	Initiator is ready to complete the last data transfer of a transaction, but it has not yet completed.
asserted	deasserted	A transaction is in progress and the initiator is not ready to complete the current data phase.
asserted	asserted	A transaction is in progress and the initiator is ready to complete the current data phase.

If CGNT# is deasserted and CFRAME# is asserted the transfer is valid and will continue. The deassertion of CGNT# by the arbiter indicates that the master will no longer own the bus at the completion of the transaction currently in progress. The master keeps CFRAME# asserted while the current transaction is still in progress. It deasserts CFRAME# when it is ready to complete the final data phase. The CGNT# to one master can be deasserted simultaneously with the assertion of another master's CGNT# if the bus isn't in the idle state.

Arbitration Algorithm

The CardBus standard does not define the scheme used by the CardBus arbiter to decide the winner of the competition when multiple masters simultaneously request bus ownership. The arbiter may utilize any scheme, such as one based on fixed or rotational priority or a combination of the two (rotational between one group of masters and fixed within another group). The goal of the arbiter design should be to minimize access latency, considering all bus masters in the system (bus masters embedded in the system along with those residing on add-in cards).

Bus Access Latency

When a bus master wishes to transfer a block of data between itself and a target PCI device, it must request the use of the bus from the bus arbiter. Bus access latency is defined as the amount of time that passes from the moment a bus master requests the use of the PCI bus until it completes the first data transfer of the transaction. Table 7-2 describes each latency component.

Table 7-2: Access Latency Components

Latency Component	Description
Arbitration Latency	Defined as the period of time from the bus master's assertion of CREQ# until the bus arbiter asserts the bus master's CGNT#. This period is a function of the arbitration algorithm, the master's priority and whether any other masters are requesting access to the bus.
Bus Acquisition Latency	Defined as the period time from the reception of CGNT# by the requesting bus master until the current initiator surrenders the bus. The requesting bus master can then initiate its transaction by asserting CFRAME#. The duration of this period is a function of how long the current bus master's transaction-in-progress takes to complete. This parameter is the larger of either the current master's LT value (in other words, its timeslice) or the longest latency to first data phase completion in the system (16 clocks for 2.1 devices).
Target Latency	Defined as the period of time from the start of a transaction until the currently-addressed target is ready to complete the first data transfer of the transaction. This period is a function of the access time for the currently-addressed target device, but may not exceed 16 clocks from the assertion of CFRAME# for a 2.1-compliant PCI device).

CardBus initiators should always use burst transfers to transfer blocks of data between themselves and a target CardBus or PCI device (some poorly-designed masters use a series of single-data phase transactions to transfer a block of data). The transfer may consist of anywhere from one to an unlimited number of bytes. A bus master that has requested and has been granted the use of the bus (its CGNT# is asserted by the arbiter) cannot begin a transaction until the current bus master completes its transaction-in-progress. If the current master were permitted to own the bus until its entire transfer were completed, however, it would be possible for the current bus master to lock out other bus masters from using the bus for extended periods of time. The extensive delay incurred could cause other bus masters (and/or the application programs they serve) to experience poor performance or even to malfunction (buffer overflows or starvation may be experienced).

As an example, a bus master could have a buffer-full condition and is requesting the use of the bus in order to off-load its buffer contents to system memory. If it experiences an extended delay (latency) in acquiring the bus to begin the transfer, it may experience a data overrun condition as it receives more data from its associated device (such as a network) to be placed into its buffer.

In order to ensure that the designers of bus masters are dealing with a predictable and manageable amount of bus latency, the 2.1 PCI specification defines several mechanisms:

- **Master Latency Timer**—prevents master from monopolizing bus.
- **Limit on initiator's latency**—initiator is not permitted to keep CIRDY# deasserted for longer than eight clock periods during any data phase.
- **Target-Initiated Termination**—prevents slow targets from consuming bus bandwidth.

Master Latency Timer

The master latency timer, or LT, is implemented as a CardBus configuration register in the bus master's configuration space. It is either initialized by the configuration software at start-up time, or contains a hardwired value. The value contained in the LT defines the minimum amount of time (in CCLK periods) that the bus master is permitted to retain ownership of the bus whenever it acquires bus ownership and initiates a transaction.

How LT Works

When the bus master detects bus idle (CFRAME# and CIRDY# deasserted) and its CGNT# asserted, it has bus acquisition and may initiate a transaction. Upon initiation of the transaction, the master's LT is initialized to the value written to the LT by the configuration software at start-up time (or its hardwired value). Starting on the next rising-edge of the CCLK and on every subsequent rising-edge, the master decrements its LT by one.

If the master is in the midst of a burst transaction and the arbiter removes its CGNT#, this indicates that the arbiter has detected a request from another master and is granting ownership of the bus for the next transaction to the other master. In other words, the current master has been preempted.

If the current master's LT has not yet been exhausted (decremented all the way down), it has not yet used up its timeslice and may retain ownership of the bus until it either: completes its burst transaction or its LT expires, whichever comes first. If it is able to complete its burst before expiration of its LT, the other master that has its CGNT# may assume bus ownership when it detects that the current master has returned the bus to the idle state. When the preempted master has exhausted its LT, it is permitted to complete one more data transfer and must then yield the bus.

If the current master has exhausted its LT, still has its CGNT# and has not yet completed it burst transfer, it may retain ownership of the bus and continue to burst data until it either: completes its overall burst transfer, or its CGNT# is removed by the arbiter. In the latter case, the current master is permitted to complete one more data transfer and must then yield the bus.

It should be noted that when forced to prematurely terminate a data transfer, the bus master must "remember" where it was in the transfer. After a brief period, it may then reassert its CREQ# to request bus ownership again so that it may continue where it left off.

Implementation of the LT register is mandatory for CardBus initiators. They must be implemented as a read/writable register by any master that performs more than two data phases per transaction. The LT register contents can be hardwired (read-only) for a master that only performs one or two data phases per transaction, but the hardwired value may not exceed 16.

The initiator may not keep CIRDY# deasserted for more than eight CCLKs during any data phase. If the initiator has no buffer space available to store read data, it must delay requesting the bus until is has room for the data. On a write transaction, the initiator must have the data available before it asks for the bus.

How Software Determines Timeslice

Configuration software determines the timeslice requested by the bus master designer by reading the hardwired, read-only value from the device's Min_Gnt (Minimum Grant) configuration register. The designer indicates the desired timeslice in increments of 250ns. The configuration software evaluates the bus master's bus need against those of the other masters that reside on the bus and tries to match, as closely as possible, the master's request. The configuration software "knows" the speed of the PCI bus and converts the request into the equivalent number of clock periods.

Preventing Target from Monopolizing Bus

A target with very slow access time may require a number of clock cycles to transfer a data item (during a given data phase) between itself and the current master. The target does not allow the transfer of a data item to complete until it is ready. This is accomplished by holding off assertion of the target ready signal, CTRDY#, until the addressed device is ready to complete the transfer of the data item. If a target were permitted an unlimited number of time to transfer each data item, it could tie up the bus.

This problem is addressed by requiring slow targets to terminate a transfer prematurely if it will tie up the bus for long periods. There are three possible cases:

1. If the **time to complete the first data phase** will be **greater than 16 clocks** (from the assertion of CFRAME#), the target must immediately issue a retry to the master. An example would be a master's access to a very slow target to get data. The 16 clock rule forces the target to terminate the transaction with no data transferred, thus freeing up the bus for other masters to use. After a minimum of two CCLKs have elapsed, the master that received the retry can reassert its request and, when it receives its CGNT# (and the bus is idle), reinitiate its transaction again. The start address it issues is the address of the data item that was retried.
2. If the target ascertains that it will take it **more than eight CCLKs to complete the current data phase** (this is referred to as the incremental latency timeout) and it is not the final data phase (CFRAME# is still asserted), the target issues a disconnect type "C" to the master. If the target can transfer the current data item within eight CCLKs but knows in advance that it can-

not transfer the next data item within eight CCLKs, it must issue a disconnect (type "A" or "B") to the initiator when the current data item is transferred. The master terminates the transaction when the current data item is transferred and "remembers" the point of disconnection. After two CCLKs have elapsed, the master that received the disconnect can reassert its request and, when it receives its CGNT#, reinitiate its transaction again. The start address it issues is the address of the data item after the one that the disconnect was detected on earlier.

3. If an attempt to communicate with a target results in a **collision on a busy resource** (e.g., a CardBus master is attempting a data transfer with an EISA target, but the EISA bridge recognizes that an EISA master currently owns the EISA bus), the target should immediately issue a retry to the master. This forces the master to terminate the transaction with no data transferred, thus freeing up the PCI bus for other masters to use. After a minimum of two CCLKs have elapsed, the master that received the retry can reassert its request and reinitiate its transaction again. The start address it issues is the address of the data item that was retried.

It should be noted that the target-related rules are completely independent of the master's LT. The target has no visibility to the master's LT (and visa versa) and therefore cannot tell whether it has timed out or not. This means that slow access targets (greater than eight clocks from the start of one data transfer to the start of the next) always (before or after LT expiration) disconnect from the master after each slow access, thereby fragmenting the overall burst transaction into a series of single data phase transactions. Two examples of devices that might perform disconnects are:

- Targets that are very slow all of the time (virtually all 16-bit PC Cards would fall into this category).
- A target that exhibits very slow access sometimes (perhaps because of a buffer full condition or the need for mechanical movement) and would therefore tie up the PCI bus.

Target Latency on First Data Phase

The following rule was stated earlier: if the time to complete the first data phase will be greater than 16 PCI CLKs, the target must immediately issue a retry to the master.

Target Latency on Subsequent Data Phases

If the target ascertains that it will take it more than eight CCLKs to complete the current data phase (this is referred to as the incremental latency timeout) and it is not the final data phase (CFRAME# is still asserted), the target issues a disconnect type "C" to the master. If the target can transfer the current data item within eight CCLKs but knows in advance that it cannot transfer the next data item within eight CCLKs, it must issue a disconnect (type "A" or "B") to the initiator when the current data item is transferred.

Delayed Transactions

If a target cannot meet the 16 clock rule most of time, it must be designed to "memorize" the transaction, issue a retry to the initiator, and process the request off-line. This frees up the bus for other bus masters. The latched transaction is referred to as a delayed read or write request. The target completes the transaction locally and waits for the bus master to retry the transaction. It can then respond within 16 clocks. A detailed description of delayed transactions can be found in the MindShare book entitled *PCI System Architecture* (Addison-Wesley).

Fast Back-to-Back Transactions

Assertion of its grant by the PCI bus arbiter gives a PCI bus master access to the bus for a single transaction. If a bus master desires another access, it should continue to assert its CREQ# after it has asserted CFRAME# for the first transaction. If the arbiter continues to assert its CGNT# at the end of the first transaction, the master may then immediately initiate a second transaction. However, a bus master attempting to perform two, back-to-back transactions usually must insert an idle cycle between the two transactions. This is illustrated in Figure 7-4 on page 95. When it doesn't have to insert the idle cycle between the two bus transactions, this is referred to as fast back-to-back transactions. This can only occur if there is a guarantee that there will not be contention (on any signal lines) between the masters and/or targets involved in the two transactions. There are two scenarios where this is the case.

In the first case, the master guarantees that there will be no contention. In the second case, the master and the community of PCI targets collectively provide the guarantee. Figure 7-5 on page 96 illustrates two fast back-to-back transactions.

A detailed description of fast back-to-back transactions can be found in the MindShare book entitled *PCI System Architecture* (Addison-Wesley).

Figure 7-4: Typical Back-to-Back Writes

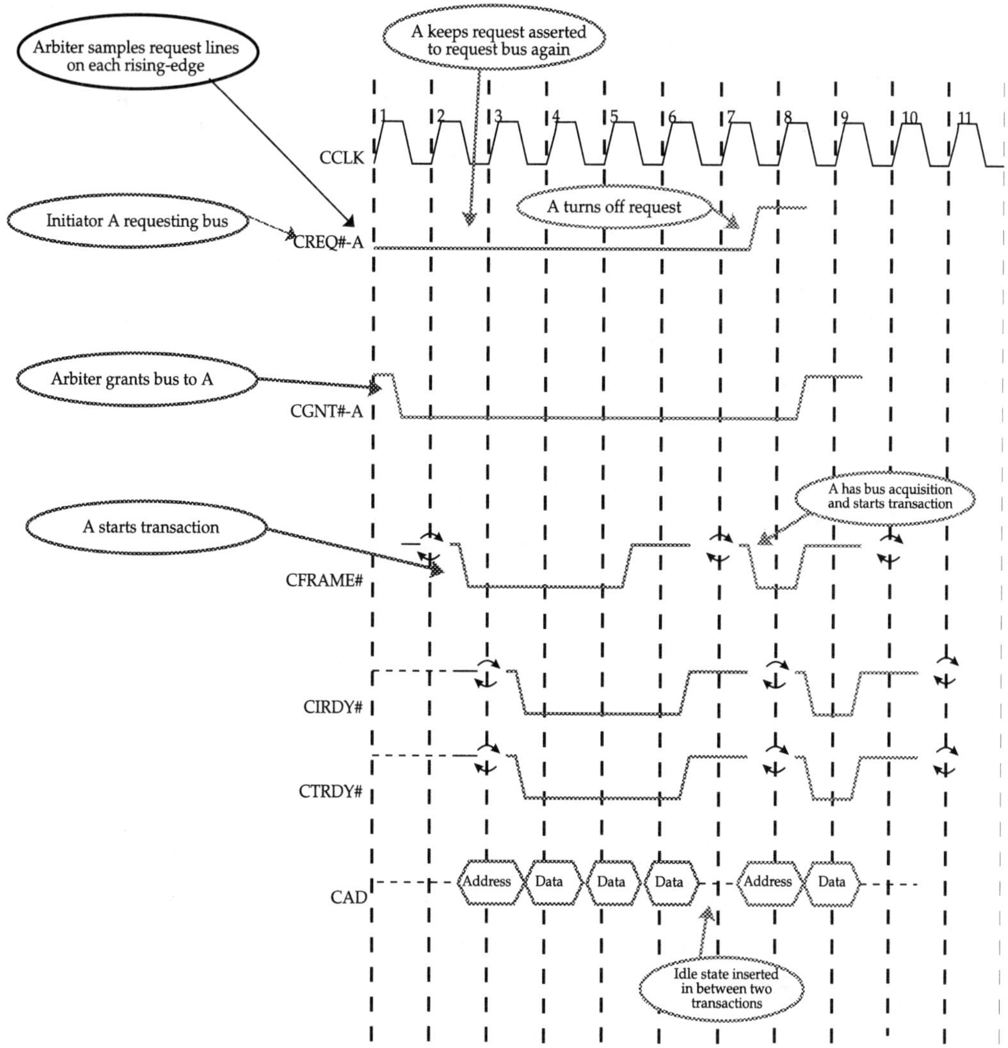

Figure 7-5: Fast Back-to-Back Writes

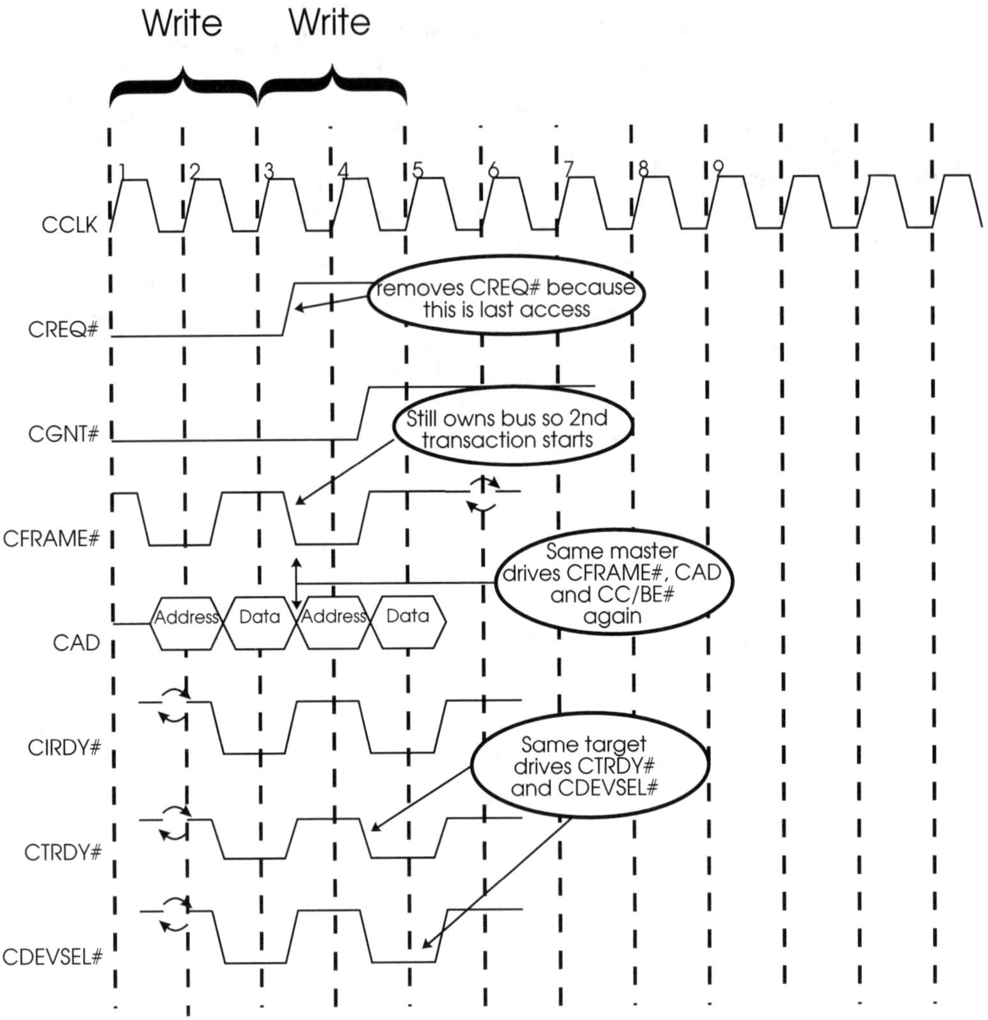

8 Intro to CardBus Transfers

The Previous Chapter

The previous chapter described the bus arbitration process, including the arbitration signaling protocol, timing, and the arbitration algorithm.

This Chapter

This chapter defines the commands supported by CardBus and describes the corresponding transactions.

The Next Chapter

The next chapter details CardBus memory transactions and related transfer protocols.

Review of CardBus Transactions

CardBus employs the same basic transaction protocol as the PCI bus. All Cardbus actions are synchronized to the CardBus CCLK signal. All CardBus bus transactions consist of an address phase followed by one or more data phases. An address phase is one CCLK in duration. The number of data phases depends on how many data transfers are to take place during the overall burst transfer. Each data phase has a minimum duration of one CCLK. Each wait state inserted in a data phase extends it by an additional CCLK.

The Address Phase

When a CardBus initiator starts a transaction it identifies the target device and the type of transaction during the address phase. The target device is identified by the start address driven over the CardBus address/data bus (CAD). At the same time, the initiator identifies the type of transaction by driving the command type onto the CardBus Command/Byte Enable bus (CC/BE[3:0]#). In addition, the initiator asserts the CFRAME# signal, indicating the presence of a valid start address and transaction type on the bus. Since the initiator only presents the start address for one CCLK cycle, it is the responsibility of every CardBus target device to latch the address to be decoded.

By decoding the address latched from the CAD bus and the command type latched from the CC/BE# bus, a target device can determine if it is being addressed and the type of transaction in progress. It's important to note that the initiator only supplies a start address to the target (during the address phase). Upon completion of the address phase, the address/data bus is then used to transfer data in each of the data phases. It is the responsibility of the target to latch the start address and to auto-increment it to point to the next group of locations during each subsequent data transfer (if there is more than one data phase).

Data Phase(s)

When a CardBus target determines that it is the target of a transaction, it claims the transaction by asserting CDEVSEL# (device select). If the initiator doesn't sample CDEVSEL# asserted within a predetermined amount of time, it aborts the transaction. A normal target may claim the transaction by asserting CDEVSEL# during either clock period two, three, or four (from the initiation of the transaction). Assuming no normal target asserts CDEVSEL# during that period, the only device permitted to assert CDEVSEL# during clock period five is the subtractive decoder (e.g., the ISA bus bridge). The subtractive decoder can claim transactions unclaimed by other devices if the target device may be on its other bus. If the subtractive decoder chooses not to claim the transaction, the master must abort the transaction and return the bus to the idle state in a graceful fashion. It must also set its MASTER ABORT DETECTED bit in its configuration status register.

Both the initiator and the target must indicate that they are ready to complete a data phase by asserting their respective ready lines (CIRDY# and CTRDY#). If either the initiator or target device has not asserted its ready signal, then the data phase is extended by one CCLK period (i.e., a wait state is inserted).

The number of data bytes transferred during a data phase is determined by the Command/Byte Enable signals asserted by the initiator during the data phase.

The initiator asserts CFRAME# at the start of the transaction and keeps it asserted until it's ready to complete the final data phase. The initiator indicates that the last data transfer is in progress by deasserting CFRAME# and asserting CIRDY#. When the last data transfer has been completed, the initiator returns the bus to the idle state by deasserting its ready line (CIRDY#).

If another bus master had previously been granted ownership of the bus (i.e., its CGNT# pin is asserted) by the bus arbiter and is waiting for the current initiator to surrender the bus, it detects that the bus has returned to the idle state by sampling CFRAME# and CIRDY# both deasserted on the same CCLK rising-edge.

Parity

Parity generation, checking, error reporting and timing are covered in detail in the chapter entitled "Error Handling" on page 171.

Transaction Types

During the address phase, a CardBus initiator identifies the type of transaction it wishes to perform using CC/BE[3:0]#. Table 8-1 defines the transaction types. The following sections provide a description of each of the command types.

Table 8-1: CardBus Command Types

CC/BE3#	CC/BE2#	CC/BE1#	CC/BE0#	Command Type
0	0	0	0	Interrupt Acknowledge (Allocated)
0	0	0	1	Special Cycle
0	0	1	0	I/O Read
0	0	1	1	I/O Write
0	1	0	0	Reserved
0	1	0	1	Reserved
0	1	1	0	Memory Read
0	1	1	1	Memory Write

Table 8-1: CardBus Command Types (Continued)

CC/BE3#	CC/BE2#	CC/BE1#	CC/BE0#	Command Type
1	0	0	0	Reserved
1	0	0	1	Reserved
1	0	1	0	Configuration Read
1	0	1	1	Configuration Write
1	1	0	0	Memory Read Multiple
1	1	0	1	Dual Address (Allocated)
1	1	1	0	Memory Read Line
1	1	1	1	Memory Write and Invalidate

Allocated Commands

Allocated commands are used by PCI devices, but not by CardBus. They are treated as allocated so that common silicon parts can be implemented for use in either the CardBus and/or PCI environments.

Special Cycle Command

The special cycle command is issued by an initiator to broadcast a message to one or more target CardBus or PCI devices. Each target must examine the message to determine whether the message applies to it (a target may be designed not to recognize any messages or to recognize only specific messages). Via its configuration command register, a target's ability to monitor special cycle messages can be enabled or disabled.

During the address phase, a valid address is not driven onto the CAD bus. The CAD bus and CPAR must be driven with a stable pattern, however, so that the parity of the CAD bus and the command on CC/BE[3:0]# can be checked for correctness. The initiator uses the CC/BE bus to indicate that this is a special cycle transaction.

During the data phase, the initiator broadcasts the message type on CAD[15:0] and an optional, message-dependent data field may be presented on

CAD[31:16]. The message and associated data are only valid during the clock when CIRDY# is asserted. The data contained in, and the timing of subsequent data phases is message-dependent (the subject of multiple data phase special cycles is discussed under the section entitled "Special Cycle Transaction"). If necessary, the initiator may insert wait states into the transaction by deasserting CIRDY#, but targets cannot insert wait states. In addition, no target should assert CDEVSEL# when it recognizes a message. Since multiple targets can recognize the message type, there would be contention on the CDEVSEL# line if they all tried to claim the transaction by asserting CDEVSEL#. The targets must watch CIRDY# to determine the presence of the message being sent by the initiator. It should be noted that the message type (and any associated data on CAD[31:16]) is only valid during the first data phase.

Since no target responds to the special cycle (CDEVSEL# is not asserted), another means must be used to end the transaction. The initiator must perform a master-abort to end the transaction. It must be noted that when the initiator terminates the transaction with a master-abort (because CDEVSEL# was not asserted by a target), it must not set the MASTER-ABORT DETECTED bit in its configuration status register. That bit should only be set in a transaction where a CDEVSEL# is expected but not received.

Allocation of message codes is handled through the PCI Special Interest Group (SIG) and requests for allocation of new message codes should be submitted to the PCI SIG in writing. Refer to MindShare book entitled *PCI System Architecture* (Addison-Wesley) for a list of the currently-defined messages.

During system design, each CardBus device that is capable of recognizing or broadcasting message codes must be hardwired with the message codes it recognizes or broadcasts. Upon recognition of any of its assigned message codes, a target should take the application-specific action defined by the message code received.

The special cycle command takes a minimum of six clocks to complete (more if the initiator inserts wait states by delaying the assertion of CIRDY#). One additional clock is required for the turn-around cycle before the next transaction is initiated on the bus. Therefore, a total of seven clock cycles are required from the start of the special cycle to the start of the next cycle.

Special Cycle Transaction

Single-Data Phase Special Cycle Transaction

Figure 8-1 on page 104 illustrates the special cycle transaction timing. During the address phase, the initiator drives a stable pattern onto the CAD bus and CPAR. This is only for parity checking purposes. No actual address is driven. In addition, the initiator drives the special cycle command onto the CC/BE bus during the address phase.

At the end of the address phase, the data phase begins. The initiator drives the message code onto CAD[15:0] and any optional, message-related data onto CAD[31:16]. It also asserts the appropriate byte enable lines (i.e., CC/BE[1:0]# or [3:0]#). The message is only guaranteed to be present on the CAD bus for one clock when the initiator asserts CIRDY#. The initiator can insert wait states into the data phase by delaying the assertion of CIRDY#. When the message is driven onto the CAD bus, the initiator asserts CIRDY# to indicate its presence. The targets that are designed to recognize special cycles latch the message information from the CAD bus when CIRDY# is sampled asserted.

Since a target is not expected to claim a special transaction, CDEVSEL# is sampled deasserted (by the initiator) at the end of clocks three through six. Since the transaction isn't claimed on any of these clocks, the initiator executes a master-abort to return the bus back to the idle state. If the master inserted one or more wait states before presenting the message and asserting CIRDY#, the master must extend the master abort timeout period by at least the number of wait states inserted (before performing the master abort to return the bus to the idle state). The specification states that this time period is required to give the target(s) sufficient time to "process" the message. This period of time is necessary to ensure that the target(s) have completed all internal actions related to reception of the message and are prepared to handle another transaction. When it occurs, the master abort is accomplished by first deasserting CFRAME# and then CIRDY#.

Multiple Data Phase Special Cycle Transaction

It is permissible for an initiator to deliver multiple packets of message information during the special cycle. No messages are currently defined that provide this capability, however. The target(s) latch the first message packet on the rising-edge of the clock when CIRDY# is first sampled asserted. CFRAME# would remain asserted because there would be at least one more data phase. The message type encoded on CAD[15:0] may imply the number of additional message packets to be delivered or the data field encoded on CAD[31:16] may state the number of packets. The second data phase starts during the clock cell immediately following the first assertion of CIRDY#. Although the specification doesn't clearly state so, the author interprets the specification as indirectly stating that the initiator can deassert CIRDY# during the second (and any subsequent) data phase until it has placed the next message packet on the CAD bus. Each additional data phase completes when CIRDY# is sampled asserted. When the final data transfer completes, the initiator must keep CIRDY# asserted for at least four additional clocks before performing a master abort to return the bus to the idle state. This time period is required to give the target(s) sufficient time to "process" the message. The specification does not explain what form this "processing" might take.

Figure 8-1: The Special Cycle Transaction

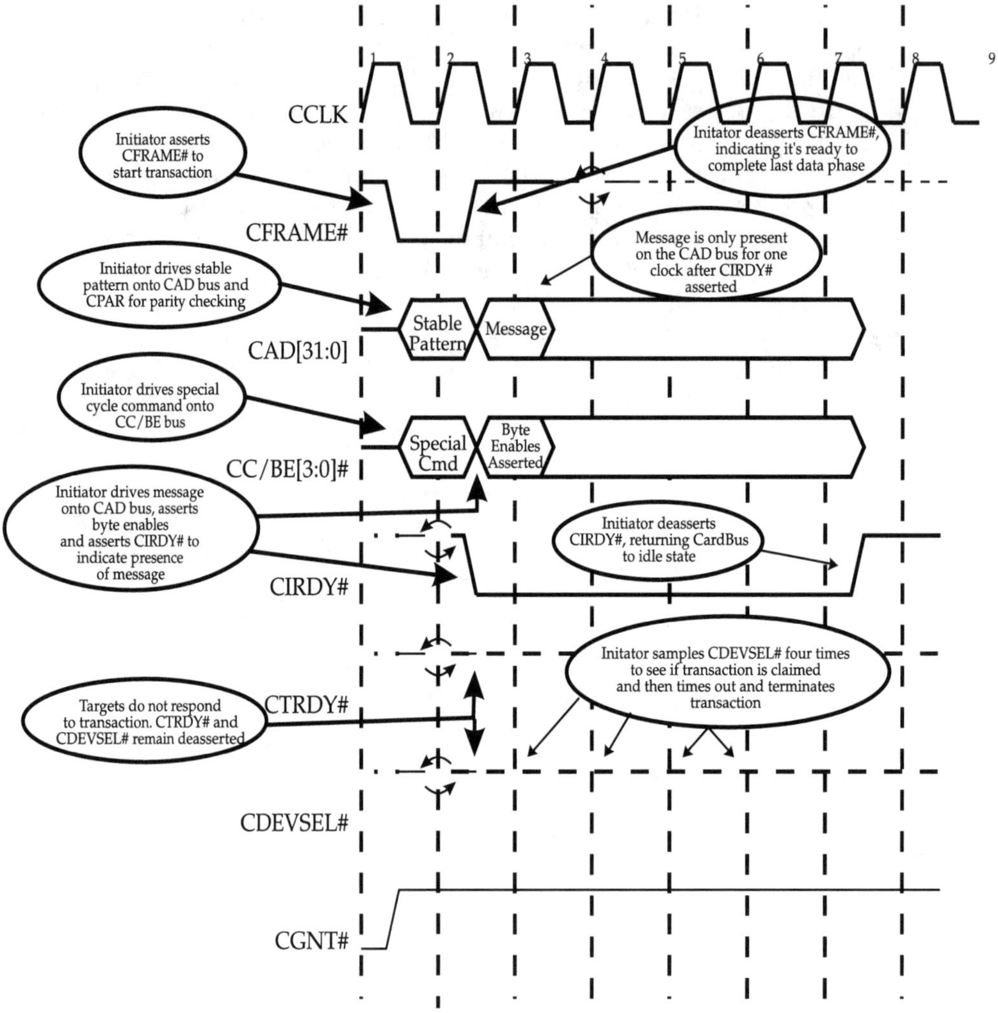

I/O Read and Write Commands

The I/O read and write commands are used to transfer data between the initiator and the currently-addressed I/O target. The target must decode the entire 32-bit address. Refer to Chapter 10 on page 149 for details regarding I/O transactions.

Accessing Memory

The PCI specification defines five commands utilized to access memory:

- Memory read command.
- Memory read line command.
- Memory read multiple command.
- Memory write command.
- Memory write and invalidate command.

The specification says that the cache line size configuration register (described in the chapter entitled "Configuration Registers") must be implemented by bus masters that utilize the memory write and invalidate command (described later in this chapter). It also strongly recommends that this register be implemented for bus masters that utilize the memory read, memory read line and memory read multiple commands.

If the cache line size configuration register is implemented, the initiator should follow the usage guidelines outlined in Table 8-2 on page 106 when performing memory reads. If an initiator accesses memory and does not implement the cache line size configuration register, it should follow the same guidelines, assuming a cache line size of 16 or 32 bytes.

When a bus master uses the memory read line or the memory read multiple commands, it is indicating that it knows the target memory is well-behaved (not memory-mapped I/O). It should use the memory read command when reading from memory-mapped I/O. If the read traverses a bridge, use of the bulk read commands gives the bridge permission to prefetch data within the addresses area. This would permit the bridge to establish a buffered link through the bridge between the initiator and the target, with the bridge loading the prefetch buffer from the memory on the destination bus and the initiator reading the data from the other end of the buffer on the initiating bus. This would result in a dramatic improvement in performance.

The specification strongly recommends that the bulk read/write commands be used when transferring large blocks of data to or from memory. These commands are memory write and invalidate, memory read line and memory read multiple.

Table 8-2: Preferred Use of Memory Read Commands

Read Command Type	To Be Used When
Memory Read	Reading data from non-prefetchable memory (e.g., memory-mapped I/O) or reading a single doubleword.
Memory Read Line	Reading more than one doubleword but no more than a cache line in prefetchable memory space.
Memory Read Multiple	Read crosses a cache line boundary in a prefetchable memory range.

Writing Memory

The initiator may use the memory write or the memory write and invalidate command to update data in memory.

Memory Write Command

This command is used to transfer one or more data objects to memory. When the target asserts CTRDY#, it has assumed responsibility for maintaining the coherency of the data. This can be done by ensuring that any software-transparent posting buffer is flushed prior to synchronization events such as interrupts, or the updating of an I/O status register or memory flag being passed through the device that contains the posted-write buffer (i.e., a bridge).

Memory Write and Invalidate Command

Problem. Assume that another CardBus master is performing a memory write and the processor's write back cache(s) is snooping the transaction. It experiences a snoop hit on a modified line. This means that the initiator is about to update a stale line in memory. Assuming that the cache is not capable of data snarfing (latching the data from the CAD bus) to keep the cache line updated, it could invalidate the cache line. This, however, would be a mistake. The fact that the line is marked modified indicates that some or all of the information in the line is more current than the corresponding line in memory. The memory write being performed by the current initiator is updating some item(s) in the memory line. Trashing the line from the cache would quite probably trash some data that is more current than that in the memory line.

If the cache permits the initiator to complete the memory write and then flushes the modified cache line to memory, the data just written by the initiator is overwritten by the stale data in the cache line. The correct action would be to force the initiator that is attempting the write to get off the bus (abort the transaction). The cache then acquires the bus and performs a memory write to transfer, or flush, the modified cache line to memory. In the cache directory, the cache line is then invalidated because the initiator will subsequently update the memory line immediately after the cache line is flushed to memory. The cache then removes the back off, permitting the initiator to re-initiate the memory write. The memory line now contains the most current data. The cache snoops this transaction as well, but it now results in a cache miss (because the cache line was invalidated after it was deposited in memory). The cache does not interfere in the memory write this time.

Solution. The memory write and invalidate command is identical to the memory write command except that it guarantees the transfer of a complete cache line (or multiple cache lines) during the current transaction. This implies that the cache line size configuration register must be implemented in the initiator so that it can make the determination that an entire cache line (or lines) will be written.

If, when snooping, the write-back cache detects a memory write and invalidate initiated and experiences a snoop hit on a modified line, the cache can just invalidate the line and doesn't need to back off the initiator in order to perform the flush to memory. This is possible because the initiator has indicated that it is updating the entire memory line and all of the data in the modified cache line is therefore stale and can be invalidated. This improves performance by eliminating the requirement for the back off and line flush.

It is a requirement that the initiator must assert all of the byte enable signals during each data phase of the memory write and invalidate transaction. It also required that linear addressing be used. For information on the byte enables and on linear addressing, refer to the chapter entitled "The Read and Write Transfer."

Configuration Read and Write Commands

Each CardBus device may implement up to 64 doublewords of configuration registers that are used during system initialization to configure the CardBus device for proper operation in the system. To access a CardBus agent's configuration registers, a configuration read or write command must be initiated. CAD[10:8] select the function within the device and the contents of CAD[7:2] (during the address phase) are used to select one of the target's 64 doublewords of configuration space.

The x86 processor family implements two address spaces: memory and I/O. CardBus requires the implementation of a third address space: configuration space. The mechanism used to generate configuration transactions is described in the chapter entitled "Configuration Transfers" on page 237.

Reserved Bus Commands

Targets must not respond (assert CDEVSEL#) to reserved bus commands. This means that use of a reserved bus command will result in the initiator experiencing a master abort.

Address/Data Stepping

Advantages: Diminished Current Drain and Crosstalk

Turning on a large number of signal drivers simultaneously (e.g., driving a 32-bit address onto the CAD bus along with a four-bit command a parity bit) can result in:

- a large spike of current drain.
- a significant amount of crosstalk within the driver chip and on adjacent external signal lines.

The designer could choose to alleviate both of these problems by turning on the drivers associated with non-adjacent signal drivers in groups over a number of steps, or clock periods.

As an example, assume that the system board designer lays out the 32 CAD lines as adjacent signal traces in bit sequential order. By simultaneously driving all 32 lines, crosstalk would be generated on the traces (and within the driver chip). Now assume that there are four 8-bit groups of signal drivers connected as follows:

- driver group one is connected to CAD lines 0, 4, 8, 12, 16, 20, 24, 28.
- driver group two is connected to CAD lines 1, 5, 9, 13, 17, 21, 25, 29.
- driver group three is connected to CAD lines 2, 6, 10, 14, 18, 22, 26, 30.
- driver group four is connected to CAD lines 3, 7, 11, 15, 19, 23, 27, 31.

The initiator could turn on the first driver group in clock cell one of a transaction, followed by group two in clock cell two, group three in clock cell three, and group four in clock cell four. Using this sequence, non-adjacent signal lines are being switched during each clock cell, reducing the interaction and crosstalk.

Since the entire address is not present on the bus until clock cell four, the initiator must delay assertion of the CFRAME# signal until clock cell four when the final group driver is switched on. Because the assertion of CFRAME# qualifies the address as being valid, no targets latch and use the address until CFRAME# is sampled asserted.

Data Stepping

The data presented by the initiator during each data phase of a write transaction is qualified by the assertion of the CIRDY# signal by the initiator. The data presented by the target during each data phase of a read transaction is qualified by the assertion of the CTRDY# signal by the target. In other words, data can be stepped onto the bus, as well as address.

How Device Indicates Ability to Use Stepping

A device indicates its ability to perform stepping via the WAIT CYCLE CONTROL bit in its configuration command register. There are three possible cases:

- If the device is not capable of stepping, the bit is hardwired to zero.
- If the device always using stepping, the bit is hardwired to one.
- If the device's ability to use stepping can be enabled and disabled via software, the bit is implemented as a read/writable bit. If the bit is read/writable, reset sets it to one.

Continuous and Discrete Stepping

The initiator (or the target) may use one of two methods to step a valid address or data onto the CAD bus, or a valid level onto the CPAR.

Continuous Stepping

If the device driving the CAD bus and the parity pin, either initiator or target, uses very weak output drivers, it may take several clocks for it to drive a valid level onto these bus signals (i.e., the propagation delay may be lengthy because it may take several reflections, with the resultant voltage-doubling effect, before the address (or data) is in the correct state on the bus). Although not forbidden, continuous stepping is frowned upon, while discrete stepping is the preferred method.

Discrete Stepping

The device driving the CAD bus and the parity pin, either initiator or target, may have strong output drivers and may drive a subset of them on each of several clock edges until all of them have been driven.

Disadvantages of Stepping

There are two disadvantages associated with stepping:

- Due to the prolonged period it takes to set up the address or data on the bus, there is a performance penalty associated in any address or data phase where stepping is used.
- In the midst of stepping the address onto the bus, the arbiter may remove the grant from the stepping master.

Preemption While Stepping in Progress

When the bus arbiter grants the bus to a bus master, the master then waits for bus idle before initiating its transaction. If, during this period of time, the arbiter detects a request from a higher priority master, it can remove the grant from the first master before it begins a transaction (i.e., before it asserts CFRAME#).

Assuming that this doesn't occur, the master retains its grant and awaits bus idle. Upon detection of the bus idle state, the master begins to step the address onto the CAD bus, but delays the assertion of CFRAME# for several clocks until the address is fully driven. During this period of time, the arbiter may still remove the grant from the master. The arbiter hasn't detected CFRAME# asserted and may therefore assume that the master hasn't yet started a transaction. If the arbiter receives a request from a higher-priority master, it may remove the grant from the master that is currently engaged in stepping an address onto the CAD bus. In response to the loss of grant, the stepping master must immediately tri-state its output drivers.

It is a rule that the arbiter cannot deassert one master's grant and assert grant to another master during the same clock cell if the bus appears to be idle. The bus may not, in fact, be idle. A master may not have asserted CFRAME# yet because it is in the act of stepping the address onto the CAD bus. If the arbiter were to simultaneously remove the stepping master's CGNT# and issue CGNT# to another master, the following problem would result.

On the next rising-edge of the clock, the stepping master detects removal of its CGNT# and begins to turn off its address drivers. At the same time, the other master detects its CGNT# asserted and bus idle (because the stepping master had not yet asserted CFRAME#) and initiates a transaction. This results in a collision on the CAD bus.

When the bus appears to be idle, the arbiter must remove the grant from one master, wait one clock cell, and then assert grant to the other master. This provides a one clock cell buffer zone for the stepping master to disconnect completely before the other master detects its grant plus bus idle and starts its transaction.

It is permissible for the arbiter to simultaneously remove one master's grant and assert another's during the same clock cell if the bus isn't idle (i.e., a transaction is in progress). There is no danger of a collision because the master that has just received the grant cannot start driving the bus until the current master idles the bus.

Broken Master

The arbiter may assume that a master is broken if the arbiter has issued CGNT# to the master, the bus has been idle for 16 clocks, and the master has not asserted CFRAME# to start its transaction. The arbiter is permitted to ignore all further requests from the broken master and may optionally report the failure to the operating system (in a device-specific fashion).

Stepping Example

Figure 8-2 on page 112 provides an example of an initiator using stepping over a period of three clocks to drive the address onto the CAD bus. The initiator can start the transaction on clock three (CGNT# sampled asserted and bus idle—CFRAME# and CIRDY# sampled deasserted). It then begins to drive the address onto the CAD bus and the command onto the CC/BE bus. During clock cell four, it continues to drive the address onto the CAD bus. During clock cell five, it finalizes the driving of the address and asserts CFRAME#, indicating the presence of the address and command. When the targets sample CFRAME# asserted on the rising-edge of clock six (the end of the address phase), they latch the address and command and begin the address decode. Since this is an example of a write transaction, the initiator begins to drive the data onto the CAD bus at the start of the data phase (clock six). Once again, it uses stepping, asserting the write data over a period of two clocks. It withholds the assertion of CIRDY# until the data has been fully driven.

Figure 8-2: Example of Address Stepping

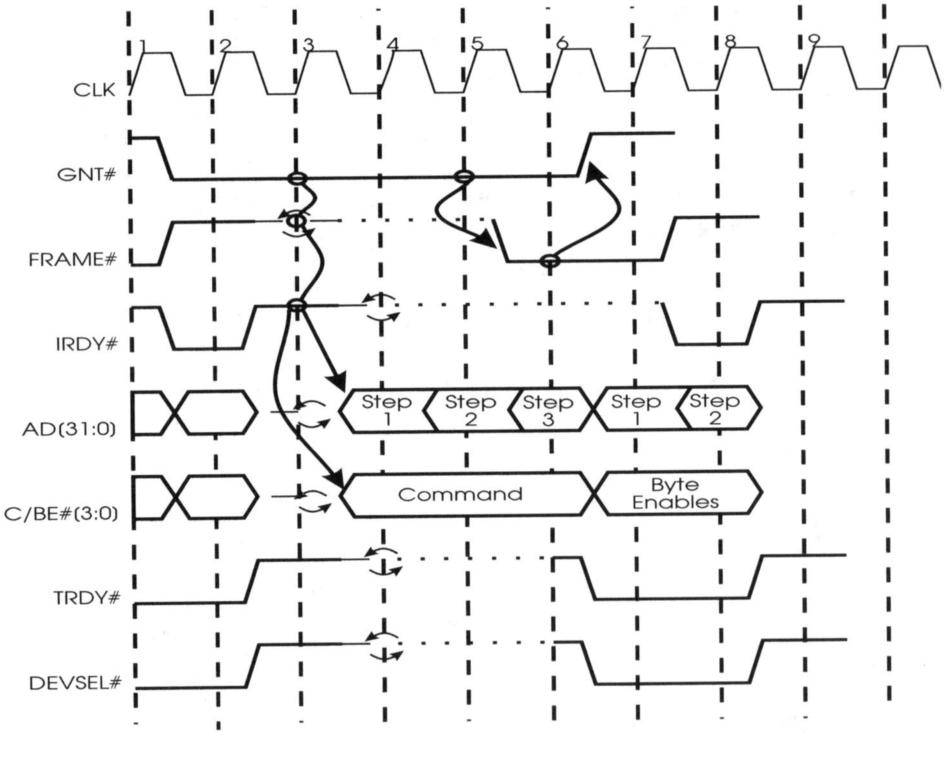

Who Must Support Stepping?

All CardBus devices must be able to handle address and data stepping performed by the other party in a transaction. The ability to use stepping, however, is optional.

Response to Illegal Behavior

Upon detection of illegal use of bus protocol, all CardBus devices should be designed to gracefully return to the idle state (i.e., cease driving all bus signals) as quickly as possible. The specification is understandably vague on this point. It depends on the nature of the protocol violation as to whether the devices can gracefully return to their idle states and still function properly. As an example, the specification cites the case where the initiator simultaneously deasserts CFRAME# and CIRDY#. In this case, when the target detects this illegal end to the transaction, it is suggested that the target deassert all target-related signals and return its state machine to the idle state. In the event that a protocol violation leaves a target device questioning its ability to function correctly in the future, it can respond to all future access attempts with a target abort. If the target thinks that the protocol violation has not impaired its ability to function correctly, it just surrenders all signals, returns to the idle state, and does not indicate any type of error.

Target-Initiated Termination

CSTOP# Signal

A target may use the CSTOP# signal to instruct the initiator to prematurely end the transaction on the current data phase. Using the CDEVSEL# and CTRDY# signals in conjunction with CSTOP#, the target can indicate one of the following to the initiator:

- Disconnect upon completion of the current data phase (the current doubleword is transferred). There are two variants: **disconnect A and B**. The initiator may choose to continue the transfer (starting with the next doubleword) at a later time, or may choose not to resume the transaction (this might occur if it were prefetching and did not really need the data).
- Disconnect during the current data phase without transferring the current

doubleword. This is referred to as **disconnect C**. The initiator may choose to continue the transfer (starting with the current doubleword) at a later time, or may choose not to resume the transaction (this might occur if it were prefetching and did not really need the data).

- Issue a **retry** during the first data phase. No data is transferred during the transaction and the initiator is obliged to retry the transaction later.
- **Target abort** the transaction and do not retry (no data is transferred).

Disconnect

Disconnect A and B

Disconnect A or B is indicated to the initiator by asserting CTRDY# and CSTOP# while keeping CDEVSEL# asserted. This tells the initiator that the target is ready to transfer the current data item (CTRDY# asserted) and then stop the transfer (CSTOP# asserted). CDEVSEL# remaining asserted gives the initiator permission to resume the transaction at a later time (if so desired; resumption is not mandatory) at the point that it left off (on the doubleword that would have been transferred in the next data phase).

Disconnect A and B are differentiated from each other by the state of CIRDY# at the point where the disconnect is indicated. It is a disconnect A if CIRDY# is not asserted when CSTOP# and CTRDY# are asserted. See clock two in Figure 8-3 on page 116. In this case, the current doubleword cannot be transferred until the initiator asserts CIRDY#. When CIRDY# is asserted (on clock three), the initiator also deasserts CFRAME#, indicating that this is the final data phase. The current doubleword is transferred and the transaction ends. The target deasserts CSTOP#, CTRDY# and CDEVSEL# in clock three.

It is a disconnect B (see Figure 8-4 on page 117) if CIRDY# is asserted when CSTOP# and CTRDY# are asserted. In this case, the current doubleword is transferred on that clock (clock two) and no more data is transferred. CFRAME# is still asserted. Normally, the initiator deasserts CFRAME# when it asserts CIRDY# for the last data phase, but in this case the initiator did not know this was the last data phase when it asserted CIRDY#. For this reason, in clock two the initiator keeps CIRDY# asserted and deasserts CFRAME#, indicating that it is ready to complete the final data phase. Both the initiator and the target know that no data will be transferred in this "null" data phase, however. The target deasserts CTRDY# to enforce this fact. In clock three, CIRDY# is deasserted to return the bus to the idle state. The target deasserts CSTOP# and CDEVSEL# (the target is not permitted to deassert them until it samples CFRAME# deasserted).

Assuming that the master decides to resume the transfer, after keeping its CREQ# deasserted for a minimum of two clocks, the master should then reassert its CREQ# and re-arbitrate for bus ownership. When it has successfully reacquired bus ownership, the initiator should re-initiate the transaction using the doubleword address of the next data item that would have been transferred if the disconnect had not occurred. In other words, the initiator should resume the transfer where it left off. This implies that the master must "remember" the address to resume at.

A master that experiences a disconnect has transferred at least one data item. The master is not required to resume the transaction later (because it may have been prefetching).

Some targets only support single data phase transactions. When a master attempts a multiple data phase transaction, the target asserts CSTOP# along with CTRDY# during the first data phase of the burst. This informs the master that the target is ready to transfer the current data item, but is also instructing the master to disconnect from it after the transfer has taken place. The master terminates the transaction as instructed. If the master intends to continue the data transfer, it arbitrates for the bus again and then reinitiates the burst starting with the next doubleword.

Cacheable memory target are not permitted to disconnect a memory write and invalidate transaction except at cache line boundaries. This is necessary because the snooper (the host/PCI bridge) may have already eliminated a modified copy of the line based on the master's promise to overwrite the entire line in memory).

Figure 8-3: Type "A" Disconnect

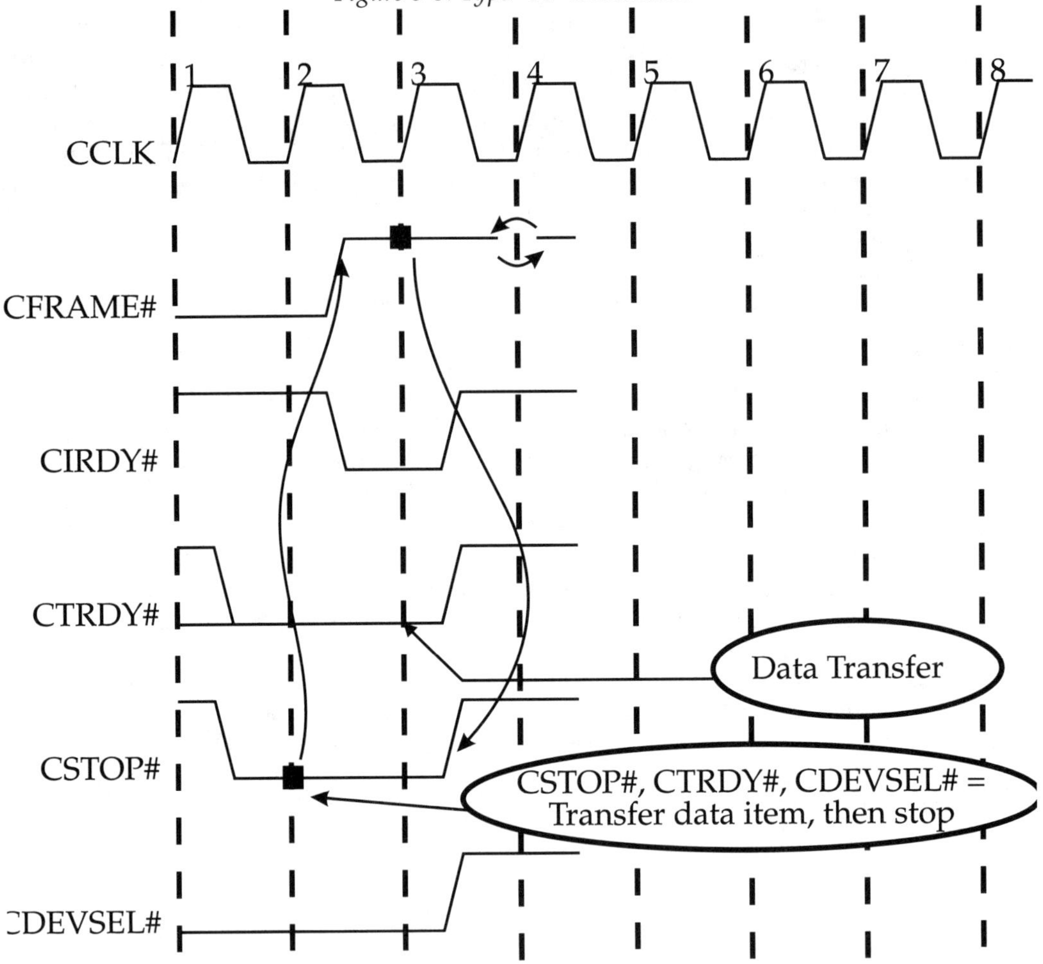

Figure 8-4: Type "B" Disconnect

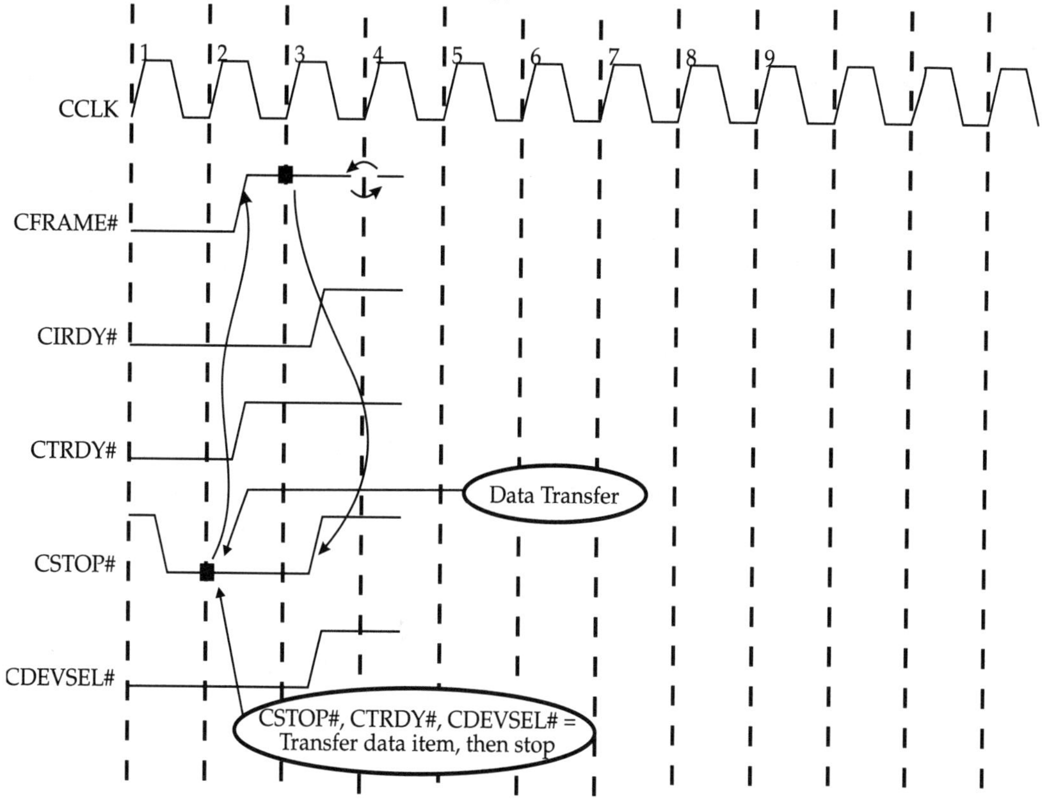

Disconnect C

Refer to Figure 8-5 on page 118. Assume that at least one data phase has completed (on clock one) and at least one doubleword has therefore been transferred. When the initiator completed the previous data phase and entered the current one (in clock one), it kept CIRDY# asserted to indicate that it is ready to complete the current data phase. It did not, however, deassert CFRAME# because this isn't the final data phase. In this data phase, the target asserts CSTOP# (during clock one) and deasserts CTRDY#, indicating that it wants the initiator to terminate the transaction on this data phase with no data transferred. In response, the initiator keeps CIRDY# asserted (in clock two) and deasserts CFRAME#, indicating that the final data phase in progress. No data is transferred in this last data phase, however, because the target has CTRDY# deasserted. In clock three, the initiator deasserts CIRDY#, returning the bus to the idle state. The target deasserts CSTOP# and CDEVSEL#.

Figure 8-6 on page 119 also illustrates a disconnect C, but the initiator has deasserted CIRDY# upon entry to the current data phase. When the initiator discovers (on the rising-edge of clock two) that the target wants it to stop on this data phase without transferring the current doubleword, it responds by asserting CIRDY# and deasserting CFRAME#. This signals the final data phase (a null data transfer). The initiator deasserts CIRDY# one clock later to return the bus to the idle state and the target deasserts CSTOP# and CDEVSEL#.

Upon receipt of a disconnect C, the initiator has the option of resuming the transaction later or not. If it was prefetching data that wasn't explicitly required, it may choose not to.

Figure 8-5: Disconnect C Issued with CIRDY# Asserted

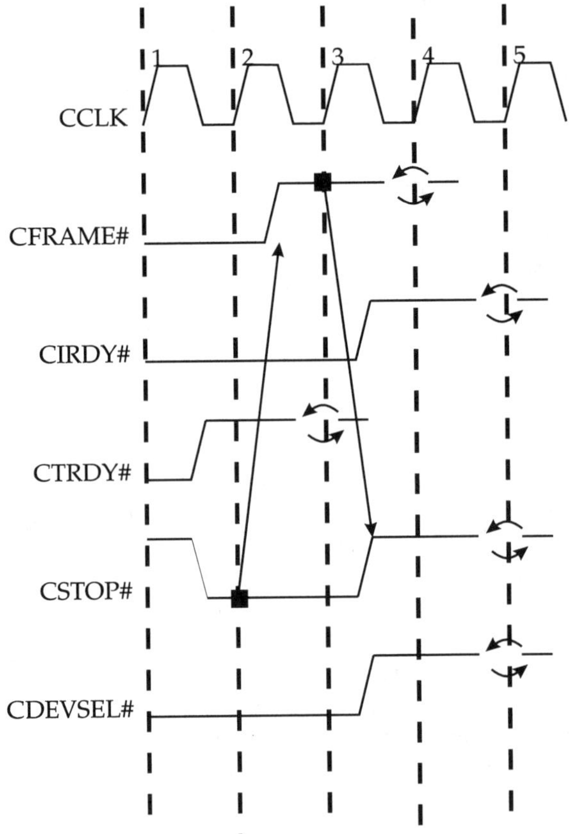

Figure 8-6: Disconnect C Issued without CIRDY# Asserted

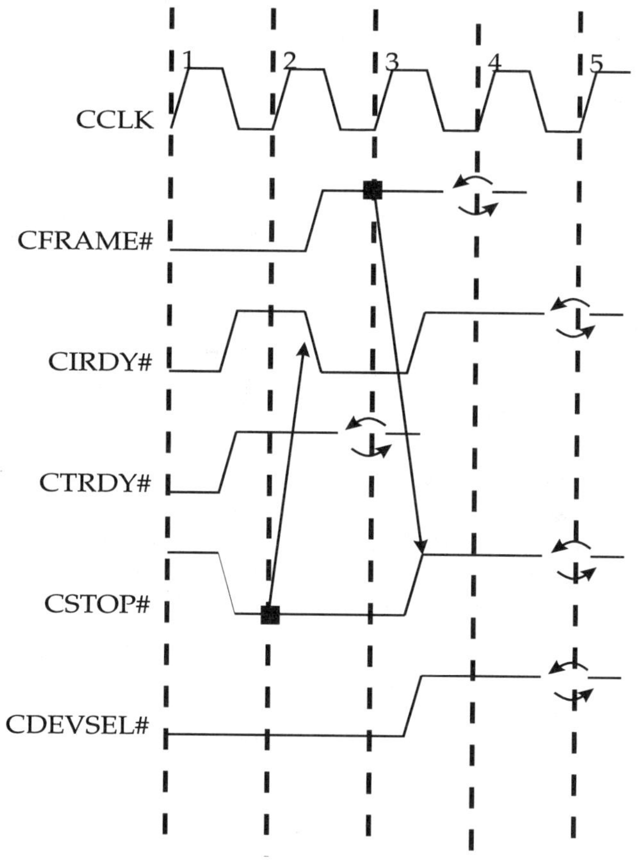

Reasons Target Issues Disconnect

Target Slow to Complete Data Phase. Assume that the target determines that the latency to complete any data phase (including the first) will be longer than eight clocks and the initiator intends to perform another data phase (CFRAME# is still asserted). The target must issue a disconnect C to the initiator on or before the eighth clock of the current data phase. It should be noted that this rule is new in revision 2.1 of the specification. The target used to be permitted to take as long as it needed to transfer a data item and would then issue a disconnect A or B to the initiator. In essence, the old wording of this rule permitted a target to tie up the bus for long periods of time.

This rule ensures that a slow target will not tie up the bus for extended periods of time. This subject is covered in the chapter entitled "PCI Bus Arbitration" in the section entitled "Preventing Target From Monopolizing Bus."

Target Doesn't Support Burst Mode. If a target doesn't support burst mode and it detects that the master intends to perform a second data phase (CFRAME# is still asserted), it must issue a disconnect A or B to the initiator during the first data phase. Alternately, it may issue a disconnect C in the second data phase.

Memory Target Doesn't Understand Addressing Sequence. If a memory target doesn't understand the addressing sequence indicated by the initiator via AD[1:0] during the address phase, the target must issue a disconnect A or B to the initiator when it is ready to complete the first data phase, or, as an alternative, may issue a disconnect C during the second data phase. This forces the initiator to fragment a burst transaction into single data phase transactions that the target can handle. The initiator may be using an AD[1:0] pattern defined in a later revision of the specification than the target was designed to. This subject is covered in the chapter entitled "The Read and Write Transfers" in the section entitled "Addressing Sequence During Memory Burst".

Transfer Crosses Over Target's Address Boundary. If a target determines during the current data phase that the initiator intends to perform another data phase (CFRAME# is still asserted) and that the current data item is the last within its address boundaries, it must issue a disconnect A or B when it is ready to complete the current data phase. This forces the master to terminate the transaction upon transferring the last data item in this target's space. Alternately, the target could issue a disconnect C in the data phase after the target's last doubleword is transferred. The master then waits a minimum of two clocks and reasserts its CREQ# to request ownership of the bus again. When it has reacquired bus ownership, it resumes its transaction using the next doubleword address. This gives an opportunity to another target that implements the next sequential doubleword address to claim the transaction, thereby permitting the transfer to continue across target boundaries.

Burst Memory Transfer Crosses Cache Line Boundary. During a memory burst transaction, a cacheable PCI memory target detects that the initiator intends to perform another data phase (CFRAME# is still asserted) after completion of the current data phase and is transferring the last doubleword within the current cache line in the current data phase. In order to force the bus master to generate the start address of the next cache line to be snooped by the host/PCI bridge, the target must issue a disconnect A or B when it is ready to transfer the last doubleword of the current line. This forces the bus master to yield bus ownership, re-arbitrate for ownership again, and then initiate a new memory transaction starting at the first doubleword of the next cache line. This permits the snooper (the host/PCI bridge) to snoop the next line address in the processor's L1 and L2 caches.

Retry

A target only issues retry to the initiator if cannot permit any data to be transferred during the current transaction. In other words, it is a rule that if a target is going to issue a retry to the initiator, it must do it on the first data phase. The signaling for a retry is identical as that for a disconnect C except that it occurs in the first data phase. Unlike the disconnect C, however, the initiator is required to re-attempt the transaction at a later time when it receives a retry.

Retry is indicated to the initiator (by the target) by asserting CSTOP# and deasserting CTRDY# while keeping CDEVSEL# asserted. This tells the initiator that the target does not intend to transfer the current data item (CTRDY# deasserted) and that the initiator must stop the transaction on this data phase (CSTOP# asserted). The continued assertion of CDEVSEL# indicates that the initiator must retry the transaction at a later time. Furthermore, it must use the exact same address, command and byte enables. If it's a write, it must use exactly the same data in the first data phase. This rule is unconditional. The access must be retried as many times as it takes to complete the transfer. If the master also has target capability, it must respond to accesses by other masters that occur in between its attempts to retry the transaction.

The specification cites the example of a multi-function device with three functions. More than one function in a multi-function device may have bus master capability. Assume that the device has three functions all having bus master capability. Such a device only has one pair of CREQ#/CGNT# signals, however. Assume that function zero initiates a transaction and receives a retry. It must try the transaction again later. If the CGNT# line is still asserted, function one can perform a transaction, and, when it's finished, function three can perform a transaction. Assume that function one's transaction completes, but function two's transaction receives a retry. Both function zero and function two must periodically re-attempt their retried transactions until they are able to complete them.

Figure 8-7 on page 122 and Figure 8-8 on page 123 illustrate two variants on the retry. In Figure 8-7 the initiator has already asserted CIRDY# when the target issues the retry. When the retry is received, the initiator responds by keeping CIRDY# asserted (in clock two) and deasserting CFRAME#. One clock later it deasserts CIRDY# to return the bus to the idle state. The target deasserts CSTOP# and CDEVSEL#. In Figure 8-8 the initiator has not yet asserted CIRDY# when it receives the retry from the target. In response, the initiator asserts CIRDY# (in clock two) and deasserts CFRAME#. One clock later, it deasserts CIRDY# to return the bus to the idle state. The target deasserts CSTOP# and CDEVSEL#.

Figure 8-7: Retry Received with CIRDY# Asserted

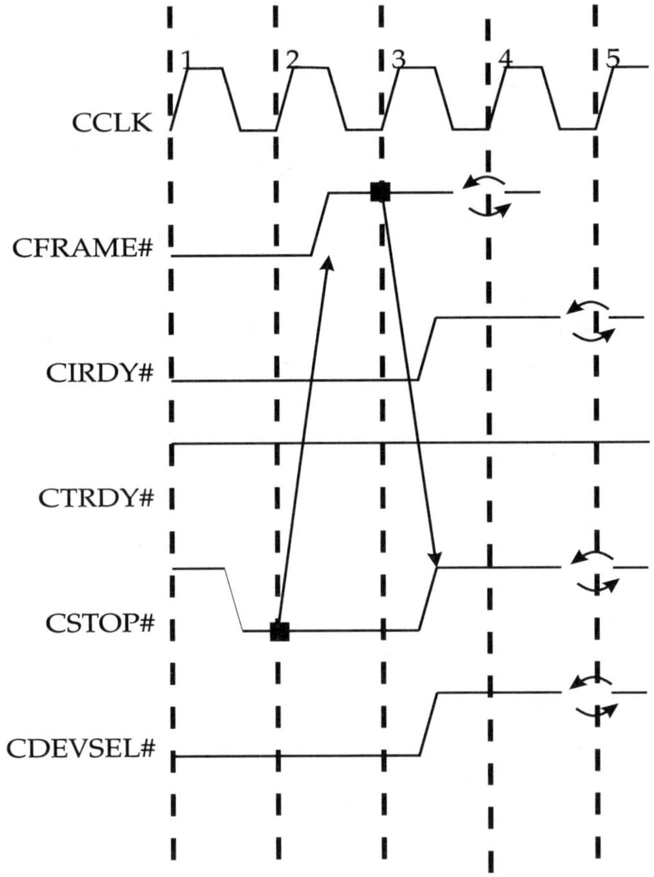

Figure 8-8: Retry Received without CIRDY# Asserted

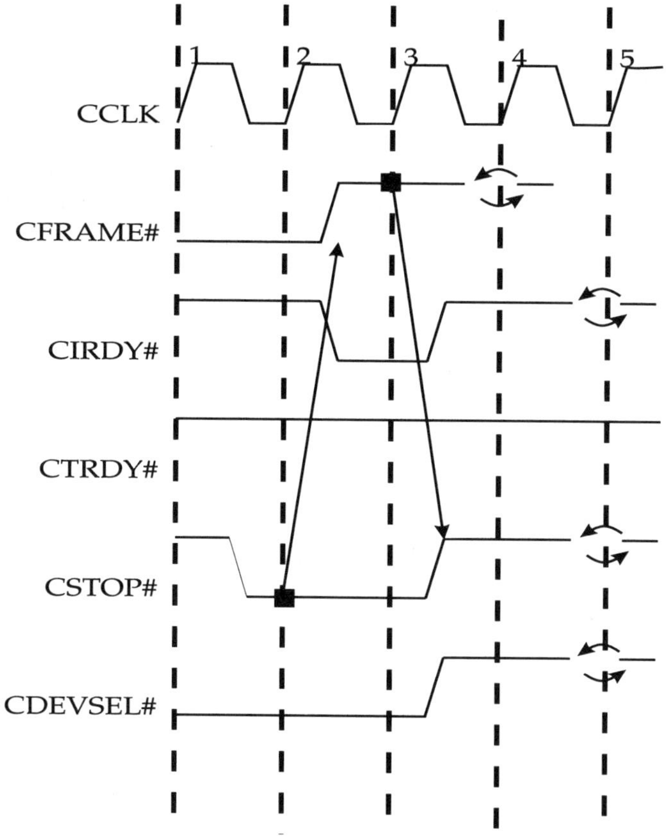

Reasons Target Issues Retry

Target Very Slow to Complete First Data Phase. If the latency to first data phase completion will be longer than 16 clocks, the target must issue a retry to the initiator. This rule prevents a target with a very long latency to first data phase completion from monopolizing the bus. This subject is covered in the chapter entitled "PCI Bus Arbitration" in the section entitled "Preventing Target From Monopolizing Bus."

Snoop Hit on Modified Cache Line. A cacheable PCI memory target is not permitted to accept or supply data (i.e., it may not assert CTRDY#) until the snoop result is presented (on SDONE and SBO#) by the snooper. If a cacheable PCI memory target determines that the snooper (the processor's L1 or L2 cache) experienced a snoop hit on a modified line (SDONE and SBO# asserted), the target must retry the initiator. The cache then arbitrates for bus ownership and writes the modified cache line into the cacheable PCI memory target. The snooper then either eliminates the line from its cache (if snooping a memory write by the master), or marks its copy clean (if snooping a memory read by the master). The retried master then re-attempts its access. The transaction is snooped again, resulting in a clean snoop this time (SDONE asserted and SBO# deasserted). The target asserts CTRDY# and accepts data from or supplies data to the master. This subject is covered in the chapter entitled "PCI Cache Support."

Resource Busy. If a target recognizes that a necessary resource is currently busy, it should immediately issue a retry to the initiator. An example would be an attempt by a PCI master to access an EISA target while the EISA bus is currently owned by an EISA bus master. In that case, the PCI/EISA bridge should immediately issue a retry to the PCI master to force it to free the PCI bus for use by other masters. This subject is covered in the chapter entitled "PCI Bus Arbitration" in the section entitled "Preventing Target From Monopolizing Bus."

Memory Target Locked. A locked memory target must issue a retry when a master other than the one that locked it attempts to access it. This subject is covered in the chapter entitled "Shared Resource Acquisition."

Host Bridge Retry Counter

The specification recommends (not a requirement) that the host/PCI bridge implement a retry counter. The counter is initialized whenever the bridge successfully transfers data during a transaction. Each time that the bridge experiences a retry during a data transfer, the counter is decremented (or incremented). When the retry count limit (implementation-specific) has been reached, the bridge should discontinue retries of the transaction and should permit the host processor to complete the transaction in progress. On a read, the bridge should supply dummy data to the processor. On a write, the bridge should pretend that the write completed with no problems. After permitting the processor to complete the transaction, the bridge would then generate an interrupt to alert the processor that a problem exists.

This recommendation exists for the following reason. Assume that the host processor initiates a host bus transaction to perform a read from a PCI target device. The bridge arbitrates for ownership of the PCI bus and initiates the transaction. In response, the addressed target issues a retry, causing the bridge to terminate the PCI transaction without transferring the requested data to the processor. After two clocks, the bridge re-arbitrates for ownership of the PCI bus, retries the read transaction and again receives a retry in response.

The bridge keeps inserting wait states into the host processor's bus transaction while it awaits the requested data. If the target continues to issue retries for an extended period, the host processor cannot recognize an external interrupt that is awaiting servicing during this period (the interrupt the host/PCI bridge generates to signal the excessive retry condition). The processor cannot recognize the interrupt and use its bus to fetch and execute the interrupt service routine until the current bus cycle is permitted to complete.

Target Abort

Description

If a target detects a fatal error or will never be able to respond to the transaction, it may signal a target-abort. This instructs the initiator to end the transaction and indicates that the target does not want the transaction retried. It also means that any data already transferred during this transaction may be corrupted. The initiator should set the TARGET-ABORT DETECTED bit in its configuration status register and the target should set the SIGNALED TARGET-ABORT bit in its configuration status register.

Target abort is indicated to the initiator by asserting CSTOP#, deasserting CTRDY# and deasserting CDEVSEL# early. This tells the initiator that the target will not transfer the current data item (CTRDY# deasserted) and that the initiator must stop the transaction on the current data phase (CSTOP# asserted). The early deassertion of CDEVSEL# instructs the initiator not to re-attempt the transaction (no retry).

Reasons Target Issues Target Abort

Broken Target. If a target is broken and unable to transfer data, it may indicate this by issuing a target abort to the master.

I/O Addressing Error. This subject is covered in the section entitled See "I/O Data Phase" on page 152.

Address Phase Parity Error. One of the ways in which a target can respond to a parity error detected at the completion of the address phase is to issue a target abort to the initiator (it must also assert CSERR# if enabled to do so).

Master's Response to Target Abort

In response to a target abort, the initiator takes one of the following actions:

- Generates an interrupt to alert its related device driver to check its status.
- Generates SERR# (assuming the master's SERR ENABLED bit is set to one in its configuration command register). For more information on SERR#, refer to "System Errors" on page 187.

Target Abort Example.

Figure 8-9 on page 127 illustrates a target signaling a target-abort. To indicate that it wishes to abort the transaction, the target asserts CSTOP# and deasserts CTRDY# (if it wasn't already deasserted) and CDEVSEL#. This instructs the initiator to stop on the current data phase (CSTOP# asserted) with no data transferred (CTRDY# deasserted) and not to retry the transaction again (CDEVSEL# deasserted early).

The initiator samples the state of CSTOP#, CTRDY# and CDEVSEL# at the rising-edge of clock two and responds by deasserting CFRAME# and asserting CIRDY# (if it wasn't already asserted) during clock cell two. This indicates that the initiator is ready to complete the final data phase (a null data phase). During clock three, the target deasserts CSTOP# (in response to sampling CFRAME# deasserted). At the same time, the initiator deasserts CIRDY#, returning the bus to the idle state on clock four.

Figure 8-9: Target-Abort

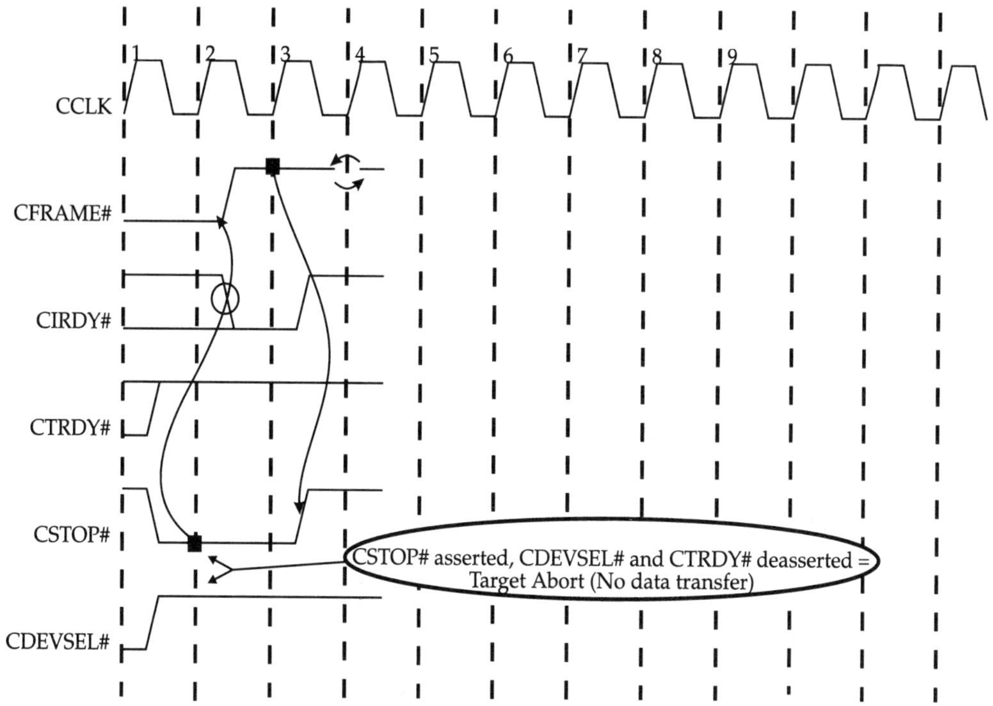

How Soon Does Initiator Attempt to Re-Establish Transfer After Retry or Disconnect?

In the event of a target-initiated retry or disconnect, the initiator must restart the transaction again. The initiator must deassert its CREQ# line for a minimum of two CardBus clocks: one when the bus goes idle (CFRAME# and CIRDY# deasserted) and another either the clock immediately before or after the return to idle. This provides lower-priority bus master with an opportunity to gain bus ownership. If the initiator intends to complete the data transfer that was disconnected or retried, it should reassert its CREQ# again after its two clock deassertion (or it may experience starvation). The 2.1 PCI spec says the master should retry the transaction within 33 clocks.

9 Memory Transfers

The Previous Chapter

This chapter defined the commands supported by CardBus and described the corresponding transactions.

This Chapter

This chapter discusses memory ready and write transactions and related protocols. It also discusses issues related to memory write buffer implementation, including byte merging, combining, and collapsing write data.

The Next Chapter

The next chapter discusses I/O transactions and the special address mechanism used.

Some Basic Transfer Protocol Rules

Prior to beginning the discussion of memory read and write transactions, the following basic rules are introduced that apply to all read/write transfers. The ready signal from the device sourcing the data must be asserted when it is driving valid data onto the data bus. The CardBus agent receiving the data can keep its ready line deasserted until it is ready to receive the data. Once a device's ready signal is asserted, it must remain so until the end of the current data phase.

The PCI 2.1 spec defines the maximum amount of time that the initiator or target is permitted to keep its ready signal deasserted. Since the CardBus spec is a derivative of the PCI spec, these rules apply for CardBus as well. The initiator is not permitted to keep CIRDY# deasserted for longer than eight clocks during any data phase. The target may keep CTRDY# deasserted for up to 16 clocks in the first data phase, but may not deassert it for longer than eight clocks in any subsequent data phase.

An agent may not alter its control line settings once it has indicated that it is ready to complete the current data phase. Once the initiator has asserted CIRDY#, it may not change the state of CIRDY# or CFRAME# regardless of the state of CTRDY#. Once a target has asserted CTRDY# or CSTOP#, it may not change CTRDY#, CSTOP# or CDEVSEL# until the current data phase completes.

Memory Read Transactions

This section discusses the timing and protocols associated with memory read transfers. During the following description of the read transaction, refer to Figure 9-1 on page 131. Each clock cycle is numbered for easy reference and begins and ends on the rising-edge. It is assumed that the CardBus initiator has already arbitrated for and been granted access to the bus. The initiator then must wait for the bus to become idle. This is accomplished by sampling the state of CFRAME# and CIRDY# on the rising-edge of each clock (along with CGNT#). When CFRAME# and CIRDY# are sampled deasserted (clock edge one) along with CGNT# asserted, the bus is idle and a transaction may be initiated by the bus master.

Address Phase

At the start of clock one, the initiator asserts CFRAME#, indicating that the transaction has begun and that a valid start address and command are on the bus. CFRAME# must remain asserted until the initiator is ready to complete the last data phase. As the initiator asserts CFRAME#, it also drives the start address onto the CAD bus (i.e. CAD31:2; CAD1:0 are not part of the address) and the transaction type onto the Command/Byte Enable lines, CC/BE[3:0]#. The address and transaction type are driven onto the bus for the duration of clock one.

A turn-around cycle (i.e., a dead cycle) is required on all shared signals. This period is required to avoid a collision when one agent is in the process of turning off its output drivers and another agent begins driving the same signal(s). During clock one, CIRDY#, CTRDY# and CDEVSEL# are not driven (in preparation for takeover by the new initiator and target). They are kept in the deasserted state by keeper resistors (required bridge resource).

CAD Turn-Around Cycle

At the start of clock two, the initiator ceases driving the CAD bus. This will allow the target to take control of the CAD bus to drive the first requested data item (between one and four bytes) back to the initiator. During a read, clock two of every transaction is defined as the turn-around cycle because ownership of the CAD bus is changing from the initiator to the addressed target. It is the responsibility of the addressed target to keep CTRDY# deasserted to enforce this period, thus preventing a collision on the CAD bus.

Figure 9-1: Example Memory Read Transfer Initiated by CardBus Card

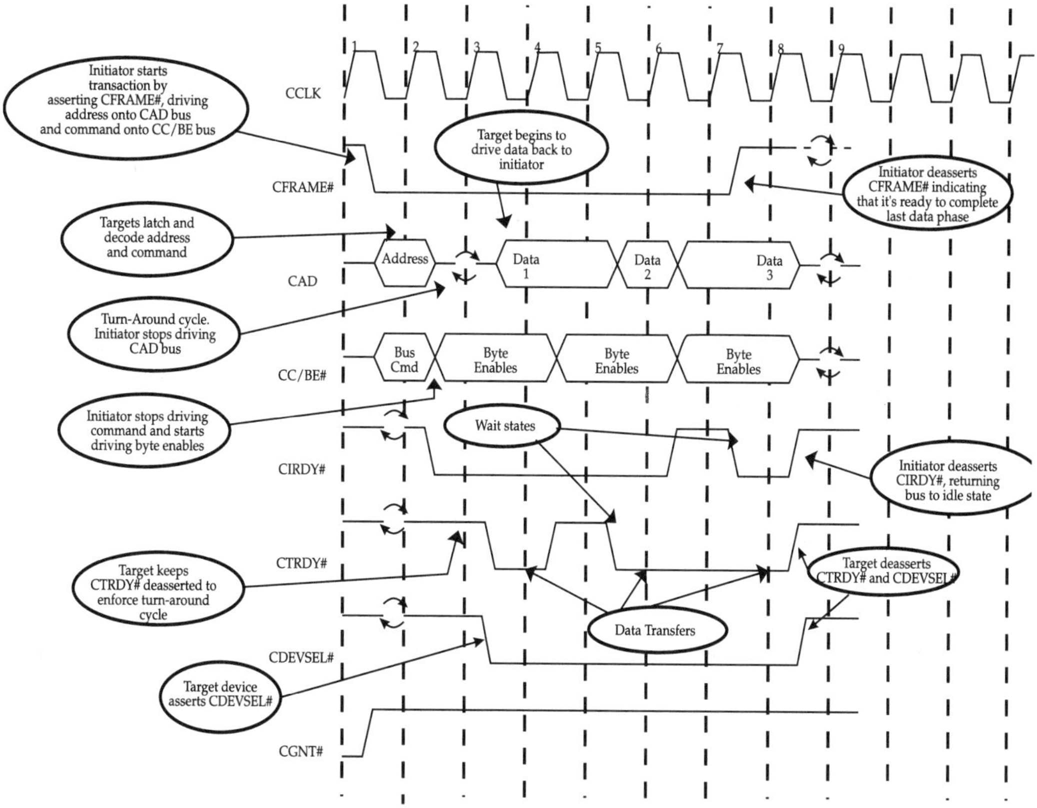

Also at the start of clock two, the initiator ceases to drive the command onto the Command/Byte Enable lines and uses them to indicate the bytes to be transferred in the currently-addressed doubleword (as well as the data paths to be used during the data transfer). No turn-around cycle is required for the CC/BE lines (since the initiator drives both the command and byte enables). Typically, the initiator asserts all of the byte enables during a read from main memory.

The initiator also asserts CIRDY# to indicate that it is ready to receive the first data item from the target. Upon asserting CIRDY#, the initiator keeps CFRAME# asserted, thereby indicating that it wants to transfer another data item. If this were the final data phase, the initiator would assert CIRDY# but deassert CFRAME# simultaneously to indicate that it is ready to complete the final data phase.

It should be noted that the initiator does not have to assert CIRDY# immediately upon entering a data phase. It may require some time before it's ready to receive the first data item (e.g., it has a buffer full condition).

First Data Transfer

During clock cell three, the target asserts CDEVSEL# to indicate that it has recognized its address and will participate in the transaction. The target begins to drive the first data item (one to four bytes, as indicated by the CC/BE lines) onto the CAD bus and asserts CTRDY# to indicate the presence of the requested data.

When the initiator and the currently-addressed target sample CTRDY# and CIRDY# both asserted at the rising-edge of clock four, the first data item is read from the bus by the initiator, completing the first data phase. The first data phase consists of clock cells two (turnaround cycle) and three.

It is the responsibility of the target to latch the start address into an address counter and to manage the address from data phase to data phase. As an example, upon completion of one data phase, the target would increment the latched address by four to point to the next doubleword. It then examines the initiator's byte enable settings to determine the bytes to be transferred within the currently-addressed doubleword. This subject is covered in more detail later in this chapter.

Second Data Transfer

At the start of the second data phase (clock edge four), the initiator sets the byte enables to indicate the bytes to be transferred within the next doubleword.

It is a rule that the initiator must immediately output the byte enables for a data phase upon entry to that data phase. If for some reason the initiator doesn't know what the byte enable setting will be for the next data phase, it should keep CIRDY# deasserted and not let the current data phase end until it knows what they will be.

In this example, the initiator keeps CIRDY# asserted upon entry into the second data phase, but does not deassert CFRAME#. This indicates that the initiator is ready to read the second data item, and once again this is not the final data phase.

Also in this example, the target needs additional time to fetch the second data item requested, so it deasserts CTRDY# to insert a wait state (clock cell five) into the second data phase. In order to keep the data paths from floating, the target must continue to drive a stable data pattern, usually consisting of the previous data item, onto the CAD bus until it has acquired and is presenting the second requested data item. This is illustrated in clock four. It is necessary to keep the CAD bus from floating in order to prevent CMOS input buffers from oscillating and drawing excessive current.

At the rising-edge of clock five, the initiator samples CTRDY# deasserted and, recognizing that the target is requesting more time for the transfer of the second data item, it inserts a wait state into the second data phase (clock cell five).

During the wait state, the target begins to drive the second data item onto the CAD bus and asserts CTRDY# to indicate its presence. When the initiator samples both CIRDY# and CTRDY# asserted at the rising-edge of clock six, it reads the second data item from the bus. This completes the second data phase. The second data phase consists of clock cells four and five.

Third and Final Data Transfer

At the start of the third data phase, the initiator sets the byte enables to indicate the bytes to be transferred in the next doubleword. It also deasserts CIRDY#, indicating that it requires more than one clock cell before it will be ready to receive the data. In other words, the initiator forces a wait state into the third data phase.

During clock cell six, the target keeps CTRDY# asserted, indicating that it is driving the third requested data item onto the CAD bus. In this example, however, the initiator requires more time before it will be able to read the data item (probably because it has a temporary buffer full condition). The target must continue to drive the third data item onto the CAD bus during the wait state (clock cell seven).

During clock cell seven, the initiator asserts CIRDY#, indicating that it is ready to accept the third data item on the next rising clock edge. It also deasserts CFRAME#, indicating that this is the final data phase. The target, having sampled CFRAME# deasserted, knows that this is the final data phase in the burst transaction.

The initiator samples both CIRDY# and CTRDY# asserted at the rising-edge of clock eight and reads the third data item from the bus. The third data phase consists of clocks six and seven.

The overall burst transfer consisting of three data phases has been completed. The initiator deasserts CIRDY#, returning the bus to the idle state (on the rising-edge of clock nine), and the target deasserts CTRDY# and CDEVSEL#.

Performance During Read Transactions

As described earlier, a turn-around cycle must be included in the first data transfer of a read transaction. This being the case, a single data phase read from a target consists of at least three cycles of the CardBus clock (one clock cell for the address phase and two clock cells for the data phase). At a clock rate of 33MHz, a read transaction consisting of a single data transfer takes 90ns to complete. An idle cycle (at 33MHz, 30ns in duration) must be included between transactions, resulting in 120ns from the start of one transaction to the start of the next. Using back-to-back single data phase read transfers, the data throughput would be 8.33 million transfers per second. If each transfer involved four bytes, the resultant transfer rate would be 33.33Mbytes per second.

In actual practice, though, most read transactions involve the transfer of multiple objects between the initiator and the currently-addressed target. The read transaction involving multiple data phases only requires the turn-around cycle during the first data phase. The second through the last data phases can each be accomplished in a single clock cycle (if both the initiator and the currently-addressed target are capable of zero wait state transfers). The achievable transfer rate during the second through the last data phases is thus one transfer every 30ns (at a bus speed of 33MHz), or 33 million transfers per second. If each data phase involves the transfer of four bytes, the resultant data transfer rate is 132Mbytes per second. Figure 9-2 on page 135 illustrates a read transaction consisting of three data phases, two of which complete with zero wait states.

Figure 9-2: CardBus Burst Read without Wait States

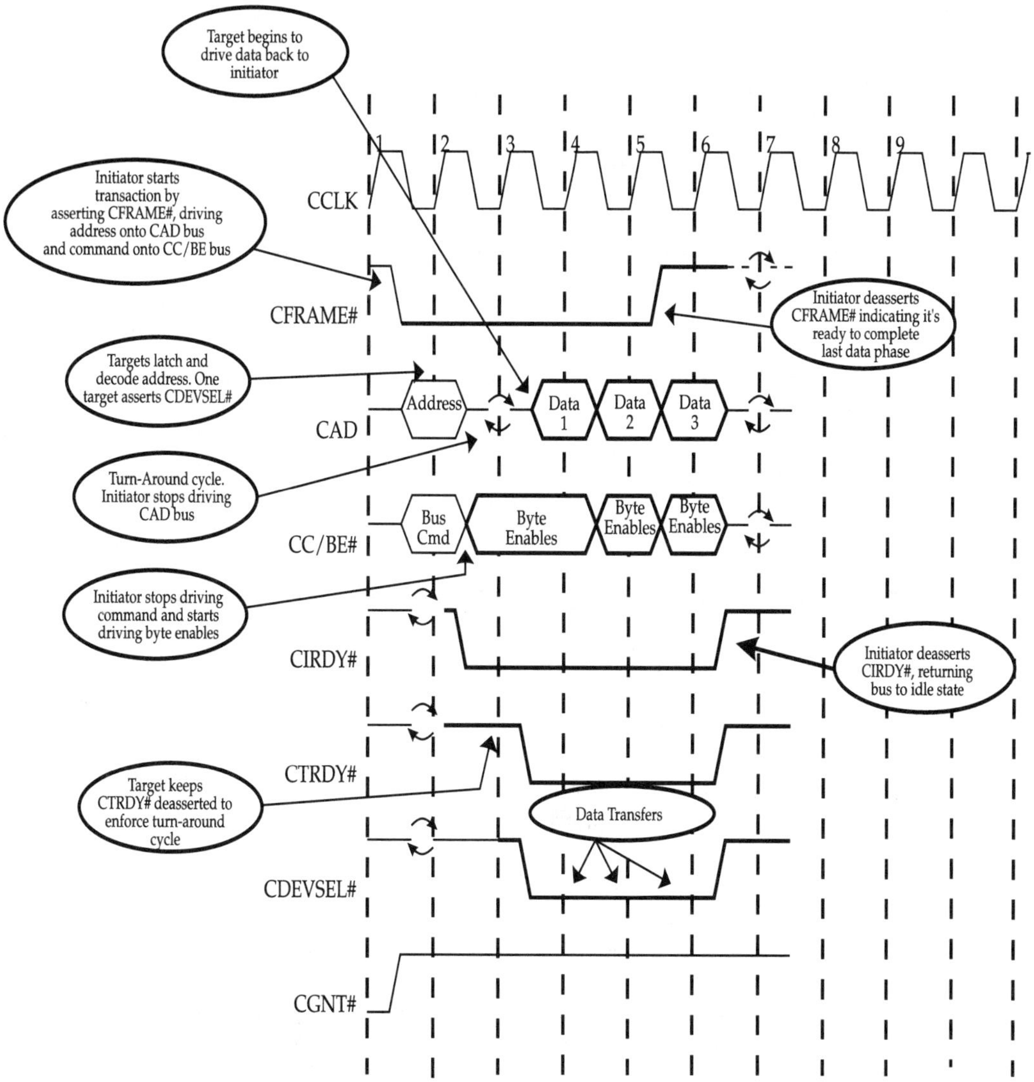

Treatment of Byte Enables During Reads

Byte Enable Settings During Each Data Phase

CardBus permits burst transactions in which the byte enables (CC/BE[3:0]#) change from one data phase to the next. Furthermore, the initiator may use any byte enable setting, consisting of contiguous or non-contiguous byte enables. During a read transaction, the initiator typically asserts all of the byte enables during each data phase, but it may use any combination.

It should be noted that all targets may not be capable of handling non-contiguous byte enables. An example would be a bridge that interface to 8- or 16-bit devices. In this case, the target could take one of the following actions:

- assert SERR#.
- break the transaction into two 16-bit transfers.

Data Phase with No Byte Enables Asserted

As stated in the previous paragraph, any combination of byte enables is valid in any data phase. This includes a data phase with no byte enables asserted (a null data phase). This can occur for a number of reasons. Some examples would be:

- During a burst transfer, the programmer may wish to "skip" a doubleword. This would be accomplished by keeping all byte enables deasserted during that data phase.
- The last data phase of a block transfer may consist of invalid data, requiring that all byte enables be deasserted. For example, assume that an expansion bus master (EISA or Micro Channel) has initiated a series of accesses with a CardBus target. The bridge between the expansion bus and CardBus will frequently packetize this series of bus master accesses into a CardBus burst transfer. When the expansion bus master has completed its last data transfer, the bridge signals this to the target by deasserting CFRAME#. This informs the target that the last data transfer is in progress. Since the bus master has already transferred all of the data. To prevent invalid data from being transferred to the target, the bridge will not assert any of the byte enables during this last data phase.

When none of the byte enables are asserted, the target must react as follows:

- **On a read:** the target must ensure that no data or status is destroyed or altered as a result of this data transfer. The target must supply a stable pattern on all data paths and must generate the proper parity (for the CAD and CC/BE buses) on the CPAR bit.
- **On a write:** the target must not store any data and the initiator must supply a stable pattern on all data paths and ensure that CPAR is valid for the CAD and CC/BE buses.

Target with Limited Byte Enable Support

Memory and I/O targets may support restricted byte enable settings and may respond with target abort for any other pattern. All devices must support any byte enable combination during configuration transactions, however.

Rule for Sampling of Byte Enables

If the target requires sampling of the byte enables (in order to precisely determine which bytes are to be transferred within the currently-addressed doubleword) during each data transfer, it must wait for the byte enables to be valid during each data phase before completing the transfer. An example of a device that requires sampling of byte enables would be a memory-mapped I/O device. It should not accept a write to or a read from 8-bit ports within the currently-addressed doubleword until it has verified (via the byte enables) that the initiator is in fact addressing those ports.

If a target does not require examination of the byte enables on a read, the target must supply all four bytes. An example of a device that would not have to wait to sample the byte enables would be a typical memory target. Memory typically yields the same data from a location no matter how many times the location is read from. In other words, performing a speculative read from the memory does not alter the data stored in the location. This type of memory target can be designed to supply all four bytes in every data phase of a read burst. The initiator only take the bytes it's addressing and ignores the others.

Ignore Byte Enables During Line Read

If the initiator is reading a line of data from memory, the memory target must return all four bytes regardless of the byte enable settings. This action is guaranteed in one of the following manners:

- If the cacheability of the target memory is determined by the initiator, the initiator must ensure that all byte enables are asserted so that the target will return all four bytes.
- If the target memory determines that the access is cacheable, it should ignore the byte enable settings during each data phase (except for parity generation) and return all four bytes.

Prefetching

If a target does not support caching but does support prefetching (indicated by hardwiring the prefetchable attribute bit in its base address configuration register to a one), it must return all four bytes (on a read) regardless of the byte enable settings. A target only supports this feature if there are no side effects from the read (for example, data destroyed or a status change in a memory-mapped I/O register).

Memory Write Transactions

During the following description of the write transaction, refer to Figure 9-3. It is assumed that the bus master has already arbitrated for and been granted access to the bus. The bus master then must wait for the bus to become idle. This is accomplished by sampling the state of CFRAME# and CIRDY# on the rising-edge of each clock. When both are sampled deasserted (on the rising-edge of clock one), the bus is idle and a transaction may be initiated by the bus master whose grant signal is currently asserted by the bus arbiter.

Figure 9-3: Example Burst Write Transaction

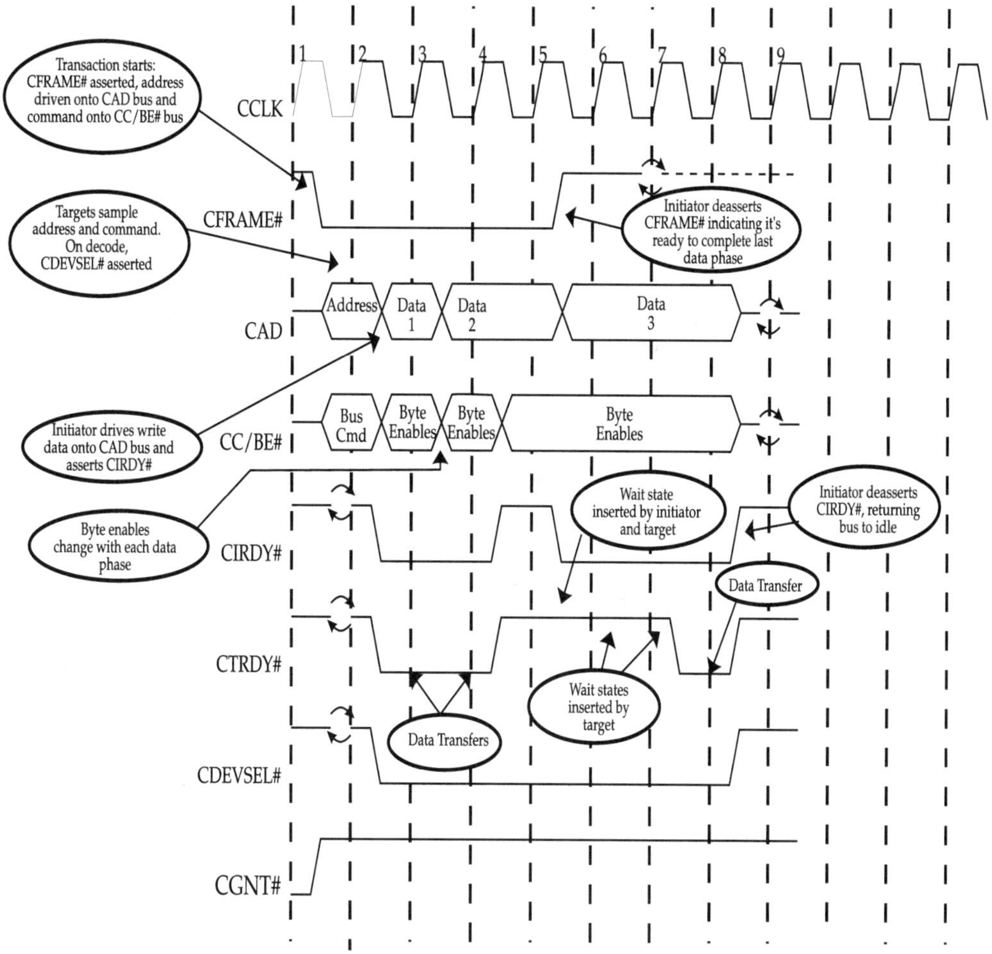

Address Phase

At the start of clock cell one, the initiator asserts CFRAME# to indicate that the transaction has begun and that a valid start address and command are present on the bus. CFRAME# remains asserted until the initiator is ready to complete the last data phase. At the same time that the initiator asserts CFRAME#, it drives the start address onto the CAD bus and the transaction type onto the Command/Byte Enable bus. The address and transaction type are driven onto the bus for the duration of clock one.

A turn-around cycle is required on all shared signals. This period is required to avoid a collision if a device turned on its output drivers at the same time that another device's output drivers are disconnecting from the signal(s). During clock cell one, CIRDY#, CTRDY# and CDEVSEL# are not driven (in preparation for takeover by the new initiator and target).

First Data Transfer

At the start of clock cell two, the initiator changes the information that it is presenting to the target over the CAD bus. During a write transaction, the initiator is driving the CAD bus during both the address and data phases. Since it doesn't have to hand off control of the CAD bus to the target, as it does during a read, a CAD turn-around cycle is unnecessary. The initiator may begin to drive the first data item onto the CAD bus at the start of clock cell two. In addition, during clock cell two the initiator uses the Command/Byte Enable lines to indicate the bytes to be transferred to the currently-addressed doubleword and the data paths to be used during the first data phase.

The initiator drives the write data onto the CAD bus and at the same time asserts the respective byte enables to indicate the data path(s) that carry valid data. It also asserts CIRDY# to indicate the presence of the data on the bus. The initiator doesn't deassert CFRAME# when it asserts CIRDY# (because this is not the final data phase).

It should be noted that the initiator does not have to assert CIRDY# immediately upon entering a data phase. It may require some time (but nor more than eight clocks) before it's ready to source the first data item (e.g., it has a buffer empty condition).

During clock cell two, the target decodes the address and command and asserts CDEVSEL# to claim the transaction. In addition, it asserts CTRDY#, indicating its readiness to accept the first data item.

At the rising-edge of clock three, the initiator and the currently-addressed target sample both CTRDY# and CIRDY# asserted, indicating that they are both ready to complete the first data phase. This is a zero wait state transfer. The target accepts the first data item from the bus on the rising-edge of clock three (and samples the byte enables in order to determine which bytes are being written), completing the first data phase.

Second Data Transfer

During clock cell three, the initiator drives the second data item onto the CAD bus and sets the byte enables to indicate the bytes to be transferred and the data paths to be used during the second data phase. It also keeps CIRDY# asserted and does not deassert CFRAME#, thereby indicating that it is ready to complete the second data phase and that this is not the final data phase. Assertion of CIRDY# indicates that the write data is present on the bus.

At the rising-edge of clock four, the initiator and the currently-addressed target sample both CTRDY# and CIRDY# asserted, indicating that they are both ready to complete the second data phase. This is a zero wait state data phase. The target accepts the second data item from the bus on the rising-edge of clock four (and samples the byte enables), completing the second data phase.

Third Data Phase

In this example, the initiator requires more time before it drives the next data item onto the CAD bus (it has a buffer empty condition). It inserts a wait state into the third data phase by deasserting CIRDY# at the start of clock cell four. This allows the initiator to delay presentation of the new data by one clock, but it must set the byte enables to the proper setting for the third data phase at the start of clock cell four.

The target also requires more time before it will be ready to accept the third data item. To indicate the requirement for more time, the target deasserts CTRDY# during clock cell four. When the initiator and target sample CIRDY# and CTRDY# deasserted at the rising-edge of clock five, they insert a wait state (clock cell five) into the third data phase.

During clock cell four, although the initiator does yet have the third data item available to drive, it must drive a stable pattern onto the data paths rather than let the CAD bus float. The specification doesn't dictate the pattern to be driven during this period. It is usually accomplished by continuing to drive the previous data item. The target will not accept the data being presented to it for two reasons:

- By deasserting CTRDY#, it has indicated that it isn't ready to accept data.
- By deasserting CIRDY#, the initiator has indicated that it is not yet presenting the next data item to the target.

During clock cell five, the initiator asserts CIRDY# and drives the final data item onto the CAD bus. It also deasserts CFRAME# to indicate that this is the final data phase. The target keeps CTRDY# deasserted, indicating that it is not yet ready to accept the third data item.

At the rising-edge of clock six, the initiator samples CIRDY# asserted, indicating that it is presenting the data, but CTRDY# is still deasserted (because the target is not yet ready to accept the data item). The target also samples CFRAME# deasserted, indicating that the final data phase is in progress. The only thing impeding the completion of the final data phase now is the target (by keeping CTRDY# deasserted until it is ready to accept the final data item).

In response to sampling CTRDY# deasserted on clock edge six, the target and initiator insert a second wait state (clock cell six) into the third data phase. During the second wait state, the initiator continues to drive the third data item onto the CAD bus and maintains the setting on the byte enables. The target keeps CTRDY# deasserted, indicating that it's not yet ready.

At the rising-edge of clock seven, the target and initiator sample CIRDY# asserted, indicating that the initiator is still presenting the data, but CTRDY# is still deasserted. In response, the target and initiator insert a third wait state (clock cell seven) into the third data phase. During the third wait state, the initiator continues to drive the third data item onto the CAD bus and maintains the setting on the byte enables. The target asserts CTRDY#, indicating that it is ready to complete the final data phase.

At the rising-edge of clock eight, the target and initiator sample both CIRDY# and CTRDY# asserted, indicating that both the initiator and the target are ready to end the third and final data phase. In response, the third data phase is completed on the rising-edge of clock eight. The target accepts the third data item from the CAD bus. The third data phase consisted of four clock periods (the first clock cell of the data phase, clock cell four, plus three wait states).

During clock cell eight, the initiator ceases to drive the data onto the CAD bus, stops driving the CC/BE bus, and deasserts CIRDY# (returning the bus to the idle state). The target deasserts CTRDY# and CDEVSEL#.

Performance During Write Transactions

Transactions wherein an initiator performs a single data phase write to a target consist of at least two cycles of the CardBus clock (the address phase and a one clock data phase). An idle cycle (at 33MHz, 30ns in duration) must be included between transactions. At a clock rate of 33MHz, then, a single data phase write transaction takes 90ns to complete. Using back-to-back single data phase write transfers, the data throughput would be 11.11 million transfers per second. If each transfer involved four bytes, the resulting transfer rate would be 44.44Mbytes per second.

The first through last data transfer of a write transaction involving multiple data phases can each be accomplished in a single clock cycle (if both the initiator and the currently-addressed target are capable of zero wait state data phases). The achievable transaction rate during the first through last data phases is thus one transfer every 30ns (at a bus speed of 33MHz), or 33 million transfers per second. If each transfer involves the transfer of four bytes, the data transfer rate is 132Mbytes per second. Figure 9-4 on page 143 illustrates a write transaction consisting of three zero wait state data phases.

Figure 9-4: Optimized Write Transaction (no wait states)

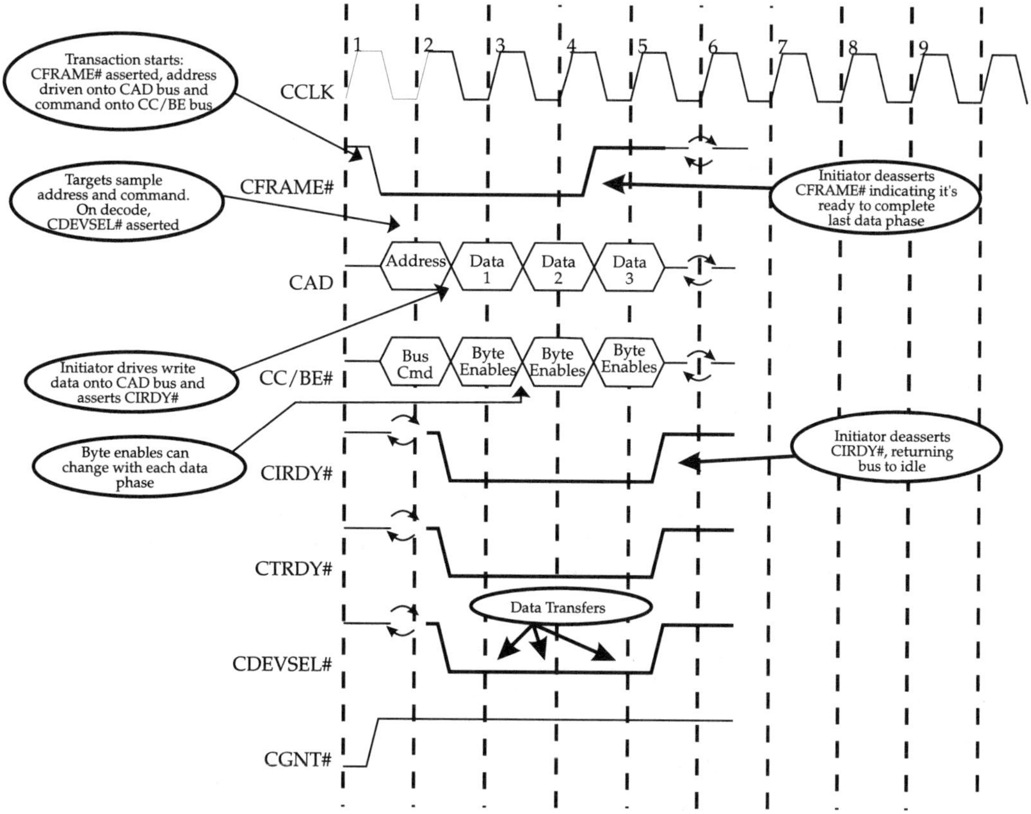

Posted-Write Buffer

General

A bridge (e.g., PCI-to-CardBus bridge or a host/CardBus) may incorporate a posted-write buffer that allows a bus master to complete a memory write quickly. The transaction and the write data are latched within the bridge's posted-write buffer and the master is permitted to complete the transaction. When a bridge implements a posted-write buffer, a potential problem exists. Another bus master (or the same one) may initiate a memory read from the target of the posted write before the data is actually written to the memory target. If this were permitted, the master performing the read would not receive the freshest copy of the information. In order to prevent this from occurring, the bridge designer must first flush all posted writes to their destination memory targets before permitting a read to occur on the bus. A device driver can ensure that all memory data has been written to its device by performing a read from the device. This will force the flushing of all posted write buffers in bridges that reside between the processor executing the read and the target device before the read is permitted to complete.

It is also a requirement that the bridge must perform all posted writes in the same order in which they were originally posted. A bridge is only permitted to post writes to regular memory targets. Software must be assured real-time communication with I/O and memory-mapped I/O devices, as well as with configuration registers.

Combining

A bridge may combine posted memory writes to successive doublewords into a single burst memory write transaction using linear addressing ("Linear and Cacheline Wrap Addressing" on page 146). This feature is recommended to improve performance. The doublewords must be written in the same order in which they were posted. This means that writes posted to doublewords zero, one and two (they were posted in that order) can be combined into a linear burst write, while writes posted to doublewords two, one, zero cannot. Instead, these three writes would have to be performed as three separate single data phase memory write transactions. Writes posted to doublewords zero, one, and three (in that order) can be combined into a linear burst write with no byte enables asserted in the third data phase. The specification recommends that bridges that permit combining include a control bit to allow this feature to be disabled.

Byte Merging

A bridge may combine writes to a single doubleword to be merged within one entry in the posted-write buffer. This feature is recommended to improve performance and is only permitted in memory address ranges that are prefetchable. As an example, assume that a bus master performs two memory writes: the first writes to locations 00000100h and 00000101h and the second writes to locations 00000102h and 00000103h. These four locations reside within the same doubleword. The bridge could absorb the first two-byte write into a doubleword buffer entry and then absorb the second two byte write into the same doubleword buffer entry. When the bridge performs the memory write, it can complete it in a single data phase.

Collapsing (Forbidden)

Multiple writes to the same location(s) cannot be performed as a single write on the other side of the bridge. Two sequential writes to the same doubleword where at least one of the byte enables was asserted in both transactions must be performed as two separate transactions on the other bus. Collapsing of writes is forbidden for any type of write transactions.

The specification states that a bridge may allow collapsing within a specific range when a device driver indicates that this will not cause operational problems. How the device driver would indicate this to a bridge is outside the scope of the specification.

Cache Line Merging

The bridge may perform cache line merging within an area of memory that the bridge knows is cacheable or when it uses combining and/or byte merging to create a burst write of a cache line. It captures (i.e., posts) individual memory writes performed by bus masters on one bus to build a cache line to be written on the other bus using a memory write and invalidate transaction or a linear memory write transaction. Note that the specification doesn't specifically state that a memory write and invalidate command would be used.

Addressing Sequence During Memory Burst

Linear and Cacheline Wrap Addressing

The start address issued during any form of memory transaction is a doubleword-aligned address presented on CAD[31:2] during the address phase. The memory target latches this address into an address counter and uses it for the first data phase. Upon completion of the first data phase and assuming that it's not a single data phase transaction, the memory target must update its address counter to point to the next doubleword to be transferred (if the target supports bursting).

On a multiple data phase memory access, a memory target must check the state of address bits one and zero (CAD[1:0]) to determine the policy to use when updating its address counter at the conclusion of each data phase. Table 9-1 on page 147 lists the addressing sequences defined in the revision 2.1 specification and encoded in the first two address bits. Only two addressing sequences are currently defined:

- **Linear, or sequential, address mode**. All memory devices that support multiple data phase transfers must implement support of linear, or sequential, addressing (and must start at the beginning of a memory line). The memory write and invalidate command must use linear addressing. At the completion of each data phase, the memory target increments its address counter by four to point to the next sequential doubleword for the next data phase.
- **Cacheline wrap mode**. Support for cacheline wrap mode is optional and is only used for memory reads. At the start of each data phase of the burst read, the memory target increments the doubleword address in its address counter. When the end of the cache line is encountered and assuming that the transfer did not start at the first doubleword of the cache line, the target wraps to the start doubleword address of the cacheline and continues incrementing the address in each data phase until the entire cache line has been transferred. If the burst continues past the point where the entire cache line has been transferred, the target starts the transfer of the next cache line at the same address that the transfer of the previous line started at.

Implementation of the cacheline wrap mode is optional for memory and meaningless for I/O and configuration targets. The addressing sequence used during a cache line fill is established at the start of the transfer based on the start memory address and the length of the transfer. This implies that the memory target must know that a cache line fill is in progress (wrap mode indicated) and the size of a cache line (established at start-up when the platform-specific configuration program writes the system cache line size to the memory target's cache line size configuration register).

The 486 processor's internal cache has a line size of sixteen bytes (four doublewords) and has a 32-bit data bus. It must therefore perform four 32-bit transfers to fill a cache line. The first doubleword address output by the processor is the one that resulted in an internal cache miss. This could be any of the four doublewords within the line. For a detailed description of the 486 cache line fill addressing sequence, refer to the Addison-Wesley publication entitled *80486 System Architecture*. For that used by the Pentium processor, refer to the Addison-Wesley publication entitled *Pentium Processor System Architecture*. For that used by the PowerPC 60x processors, refer to the Addison-Wesley publication entitled *PowerPC System Architecture*.

As an example, assume that the cache line size is 16 bytes and the start doubleword address issued by the master is 00000104h. This doubleword resides within the 16-byte aligned cache line that occupies memory locations 00000100h through 0000010Fh. The sequence of the doubleword transfers would be 00000104h, 00000108h, 0000010Ch and 00000100h. If the burst continues past this point, the next series of doublewords transferred would be 00000114h, 00000118h, 0000011Ch and 00000110h.

If the target does not implement the cache line size register, the target must issue a disconnect (A or B) on the first data phase or a type C disconnect on the second one (it can't handle wrap mode because it doesn't know the line size).

If the master wants to use linear addressing after the first line has been read, it must end the transaction and begin a new one indicating linear addressing.

Table 9-1: The Burst Addressing Sequence

CAD1	CAD0	Addressing Sequence
0	0	Linear, or sequential, addressing sequence during the burst.
0	1	Reserved. When detected, the memory target should signal a target disconnect after the first data phase or a retry on the second data phase.
1	0	Cacheline wrap mode.

Table 9-1: The Burst Addressing Sequence (Continued)

CAD1	CAD0	Addressing Sequence
1	1	Reserved. When detected, the memory target should signal a target disconnect after the first data phase or a retry on the second data phase.

Target Response to Reserved Setting on CAD[1:0]

Assuming that the initiator has started a multi-data phase memory transaction and that it has placed a reserved pattern on CAD[1:0] in the address phase (01b or 11b pattern), the revision 2.x-compliant PCI memory target must either issue a disconnect (type A or B) on the transfer of the first data item, or a disconnect type C during the second data phase. This is necessary because the initiator is indicating an addressing sequence that is unfamiliar to the target.

10 I/O Transfers

The Previous Chapter

The previous chapter discussed memory transactions. Memory read and write transfers were detailed as well as the mechanisms used to enhance performance, such as combining, byte merging, and write-posting.

This Chapter

This chapter discusses the I/O transfer protocol and its differences from memory transfers.

The Next Chapter

The next chapter introduces the locking protocol defined by CardBus to permit exclusive access to a given range of memory address space.

CardBus I/O Addressing

The address placed on the CAD bus during the address phase is decoded by the target device. A positive decode results in CDEVSEL# being asserted so that the initiator can detect that a target device has responded. The address decoded by I/O devices differs from a memory address:

- A memory address consist of CAD[31:2]. Note that CAD[1:0] defines the burst sequence and are not used during the address decode. CAD[31:2] identifies the 32-bit memory device.
- I/O addresses consist of CAD[31:0]. I/O decoders examine the entire 32-bit address to determine whether CDEVSEL# should be asserted. In this way, a target, byte-specific location can be identified.

This I/O mapping permits different CardBus and PCI devices to implement 8- or 16-bit registers in their designs that are mapped into the same 4-byte block of address space (provides support for legacy I/O addressing). Consider the following example of CardBus I/O addressing.

Example I/O Decode and CDEVSEL# Assertion

To illustrate the advantages of the I/O addressing scheme, assume that the CardBus card has implemented two 8-bit registers associated with a legacy device (CB Reg A and B) as illustrated in Figure 10-1. Also assume that legacy software expects these registers to be mapped into contiguous I/O locations within the same four byte block of address space, as illustrated.

Figure 10-1: Legacy Device Mapped into CardBus I/O Address Space

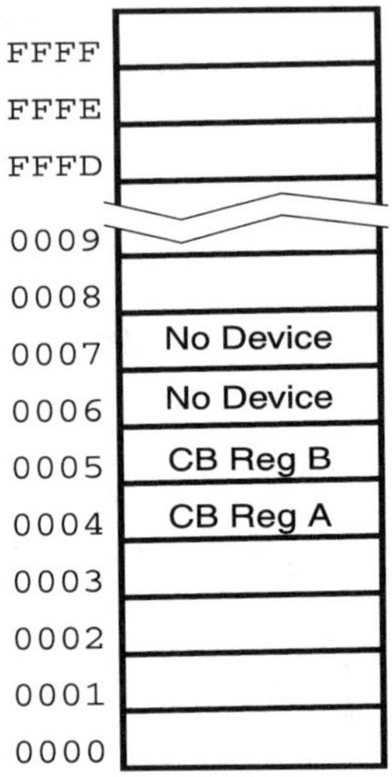

If memory-like address decoding were used (i.e., decoding only CAD[31:2]) any access within the four bytes block of address space that starts at IO location 0004h would result in CDEVSEL# being asserted. However, it would be a mistake to assert CDEVSEL# if an attempted access were made to one of the upper two locations within this doubleword (because the target device has no physical device mapped into those locations). The card would not recognize that it was not the target of the transaction until CC/BE[3:0]# are checked during the data phase.

The problem is solved using the I/O address mechanism. While only two I/O locations are needed by the CardBus card, the smallest range of I/O addresses that can be mapped using the CardBus Base Address Register (BAR) is four bytes (see Chapter 18 on page 297.) As illustrated in Figure 10-2, the I/O addressing mechanism requires address decoding down to the byte location, using CAD[31:0]. The CardBus card asserts CDEVSEL# only when a target register occupies the byte address specified by CAD[1:0]. If the start address indicates that either or both of the upper two bytes are being accessed (i.e., CAD[1:0] are set to 10b or 11b), CDEVSEL# will not be asserted.

Figure 10-2: Assertion of CDEVSEL during I/O Address Decode

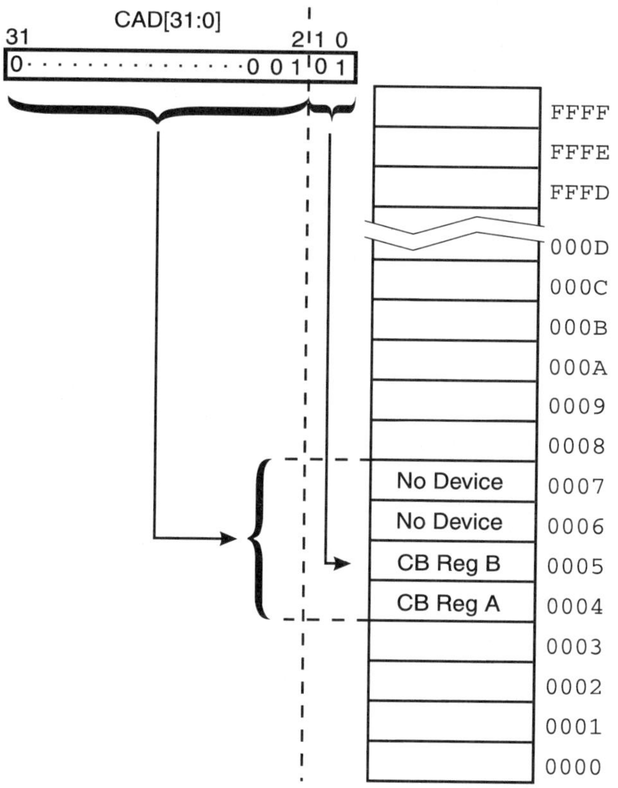

I/O Address Phase

The initiator asserts CFRAME# and drives the address CAD[31:0] to the CardBus pins, along with either the I/O read or write command on CC/BE[3:0]#. At the end of the address phase, the target latches the start address and the I/O read or write command and begins the address decode. An I/O target claims the transaction (asserts CDEVSEL#) based on the byte-specific start address that it latched. If the indicated 8-bit I/O port is implemented in the target, the target asserts CDEVSEL# and claims the transaction. If the target owns all locations within the entire four bytes of address space, the decode may be performed using only CAD[31:2]. CC/BE[3:0]# can then be used to identify the specific location(s) targeted within the doubleword.

I/O Data Phase

The byte enables asserted during the first data phase identify the least-significant byte addressed within the doubleword (the same one indicated by the setting of CAD[1:0]) as well as any additional bytes (within the addressed doubleword) that the initiator is addressing. It is illegal (and makes no sense) for the initiator to assert any byte enables of lesser significance than the one indicated by the CAD[1:0] setting. If the initiator does assert any illegal byte enable pattern, the target must terminate the transaction with a target abort. Table 10-1 on page 152 illustrates the legal CC/BE[3:0]# combinations.

Table 10-1: Legal CAD[1:0] and CC/BE[3:0]# Combinations during I/O Addressing

CAD1	CAD0	CC/BE3#	CC/BE2#	CC/BE1#	CC/BE0#
0	0	X	X	X	0
0	1	X	X	0	1
1	0	X	0	1	1
1	1	0	1	1	1

Consider the following example of an illegal I/O address, in which a PC Card implements two registers (labeled CB Reg A and CB Reg B) located in the upper two bytes of a four byte block of I/O address space (see Figure 10-3 on page 153.) If CAD[31:2] identify the four byte block that the two target registers reside in and CAD[1:0] are set to 10b respectively, then CB Reg A is selected. The CardBus card having decoded the entire 32-bit address recognizes that it is the target device and asserts CDEVSEL#. The byte enable lines CC/BE[3:0]# must then be examined by the card to verify the address. Assertion of either CC/BE1# or CC/BE0# indicates access to a location outside the range of addresses mapped to the card and contradicts the initial start address, thus the transaction should be target aborted by the CardBus card.

If an I/O target claims a transaction (asserts CDEVSEL#) based on the byte-specific start address issued during the address phase, then subsequently examines the byte enables (issued during the data phase) and determines that it cannot fulfill the initiator's request, the target must respond by indicating a target-abort (CSTOP# asserted, CTRDY# and CDEVSEL# deasserted) to the initiator. The target-abort is covered under the heading "Target Abort" on page 125."

Figure 10-3: Example of Illegal I/O Address

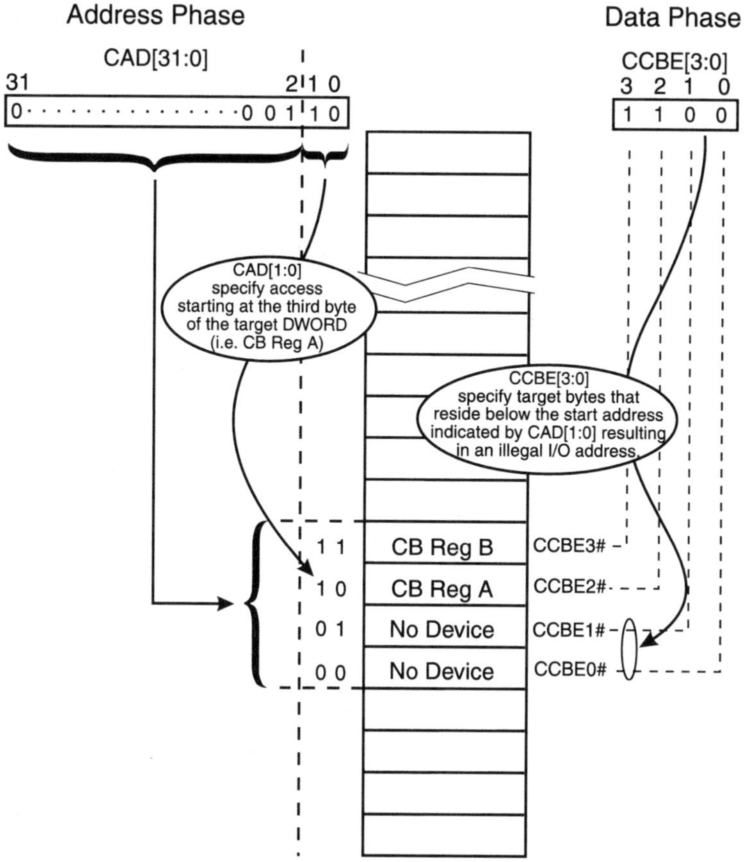

I/O Targets Supporting Only Single Data Phase Transactions

Many PCI I/O targets are not designed to handle multi-data phase transactions. A target can determine that the initiator intends to perform a second data phase upon completion of the first by checking the state of CFRAME# when CIRDY# is sampled asserted in the first data phase. If CIRDY# has been asserted by the initiator and it still has CFRAME# asserted, this indicates that this is not the final data phase in the transaction.

If an I/O target doesn't support multi-data phase transactions and the initiator indicates that a second data phase is forthcoming, the target must respond in one of two ways:

- When it's ready to transfer the first data item, terminate the first data phase with a disconnect type A or B (CSTOP#,CTRDY# and CDEVSEL# asserted). The first data item is transferred successfully, but the initiator is forced to terminate the transaction at that point. It must then re-arbitrate for bus ownership and re-address the target using a byte-specific start address within the next I/O doubleword.
- Terminate the second data phase with a type C disconnect (CSTOP# and CDEVSEL# asserted, CTRDY# deasserted). The first data phase completes normally. The initiator is then forced to terminate the transaction during the second data phase without transferring any additional data. The initiator then re-arbitrates for bus ownership and re-addresses the target using a byte-specific start address within the next I/O doubleword.

I/O Address Management

As in any CardBus read/write transaction, it is the responsibility of the I/O target to latch the start address delivered by the initiator. In a burst transaction, it then assumes responsibility for managing the address for each subsequent data phase that follows the first data phase. Unlike memory address management, however, there is no explicit or implicit I/O address sequencing from one data phase to the next. The initiator and the target must both understand and utilize the same I/O address management. Two examples would be:

1. Both the initiator and the target understand that the doubleword address (on CAD[31:2]) delivered by the initiator is to be incremented by four at the completion of each data phase. In other words, the read or write transaction proceeds sequentially through the target's I/O address space a doubleword at a time.
2. Both the initiator and the target understand that the target doesn't increment the doubleword address for each subsequent data phase. This is how a designer would implement a FIFO port.

Processors typically do not perform burst I/O operations. It's easy to assume that the Intel x86 INS (input string) and OUTS (output string) instructions cause the processor to generate a burst I/O read or write transaction series, but this isn't so. When a REP INS (i.e., repeat IN string instruction until count exhausted) instruction is executed by the x86 processor, it results in a series of back-to-back I/O read and memory write bus cycle pairs. The REP OUTS instruction results in a string of back-to-back memory read and I/O write bus cycle pairs.

11 Locked Transfers

The Previous Chapter

The previous chapter discussed I/O transfers and the addressing protocol used.

This Chapter

This chapter describes the locking support provided by CardBus cards.

The Next Chapter

The next chapter discusses parity generation, error detection, and error handling.

Introduction

The PC Card standard defines a locking mechanism that provides exclusive access to a region of memory to support software semaphores. Locking permits a CardBus initiator to gain exclusive access to another CardBus memory region or to PCI memory. Conversely, the locking mechanism provides a mechanism for CardBus memory targets to ensure the exclusive access is honored.

The CardBus locking protocol uses essentially the same protocol as the PCI bus, with slight variation. If you are already familiar with the PCI mechanism for establishing the bus lock and resource lock implementations, you may want to go directly to the summary of CardBus and PCI differences in "Appendix B—PCI & CardBus Differences" on page 383.

Locked Transactions and Semaphores

Memory Semaphore Definition

In some circumstances a master must perform a series of accesses to a particular memory target with the assurance that no other master will access the same target until the master's series of accesses have been completed. This is often referred to as an atomic series of transactions.

The following is an example of a situation that would require this ability to lock out other masters from accessing a particular target. Assume that the host system is executing multiple tasks under a multiprocessing operating system (such as OS/2, Unix, or Windows NT). A memory location is used to indicate the availability of a central resource, such as the page table in memory. A memory location that is used to reflect the availability or unavailability of a shared resource is referred to as a memory semaphore. When a task executing on a processor needs to access the page table, it must first determine that the page table isn't currently owned by another task.

To ascertain the availability of the page table, the task must first read from the memory semaphore associated with the page table and check the state of the semaphore byte to determine the page table's availability. If the byte is zero, this typically indicates that the page table is available. The task then sets the byte to a non-zero value and writes the byte back into the memory semaphore. In this manner, the task has acquired exclusive ownership of the page table and may initiate a series of one or more page table accesses without fear that another task will attempt to access the page table during this period. If any other task should check the state of the respective memory semaphore during this period, the state of the semaphore (i.e., non-zero) informs it that the page table is currently unavailable. When the current table owner has completed its series of page table accesses, it writes a zero into the memory semaphore, thereby marking the page table available again.

Synchronization Problem

Assume that one task is executing on processor A and another task is executing on processor B. The task on processor A must access the page table in memory. Using the bus to communicate with memory, processor A first initiates and completes a memory read bus cycle to read the page table's memory semaphore. The state of the semaphore is zero, indicating that the page table is available. The task sets the semaphore to a non-zero value in processor A's register (to mark the page table unavailable to other tasks) and processor A then requests the use of the bus to perform the memory write bus cycle to update the semaphore in memory.

At this time, processor B is also requesting the use of the bus and is granted access to the bus before processor A (because it has higher priority or is next in line for a bus access). Upon acquiring bus ownership, processor B then initiates a memory read bus cycle to read the page table's semaphore and determine the availability of the page table. When the task on processor B completes its memory read and is then testing the state of the semaphore, processor A gains access to the bus and performs the memory write to change the semaphore to a non-zero value. Upon completion of the write, the task on processor A believes that it now has gained exclusive ownership of the page table.

Meanwhile, the task on processor B determines that the current state of the semaphore is zero. It has no knowledge that processor A has already updated the semaphore in memory. Thinking that the semaphore is still zero, it initiates a memory write to write a non-zero value into the same semaphore. When processor A has completed the memory write to update the semaphore, processor B then acquires bus ownership and also writes a non-zero value into the same semaphore.

The tasks on processors A and B now each believe that the page table belongs solely to them. This situation would be prevented if processor A were able to perform the semaphore read, modification and update as an atomic, indivisible operation with the assurance that no other master can access the same memory semaphore until the atomic transaction series has been completed.

CardBus/PCI Solutions: Bus and Resource Locking

CBLOCK# Signal

The bus locking mechanism is implemented via the CardBus CBLOCK# signal. There is only one CBLOCK# signal and only one master can use it at a time. This means that only one master may perform a locked transaction series during a given period of time. The CBLOCK# signal is a sustained tri-state signal. As with all CardBus sustained tri-state signals, the system board designer is required to provide a pullup resistor on the CBLOCK# signal. When not in use, the state of CBLOCK# is therefore deasserted.

Bus Lock: Permissible but Not Preferred

If a bus master could instruct the CardBus bus arbiter to lock the bus when the semaphore is read from memory and not grant the bus to any other master until so instructed by the bus master, the synchronization problem described earlier would be solved. This is referred to as a bus lock.

CardBus permits this implementation. The CardBus master initiates the memory read and asserts CBLOCK#. When the CardBus bus arbiter samples CBLOCK# asserted by the current initiator, it recognizes this as a request for exclusive bus ownership. Assuming that the first data phase of the memory read transaction completes normally (no target abort or retry issued by the target), the initiator may assume that no other bus master will be able to access the memory target until it completes the update of the semaphore. After completion of the read and while the master is internally testing the state of the semaphore, the master continues to assert the CBLOCK# signal (even though it's not currently using the bus).

While CBLOCK# remains asserted, the arbiter ignores CardBus bus requests from all masters other than the one that established the lock. The arbiter knows which master established the lock because each master has a dedicated CREQ#/CGNT# signal pair and it knows which master asserted CBLOCK# when it was granted bus ownership.

When the master that established the lock later requests ownership of the CardBus again to perform the memory write to update the semaphore, the arbiter grants it the bus. The master performs the memory write and then releases the CBLOCK# signal. This instructs the arbiter to cease the bus lock. It also instructs the locked memory target to unlock itself. A CardBus memory target that is locked unlocks itself whenever it detects CFRAME# deasserted with CBLOCK# deasserted.

In the event that the master reads the semaphore and determines that it has already been set to a non-zero value by another master, it just ceases to assert the CBLOCK# signal (and the target unlocks itself).

The bus lock implementation impedes other masters from accessing any targets just to prevent anyone from accessing the small area of the memory target that the semaphore resides in. For this reason, this approach is considered to be less than optimal. The next section describes the preferred approach, resource locking.

Resource Lock: Preferred Solution

Introduction

CardBus implements a signal, CBLOCK#, that a master can use to prevent the synchronization problem described earlier. It allows a master to reserve a particular memory target (or a portion of it) for its sole use until it completes a series of accesses to the target. When the final access of the atomic transaction series has been completed, the master indicates that it no longer requires exclusive ownership of the target by deasserting CBLOCK#. CardBus permits other masters to use the bus to access targets other than the locked target during the period that a master has exclusive ownership of a particular target.

Determining Lock Mechanism Availability

There is only one CardBus CBLOCK# signal line and it may only be used by one master at a time. If a master wishes to use the CBLOCK# signal to reserve a target for exclusive access, it must first determine that the CBLOCK# signal is not already in use by another master. This is accomplished in the following manner:

- Do not assert CREQ# if CBLOCK# is currently asserted.
- If CFRAME# and CBLOCK# are sampled deasserted, the locking resource is not busy. The master may assert its CREQ#.
- While waiting for CGNT#, the master must continue to monitor CBLOCK#. If CBLOCK# is sampled asserted, the master deasserts its CREQ# (because another master has already started using CBLOCK#).
- When the master samples bus idle (CFRAME# and CIRDY# deasserted) and CBLOCK# deasserted, it has acquisition of the bus and of the CBLOCK# signal. It may start the memory read transaction to read the semaphore from memory for testing.

Note that the same steps are required for determining the availability of the CBLOCK# pin for both resource and bus locks.

Establishing Lock on Memory Target

Figure 11-1 on page 162 illustrates the process of gaining exclusive ownership of a memory target. The specification states that the master may only access the target that it has locked (no other targets) for the duration of the exclusive transaction series. This rule exists to ensure that the master accomplishes the read/modify/write of the semaphore in an expeditious fashion so as to have minimal impact on other masters that may need to access the memory target (or any other target, if the system implements bus locking).

Figure 11-1: Establishing the Lock

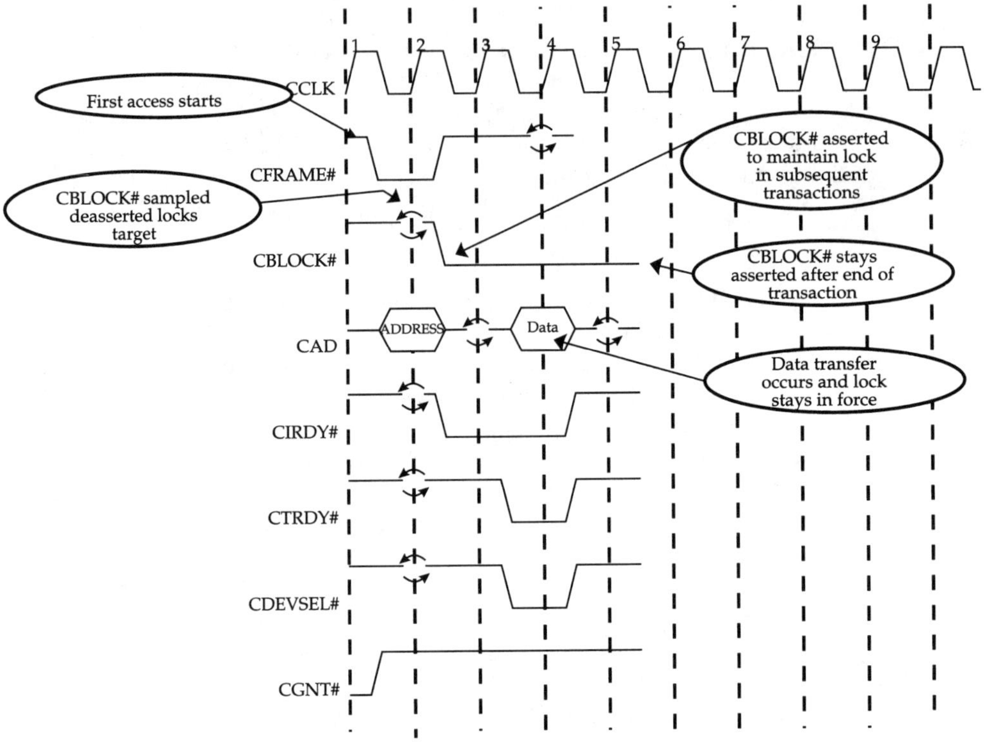

Assume that a master wishes to acquire exclusive ownership of a memory target to perform a semaphore read/modify/write operation. When the master has established that the CBLOCK# signal is not currently in use (see previous section) by another master, it asserts CREQ# to the arbiter to request access to the bus. While waiting for the grant (CGNT#), the master must continue to monitor the CBLOCK# signal. If CBLOCK# is sampled asserted, another master has gained ownership of CBLOCK# and the master must deassert CREQ# until CBLOCK# is available.

Assuming that the master has acquired the bus (its CGNT# is asserted and the bus is idle), the master initiates the transfer at the start of clock one by asserting CFRAME#, leaving CBLOCK# deasserted to request the lock (this sounds contradictory, but continue reading), and driving the address and command type (memory read) onto the CAD bus and the Command/Byte Enable lines, respectively.

The target latches the address and command and samples CBLOCK# deasserted at the rising-edge of clock two. It proceeds with the address decode.

The master asserts CBLOCK# during clock two to instruct the target to stay locked after this transaction completes.

The target decodes the address and asserts CDEVSEL# and CTRDY# during clock three (medium speed decoder). It also "remembers" that CBLOCK# was sampled deasserted at the end of the address phase. This instructs the target to lock itself. In fact, the target will only lock itself if the first data phase of the transaction completes successfully (the lock is formally established at the completion of the first data phase). If the first data phase doesn't complete (for example, the target issues a retry because it cannot complete the access yet), the master has not gained exclusive ownership of the target. It must terminate the transaction, release CBLOCK#, and try again later.

The master asserts CBLOCK# at the rising-edge of clock two to maintain the lock past the end of this transaction. CFRAME# is deasserted because the one (and only) data phase is in progress (note that it doesn't have to be a single data phase transaction).

At the rising-edge of clock four, the first (and only) data item is available for transfer (CIRDY# and CTRDY# are asserted) and the master reads the data (the semaphore) from the target. The successful completion of the data phase formally establishes the target lock. In this example, the master was only transferring one data item, so the transaction is terminated during clock four (CIRDY#, CDEVSEL# and CTRDY# are deasserted).

The master continues to assert CBLOCK# to indicate that CBLOCK# is now in use. The target samples CBLOCK# asserted and CFRAME# deasserted on the rising-edge of clock five. This target (or a portion of it) is now locked and cannot be accessed by any other master. The target remains locked until it samples CBLOCK# and CFRAME# deasserted on a rising-edge of the clock.

At a minimum, the memory target locks the 16-byte aligned block accessed during the read in which the lock is established. A memory target can be designed to lock an area from the accessed 16-byte aligned block up to the entire memory target. The optimum would be to lock just the 16-byte aligned block accessed during the initial read. Other masters that don't require the locking mechanism could then successfully access locations outside the bounds of the locked region while the lock is still in force.

When a target (or a portion of it) has been locked, the target must only permit the master that established the lock to access to the locked area. Any attempt by any other master to access the locked area must result in a retry to the master. If the memory is multi-ported, the lock also precludes any memory accesses by entities within the device itself until the lock is removed.

Unlocked Targets May Be Accessed by any Master

During the period of time that a target is locked, masters that don't require use of the locking signal can successfully acquire the bus (assuming that the arbiter doesn't implement bus locking) and perform transfers with unlocked targets (including unlocked portions of the memory target that contains the locked area). A locked target refuses (retries) access attempts within its locked area that are initiated by other masters, but permits access attempts by the master that locked it.

Access to Locked Target by Master Other than Owner: Retry

Figure 11-2 on page 165 illustrates an attempt by a master other than the one who locked it to access a locked target. The master performing this bus transaction is not performing an atomic transaction series, so it is not required to sample CBLOCK# prior to assuming bus ownership. The illustration shows the CBLOCK# signal being held asserted by the master that locked the target.

The current master initiates the transfer attempt at the start of clock one by asserting CFRAME# and driving the address and the command onto the CAD and Command/Byte Enable buses, respectively. The CBLOCK# signal is still asserted by the master that read the semaphore from memory at an earlier point in time.

The target latches the address, command and the state of the CBLOCK# signal at the rising-edge of clock two and begins the address decode.

The initiator deasserts CFRAME# during clock two, indicating that the one (and only) data phase is in progress.

When the target decodes its address, it asserts CDEVSEL# in clock three to claim the transaction. It has also determined that the master attempting to access it is not the one that locked it. The master that locked it would have demonstrated its control of the CBLOCK# signal by deasserting CBLOCK# during the address phase. The locked memory target must therefore reject the access by issuing a retry to the current master. CSTOP# is asserted along with CDEVSEL#, and CTRDY# stays deasserted. This combination indicates that the initiator is to stop the transaction on the current data phase (CSTOP# asserted) with no data transferred (CTRDY# deasserted) and that the initiator is to retry the transaction again later (CDEVSEL# asserted).

When the initiator samples CSTOP# and CDEVSEL# asserted and CTRDY# deasserted at the rising-edge of clock four, it terminates the transaction without a data transfer and will re-attempt the access later. For more information on retry, refer to the section entitled "Target-Initiated Termination" on page 113. The initiator then deasserts CIRDY#, returning the bus to the idle state. The target deasserts CSTOP# and CDEVSEL#.

Figure 11-2: Preventing Access to the Locked Memory Range

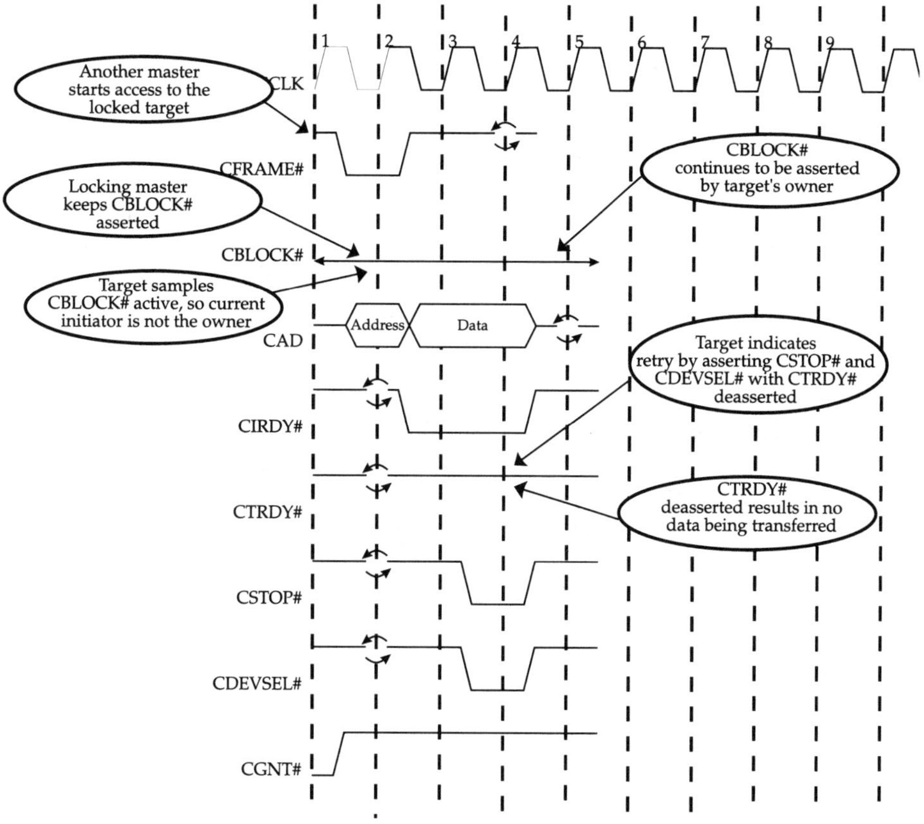

Continuation and/or End of Locked Transaction Series

Figure 12-3 illustrates the continuation and/or the end of an exclusive access series. In this example, the master had accessed the target earlier (to read the memory semaphore) and locked it for its exclusive use (CBLOCK# was left asserted by the master when it ended the earlier read access). When the locking master gains bus ownership again (CGNT# asserted by the arbiter and the bus is idle), it starts the next access in the locked series (the memory write to update the memory semaphore).

At the start of the transaction (the rising-edge of clock one), the initiator asserts CFRAME# and deasserts CBLOCK#. It deasserts CBLOCK# to reestablish its lock on the target and identify itself as the target's owner.

The target latches the address, command and the state of the CBLOCK# signal at the end of the address phase (on the rising-edge of clock two) and begins the address decode. Upon decoding the address and asserting CDEVSEL#, the target locks itself again (because CBLOCK# was sampled deasserted at the end of the address phase).

During clock two, the initiator reasserts CBLOCK# to continue the lock through the end of this transaction. If the initiator left CBLOCK# deasserted during the data phase and the target were to issue a retry for some reason, the master has lost control of the target. In other words, after the master terminated the transaction (due to the retry), the target would sample CFRAME# and CBLOCK# deasserted, thereby instructing it to unlock itself.

The data is written into the memory semaphore at the rising-edge of clock three when CTRDY# and CIRDY# are both sampled active. The initiator and target release CIRDY# and CTRDY#, respectively. If the master must maintain the lock on the target for one or more additional accesses, it continues to assert CBLOCK# after the end of the transaction. If, on the other hand, the master has completed its exclusive series of accesses to the target, it releases CBLOCK# at the end of the current transaction. When the target samples CFRAME# and CBLOCK# both deasserted (on clock four in the example), it clears its lock.

Figure 11-3: Completing the Locked Transaction

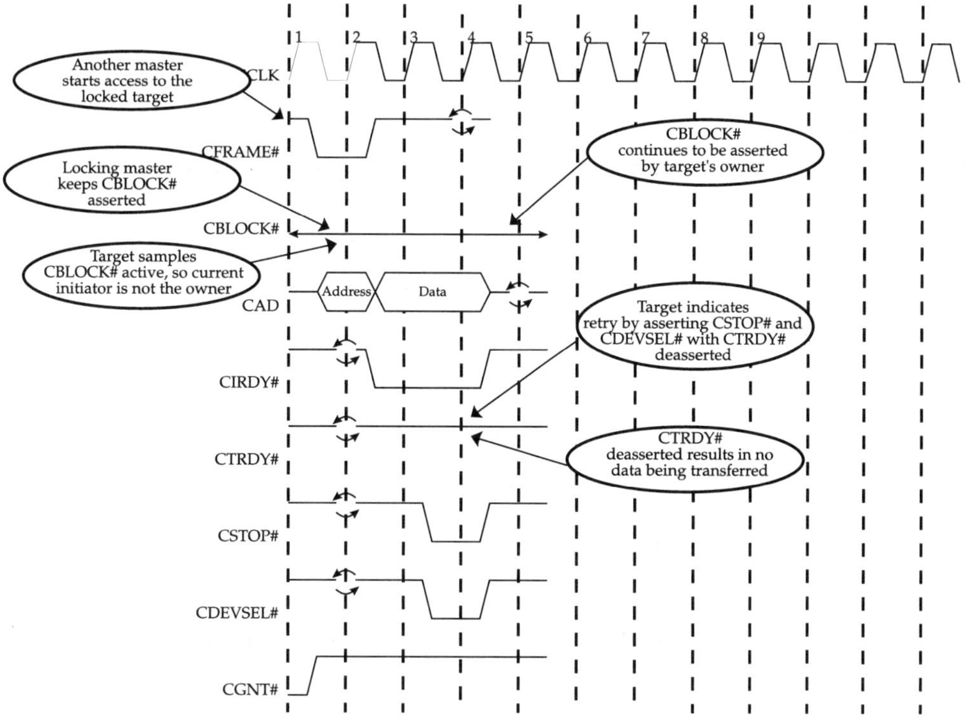

Devices that Must Implement Lock Support

All CardBus memory targets that contain system memory must support locking. Similarly, all host/CardBus bridges that have CardBus cards that implement system memory must also support the locking mechanism. All CardBus masters that must have the ability to gain exclusive ownership of a block of memory must also implement locking capability.

Caution—You Can't Trust Lock!

Now that the discussion of locking is done, here's an interesting sidebar—the revision 2.1 PCI spec warns that some host processor bus environments (e.g., PowerPC PC-compatible platforms) do not permit main memory (which typically resides on the host bus) to be locked. In other words, the host/PCI bridge just ignores the bus master's request to lock memory. It advises the bus master designer to use some other mechanism to guarantee exclusive access to a resource.

Summary of Locking Rules

Implementation Rules for Masters

Any master that implements locking capability must adhere to the following rules:

1. The master may only access a single target for the duration of the lock. This rule exists to force masters to expeditiously return a locked resource to the available state.
2. A lock cannot straddle device boundaries. The 16 byte block (minimum) to be locked must reside completely within one memory target.
3. The maximum memory area that a master can count on locking is a 16 byte block (aligned on a 16 byte boundary). In fact, a target may lock a larger area (up to and including the entire memory target), but a master has no way of knowing this. An access anywhere within a 16 byte block locks the entire 16 byte block.
4. The first transaction of a locked transactions series must be a memory read (to read the semaphore from memory).
5. Lock must be asserted during the clock immediately following the address phase and must be kept asserted after the transaction has concluded (in order to keep the target locked).
6. The CBLOCK# signal must be deasserted if the first data phase ends in a retry. In this case, the master has not locked the target. Other masters can successfully access it.
7. CBLOCK# must be deasserted whenever a transaction is terminated by a target abort (in any data phase). This basically indicates that the target is broken or can never complete the access.
8. CBLOCK# must also be deasserted if the transaction is terminated by a master abort (no target has responded).
9. CBLOCK# must be deasserted for at least one idle cycle between consecutive locked transaction series.

Implementation Rules for Targets

PCI memory targets that support locking must adhere to the following rules:

1. The target of a transaction locks itself when CBLOCK# is sampled deasserted at the end of the address phase.

2. Once a target is locked, the target must remain locked until it samples both CFRAME# and CLOCK# deasserted or until it issues a target abort to the initiator.
3. The target must, at a minimum, lock the 16 byte aligned area of memory that the first data item of the read resides within. It may, however, lock a larger area, up to and including the entire target.
4. Cacheable PCI memory targets that support a write-back cache associated with the host processor must permit the host/PCI bridge to perform a write-back to memory even when the target is locked.

12 Error Handling

The Previous Chapter

The previous chapter described the locking support provided by CardBus. It described both bus locking and resource locking implementations and defined the behavior of CardBus target and initiators that support locking.

This Chapter

CardBus architecture provides two error reporting mechanisms: one for reporting data parity errors and the other for reporting more serious system errors. This chapter provides a discussion of error detection, reporting and handling using these two mechanisms.

The Next Chapter

The next chapter describes the interrupt support provided by the CardBus interface and possible interrupt routing mechanisms.

Introduction to CardBus Parity

All transactions that take place across CardBus are parity-checked. This checking occurs during the address phase and during each data phase. A single parity bit, CPAR, is generated by the device sourcing the address and/or data. CPAR is driven to ensure even parity on CAD[31:0] and CC/BE[3:0]#. The CardBus device receiving the address or data is responsible for checking the parity to verify that an even number of one bits was received via CAD[31:0], CC/BE[3:0]#, and CPAR. If an error is detected, an error signal is asserted: CPERR# is asserted for most data parity errors and CSERR# is asserted for address parity errors and some data parity error. The exact cases are covered in the following sections.

CardBus agents driving the CAD bus during the address phase or any data phase of a transaction must always drive a stable 32-bit pattern onto the CAD bus and CC/BE# bus (because parity is based on the full content of the CAD bus and the CC/BE# bus). This includes:

- Special and interrupt acknowledge transactions. The address bus is not used to address the target device (e.g., the CAD lines are don't care but must be driven with a stable pattern), and during type zero configuration transactions where CAD[31:11] do not contain valid information.
- Data phases where the device supplying data isn't supplying all four bytes (all four byte enables are not asserted).

Refer to Figure 12-1 during the following discussion. The CardBus device driving the CAD bus during the address phase or any data phase of a transaction is responsible for calculating and driving even parity onto the CPAR line. Note however, that CPAR lags its associated address or data by one clock cycle. That is, CPAR must be driven one clock cycle after the address or data is first driven onto the bus (when CTRDY# is asserted during a read data phase to indicate the presence of the read data on the bus, or CIRDY# is asserted during a write data phase to indicate the presence of the write data on the bus). The computed parity bit supplied on CPAR must be set (or cleared) so that the 37 bits consisting of CAD[31:0], CC/BE[3:0]# and CPAR contains an even number of one bits.

Figure 12-1: Example of Parity Generation and Reporting

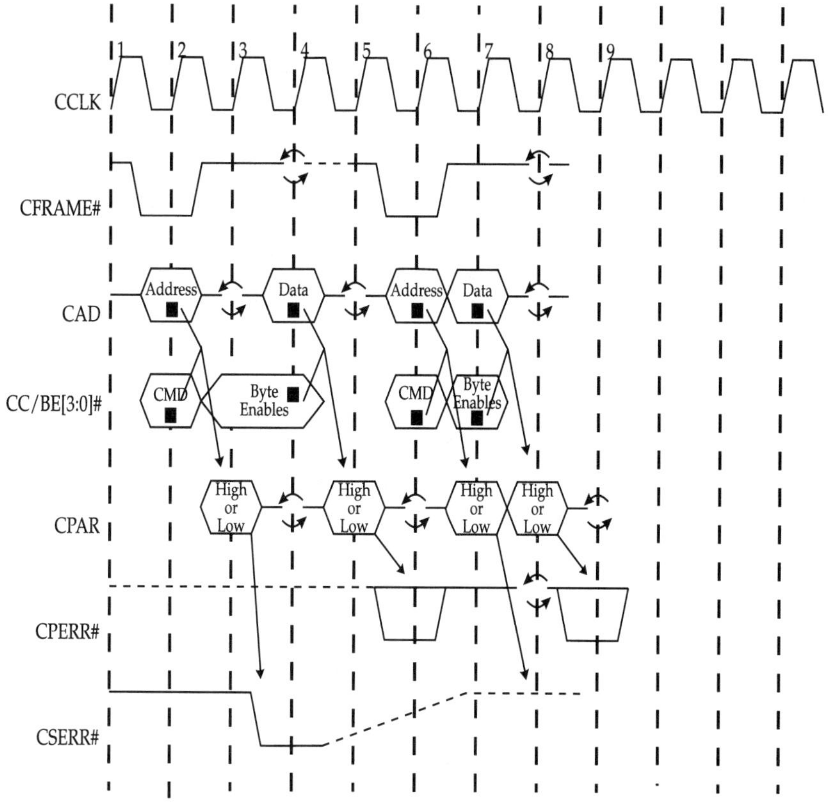

During the CardBus clock cycle immediately following the conclusion of the address phase or the assertion of ready by the device sourcing the data during any data phase of a transaction, the CardBus agent receiving the address or data computes expected parity based on the information latched from CAD[31:0] and CC/BE[3:0]#. The agent supplying the parity bit must present it on the rising clock edge immediately following the conclusion of the address phase or the assertion of ready by the device sourcing the data during the data phase that it is associated with. The device(s) receiving the address or data expect it to be present and stable at that point and latch it. The computed parity bit is then compared to the parity bit actually received on CPAR to determine if address or data corruption has occurred. If the parity is correct, no action is taken. If the parity is incorrect, the error must be reported. This subject is covered in the sections that follow.

Address Phase Parity

Address Parity Generation and Checking

Refer to Figure 12-2 on page 175 during the following discussion. Every CardBus transaction starts with the address phase (clock one in the figure). During the address phase, the initiator drives the start address onto CAD[31:0] and the command (transaction type) onto CC/BE[3:0]#. It also asserts CFRAME# to indicate the presence of a valid start address and transaction type on the bus. At the end of the address phase (on the rising-edge of clock two), the CardBus target latches the address, command, and state of the CFRAME# signal. Sampling CFRAME# asserted at this point qualifies the address and command as valid. The target then begins address decode during clock two.

In addition, the following actions are also taken during clock two:

- The target calculates whether CAD[31:0] and CC/BE[3:0]# contain an even or an odd number of ones thereby determining the value it expects to latch from the CPAR signal on clock three.
- The initiator drives CPAR to either a one or a zero to force even parity on the 37 bits consisting of CAD[31:0], CC/BE[3:0]# and CPAR.

On the rising-edge of clock three, the target latches the state of the CPAR signal. During clock three, the targets compare the expected parity to the actual parity bit supplied by the initiator on the CPAR signal. If it results in a good compare, the targets take no action.

If, however, it results in a miscompare, the address and/or command were corrupted in flight. This is considered to be a destabilizing event in the CardBus environment. The initiator is reaching out and touching a location within the target that it never meant to touch or is touching it in a way it never meant to. CSERR# is the reporting mechanism used by targets when they detect an address parity error.

Figure 12-2: Timing of Address Parity Generation and Error Reporting

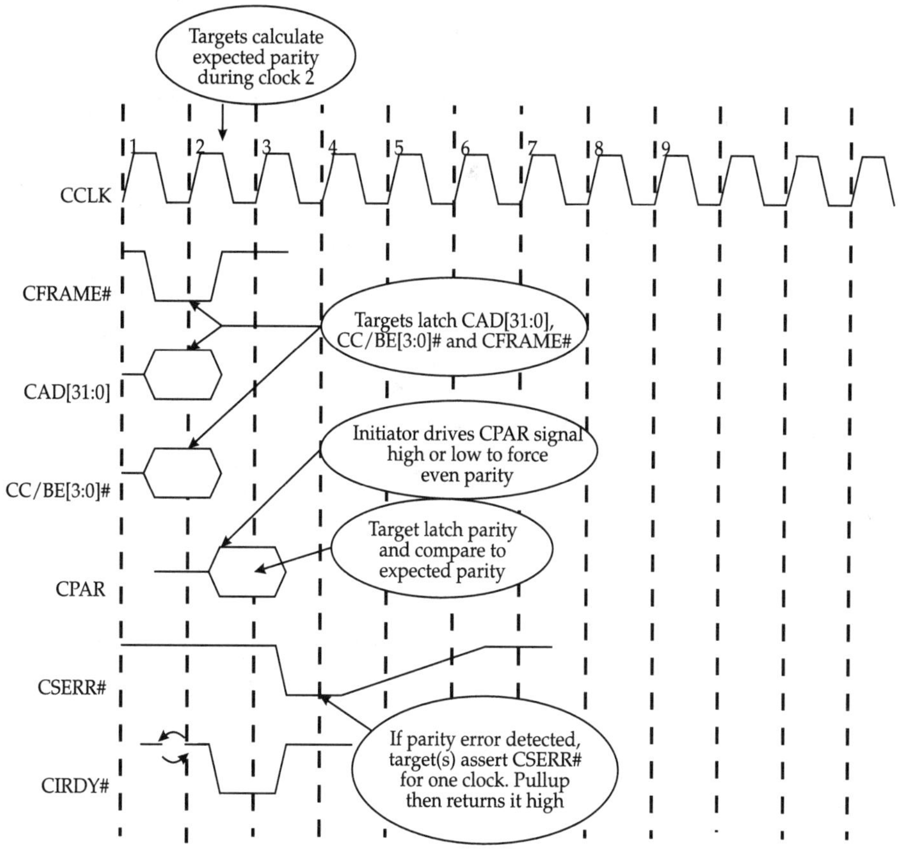

Address Phase Parity Error Reporting

A target that detects an address phase parity miscompare must assert CSERR# for one clock (if the device's CSERR# ENABLE bit is set to one in its configuration command register). Any device that asserts CSERR# must also set the SIGNALED SYSTEM ERROR bit in its configuration status register to one. The device's DETECTED PARITY ERROR status bit must also be set to one (even if CSERR# isn't signaled by the device due to the state of its CSERR# ENABLE bit). The CardBus configuration command register is pictured in Figure 12-3. The status register is pictured in Figure 12-4.

Figure 12-3: CardBus Function's Configuration Command Register

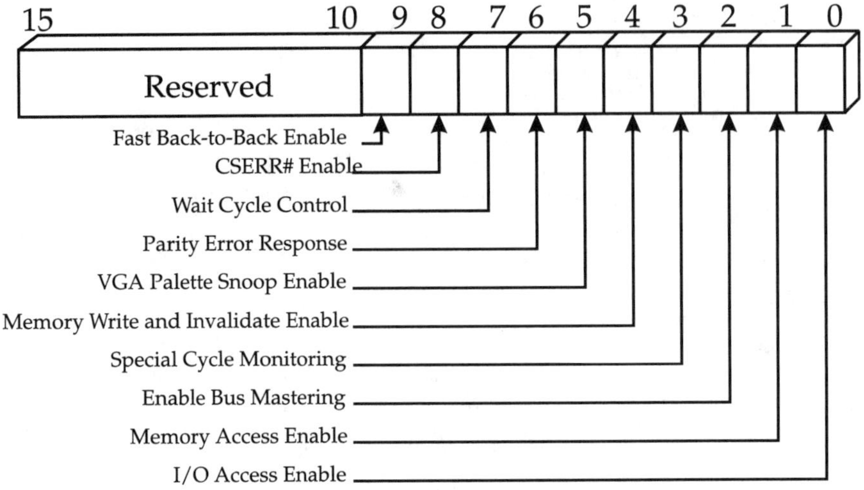

Figure 12-4: CardBus Function's Configuration Status Register

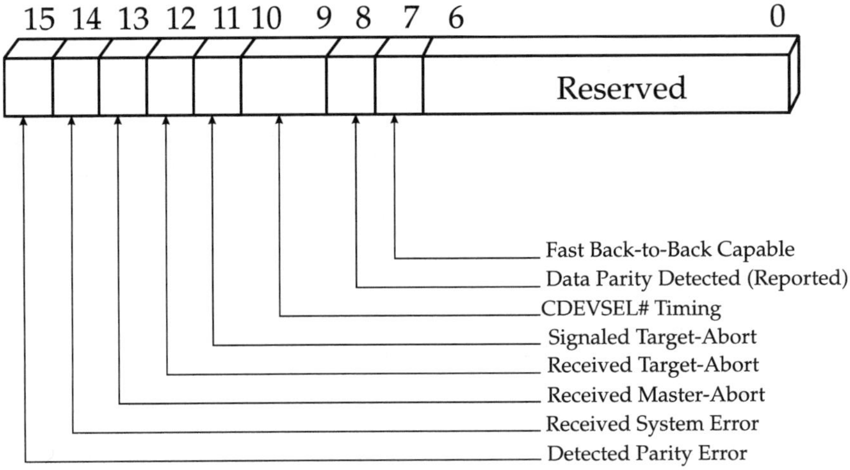

As stated earlier, the specification recommends that CSERR# be asserted within two CardBus clocks of error detection. The earliest that CSERR# would therefore be asserted would be during clock three of Figure 12-2 on page 175, but it could be during clock four, five, or later (although not recommended).

In addition to the assertion of CSERR#, a target device that receives a corrupted address/command can react in one of the following ways:

- assert CDEVSEL# and terminate the transaction with a target abort.
- not assert CDEVSEL# and let the master time out and execute a master abort.

The target is not permitted to terminate the transaction with a retry or a disconnect.

Data Parity

Data parity is generated and checked for all data phases within a burst read or write transaction. All initiators are required to generate data parity; however, not all targets are required to check data parity. The exclusion is discussed under the heading entitled, "Devices Excluded from CPERR# Requirement" on page 186.

A CardBus agent responsible for checking data parity can begin checking parity as soon as it detects that valid data and parity are present. Consider the following examples for a read and write transaction.

- During a read transaction the initiator momentarily has a buffer full condition and is inserting wait states (CIRDY# is deasserted) into the data phase. In this instance, the initiator can be designed to sample the target's data when it detects CTRDY# asserted (i.e., the target has driven valid data onto CAD[31:0]). The initiator knows that the target must drive CPAR in the next clock cycle, and thus can calculate parity and assert CPERR# (if the parity is incorrect). In this case, the initiator must keep CPERR# asserted until two clocks after the completion of the data phase.
- During a write transaction where the target is inserting wait states by delaying assertion of CTRDY#, the target can be designed to sample the initiator's data (when CIRDY# is sampled asserted), sample CPAR (on the clock edge after CIRDY# sampled asserted), calculate parity and assert CPERR# (if the parity is incorrect). In this case, the target must keep CPERR# asserted until two clocks after the completion of the data phase.

This section details the exact protocol for generating, checking, and reporting parity errors that occur during a data phase.

Data Parity Generation and Checking on Read

Introduction

During each data phase of a read transaction, the target drives data onto the CAD bus. It is therefore the target's responsibility to supply correct parity to the initiator on CPAR during the clock immediately following its assertion of CTRDY# during each data phase. At the conclusion of each data phase (or, alternately, one the clock after CTRDY# is asserted), the initiator latches the contents of CAD[31:0] and CC/BE[3:0]# and calculates the expected parity during the clock cycle immediately following the conclusion of the data phase (or, alternately, the assertion of CTRDY#). The initiator then latches the parity bit supplied by the target from the CPAR signal on the next rising-edge of the CardBus clock and compares computed vs. actual parity. If a miscompare occurs, the initiator then asserts CPERR# during the next clock. At the latest, the assertion of CPERR# lags the conclusion of each data phase by two CardBus clock cycles.

The master may take other actions in addition to the assertion of CPERR#. The section (in this chapter) entitled "Data Parity Reporting" provides a detailed discussion of the possible actions taken by a bus master upon receipt of bad data.

Example Burst Read

Refer to the read burst transaction illustrated in Figure 12-5 on page 180 during this discussion. The initiator drives the address and command onto the bus during the address phase (clock one). The target latches the address and command on clock two and begins address decode. In this example, the target has a fast address decoder and asserts CDEVSEL# during clock two. In addition, the following occurs during clock two:

- Having latched the address and command, the targets compute the expected parity based on the information from CAD[31:0] and CC/BE[3:0]#.
- The initiator sets the parity signal, CPAR, to the appropriate value to force even parity.

The target keeps CTRDY# deasserted to insert the wait state necessary for the turnaround cycle on the CAD bus.

On clock three, the target latches the CPAR bit and compares it to the expected parity computed during clock two. If the target experiences a miscompare, it asserts CSERR# (if the PARITY ERROR RESPONSE and CSERR# ENABLE bits in its configuration command register are set to one) within two clocks (recommended) after the error was detected. This subject is covered in the section entitled "Address Phase Parity" on page 174.

During clock three, the target drives the first data item onto the CAD bus and asserts CTRDY# to indicate its present. The initiator latches the data on clock four (CIRDY# and CTRDY# are sampled asserted).

During clock four, the target drives the CPAR signal to the appropriate state for first data phase parity. The initiator computes the expected parity. The initiator latches CPAR on clock five and compares it to the expected parity. If the parity is incorrect, the initiator asserts CPERR# during clock five (if enabled by software).

The second data phase begins during clock four. The target drives the second data item onto the bus and keeps CTRDY# asserted to indicate its presence. The initiator latches the data on clock five (CIRDY# and CTRDY# sampled asserted). During clock five, the initiator computes the expected parity. The actual parity is latched from CPAR on clock six and checked against the expected parity. If an error is detected, the initiator asserts CPERR# during clock six (if enabled by software).

The third data phase begins on clock five. The target drives the third data item onto the CAD bus and keeps CTRDY# asserted to indicate its presence. The initiator deasserts CIRDY# to indicate that it is not yet ready to accept the third data item (e.g., it has a buffer full condition). When the initiator samples CTRDY# asserted on clock six, this qualifies the presence of the third data item on the bus. The initiator can be designed to submit the data to its parity generator at this point. Assuming that it is designed this way, the initiator can latch the CPAR bit from the bus on clock seven (it's a rule that the target must present CPAR one clock after presenting the data). At the earliest, then, the initiator could detect a parity miscompare during clock seven and assert CPERR#. It must keep CPERR# asserted until two clocks after completion of the data phase. During the third data phase, the initiator re-asserts CIRDY# during clock seven and deasserts CFRAME# to indicate that it is ready to complete the final data phase. The final data phase completes on clock eight when CIRDY# and CTRDY# are sampled asserted. The initiator reads the final data item from the bus at that point. At the latest (if an early parity check wasn't performed), the initiator must sample CPAR one clock afterwards, on clock nine, and, in the event of an error, must assert CPERR# during clock nine.

Figure 12-5: Example of Data Parity Generation and Error Reporting during Read Burst

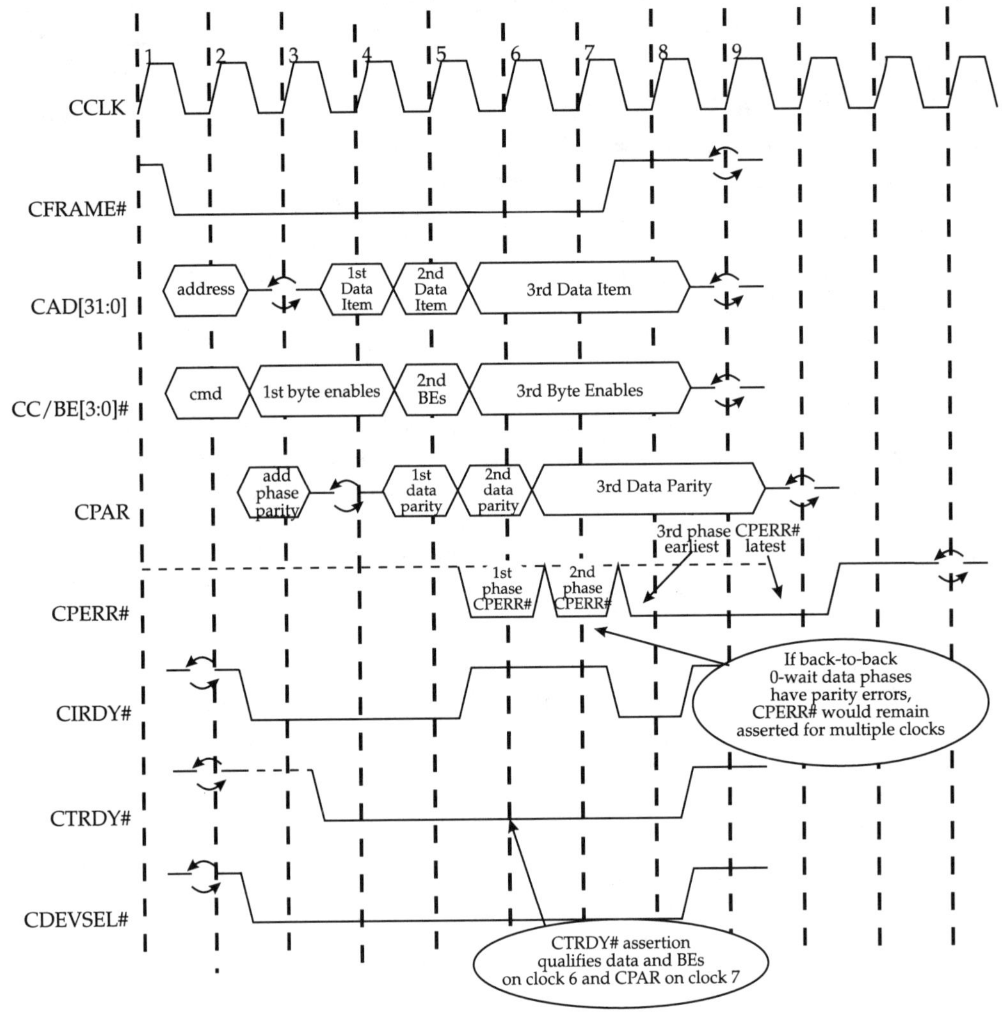

Data Parity Generation and Checking on Write

Introduction

During each data phase of a write transaction, the initiator drives data onto the CAD bus. It is therefore the initiator's responsibility to supply correct parity to the target on CPAR during the clock immediately following its assertion of

CIRDY#. At the conclusion of each data phase (or, alternately, when CIRDY# is asserted), it is the target's responsibility to latch the contents of CAD[31:0] and CC/BE[3:0]# and to calculate the expected parity during the clock cycle immediately following the conclusion of the data phase (or the assertion of CIRDY#). The target then latches the parity bit supplied by the initiator from the CPAR signal on the next rising-edge of the CardBus clock and compares computed vs. actual parity. If a miscompare occurs, the target then asserts CPERR# during the next clock. The assertion of CPERR# lags the conclusion of each data phase by two CardBus clock cycles (as noted earlier, it can be asserted earlier, but must then be held asserted until two clocks after the conclusion of the data phase). During a burst write, it is the initiator's responsibility to sample the state of the CPERR# signal on the second rising-edge of the CardBus clock after the conclusion of each data phase. If it samples CPERR# asserted by the target, this indicates that the last data item written to the target was corrupted in flight. The section entitled "Data Parity Reporting" on page 183 provides a detailed discussion of the actions taken by a bus master upon detection of a data phase parity error.

Example Burst Write

Refer to the write burst transaction illustrated in Figure 12-6 on page 183 during the following discussion. The address phase completes on clock two. All targets latch the address and command. During clock two, all targets compute the expected parity. During clock two, the initiator supplies the parity bit on the CPAR signal. The targets latch CPAR on clock three. They compare expected vs. actual parity. If an error is detected, the targets assert CSERR# (if the PARITY ERROR RESPONSE and CSERR# ENABLE bits in their configuration command register are set to one) within two clocks (recommended).

The first data phase starts during clock two. The initiator supplies the first data item on the CAD bus and asserts CIRDY# to indicate valid data is present. The first data item is latched by the target on clock two (CIRDY# and CTRDY# sampled asserted). During clock three, the initiator supplies the parity bit on CPAR. The target computes the expected parity. The actual parity is latched on clock four and is compared to the expected parity. In the event of an error, the target asserts CPERR# in clock four (if the PARITY ERROR RESPONSE bit in its configuration command register is set to one) back to the initiator to indicate that the first data item was corrupted in flight. The initiator samples CPERR# on clock five to determine if the first data item transferred without error.

The second data phase starts during clock three. The initiator drives the second data item onto the CAD bus and the second set of byte enables onto the CC/BE bus. The target latches the data and byte enables on clock four (CIRDY# and

CTRDY# sampled asserted). During clock four, the target computes the expected parity. The actual parity is latched on clock five and is compared to the expected parity. In the event of an error, the target, if enabled to respond to parity errors, asserts CPERR# (in clock five) back to the initiator to indicate that the second data item was corrupted in flight. The initiator samples CPERR# on clock six to determine if the second data item transferred without error.

The third data phase starts during clock four. The initiator drives the third data item onto the CAD bus and the third set of byte enables onto the CC/BE bus. The target deasserts CTRDY#, indicating that it isn't ready to accept the third data item (e.g., it has a buffer full condition). The initiator keeps CIRDY# asserted and deasserts CFRAME#, indicating that it is ready to complete the final data transfer. The target asserts CTRDY# and latches the data and byte enables on clock four (CIRDY# and CTRDY# sampled asserted).

The target could be designed to check parity and report a parity error while it's inserting wait states in the data phase. In this example, the target latches the data and byte enables on clock five (CIRDY# is asserted, indicating that the data is present) and submits them to its parity generator to compute the expected parity during clock five. Also during clock five, the initiator begins to drive the parity bit onto CPAR. The target then latches CPAR on clock six and compares the actual parity to the expected parity. In the event of an error, the target asserts CPERR# during clock six. It must keep CPERR# asserted until two clocks after completion of the data phase. During the third data phase, the target re-asserts CTRDY# during clock six to indicate that it is ready to complete the data phase. The final data phase completes on clock seven when CIRDY# and CTRDY# are sampled asserted. The target latches the final data item from the bus at that point. At the latest (if early parity check wasn't performed), the target must sample CPAR one clock afterwards, on clock eight, and, in the event of an error, must assert CPERR# during clock eight.

Figure 12-6: Example of Data Parity Generation and Error Reporting during Burst Write

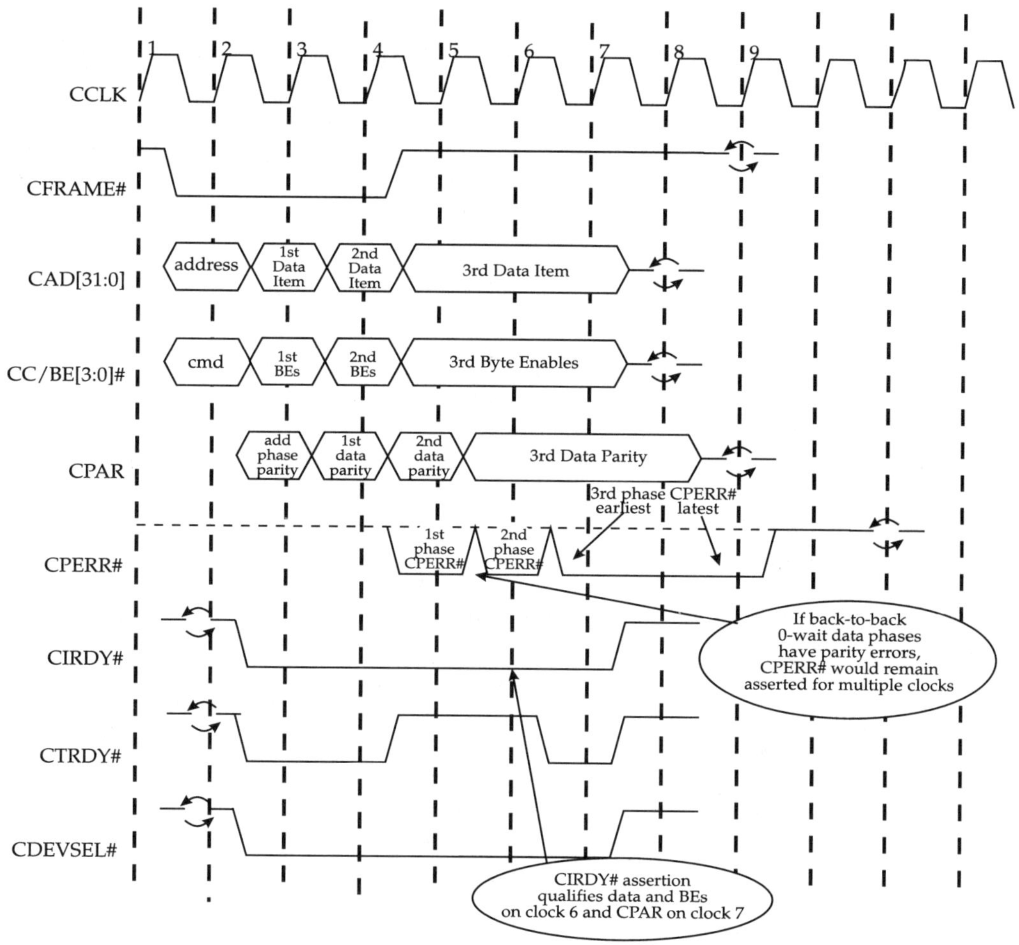

Data Parity Reporting

General

Upon detection of a data phase parity error, the CardBus device that checked the parity is responsible for asserting the DETECTED PARITY ERROR bit in its configuration status register. It also asserts CPERR# if the PARITY ERROR RESPONSE bit in its configuration command register is set to one. Only two categories of devices are excluded from the requirement to implement the CPERR#

signal and the PARITY ERROR RESPONSE bit. They are described in the section entitled "Devices Excluded from CPERR# Requirement" on page 186.

If a data phase parity error is detected, CPERR# must be asserted (at the latest) in the second clock after completion of the data phase (i.e., one clock after CPAR is latched). Once CPERR# is asserted, it must not be deasserted until during the third clock after the data phase completes. Figure 12-5 on page 180 and Figure 12-6 on page 183 both illustrate examples where the devices receiving the data checked parity and asserted CPERR# before the completion of the data phase.

Parity Error During Read

During a read transaction, the target sources the data and the parity. The initiator receives the data and parity and checks the parity for correctness. If the data is incorrect, the initiator must set the DETECTED PARITY ERROR bit in its configuration status register (irrespective of the state of its PARITY ERROR RESPONSE bit). Assuming that the initiator's PARITY ERROR RESPONSE bit is set to one, the initiator asserts CPERR# in the second clock immediately following completion of the data phase and sets the DATA PARITY REPORTED bit in its configuration status register.

Whether or not the bus master continues the transaction or terminates it is master design-dependent. The specification recommends that the transaction be continued to completion. In addition to the assertion of CPERR#, the bus master is required to report the parity error to the system software. The specification recommends utilization of an interrupt or setting a bit in a status register that is polled by the device driver. Alternately, the designer can assert CSERR#, but this approach should not be used lightly. It will more than likely result in a system shutdown. In a particular platform design, the chip set logic may convert any assertion of CPERR# into CSERR#.

Parity Error During Write

During a write transaction, the initiator sources the data and the parity. The target receives the data and parity and checks the parity for correctness. If the data is incorrect, the target must set its DETECTED PARITY ERROR bit to one (irrespective of the state of its PARITY ERROR RESPONSE bit). Assuming that the target's PARITY ERROR RESPONSE bit is set to one, the target asserts CPERR# in the second clock immediately following completion of the data phase. The initiator samples CPERR# on the second clock after completion of the data phase. If CPERR# has been asserted by the target, the initiator sets the DATA PARITY REPORTED bit in its configuration status register. Targets never set this bit because only the bus master reports the error to software.

Whether or not the bus master continues the transaction or terminates it is master design-dependent. The specification recommends that the transaction be continued to completion. In addition to the assertion of CPERR#, the bus master is required to report the parity error to the system software. The specification recommends utilization of an interrupt or setting a bit in a status register that is polled by the device driver. Alternately, the designer can assert CSERR#, but this approach should not be used lightly. It will more than likely result in a system shutdown. In a particular platform design, the chip set logic may convert any assertion of CPERR# into CSERR#.

Data Parity Error Recovery

The PC Card standard permits recovery from data phase parity errors but does not require it. Recovery from the error may be attempted by the master, the device driver, or by the operating system. The specification recommends that recovery be attempted at the lowest possible level (i.e., by the bus master). Error recovery cannot be attempted if the device reports the error by some mechanism other than CPERR# assertion (e.g., the error is reported via CSERR# assertion). If the error cannot be recovered from, the error must be reported to the operating system (if the bus master's DATA PARITY RESPONSE bit is set to one). Following are examples of recovery by the master, device driver and the operating system.

Recovery by the Bus master

The master may attempt recovery by re-attempting the transaction if it knows that it will have no side effects (e.g., if the target device is a FIFO buffer, the access should not be re-attempted). If the re-attempt of the access completes with no errors, the master does not have to report an error to the system. If the attempt (or, perhaps, several attempts) is unsuccessful, then the master must report the error. If there is a device driver associated with the master, the master alerts the driver to the error by generating an interrupt, setting a status bit, or some similar method. If there isn't a device driver associated with the master, the master may report the error by asserting CSERR#.

Recovery by the Device Driver

Assuming that the bus master reported the error to its device driver, the driver may instruct the bus master to re-attempt the transaction (once again, the driver must know that the re-attempt will not cause side effects). If the access completes with no errors, the device driver does not have to report the error to the operating system. If the access error cannot be recovered from, the driver must report the error to the operating system.

Recovery by the Operating System

How the operating system responds to the report of a data parity error is operating system-specific.

Special Case: Data Parity Error During Special Cycle

The initiator uses a special cycle to broadcast a message (during the data phase) to the entire community of targets. In the event that any of the target(s) detects a parity error related to the data phase, this indicates that the message was corrupted in flight. Since messages are used to issue instructions to subsystems, a corrupted message might place a subsystem in a state that was not intended. The PC Card standard considers this to be a destabilizing event (like an address phase parity error). CSERR# is used as the reporting mechanism.

The target that detected the error must assert CSERR# if:

- the CSERR# ENABLE bit in its configuration command register is set to one, and
- the PARITY ERROR RESPONSE bit is also set to one in its command register.

The target must set the DETECTED PARITY ERROR bit in its configuration status register. Any CardBus device that signals CSERR# is required to set the SIGNALED SYSTEM ERROR bit in its configuration status register.

CPERR# Signal

General

CPERR# is a sustained tri-state signal used to signal the detection of a parity error related to a data phase. There is one exception to this rule: a parity error detected on a data phase during a special cycle is reported using CSERR# rather than CPERR# (as discussed in the previous section).

CPERR# is implemented as an output on targets and as an input/output on masters.

Devices Excluded from CPERR# Requirement

The PC Card standard excludes one category of devices from the requirement to implement the CPERR# signal and the PARITY ERROR RESPONSE bit in the configuration command register. The excluded devices are those that do not deal with permanent data and that do not exhibit residual effects due to incorrect data being received.

An ideal example would be a video frame buffer. It is legal to build a video frame buffer that doesn't check the integrity of data written into its memory buffer. In the event that one or more data items are corrupted while being written into the buffer, the only effect is incorrect pixels on the screen. While this may be destabilizing to the end user's state of mind, the effects are not residual (i.e., it does not corrupt programs or data in memory or on permanent storage).

System Errors

The following sections outline the various causes of system errors and the assertion of CSERR#. In all cases, a device is not enabled to assert CSERR# unless the CSERR# ENABLE bit in its configuration command register is set to one.

CSERR# Signal

CSERR# is an output from all CardBus devices and is an input to the platform support logic (i.e., the chip set). A CardBus device is not permitted to assert CSERR# unless the CSERR# ENABLE bit in its configuration command register is set to one. CSERR# is implemented as an open-drain, shared signal because multiple CardBus devices may assert CSERR# simultaneously. The system designer provides a pull-up resistor on the CSERR# signal line. When any (or all) CardBus devices that are asserting CSERR# cease driving it, the pull-up has the responsibility to return CSERR# to the deasserted state. This can take several CardBus clocks.

When asserted, CSERR# is asserted on the rising-edge of the CardBus clock and is asserted for one clock and then tri-stated. It may be asserted at any time (i.e., its assertion is not tied to any type or phase of a CardBus transaction). The specification suggests that CSERR# should be asserted as quickly as possible (within two clocks of detecting an error condition is recommended).

The CSERR# signal is used to signal the following types of conditions:

- parity error on the address phase of a transaction.
- parity error on the data phase of a special cycle transaction.
- problems other than parity detected by a CardBus device.
- critical system failures detected by system board logic.

Before deciding to assert CSERR# for an error, the designer should always consider that assertion of CSERR# is considered an indication of a very serious problem. As examples, upon detection of CSERR# assertion, the platform logic may assert NMI in an Intel system or TEA# or MC# in a PowerPC system. The NMI or machine check interrupt handler is invoked and may halt the machine. The PC Card standard does not dictate the action to be taken by the system logic when CSERR# assertion is detected. As indicated earlier, it could result in a high-priority interrupt, or in the setting of a status bit to be polled by system software, etc.

Once system logic detects CSERR# asserted, it must sample CSERR# deasserted on two successive clock edges before assuming that it has been deasserted. This requirement is because open-drain signaling cannot guarantee stable signals on every clock edge.

The sections that follow contain additional discussion of CSERR# usage.

Address Phase Parity Error

This subject is discussed under the heading "Address Phase Parity" on page 174.

Data Parity Error During Special Cycle

This subject is discussed under the heading "Special Case: Data Parity Error During Special Cycle" on page 186.

Target Abort Detection

A master that doesn't have a mechanism (such as an interrupt line) to report a target abort to system software, may assert CSERR# to alert system software. The master must also set the RECEIVED TARGET ABORT bit in its status register.

Other Possible Causes of System Error

When any CardBus device suffers a serious failure that impairs its ability to operate correctly, it may assert CSERR# (if its CSERR# ENABLE bit is set to one) to inform system software of the failure. It must also set the SIGNALED SYSTEM ERROR status bit in its configuration status register.

Devices Excluded from CSERR# Requirement

The exceptions stated for CPERR# implementation in the section entitled "Devices Excluded from CPERR# Requirement" on page 186 are also exceptions for CSERR#.

Part Four

CardBus Interrupts

13 CardBus Function Interrupts

The Previous Chapter

The previous chapter discussed parity generation, error detection, and error reporting.

This Chapter

This chapter describes the interrupt support provided by the CardBus interface and possible interrupt routing mechanisms. As stated earlier in the book, additional detail regarding interrupts in the PCMCIA and PCI environments can be found in the MindShare books entitled *PCMCIA System Architecture* and *PCI System Architecture* (published by Addison-Wesley).

The Next Chapter

The next chapter describes issues related to the status change interrupt. CardBus cards generate a status change interrupt for a variety of reasons. This chapter discusses status change interrupt routing and handling.

Introduction

A single interrupt pin, CINT#, is defined by the CardBus interface for use by CardBus cards. This is in contrast with the four interrupt pins available to a PCI-compliant device. The single CardBus interrupt pin must be shared by all functions implemented within a CardBus card. The sharing protocol is defined by the PC Card standard and is discussed later in this chapter.

How CINT# gets routed to a given system IRQ line depends on the design of the CardBus bridge (PCI-to-CardBus, Host-to-CardBus, etc.) and the system board design. In other words, a CardBus bridge and system board may support a variety of interrupt routing mechanisms. See the section entitled, "Interrupt Routing Mechanisms" on page 196 for details.

Note that the capability to route a given CINT# pin to a given IRQ line does not mean that the IRQ line is available (i.e., the IRQ line may already be in use by another device, such as an ISA card).

Determining If Interrupts are Required

Each function within a CardBus card must have its own set of configuration registers occupying its function-specific configuration address space (64 dwords in size). The first 16 dwords of a function's configuration space is referred to as its configuration header. As illustrated in Figure 13-1, each configuration header contains an interrupt pin register (within dword 15d) that determines whether the respective function uses interrupts. The registers marked "allocated" are used by a PCI function, but not by a CardBus function. The interrupt pin register is read-only and its contents are interpreted by PCMCIA configuration software as follows:

- If the interrupt pin register contains 00h, an interrupt is not used.
- If the register contains a non-zero value, an interrupt is used.

If the interrupt pin register indicates that the function uses an interrupt, the function's Card Information Structure (CIS) contains an interrupt descriptor that specifies the IRQ line(s) that the designer prefers the CINT# signal be routed to.

Figure 13-1: CardBus Card Configuration Header

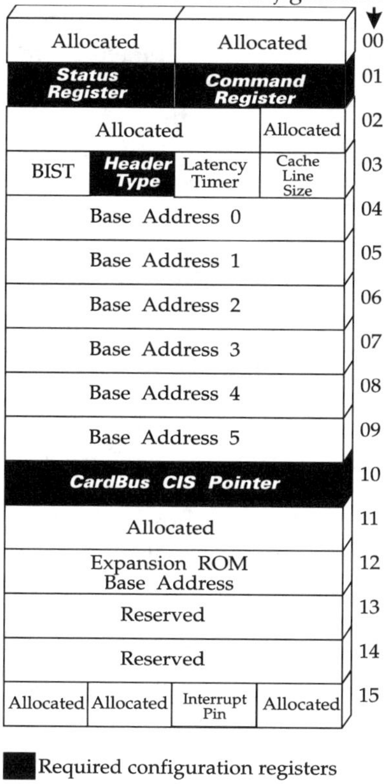

Interrupt Routing

General

Each CardBus card function that uses interrupts must contain an interrupt descriptor within the configuration table of its CIS. The CIS specifies the desired IRQ line(s) that the CINT# pin be routed to. The CardBus card's client driver parses the CIS to determine the interrupt routing and requests that one of the desired IRQs be allocated to its function by making an RequestIRQ service call to Card Services (CS). It is the job of CS to determine if the request IRQ line is available and, if so, to allocate the IRQ line to the client driver and its card function.

Once an IRQ line has been allocated to a card function and all other system resources needed by the function have been allocated, the client driver will request that the configuration be completed by making the RequestConfiguration service call. This call causes the function configuration registers to be set to the appropriate values and the CardBus bridge to be configured. The chapters that comprise Part V entitled "Configuration" on page 225 discuss the configuration process and define the function and bridge configuration registers.

Interrupt Routing Mechanisms

The PC Card standard does not specify how the interrupt routing should be accomplished. Interrupt routing is managed by the CardBus bridge and system board logic (i.e., the chipset). It is up to the system designer to determine how the interrupts will be routed from the card's CINT# pin to a given IRQ line. One of the following interrupt routing mechanisms is likely to be used:

- **Direct IRQ routing** — the CardBus bridge can include IRQ outputs that can be tied directly to the interrupt controller inputs.
- **Serialized IRQ routing** — the CardBus bridge and system board can implement a serial protocol to transfer interrupt requests between the CardBus bridge and interrupt controller. This is typically referred to a serialized interrupts.
- **Routing via PCI interrupt pins** — the CardBus bridge's PCI interrupt pins can be used to deliver interrupts. Note that only the system board designer knows the possible interrupt routing from the PCI-to-CardBus bridge's implemented interrupt pins (INTA#, INTB#, INTC#, and INTD#) to the IRQ inputs.

All of these routing methods are illustrated in Figure 13-2 on page 198 and are discussed in the following sections.

Direct IRQ routing

The CardBus bridge can be designed to provide one or more IRQ outputs that can be routed by the system designer directly to the interrupt controller inputs. This mechanism provides a great deal of flexibility since both CardBus and 16-bit PC Cards can have their interrupts routed to a wide variety of IRQ lines. This is particularly important for legacy functions implemented within PC Cards.

Serialized IRQ Routing

Some CardBus bridge and system vendors may choose to transfer interrupts to the interrupt controller via a serial transfer mechanism. Currently, two standards exist for serializing IRQ lines. These mechanisms, while similar, are implemented in different ways. Conceptually, these serial transfer mechanisms permit the serial transfer of all fifteen IRQ lines to the interrupt controller, reducing the number of pins that must be implemented. For more information regarding these mechanisms refer to the chapter entitled "The TI PCI 1130" on page 365.

IRQ Routing Via PCI Interrupt Pins

The difficulty in routing the CINT# pins via the PCI interrupt pins is that the routing depends on the system board layout. Furthermore, a given PCI interrupt pin may be physically connected to other devices that have already been assigned an interrupt (as illustrated in Figure 13-3). This figure only shows one of many possible implementations. The physical connection between the PCI interrupt pins can vary widely. If a PCI interrupt pin has already been routed to a given IRQ line (because it is shared by a PCI device that has already been configured), then the same IRQ must be used by the PC Card.

Figure 13-2: Example CardBus Interrupt Routing Methods

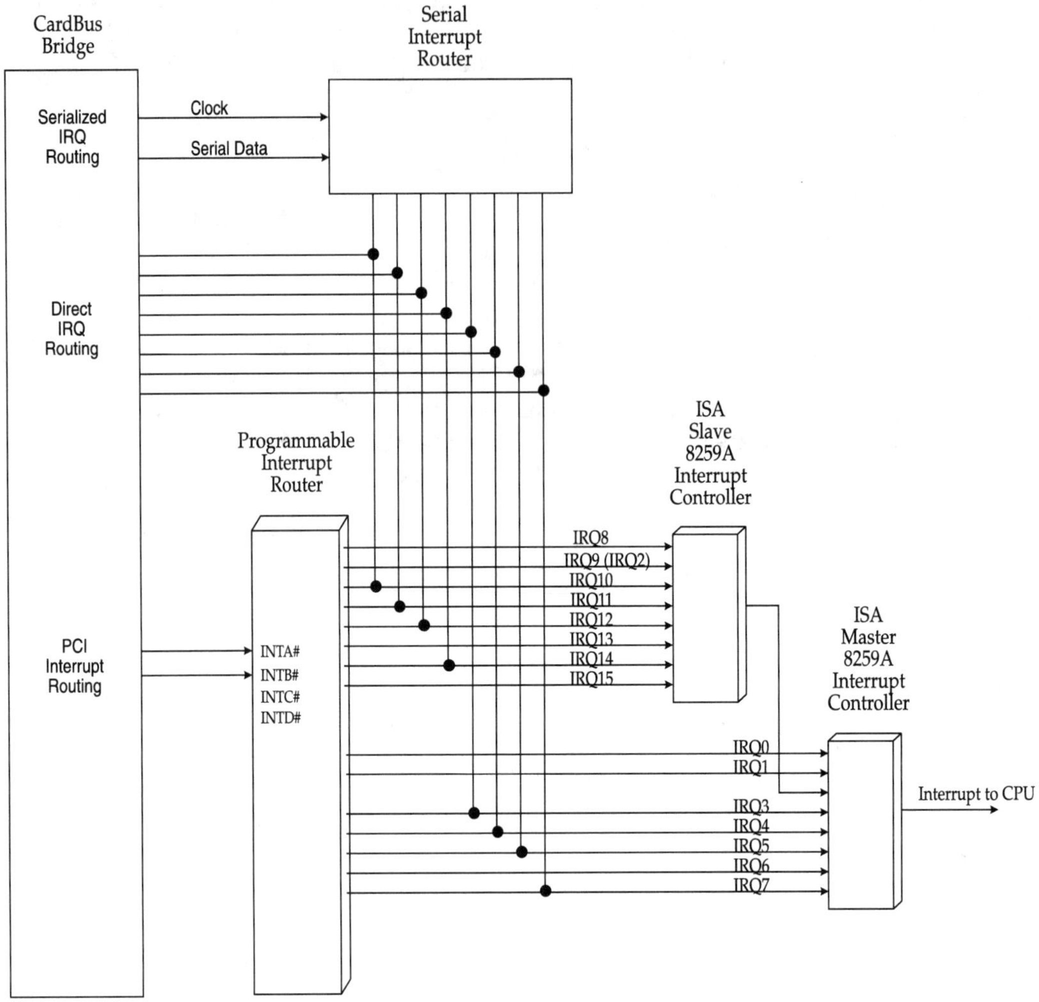

Figure 13-3: Example of PCI Interrupt Routing

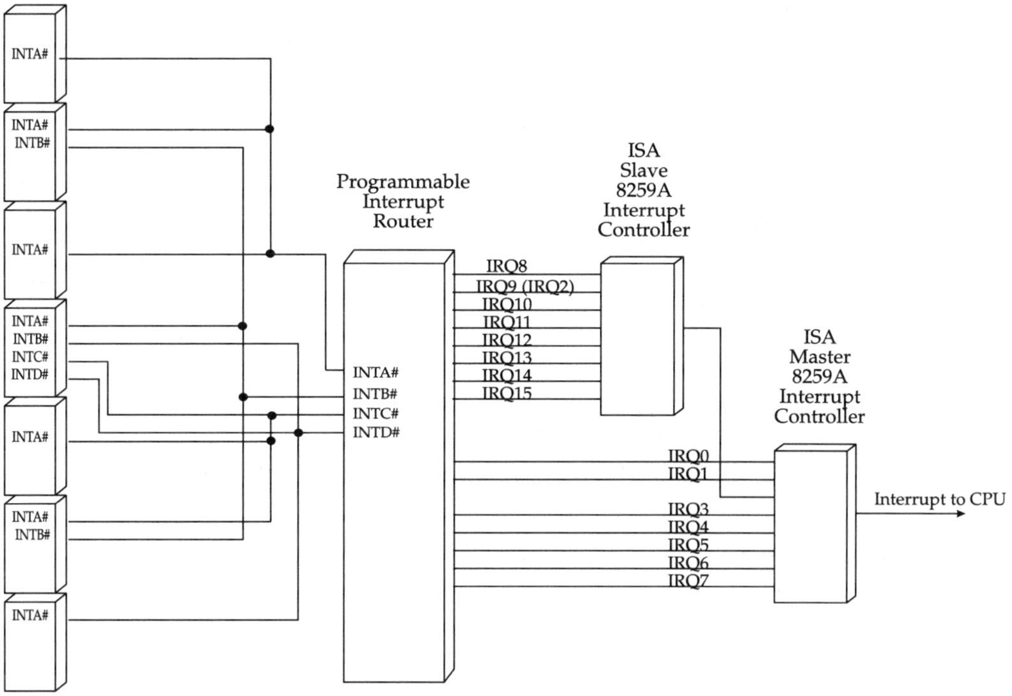

Shared Interrupt Handling

General

The PC Card standard defines an interrupt sharing mechanism that allows multiple CardBus functions to share the single CINT# pin. Each function within a multiple function PC Card has its own enabler that includes an interrupt service routine (ISR) designed specifically for that function.

Interrupt sharing is managed by card services (CS). The interrupt sharing mechanism requires that the enabler ISR for each function be registered with card services. The following sections detail the interrupt handling procedures for multifunction PC Cards.

IRQ Initialization

The card's function enabler (client driver), after having determined the configuration requirements of the card (by parsing the CIS), requests a specific IRQ line from CS by making the RequestIRQ service call. In addition, the enabler passes the starting address of its ISR to CS. CS then verifies that the requested IRQ line is available and completes the call by returning success to the function's enabler. The enabler then knows that it has acquired the IRQ, and CS has the entry point of the function's ISR.

Next, the enabler requests that CS configure the CardBus bridge so that it steers the PC Card's CINT# line to the specified interrupt output (e.g., PCI interrupt pin, serialized interrupt, or IRQ line), using the RequestConfiguration service call. CS in turn makes the appropriate calls to socket services (SS), directing it to load the appropriate registers within the CardBus bridge, thereby, setting it up to steer the PC Card's interrupt requests over the specified IRQ line.

Note that each function within a given CardBus card is initialized in the same fashion. The following is a brief description of the actions that would be taken be each enabler when initializing its function within a dual-function CardBus card.

Function Zero

When an enabler detects the presence of its function and determines that an interrupt is required, it requests that CS allocate an IRQ for its card (via the RequestIRQ service call). The enabler passes the starting address of its ISR to CS when making the service call. It also identifies the location of its function by passing CS the logical socket number and its logical function number (zero in this example).

CS then hooks the interrupt table entry that corresponds to the interrupt requested by the enabler. In this way, CS will be notified if an interrupt is generated via CINT#. CS contains a first-level interrupt handler (FLIH) that is called each time the CINT# pin is asserted. Note that the enabler registers its ISR with CS, but does not directly hook the interrupt.

Function One

When function one's enabler detects the presence of its function within the dual-function PC Card, it must also request an IRQ (via the RequestIRQ service) from CS. When making the service call, the enabler passes the entry point of its ISR to CS and specifies the logical socket and its function number (one in this example).

Since both functions share the same CINT# pin, if either generates an interrupt the CS's FLIH is called. The FLIH within CS must determine which function currently has an interrupt pending and call the corresponding device-specific enabler's ISR. After the HBA and PC Card are configured, an interrupt generated by function one will cause the FLIH within card services to execute. The specific actions taken by the FLIH and ISR are discussed in the next section.

Handling the Interrupt Request

A summary of the events that take place when a multiple-function card generates an interrupt is detailed in the following paragraphs. The example is based on a PC-compatible platform using cascaded 8259 interrupt controllers.

When a single function within a multi-function PC Card generates an interrupt request, it sets the INTR bit in its function event register and asserts the CINT# signal. The CardBus bridge steers the CINT# signal to the selected IRQ input on the interrupt controller. The interrupt controller responds by asserting the processor's interrupt request input. This causes the processor to cease normal program execution and to interrogate the interrupt controller to find out which interrupt has occurred (in an x86 environment, by performing back-to-back interrupt acknowledge bus cycles). The interrupt controller responds by sending the processor the 8-bit interrupt table entry number corresponding to the highest-priority IRQ line that is currently requesting service. The processor receives the entry number (aka the vector) and performs a memory read from the specified interrupt table entry. The entry contains the starting address of the ISR associated with the IRQ line. Since CS previously hooked the interrupt, the starting address will point to the starting address of the FLIH.

The processor temporarily stores the FLIH's starting address in a special unnamed register and also saves the current status of the program that was being executed when the interrupt occurred (i.e., it pushes the Eflag, CS, and IP registers onto the stack). This is done so the processor can return to the original program after the interrupt has been serviced. Once the processor saves its place, it then moves the FLIH's starting address into the CS and IP registers, causing the processor to begin fetching and executing instructions from CS's FLIH.

The FLIH reads the function event registers to determine which function(s) currently has an interrupt request pending (i.e., the function whose INTR bit is set). The FLIH then calls the ISR for that function, by using the entry point the enabler passed to CS when the RequestIRQ function was performed.

The function's ISR does not clear the INTR bit in the function event register, nor at the interrupt controller. When the ISR completes execution, it returns to the FLIH. Before the FLIH completes, it issues an EOI command to the interrupt controller, allowing it to service additional interrupt requests. The FLIH also clears the INTR bit within the function event register (by writing a "1" to the INTR status bit), indicating that CS is ready to handle another interrupt request. If another interrupt is pending for that function, it is again free to set the INTR bit. After the EOI command has been issued, the FLIH executes the IRET instruction (or RFI in a PowerPC environment), returning the processor to normal program flow.

14 Status Change Interrupts

The Previous Chapter

The previous chapter described function interrupt support provided by the CardBus interface and some of the possible interrupt routing mechanisms.

This Chapter

This chapter discusses status change interrupts. CardBus cards generate a status change interrupts for a variety of reasons. This chapter also discusses status change interrupt routing and handling, and also defines the mandatory socket interface registers contained within a CardBus bridge.

The Next Chapter

The next chapter provides an overview of the CardBus configuration process. This process includes configuring the CardBus bridge and the CardBus card.

Introduction

Status change interrupt support is optional for CardBus cards. The status change interrupt is used only by those cards wishing to notify system software of PCMCIA-specific status changes. The conditions reported via the status change interrupt reflect changes in the:

- **Ready state** — whether the function is ready to be accessed
- **Write-protect state** — whether memory is write-protected
- **Battery voltage detect state** — whether the battery is fully charged, low, or dead.

When any of the above conditions change within a function, the card asserts its CSTSCHG pin to notify the CardBus bridge. The bridge in turn generates an interrupt to report the status change to CS.

A card function that generates status change events must also implement a set of four event-related registers. These registers are used by PCMCIA software to determine which event has occurred and to manage the event. These registers include the:

- **Function Event register** — specifies the event that changed status.
- **Function Event Mask register** — masks CSTSCHG assertion for specified events.
- **Function Present State register** — reflects the current state of each condition.
- **Force Event register** — simulates status change events for debug purposes.

The location of these status registers is specified within the configuration tuple (CISTPL_CONFIG_CB). See Chapter 19, entitled "CardBus CIS" for details.

Another optional function associated with the CSTSCHG pin is the general wakeup event used if the interface and card had previously been powered off. The intent of the general wakeup event is to notify the CardBus bridge to reapply power to the CardBus interface, which had previously been powered-down to conserve power. Once power is reapplied, the card must be reconfigured and the CSTSCHG pin once again is used to report normal status change events. See "Interface Wakeup" on page 213 for detailed information.

Each socket interface within the bridge must also include a Socket Control register that is used by PCMCIA software to request that power be applied to the socket.

A distinction should be made between the CSTSCHG signal that the CardBus card asserts when it detects an event, and a status change interrupt generated by the CardBus bridge to notify PCMCIA software that a status change has occurred (at one of its socket interfaces). The assertion of the CSTSCHG pin is but one of several events that can cause the bridge to generate a system interrupt (called generically, a status change interrupt).

The following sections detail status change interrupt handling and defines each bit within the CardBus card's function registers and the CardBus bridge's socket status registers listed above.

CSTSCHG Pin

CSTSCHG is an optional interrupt pin implemented by CardBus cards that contain at least one function that engages in status change reporting. CSTSCHG is a level-sensitive signal that is used to notify the CardBus bridge of status change events that occur within one of the card's functions. The CardBus bridge is responsible for steering the CSTSCHG to one of its interrupt outputs. In this way, the CSTSCHG interrupt can be routed to an IRQ line in much the same way as the CINT# pin. Note that the purpose of these two interrupt pins is not related and each pin has its own steering logic within the bridge.

The CSTSCHG pin may also be asserted as a pulse to notify the CardBus bridge of a wakeup event if the interface is currently powered off.

Note that CSTSCHG is asynchronous with respect to CCLK.

Handling Status Change Events

The Function Present State register (illustrated in Figure 14-1) reflects the current state of each condition that can cause a status change event. The definition of each field within the Function Present State register is described in Table 14-1 on page 206. When the state of any of these bits change, the function must set the corresponding bit within the Function Event register. Figure 14-2 on page 207 illustrates the fields within the function event register. The definition of each bit is listed in Table 14-2 on page 208.

Figure 14-1: Function Present State Register

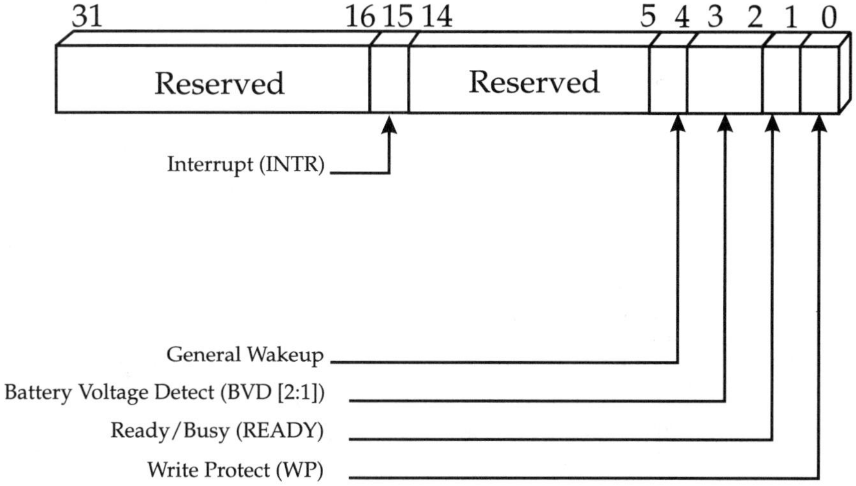

Table 14-1: Function Present State Register Bit Assignment

Bit	Name	Description
0	WP	**Write Protect**. This bit reflects the current state of the corresponding card's write-protect switch. When set, this bit indicates that the write-protect switch is in the write-protect position or that the card is read-only (in the absence of a write-protect switch). When this field is cleared, the card can be written to. This field must always retain its state, even during the assertion of CRST# and when power to the interface is cycled.
1	READY	Card function is **ready** to perform another operation. This bit reflects the ready condition of the function. When set, the function is ready for the next operation (e.g., to accept a data transfer). When cleared, the function is busy (e.g., performing initialization or performing the previous command). This field is not affected by CRST# and if the function can generate wakeup when READY changes state, it should retain its state when power to the interface is cycled.
3:2	BVD[2:1]	**Battery Voltage Detect 1 and 2**. These bits reflect the current condition of the card's battery. The bits should be interpreted as follows: **BVD2 BVD1** 1 0 Battery is operational 0 1 Battery needs to be replaced x 0 Battery cannot sustain RAM contents This field is not affected by CRST# and if the function can generate wakeup when BVD[2:1] changes state, it should retain its state when power to the interface is cycled.
4	GWAKE	**General Wakeup**. This bit reflects the current state of the wakeup event(s) that are not represented by the WP, READY, or BVD[2:1] fields. This field is set when a wakeup event (other than those just stated) has occurred and remains set until the condition causing the wakeup event has been serviced, at which time the function clears the GWAKE bit. This field is not affected by CRST#.
14:5	Reserved	Reserved for future use

Table 14-1: Function Present State Register Bit Assignment (Continued)

Bit	Name	Description
15	INTR	Card Function **Interrupt Request Pending**. This bit is set when the function has an interrupt pending and is cleared when the function recognizes that the condition causing the interrupt has been serviced. Note that this bit will typically be cleared by the function prior to the INTR in the Function Event register being cleared by system software. As a result, another interrupt pending condition may occur and be reflected by this bit field before the system is ready to accept the next interrupt request. Furthermore, the value of this field is available even if interrupts have not been configured. This field is not affected by CRST# and if the function can generate wakeup when the interrupt occurs, it should retain its state when power to the interface is cycled.
31:16	Reserved	Reserved for future use.

Figure 14-2: The Function Event Register

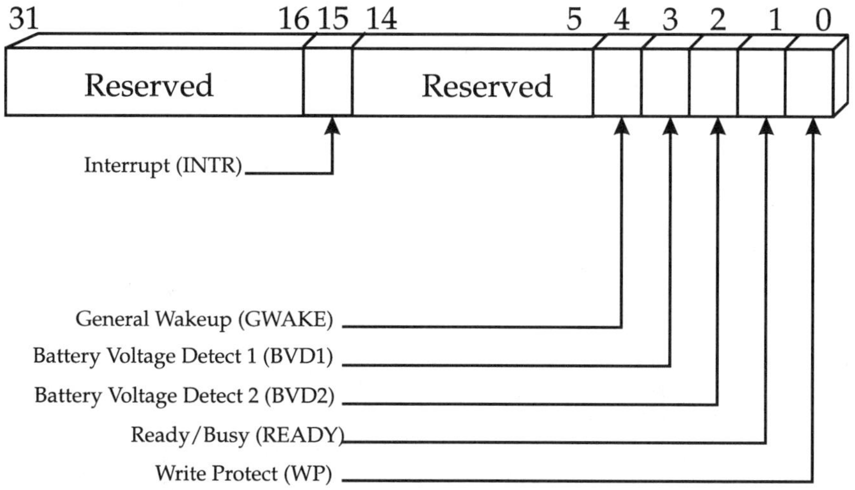

Table 14-2: Function Event Register Bit Assignment

Bit	Name	Description
0	WP	**Write Protect**. This bit is set whenever the WP field in the Function Present State register changes state. Writing a one to this field clears the field. Writing zero has no effect. If the card function implements general wakeup, then the field must retain its state during the assertion of CRST# and when power to the interface is cycled. Otherwise, the field should be cleared by CRST#.
1	READY	**Card Function Ready** to be accessed. This bit is set whenever the READY field in the Function Present State register changes state. Writing a one to this field clears the field. Writing zero has no effect. If the card function implements general wakeup, then the field must retain its state during the assertion of CRST# and when power to the interface is cycled. Otherwise, the field should be cleared by CRST#.
2	BVD2	**Battery Voltage Detect 2**. This bit is set whenever the BVD2 bit in the Function Present State register changes state. Writing a one to this field clears the field. Writing zero has no effect. If the card function implements general wakeup, then the bit must retain its state during the assertion of CRST# and when power to the interface is cycled. Otherwise, the field should be cleared by CRST#.
3	BVD1	**Battery Voltage Detect 1**. This bit is set whenever the BVD1 bit in the Function Present State register changes state. Writing a one to this field clears the field. Writing zero has no effect. If the card function implements general wakeup, then the bit must retain its state during the assertion of CRST# and when power to the interface is cycled. Otherwise, the field should be cleared by CRST#.
4	GWAKE	**General Wakeup**. This bit is set whenever the GWAKE bit in the Function Present State register changes state. Writing a one to this field clears the field. Writing zero has no effect. If the card function implements general wakeup, then the bit must retain its state during the assertion of CRST# and when power to the interface is cycled. Otherwise, the field should be cleared by CRST#.

Table 14-2: Function Event Register Bit Assignment (Continued)

Bit	Name	Description
14:5	Reserved	Reserved for future use
15	INTR	Card Function **Interrupt Request Pending**. This bit is set whenever an interrupt is pending. The bit is cleared by the host system (e.g., CS) when the interrupt has been serviced and is ready to receive another interrupt request. Writing a one to this bit clears the field, while writing zero has no effect. If the card function implements general wakeup, then the bit must retain its state during the assertion of CRST# and when power to the interface is cycled. Otherwise, the field should be cleared by CRST#.
31:16	Reserved	Reserved for future use.

When one of the status change bits within the Function Event register is set, the card may generate a status change interrupt by asserting CSTSCHG. Whether a CSTSCHG interrupt is generated is determined by the Function Event Mask register illustrated in Figure 14-3 on page 210. This register permits software to select the events that generate a status change interrupt and to mask others. The definition of each field is described in Table 14-3 on page 210.

The CardBus bridge receives the CSTSCHG signal and steers the interrupt request to the IRQ line specified during bridge configuration. This interrupt notifies CS that a status change has occurred.

CS receives a single status change interrupt for all events occurring within the sockets supported by a given CardBus bridge. As a result, CS must read the status information for each socket to determine which socket has encountered a status change. Upon determining the target socket, CS can access the Function Event register to determine which event occurred. Once read, the Function Event register field can be cleared by writing a one to the target field. CS can then take the appropriate action to handle the event (e.g., notifying the client driver of the event).

Note that the Function Event Mask register also contains control bits to select the type of audio information to be driven over the CAUDIO pin. The audio information can consist of a single-amplitude binary waveform as is used by 16-bit PC Cards, or may be a pulse width-modulated audio signal.

Figure 14-3: Function Event Mask Register

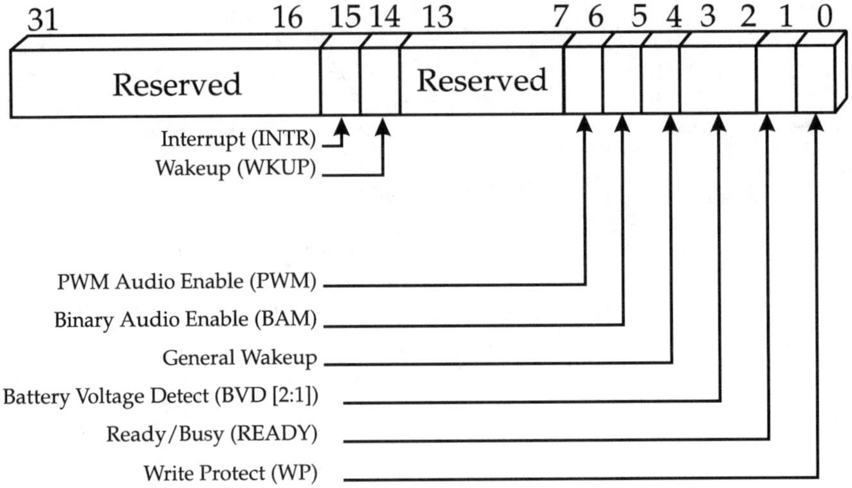

Table 14-3: Function Event Mask Register Bit Assignment

Bit	Name	Description
0	WP	**Write-Protect Mask**. This bit determines whether the CSTSCHG pin is asserted when the position of the write-protect switch is changed (as indicated by the WP bit being set in the Function Event register). When the WP mask bit is set, CSTSCHG is generated and, when cleared, WP changes do not cause an interrupt. This mask bit, in conjunction with the WKUP mask bit, also controls whether a wakeup event is generated as a result of a WP change. If the function can generate wakeup when a WP change occurs, then this bit must not be affected by CRST# or power cycling of the interface. Otherwise, the state after reset is zero.

Table 14-3: Function Event Mask Register Bit Assignment (Continued)

Bit	Name	Description
1	READY	**Ready Mask**. When set, this bit allows the CSTSCHG pin to be asserted when the READY state changes (as indicated by the READY bit being set in the Function Event register). When cleared, this bit prevents CSTSCHG from being generated as a result of READY state changes. This mask bit, in conjunction with the WKUP mask bit, also controls whether a wakeup event is generated as a result of a READY change. If the function can generate wakeup when a READY change occurs, then this bit must not be affected by CRST# or power cycling of the interface. Otherwise, the state after reset is zero.
3:2	BVD[2:1]	**Battery Condition Mask**. When set (11b), these bits allow the CSTSCHG pin to be asserted when either of the BVD bits in the Function Event register are set (indicating a state change in the battery condition). When cleared (00b), these bits prevent CSTSCHG from being generated as a result of any battery condition changes. These mask bits, in conjunction with the WKUP mask bit, also control whether a wakeup event is generated as a result of a battery condition change. Note that bit combinations of 01b and 10b are illegal. If the function can generate wakeup when a BVD change occurs, then this field must not be affected by CRST# or power cycling of the interface. Otherwise, the state after reset is zero.
4	GWAKE	**General Wakeup**. When set, this bit allows the CSTSCHG pin to be asserted when the GWAKE bit in the Function Event register is set (indicating a state change in the conditions monitored by GWAKE). When cleared, this bit prevents CSTSCHG from being generated as a result of a related condition change. This mask bit, in conjunction with the WKUP mask bit, also controls whether a wakeup event is generated as a result of a GWAKE condition change. If the function can generate wakeup when a GWAKE change occurs, then this bit must not be affected by CRST# or power cycling of the interface. Otherwise, the state after reset is zero.

Table 14-3: Function Event Mask Register Bit Assignment (Continued)

Bit	Name	Description
5	BAM	**Binary Audio Enable**. When set, binary audio mode (BAM) is enabled on the CAUDIO pin. When cleared, BAM is disabled. If the PWM bit is also set, the state of the CAUDIO pin is undetermined. The state of BAM after CRST# is zero.
6	PWM	**Pulse Width Modulation** audio enable. When set, PWM audio mode is enabled on the CAUDIO pin. When cleared, PWM audio mode is disabled. If the BAM bit is also set, the state of the CAUDIO pin is undetermined. The state of PWM after CRST# is zero.
13:7	Reserved	Reserved for future use
14	WKUP	**WakeUp mask**. When set, the wakeup function is enabled, thereby enabling wakeup events to be generated via the CSTSCHG pin. These wakeup events occur when a status change bit is set in the Function Event register and the corresponding mask bit is set. When cleared, wakeup events are disabled regardless of the event mask bit settings (bits 4:0). If the function can generate a wakeup, then this bit must not be affected by CRST#, nor by interface power being cycled. If the function does not support wakeup, this field is reserved.
15	INTR	**Function Interrupt mask**. When set, this bit enables the INTR bit in the Function Event register, permitting interrupts to be generated via the CINT# pin. This bit also enables generation of wakeup events via CSTSCHG when the interface is powered off. When cleared, this bit inhibits the generation of both CINT# when the interface is powered on (disabling function-specific interrupts) and the CSTSCHG pin when the interface is powered off (disabling wakeup events). If the function can generate a wakeup, then this bit must not be affected by CRST#, nor by the interface power being cycled. Otherwise, the state after reset is zero.
31:16	Reserved	Reserved for future use.

CardBus cards that generate status change events must also provide a Force Event register to assist in debugging the card and software. This register provides the ability to simulate events by forcing values into the Function Event register. Figure 14-4 on page 213 illustrates the Force Event register. However, this is not a physically implemented register, but rather an address port. The Force Event register address is used to write values that force bits into the Function Event register. Writing a one to any bit position of the Force Event port sets the corresponding bit in the Function Event register, thereby simulating a status change event. Note that if other functions are active, they may alter the values previously forced into the Function Event register. Writing zeroes to the Force Event port has no effect.

Figure 14-4: Force Event Register (Address Port)

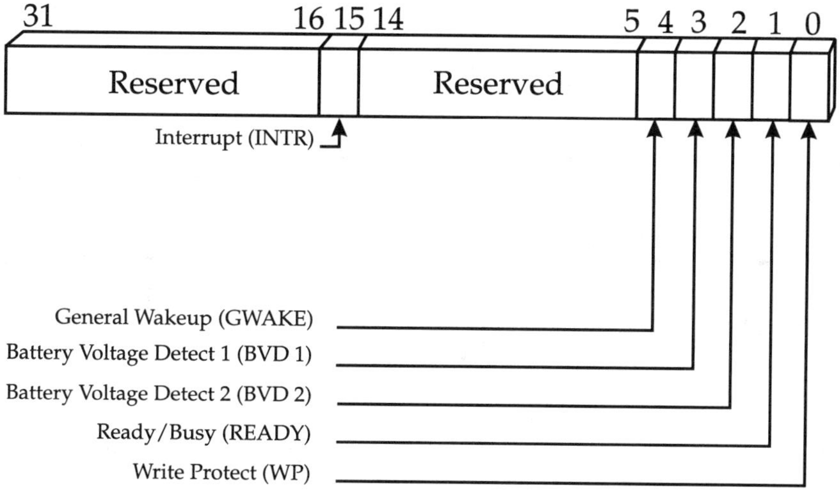

Interface Wakeup

CardBus cards have the option of implementing a wakeup protocol that can be used to request that the system reapply power to the CardBus interface and reconfigure it. When the interface is powered off, the CSTSCHG pin is used to generate the wakeup to the host system, rather than a status change interrupt.

Socket Status and Control Registers

The PC Card standard requires that a CardBus bridge include four socket status registers and one socket control register. These registers allow PCMCIA software to determine the cause of the a status change interrupt, to mask out particular events that would normally cause a status change interrupt to be generated, and to provide debug support. The control register provides a way for software to request that power be applied to the socket interface. The following sections define each socket status register and the socket control register.

Socket Event Register

Each event that can cause a status change interrupt to be generated by the CardBus bridge is illustrated in Figure 14-5 on page 214. These bits are set by the bridge in response to signals that change state at the socket interface (i.e., CCD1#, CCD2#, and CSTSCHG) or represents completion of powering up or powering down the socket interface. The definition of each field in the Socket Event register is listed in Table 14-4 on page 214.

Figure 14-5: The Socket Event Register

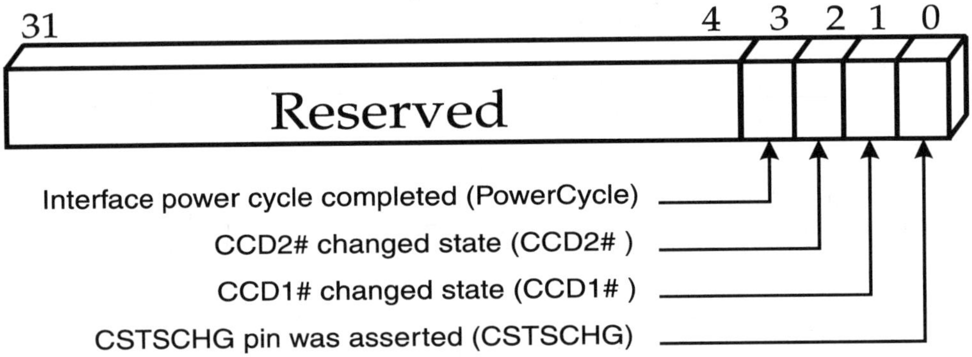

Table 14-4: Socket Event Register Bit Assignment

Bit	Field Name	Description
0	CSTSCHG	**CardBus Status Change**. The bridge sets this bit when it detects the CSTSCHG bit in the Socket Present State register change state. Writing a one clears the bit.
1	CCD1#	**CardBus Card Detect 1**. The bridge sets this bit when it detects the CCD1# bit in the Socket Present State register change state. Writing a one clears the bit.

Table 14-4: Socket Event Register Bit Assignment

Bit	Field Name	Description
2	CCD2#	**CardBus Card Detect 2.** The bridge sets this bit when it detects the CCD2# bit in the Socket Present State register change state. Writing a one clears the bit.
3	PowerCycle	The bridge sets this bit when it completes a software request to either remove or apply power to the socket interface. Writing a one clears the bit.
31:4	Reserved	Reserved for future use.

Socket Present State Register

PCMCIA software can obtain the state of the socket interface by reading the Socket Present State register. This register is read-only and reflects the status of selected interface pins as well as additional status information related to the socket's status. Each field within the Socket Present State register is illustrated in Figure 14-6, while Table 14-5 describes each field.

When a PC Card is inserted into a socket, the bridge generates a status change interrupt. This interrupt occurs after the CCD1# and CCD2# pins are asserted and the card type and Vcc have been determined by the bridge. CS, which is called as a result of the status change interrupt, must read the Socket Present State register for each socket to determine the card type and the Vcc supported by the PC Card.

Figure 14-6: The Socket Present State Register

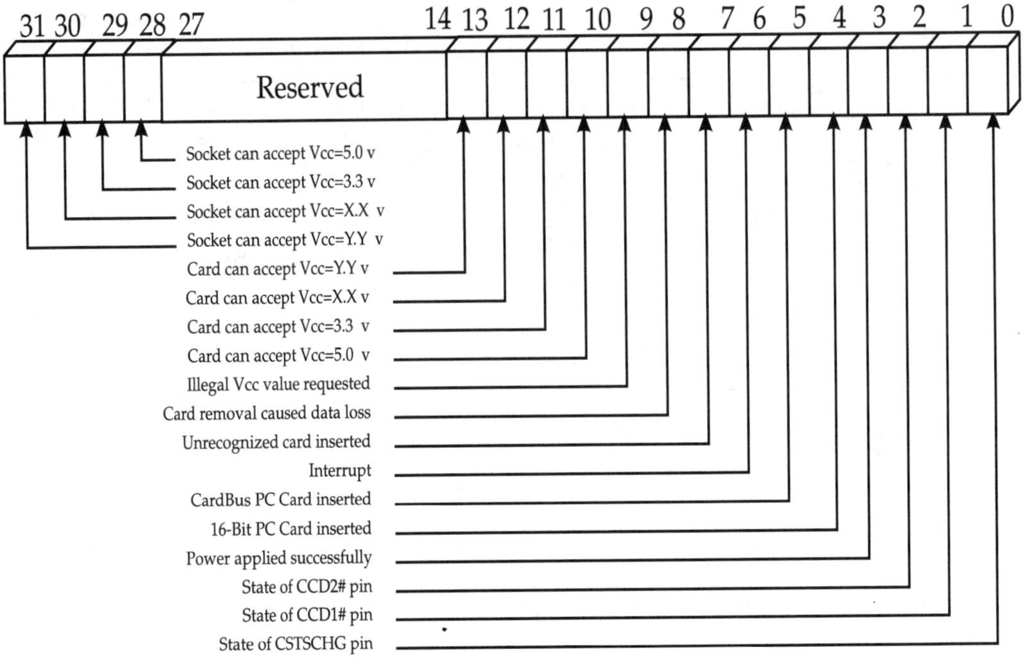

Table 14-5: Socket Present State Register Bit Assignment

Bit	Field Name	Description
0	CSTSCHG	**CardBus Status Change**. The bridge sets this bit when it detects the CSTSCHG bit in the Socket Present State register change state. Writing a one clears the bit.
1	CCD1#	**CardBus Card Detect 1**. The bridge sets this bit when it detects the CCD1# bit in the Socket Present State register change state. Writing a one clears the bit.
2	CCD2#	**CardBus Card Detect 2.** The bridge sets this bit when it detects the CCD2# bit in the Socket Present State register change state. Writing a one clears the bit.
3	PowerCycle	The bridge sets this bit when it completes a software request to either remove or apply power to the socket interface. Writing a one clears the bit.

Table 14-5: Socket Present State Register Bit Assignment (Continued)

Bit	Field Name	Description
4	16card	**16-bit PC Card**. The bridge sets the bit when it detects that a 16-Bit PC Card has been inserted. When set, the bridge configures the socket interface for a 16-bit card definition.
5	CBcard	**CardBus Card Detect**. The bridge sets the bit when it detects that a CardBus PC Card has been inserted. When set, the bridge configures the socket interface for a CardBus card.
6	Interrupt	When set, indicates the card is asserting its interrupt pin. This bit follows the state of the card's interrupt pin.
7	NotACard	The bridge sets this bit if it detects that a card has been inserted into the socket but cannot determine the type.
8	DataLost	This bit is set by the bridge when abrupt card removal may have resulted in lost data. This can occur if the card was removed during a transaction or if data is left in a buffer that had not been written to the card.
9	BadVccReq	The bridge sets this bit if software has attempted to apply a Vcc voltage not supported by the PC Card.
10	5VCard	The bridge sets this bit if the card will function properly at an initial Vcc of 5.0vdc. When cleared, the card will not operate properly if 5.0vdc is applied.
11	3VCard	The bridge sets this bit if the card will function properly at an initial Vcc of 3.3vdc. When cleared, the card will not operate properly if 3.3vdc is applied.
12	XVCard	The bridge sets this bit if the card will function properly at an initial Vcc of X.Xvdc. When cleared, the card will not operate properly if X.Xvdc is applied.
13	YVCard	The bridge sets this bit if the card will function properly at an initial Vcc of Y.Yvdc. When cleared, the card will not operate properly if Y.Yvdc is applied.
27:14	Reserved	Reserved for future use.

Table 14-5: Socket Present State Register Bit Assignment (Continued)

Bit	Field Name	Description
28	5Vsocket	When set, indicates that the bridge can supply 5vdc to the socket. When cleared, the bridge cannot supply 5vdc to the socket.
29	3Vsocket	When set, indicates that the bridge can supply 3.3vdc to the socket. When cleared, the bridge cannot supply 3.3vdc to the socket.
30	XVsocket	When set, indicates that the bridge can supply X.Xvdc to the socket. When cleared, the bridge cannot supply X.Xvdc to the socket.
31	YVsocket	When set, indicates that the bridge can supply Y.Yvdc to the socket. When cleared, the bridge cannot supply Y.Yvdc to the socket.

Socket Event Mask Register

This register provides software with the ability to mask out events that should not result in a status change interrupt being generated. Each field within the Event Mask register corresponds to a field within the Event register. See Figure 14-7 on page 218. When a bit is set in the Socket Event register, a status change interrupt is generated by the CardBus bridge (when the corresponding bit in the Event Mask register is set).

Figure 14-7: The Socket Event Mask Register

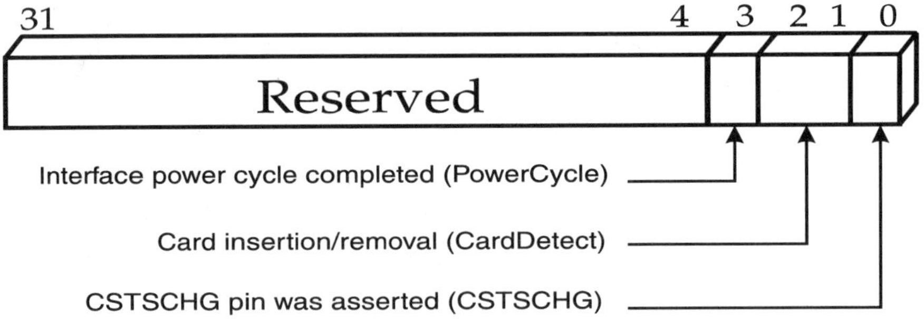

Like the other socket registers, to clear a bit the programmer must write a one to the bit position. Table 14-6 describes each field within the Event Mask register.

Table 14-6: Socket Event Mask Register Bit Assignment

Bit	Field Name	Description
0	CSTSCHG	**CardBus Status Change**. The programmer sets this bit to enable the bridge to generate a status change interrupt when the CSTSCHG bit is set in the Socket Event register. Writing a one clears the bit, causing this event to be masked.
2:1	CardDetect	The programmer sets this bit to enable the bridge to generate a status change interrupt when either of the CCD pins change state (as indicated by the Socket Event register). Writing a one clears the bit, causing these events to be masked. Note that both bits must be either set or cleared.
3	PowerCycle	The programmer sets this bit to enable the bridge to generate a status change interrupt when the bridge has completed either powering-up or powering-down the socket interface (as indicated by the Socket Event register). Writing a one clears the bit, causing these events to be masked.
31:4	Reserved	Reserved for future use.

Socket Force Event Register

The Socket Force Event register provides the ability to simulate selected events by setting the bit corresponding to the event (as illustrated in Figure 14-8). Like the Function Force Event register within a CardBus card, this register is not implemented physically. It is an address that can be written to, thereby causing the selected event to be simulated.

Writes to the Force Event port causes bits in the Socket Present State register and Socket Event register to be set. Note that other events may cause these same bits to updated before they can be read. Table 14-7 on page 220 describes each bit within the Force Event register and the resulting actions.

Figure 14-8: The Socket Force Event Register

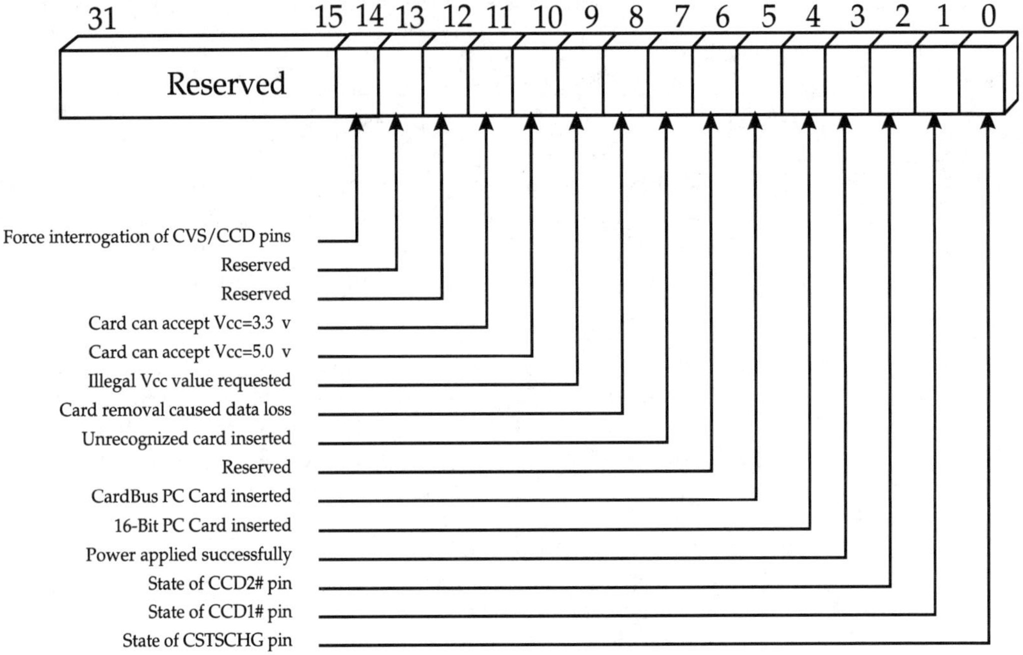

Table 14-7: Socket Force Event Register Bit Assignment

Bit	Field Name	Description
0	CSTSCHG	**CardBus Status Change**. When set, the Socket Event register's CSTSCHG bit is set, thereby simulating the assertion of the CSTSCHG pin. Note that the CSTSCHG bit in the Socket Present State register is unchanged. Writing a zero has no effect.
1	CCD1#	**CardBus Card Detect 1**. When set, the Socket Event register's CCD1# bit is set, thereby simulating a change on the CCD1# pin. Note that the CCD1# bit in the Socket Present State register is unchanged. Writing zero has no effect.
2	CCD2#	**CardBus Card Detect 2.** When set, the Socket Event register's CCD2# bit is set, thereby simulating a change on the CCD2# pin. Note that the CCD1# bit in the Socket Present State register is unchanged. Writing zero has no effect.

Table 14-7: Socket Force Event Register Bit Assignment (Continued)

Bit	Field Name	Description
3	PowerCycle	When set, the Socket Event register's PowerCycle bit is set, thereby simulating the completion of a power cycle. Note that the PowerCycle bit in the Socket Present State register is unchanged. Writing zero has no effect.
4	16card	**16-bit PC Card**. Setting this bit causes the 16card bit in the Socket Present State register to be set. If the CCD1# and CCD2# pins are asserted (i.e., a card is present in the socket), setting this bit has no effect.
5	CBcard	**CardBus Card**. Setting this bit causes the CBcard bit in the Socket Present State register to be set. If the CCD1# and CCD2# pins are asserted (i.e., a card is present in the socket), setting this bit has no effect.
6	Reserved	Reserved for future use
7	NotACard	Setting this bit causes the NotACard bit in the Socket Present State register to be set. If the CCD1# and CCD2# pins are asserted (i.e., a card is present in the socket), setting this bit has no effect.
8	DataLost	Setting this bit causes the DataLost bit in the Socket Present State register to be set.
9	BadVccReq	Setting this bit causes the BadVccReq bit in the Socket Present State register to be set.
10	5VCard	Setting this bit causes the BadVccReq bit in the Socket Present State register to be set. When set, the bridge cannot apply Vcc to the socket until the CVStest bit is set.
11	3VCard	Setting this bit causes the BadVccReq bit in the Socket Present State register to be set. When set, the bridge cannot apply Vcc to the socket until the CVStest bit is set.
12	Reserved	Reserved.
13	Reserved	Reserved.

Table 14-7: Socket Force Event Register Bit Assignment (Continued)

Bit	Field Name	Description
14	Reserved	Setting this bit causes the bridge to perform the socket interrogation (using CVS[2:1] and CCD[2:1]#) to detect the Vcc required by the card inserted. When the interrogation is complete, the bridge updates the nVCard fields in the Present State register. In addition, if the nVCard fields have previously been forced, the bridge is re-enabled to apply Vcc to the socket.
31:15	Reserved	Reserved for future use.

Socket Control Register

Socket power is applied to the socket only under software control. The CardBus bridge is not permitted to automatically apply power to the sockets without intervention from PCMCIA software. Writes to the Socket Control register request that the bridge apply the specified Vcc and/or Vpp to the socket. Figure 14-9 illustrates the Socket Control register and Table 14-8 defines each field.

Figure 14-9: The Socket Control Register

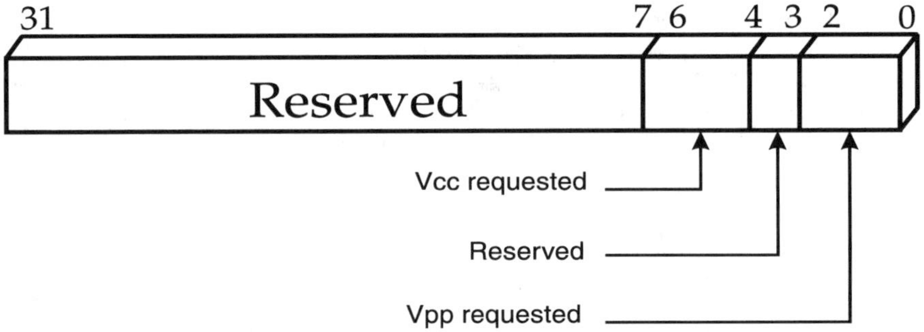

Table 14-8: Socket Control Register Bit Assignment

Bit	Field Name	Description
2:0	VppControl	CS requests that the required Vpp be applied to the socket by writing one of the following values: • 000b = Power off • 001b = 12.0vdc • 010b = 5.0vdc • 011b = 3.3vdc • 100b = Reserved • 101b = Reserved • 110 & 111 = Reserved
3	Reserved	Reserved for future use.
6:4	VccControl	This field is used to request that Vcc be applied to the socket. The bit definition is the same as Vpp except that 001b is reserved.
31:7	Reserved	Reserved for future use.

Part Five

Configuration

15 CardBus Configuration Process

The Previous Chapter

The previous chapter discussed status change interrupts. CardBus cards generate a status change interrupts for a variety of reasons. The chapter also discussed status change interrupt routing and handling.

This Chapter

This chapter provides an overview of the CardBus configuration process. This process includes configuring the CardBus bridge as well as the CardBus card(s).

The Next Chapter

The next chapter defines configuration transactions that must be performed to configure the CardBus bridge and CardBus card. It describes both type zero and type one configuration transfers required to configure CardBus cards.

Introduction

The following discussion presumes that the CardBus cards are interfaced to a PCI bus via a PCI to CardBus bridge. Figure 15-1 on page 228 illustrates such a system. During power up, configuration software is responsible for detecting and configuring the CardBus cards. The software involved in configuring CardBus cards depends on the revision level of the system firmware, the operation system, and that of CS and SS. If the software present in the system has not been upgraded to support CardBus, then the CardBus bridge and PC Cards will not be configured. For the purposes of the following discussion it is assumed that system firmware, as well as CS and SS have been updated to support the CardBus interface.

Figure 15-1: .CardBus Subsystem Connected to PCI Bus

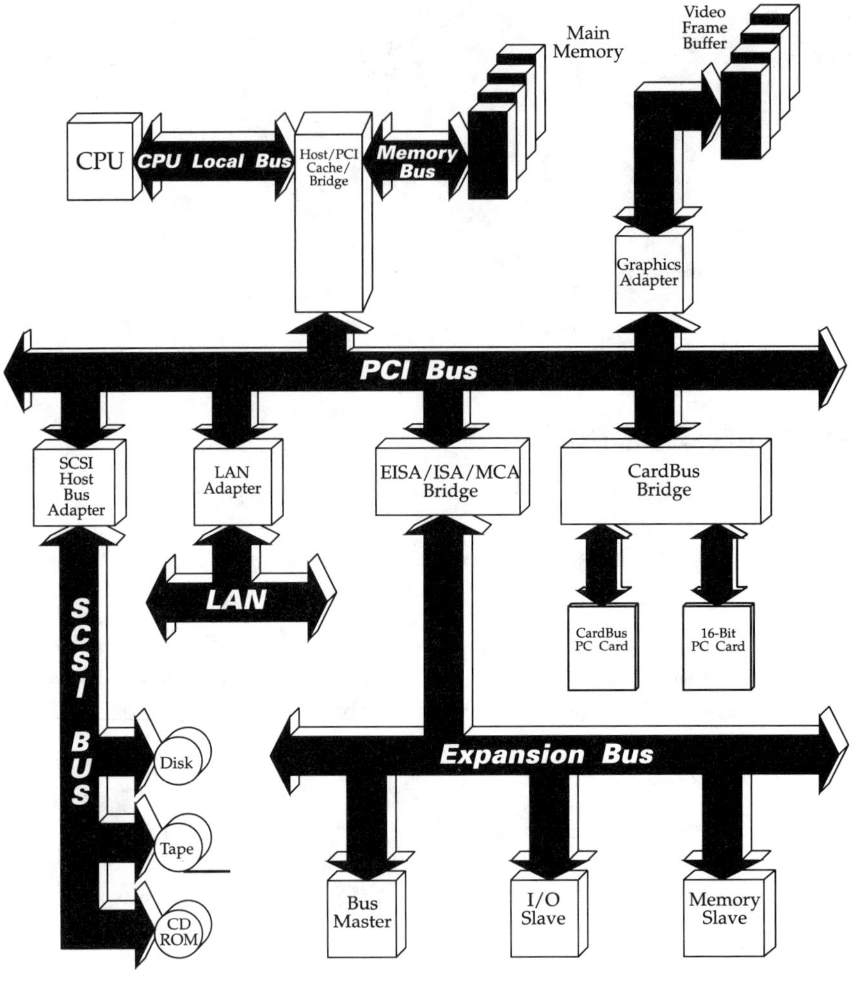

Configuring the CardBus cards must be performed in two distinct steps:

1. **PCI/CardBus bridge configuration** — Configuring the bridge is performed in essentially the same manner as any other device residing on the PCI bus. In short, PCI configuration software scans the PCI bus detecting the devices that are present and configuring them. The bridge is configured during the power-up sequence in preparation for recognition of PC Card installation and notification to PCMCIA software that a PC Card is present.
2. **PC Card and socket configuration** — Configuring CardBus cards is the responsibility of PCMCIA software. This software is designed to handle hot

insertion capability. When a PC Card is inserted into a socket, the CardBus bridge detects the card's presence and generates an interrupt to notify PCMCIA configuration software (the CardBus client driver, CS, and SS). This software is responsible for applying power to the card and for configuring the PC Card and the bridge's socket interface.

Step one above involves the typical plug and play configuration that applies to any PCI device (with the exception that it is a bridge device). A PCI-to-CardBus bridge has a unique configuration register layout (defined by an industry standards group known as Yenta).

Step two of the configuration process involves the same PCMCIA software used for 16-bit PC Cards. As is the case for 16-bit PC Cards, a client driver, or enabler, must exist for each PC Card function. Without an enabler, the PC Card functions are not configured and remain disabled. The same software elements and flow applies to both 16-bit PC Cards and CardBus cards (as illustrated in Figure 15-2).

Figure 15-2: PCMCIA Software Components and Flow

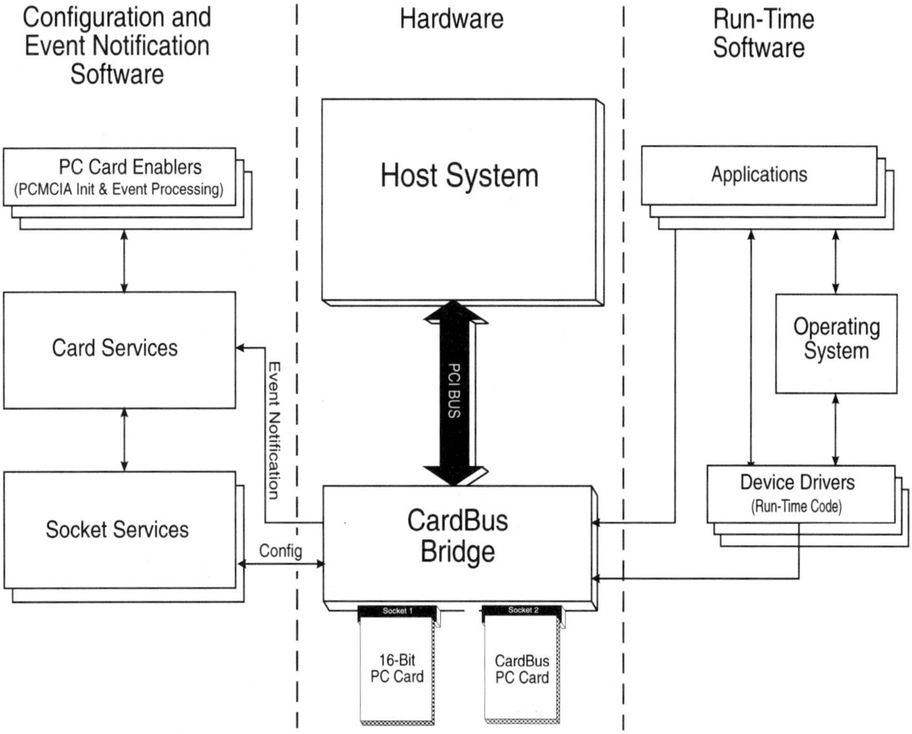

These software elements (enablers, CS, and SS) function is the same manner in a CardBus environment as they do in a 16-bit PC Card environment. A few additional services are included and others have been modified to support CardBus implementations, but the fundamental processes remain the same. Part VI, entitled "CardBus Software" on page 337 discusses SS, CS, and client drivers (enablers) used in CardBus implementations.

The term "PCMCIA configuration software" used in this chapter refers generically to one of more of the software elements: the client driver (i.e., the enabler), CS, and SS.

Configuration Address Space

All CardBus cards and PCI devices must implement a base set of configuration registers defined by the PCI and CardBus specifications. In addition, the specification sets aside additional configuration locations for implementing device-specific configuration registers. Configuration software accesses these registers to determine the configuration requirements of a given device and to allocate selected system resources. Usage of the configuration address space differs between PCI and CardBus devices:

- **PCI configuration registers** contain encoded configuration information that **defines the resource requirements** of the device. For example, PCI configuration software knows how to probe the PCI Base Address Registers to determine address space requirements. These same registers are used to configure the device's address decoders so that the device responds to the specified address range(s).
- **CardBus devices employ** PCMCIA's **CIS** (card information structure) **that specifies** the PC Card's **resource requirements**. PCMCIA configuration software must first access a PCI configuration register (the CardBus CIS Pointer register) to obtain the start address of the CIS. The CIS is then parsed (i.e., scanned) to determine the device's resource requirements. For example, BARs (Base Address Registers) tuples within the CIS defines the device's address space requirements. As is done with PCI devices, the Base Address Registers (located within the configuration address space) are used to configure the address decoders.

The differences between CardBus and PCI configuration stem from the hot insertion ability of the CardBus cards. CardBus configuration software must be prepared to detect the insertion of a CardBus card at any time, and properly configure it. An added complication of CardBus software is that is must be prepared to detect card removal and to release the socket interface configuration.

Single and Multiple Function Devices

Each CardBus card and PCI device can implement from one to eight functions (i.e., logical devices) internally. For example, a multifunction CardBus card could incorporate an ethernet LAN controller, SCSI interface, and a FAX/modem. Each of these functions requires its own set of configuration registers. These configuration registers are mapped into PCI configuration address space. Each function is allocated 256 bytes (64 dwords) of configuration address space into which their configuration registers are mapped. The definition of this 256 bytes of configuration space is defined by the PCI and CardBus specifications. Note that CardBus bridges have a specific configuration register layout and CardBus cards another. Refer to Chapter 17, entitled "CardBus Bridge Configuration Registers," on page 261 and Chapter 18, entitled "CardBus Card Configuration Registers," on page 297.

Accessing Configuration Space

Intel x86 and PowerPC 60x processors possess the ability to address two distinct address spaces: I/O and memory. CardBus and PCI bus masters use I/O and memory addressing to access CardBus and PCI devices. A third address space, configuration space, is used to access a PCI device's configuration registers. A PCI device's configuration registers must be accessed at start-up time to configure the device for proper operation in the host system. In the case of CardBus cards, configuration may occur after the system has already been started (i.e., a CardBus card can be inserted into a socket at any time).

CardBus memory space, I/O space, and configuration address space are mapped within the respective PCI address space. PCI configuration space is divided into a separate configuration address space that is allocated for each function contained within a physical device (i.e., in a chip or card). Figure 15-3 on page 232 illustrates the basic format of a PCI or CardBus function's configuration space. The first 16 doublewords of a device's space are referred to as the device's configuration header space.

The format and usage of the configuration header is defined by the PCI specification. Two header formats are currently defined: header type zero for all devices other than PCI-to-PCI bridges; and header type one for PCI-to-PCI bridges. Header type two for CardBus bridges has been defined (at the time of this printing it had not been officially adopted by the PCI Special Interest Group (SIG)). A detailed proposed description of the CardBus bridge header and Card-

Bus card header can be found in Chapters 17 and 18, respectively.

The system designer must provide some mechanism for converting pre-defined memory or I/O accesses initiated by the host processor into configuration accesses on the PCI bus and CardBus. The type one configuration mechanism defined in the PCI and CardBus specifications is described in Chapter 16, entitled "Configuration Transfers," on page 237. Access to configuration address space is provided via the configuration read and write commands.

Figure 15-3: Basic Format of Configuration Space Associated with Each Function

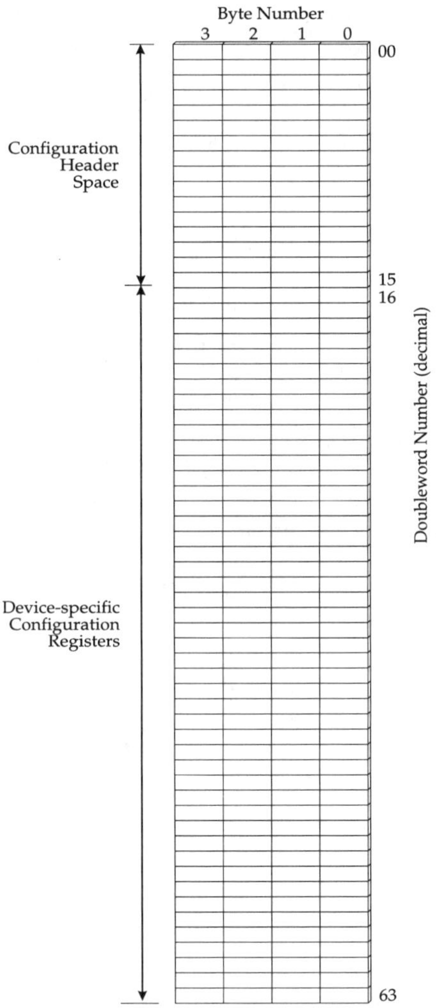

The Configuration Sequence

The CardBus bridge and PC Cards must both be configured to permit access to the target PC Cards. This configuration process involves several major steps:

1. **Socket Interface Initialization** (step one in configuring the bridge). This entails configuring and enabling the socket interface in preparation for card insertion. Specifically, PCI configuration software is responsible for configuring the socket status registers (they reflect the status of the socket interface) and for setting up the socket's status change interrupt. The status change interrupt notifies PCMCIA software of socket interface changes (e.g., card insertion), and the socket status registers reflect the cause of the interrupt (e.g., a PC Card that has been inserted into a socket). These registers must be mapped into PCI address space so that PCMCIA software can access them.
2. **PC Card Detection**. When a PC Card is inserted into a socket, the bridge generates a status change interrupt. This interrupt invokes the PCMCIA software that performs reads from the socket status registers to determine the cause of the interrupt — in this instance, card insertion.
3. **PC Card Configuration**. PCMCIA software must also determine the resources required by the PC Card (by reading its configuration registers) and configure the PC Card. Chapter 16, entitled "Configuration Transfers," on page 237 discusses access to PC Card configuration address space. PCMCIA configuration software must program the PC Card's configuration registers to assign the required address space and function-specific interrupt that are required by the PC Card. Since PC Cards are hot pluggable, PCI configuration software cannot be responsible for this portion of the configuration (because PCI configuration software is designed to configure devices only during the power-up sequence).
4. **Configuring the Bridge** to Filter Transactions and Steer the PC Card Interrupt (step two in configuring the bridge). It is the responsibility of PCMCIA configuration software to configure the bridge's socket interface so that it forwards transactions to/from a CardBus PC Card when it detects transactions that fall within the PC Card's address range (or when a CardBus card initiates a transaction).

Socket Interface Initialization

When the system powers up, all PCI devices (including CardBus bridges) are disabled and cannot be accessed except for their configuration address space. It is the responsibility of PCI configuration software to scan the PCI bus to detect the presence of all PCI devices and configure them. This is accomplished by accessing the configuration registers within the devices residing on the PCI bus. To do this, the system must provide some mechanism for generating access to PCI configuration address space. Refer to Chapter 16 for a detailed description of accessing PCI configuration address space.

A CardBus bridge provides the interface between a PC Card socket and the PCI bus. Each socket supported by a CardBus bridge requires a separate interface because each socket uses point-to-point signaling (i.e., no direct bussing between sockets). Consequently, each socket interface is treated as a separate function within the CardBus bridge. When PCI configuration software scans the PCI bus, it will detect a separate function for each socket supported by a given CardBus bridge.

When a CardBus bridge is detected, PCI configuration software determines the amount of memory and/or IO space that the bridge requires, and whether it uses interrupts to report socket status changes (e.g., card insertion or removal). The configuration program then configures the bridge by programming its address decoders to respond to memory and/or IO address ranges that are guaranteed not to conflict with those assigned to other system devices. It will also specify what IRQ line the bridge's PCI interrupt request is routed to by the system.

The CardBus bridge is partially configured by PCI configuration software to enable its PC Card socket interfaces. This entails mapping and enabling the bridge's socket status registers and routing the CardBus bridge socket status interrupt. PCI configuration software may also allocate a CardBus number that will be used later to provide access to the CardBus configuration registers. The CardBus card and its socket interface cannot be completely configured at this point (because a PC Card may not be present during power-up). The bridge configuration is completed by PCMCIA software when it detects that a PC Card is inserted into the socket and configures and enables the card.

PC Card Detection

Once the socket interface is initialized, the bridge's socket status registers will reflect whether a card is inserted into a socket or not. If a PC Card is already present when the system powers up, PCMCIA software can read the socket status registers to detect the card's presence. If however, no PC Card is present during the power-up process, then PCMCIA software awaits notification of card insertion via a status change interrupt generated by the CardBus bridge.

PC Card Configuration

Configuring a PC Card and setting up the bridge's socket interface is performed by PCMCIA configuration software. When PCMCIA software installs, it checks for the presence of a CardBus bridge. If present, software then checks the bridge's socket status registers (previously configured by PCI configuration software) to determine if a PC Card is present in any of the sockets. If a PC Card is present, it proceeds to interrogate the card to determine its resource requirements and then performs the card configuration. If no PC Cards are present, PCMCIA software remains resident in memory and awaits the insertion of a PC Card.

Configuring the CardBus card involves four steps:

1. Reading the CardBus configuration registers to find the location of the CIS.
2. Parsing the CIS (card information structure) to determine the card's configuration requirements.
3. Request the resources specified within the CIS.
4. Writing to the CardBus card's configuration registers to configure the card.

PCMCIA software consists of the CardBus card's client driver, CS, and SS. When a PC Card is detected via CS and SS, the PC Card's client driver is notified. The client driver is ultimately responsible for configuring its card.

A given client driver must first determine whether it should attempt to configure the PC Card. The client driver must parse the card's CIS to determine if the card should be configured. When a client driver requests access to the CIS, CS must first access the CardBus card's configuration address space to obtain the location of the CIS within the card. The client driver then traverses the card's tuple list to determine if it should attempt to configure the card and if so, determine the resources required by the card.

Upon determining the resources required, the client driver requests that each resource be allocated to its card via CS. If CS determines that the requested resources are available, it then allocates the resources to the client driver. The client driver, after having obtained all the resources needed by the card, requests that CS perform the configuration based on the resources previously acquired. In response, CS and SS will write to the CardBus card's configuration registers to configure the address decoders as required. CardBus cards contain PCI-like configuration registers that are accessible via PCI configuration read and write transactions.

In addition to configuring the CardBus card, CS and SS must also configure the CardBus bridge so that it can correctly forward transactions to/from the card as discussed later in this chapter.

Note that a CardBus card may contain up to eight individual functions. As a result, the configuration process defined above would be repeated for each function contained within the card.

Configuring the CB Bridge to Filter Transactions

The final stage in configuring the CardBus bridge is to set up the bridge so that is can properly forward transactions between the CardBus card and the PCI bus. The CardBus bridge contains memory and I/O address registers that must be configured so that the bridge knows the range of addresses that have been mapped to the CardBus card functions. The bridge must also be configured so that it steers interrupts from the CardBus functions to the assigned system IRQ line. Chapter 17, entitled "CardBus Bridge Configuration Registers," on page 261 contains a detailed explanation of the configuration registers.

16 Configuration Transfers

The Previous Chapter

The previous chapter provided an overview of the CardBus configuration process, including configuration of both the CardBus bridge and CardBus cards.

This Chapter

This chapter defines the configuration transactions that access configuration registers within the CardBus bridge and CardBus cards. It describes both type zero and type one configuration transfers.

The Next Chapter

The next chapter defines the CardBus bridge's configuration header, socket interface initialization, and configuring the socket interface to filter transactions between the CardBus and PCI bus. It also defines the mandatory socket interface registers contained a within CardBus bridge.

Introduction

The configuration registers within the CardBus bridge are accessed using PCI configuration accesses, while those within CardBus cards are accessed using CardBus configuration accesses. As discussed in the previous chapter, phase one of the CardBus bridge configuration must be completed to prepare the PC Card socket for card insertion. Once a Cardbus card is detected, it must be configured and the second phase of the bridge configuration must be performed so that it can pass memory and I/O transaction to and from the card, and steer interrupts. This section describes how configuration transactions are performed both to a PCI-to-CardBus bridge and to a CardBus card.

Generating Configuration Transactions

As with any other PCI device, a CardBus-to-PCI bridge permits the implementation of up to 64 doublewords (256 bytes) of configuration registers. Furthermore, each function within a CardBus card also implements up to 64 doublewords of configuration registers.

Due to the small size of the I/O space addressable by x86-compatible processors (64KB of I/O space), it's not feasible to map all of the configuration registers found within PCI devices directly into the host processor's I/O address space. The designer could implement the configuration registers within the processor's memory space, but this approach consumes a considerable amount of memory space (for example, a combination of twenty-five PCI and/or CardBus functions would require 6KB of space). The amount of memory space consumed aside, the address range utilized would be unavailable for allocation to regular memory. This would limit the system's flexibility when the mapping actual memory.

The PCI and CardBus specifications require that the system board logic must provide a specific method that permits the host processor to initiate configuration transactions. In a PC-compatible platform, this method is referred to as configuration mechanism one. Another mechanism used in earlier systems is called configuration mechanism two and is not discussed in this book. Configuration mechanism two is included in the PCI specification to support backwards compatibility. Refer to MindShare's *PCI System Architecture* book, published by Addison-Wesley, for details about configuration mechanism two.

Configuration Mechanism One

Configuration mechanism one utilizes two 32-bit I/O ports located at addresses 0CF8h and 0CFCh to initiate a configuration read or write transaction. These two ports are:

- 32-bit **configuration address port**, occupying I/O addresses 0CF8h through 0CFBh.
- 32-bit **configuration data port**, occupying I/O addresses 0CFCh through 0CFFh.

Accessing a PCI function's configuration port is a two step process:

1. Write the bus number, physical device number, function number and dword number to the configuration address port.
2. Perform an I/O read from or an write to the configuration data port.

Configuration Address Port

The configuration address port only latches information when the host processor performs a full 32-bit write to the port. A 32-bit read from the port returns its contents. The assertion of reset clears the port to all zeros. Any 8- or 16-bit access within this I/O doubleword is passed directly onto the PCI bus as an 8- or 16-bit PCI I/O access. The 32-bits of information written to the configuration address port must adhere to the template illustrated in Figure 16-1.

Figure 16-1: Contents of Configuration Address Port (0CF8h)

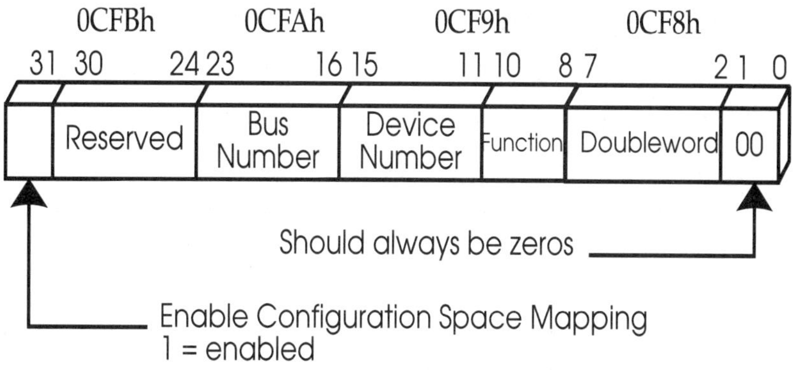

- bits [1:0] are reserved and must be zeros.
- bits [7:2] identify the target doubleword (one of 64) within the target function's configuration space.
- bits [10:8] identify the target function number (one of eight) within the target physical PCI device.
- bits [15:11] identify the target physical PCI device number (one of thirty-two).
- bits [23:16] identifies the target PCI bus number (one of 256).
- bits [30:24] are reserved and must be zero.
- bit 31 must be set to a one, enabling the translation of a subsequent host bus I/O access to the configuration data port into a configuration access on the PCI bus. If bit 31 is zero and the processor initiates an I/O read from or write to the configuration data port, the transaction is passed through to the PCI bus as a PCI I/O transaction.

Host/PCI Bridge Operation

A configuration transaction is performed by the host/PCI or host/CardBus bridge when the configuration data port is either read from or written to following a valid write to the configuration address port.

The host/PCI bridge performs a configuration read or write when it latches a valid PCI address into its configuration address port and then detects a subsequent access to its configuration data port. A valid address means that the address written to the configuration address port is targeted to a bus residing on the other side of the bridge and that the configuration enable bit (bit 31) is set.

To determine whether the target bus resides downstream from the host/PCI bridge, it implements configuration registers that specify its bus number and a subordinate bus number (highest number bus downstream). The bus number and subordinate bus number registers define the range of buses that reside downstream from the host/PCI bridge. In other words, bus numbers must be assigned sequentially going downstream from the processor.

If bit 31 in the configuration address port (see Figure 16-1 on page 239) is enabled, the bridge compares the target bus number to the range of buses that exists beyond the bridge. If the target bus is the same as the value in the bus number register, the programmer wishes to perform a configuration transaction on the bridge's PCI bus. A subsequent I/O read from or write to the bridge's configuration data port at 0CFCh causes the bridge to generate a type zero configuration read or write transaction. When the devices residing on a PCI bus detect a type zero configuration transaction in progress, this informs them that one of them is the target device.

When the target bus specified in the configuration address port does not compare with the value in its bus number register, but is equal to or less than the value in the bridge's subordinate bus number register, the bridge converts the subsequent access to the configuration data port into a type one configuration transaction on its PCI bus. When devices that reside on a PCI bus detect a type one configuration access in progress, they ignore the transaction. The only devices on that pay attention to the transaction are PCI-to-PCI or Cardbus bridges. Each of them must determine if the target bus number is within the range of PCI buses that reside beneath them. If the target bus is not within range, then a PCI-to-PCI or CardBus bridge ignores the type one access. If it's in range, the access is passed through the PCI-to-PCI or CardBus bridge as either a type zero (if the target bus compares to the bridge's bus number register) or a type one (the target bus number is equal to or less than the value in the bridge's subordinate bus number register) transaction.

Type zero and type one configuration accesses are covered in detail in subsequent sections in this chapter.

Type 0 PCI Configuration Transaction

The following discussion presumes that a PCI-to-CardBus bridge resides on a PCI bus. During the configuration process, PCI configuration software scans the PCI bus to detect devices. To simplify the discussion, assume that the CardBus bridge is device one on the PCI bus and that PCI configuration software is initiating a configuration read to function zero (socket zero interface) of the bridge.

Initiating PCI Configuration Transaction

The configuration transaction is initiated by PCI configuration software by writing to the configuration address port at I/O location 0CF8h. In this example, the address consists of:

- Bits 1:0 = Reserved (00b)
- Bits 7:2 = Dword number (000000b)
- Bits 10:8 = Function number (000b)
- Bits 15:11 = Device number (00001b)
- Bits 23:16 = Bus number (00000000b)
- Bit 31 = Configuration enable (1b)

The host/PCI bridge latches the address into the address port. Since bit 31 is set to one and the target bus number compares to the bridge's PCI bus number (or is equal to or less than the value in the bridge's subordinate bus number register), the bridge is enabled to convert a subsequent host access to its configuration data port into a PCI configuration access. The host processor then initiates an I/O read transaction to the configuration data port at 0CFCh. This is either a one, two, or four byte access (indicated by the processor's byte enable signals; or, if a PowerPC PREP environment, by A[29:31] and TSIZ[0:2]). This stimulates the bridge to arbitrate for ownership of the PCI bus and to perform a configuration read (since the processor is reading from the configuration data port). Because the target bus is the one directly on the other side of the bridge, a type zero configuration read is initiated. The bridge decodes the device number (bits 15:11 in the configuration address port) and asserts the corresponding IDSEL

(IDSEL1) pin. Figure 16-2 on page 242 illustrates the configuration registers within the host bridge and the contents of the AD bus during the address space. The following section details the address phase of a type zero configuration read transaction.

Figure 16-2: Example Type Zero Configuration Read Transaction from CardBus Bridge

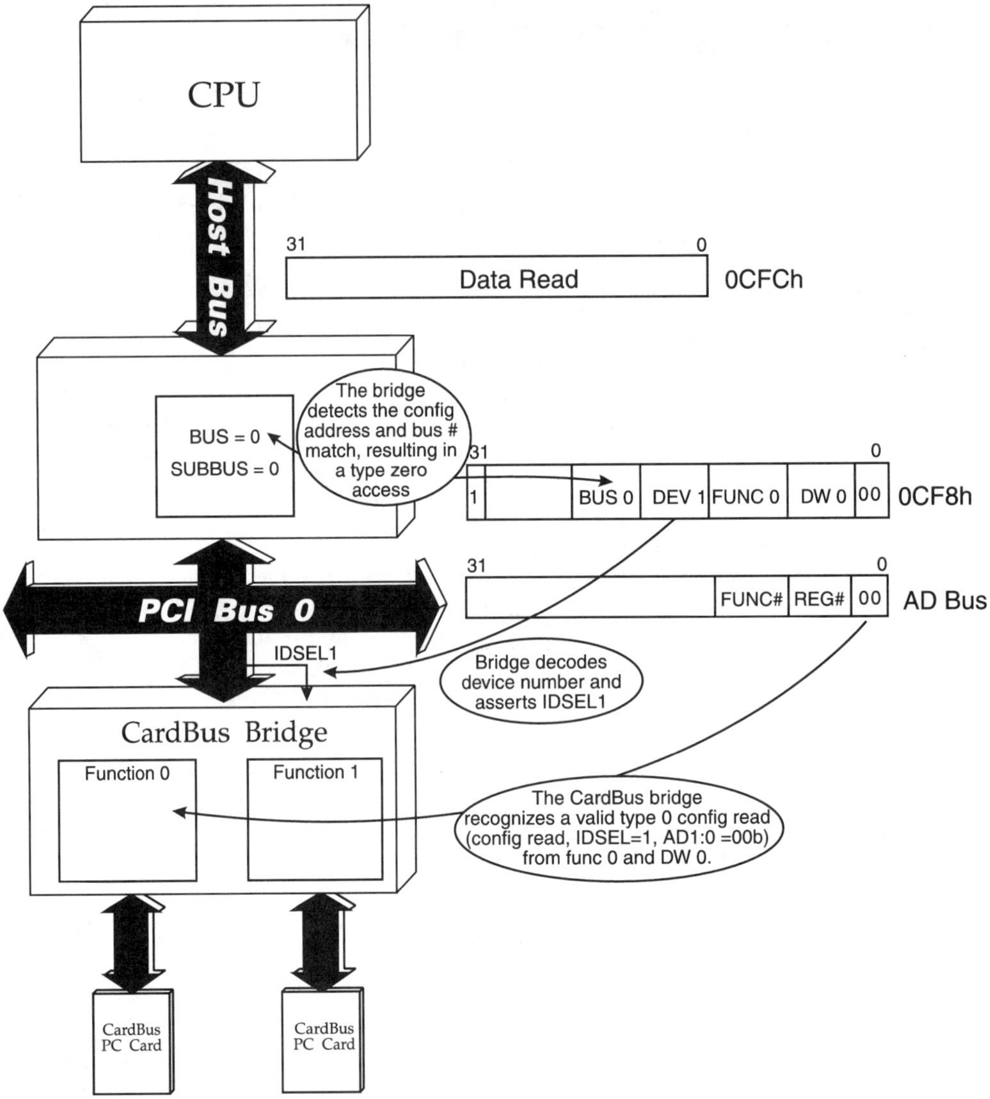

Address Phase

During a PCI configuration transaction, all PCI devices on the bus latch the following information at the end of the address phase:

- The contents of the AD bus.
- The state of the FRAME# signal (asserted, indicating that a valid address and command have been latched from the bus).
- The state of the IDSEL signal (the physical device that samples its IDSEL asserted is the target physical device).
- The command on CC/BE[3:0]# indicates that this is a configuration read or write transaction. The command type is derived from the type of access the host processor is performing with the host/PCI bridge's configuration data port. An I/O read converts to a configuration read and an I/O write converts to a configuration write.

00b on AD[1:0] indicates that this is a type zero configuration transaction targeting one of the devices on this PCI bus. When this is the case, the physical device that samples its IDSEL asserted is the target device. The AD bus information presented during a type zero configuration transaction indicates the following:

- AD[1:0] are 00b, indicating that this is a type zero transaction targeting one of the devices on this bus.
- AD[7:2] indicates the target configuration doubleword.
- AD[10:8] indicates the target function within the physical package.
- AD[31:11] are reserved and are not interpreted by any devices.

The target physical device number specified in bits [15:11] in the configuration address port are decoded and are used to assert one of the bridge's IDSEL output signal lines. The bridge implements a separate IDSEL output for each physical package on the PCI bus, including one for each PCI expansion connector. Assertion of a specific IDSEL during the address phase of a type zero configuration access selects the physical package that is the target of the configuration access.

Implementation of IDSEL

The IDSEL outputs can be implemented in one of two ways by the bridge designer:

- The upper twenty-one address lines, AD[31:11], are not used during the address phase of a type zero configuration access. The system board designer is therefore free to use these signal lines as IDSEL signals to the various physical PCI packages (up to twenty-one of them). Internally, the bridge decodes the target physical number contained in configuration address port bits [15:11] to select which AD line to set to one. Each of these address lines is connected to the IDSEL input of a separate physical PCI package. Because of the PCI rule that there can only be one load placed on each signal line by a PCI device, the package's IDSEL pin is resistively-coupled to the appropriate AD pin at the package position on the system board. As an example, AD11 could be set to one if the target physical device is device zero (the first PCI device); AD12 set to one if the target physical device is device one, etc. This method saves pins on the bridge and traces on the system board. There isn't a danger of a device misinterpreting the information on the upper part of the address (AD[31:11) because no devices look at those address bits during a type zero configuration access.

- The bridge designer can decode bits [15:11] (target physical device number) in the configuration address port and assert the target physical package's IDSEL signal line. This method requires the implementation of a separate IDSEL output pin on the bridge for each physical package on the PCI bus and a separate, point-to-point IDSEL trace on the system board between the bridge and each physical PCI package or connector.

As an example implementation approach, the PCI specification suggests the following. The bridge internally decodes the device number field in the configuration address port and selects an IDSEL signal to assert. Rather than implementing IDSEL output pins, the IDSEL signals internal to the bridge can be directed to AD[31:16] in the following manner:

- The IDSEL associated with device 0 is connected to AD16.
- The IDSEL associated with device 1 is connected to AD17.
- The IDSEL associated with device 2 is connected to AD18, etc.
- The IDSEL associated with device 15 is connected to AD31.

In this example, for devices 16 through 31, none of the upper AD lines should be asserted when the type 0 configuration transaction is performed. Since no device detects its IDSEL asserted, none respond, resulting in a master abort by the bridge.

This approach supports the implementation of 16 devices on a PCI bus.

Data Phase

As the data phase is entered, the state of the host processor's byte enables (assuming that it's an x86 processor) is copied onto the PCI C/BE# bus. The host processor byte enables are set to one of the following patterns:

- BE0# asserted indicates a one byte transfer over the lower data path with byte zero in the selected configuration doubleword.
- BE0# and BE1# asserted indicates a two byte transfer over the lower two data paths with bytes zero and one in the selected configuration doubleword.
- BE0#, BE1#, BE2# and BE3# asserted indicates a four byte transfer over all four data paths with bytes zero through three in the selected doubleword.

As the data phase is entered, the PCI devices are performing the address decode to determine which of them is the target of the transaction. Devices that sampled their IDSEL inputs deasserted at the end of the address phase ignore the transaction. The physical device that samples its IDSEL asserted decodes the target function number presented on AD[10:8] to determine if the target function exists within the package. In this example, the CardBus bridge samples its IDSEL pin asserted and determines that function zero is being accessed. Since function zero is implemented within the CardBus bridge, the bridge then asserts DEVSEL# to claim the transaction. The CardBus bridge then drives the requested bytes from dword zero of function zero to the AD bus and asserts TRDY#. The remainder of the transaction is no different from any PCI read transaction.

Type Zero Configuration Transaction Examples

The type zero configuration access is used to access the configuration registers of a PCI device on the same PCI bus on which the access is performed.

During the address phase of the transaction, the bridge places the configuration address information on the AD bus and the configuration command on the C/BE# bus. Figure 16-2 on page 242 illustrates the contents of the AD bus during the address phase of the type zero configuration access. Figure 16-3 on page 246 and Figure 16-4 on page 247 are timing diagrams of type zero read and write configuration accesses.

Figure 16-3: The Type Zero Configuration Read Access

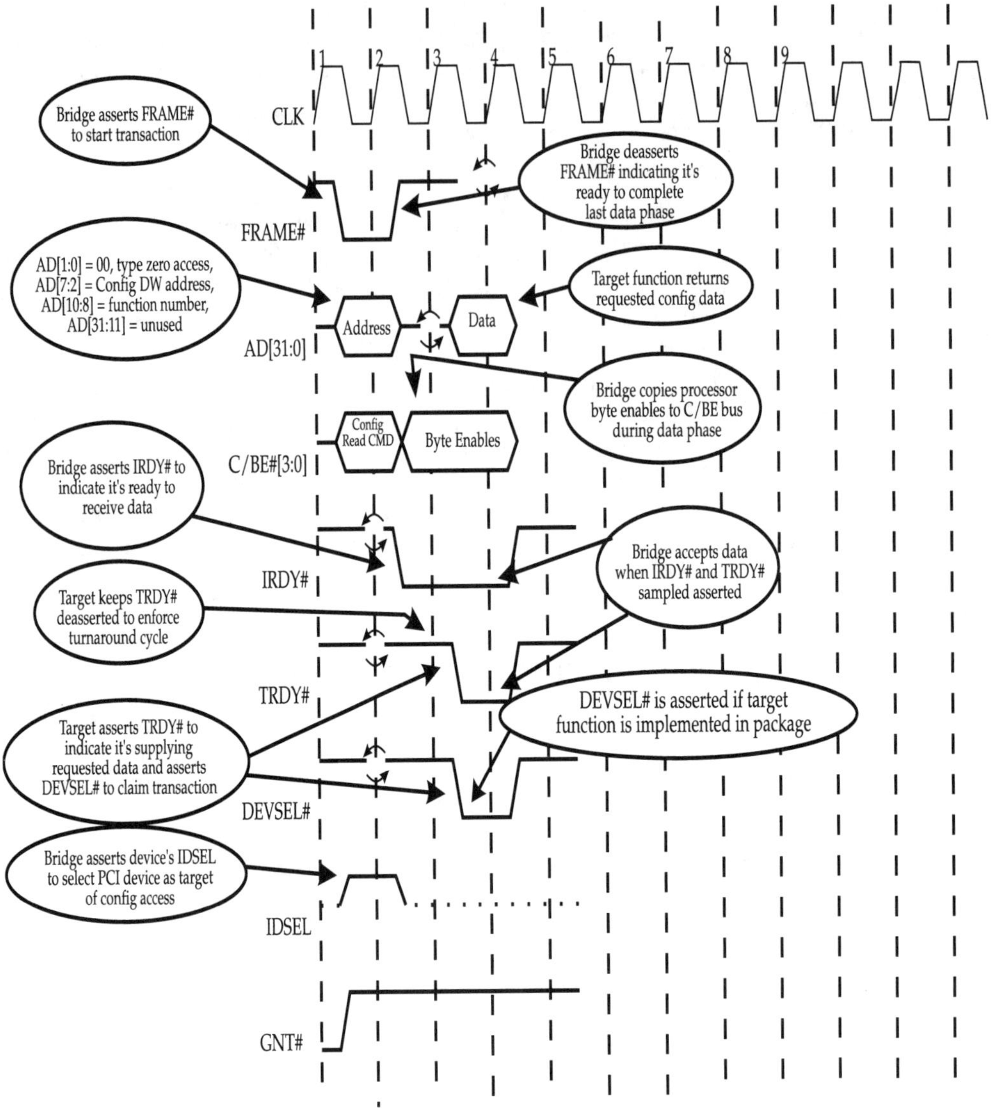

To be selected as the target of a configuration access, a PCI device must sample its device-specific IDSEL input asserted by the bridge during the address phase and detect that a type zero configuration access (AD[1:0] set to 00b) is being performed. If its IDSEL is not asserted or if AD[1:0] are not set to 00b, the device should ignore the access.

Assuming that both of these conditions are met, address bits AD[10:8] are used to select one of eight functions within the physical device. If the target function is implemented in the device, it asserts DEVSEL# (during the data phase) to claim the transaction. Address bits AD[7:2] are used to select one of sixty-four configuration doublewords within the target function's configuration space. The command on the C/BE bus during the address phase identifies it as a configuration read or write. During the data phase, the four byte enables, C/BE#[3:0], are used to select the bytes within the currently-addressed configuration doubleword. The byte enables are copied from the byte enables placed on the host bus by the processor when it initiated its read or write transaction. The data to be transferred between the bridge and the target configuration location(s) is transferred during the data phase.

Figure 16-4: The Type Zero Configuration Write Access

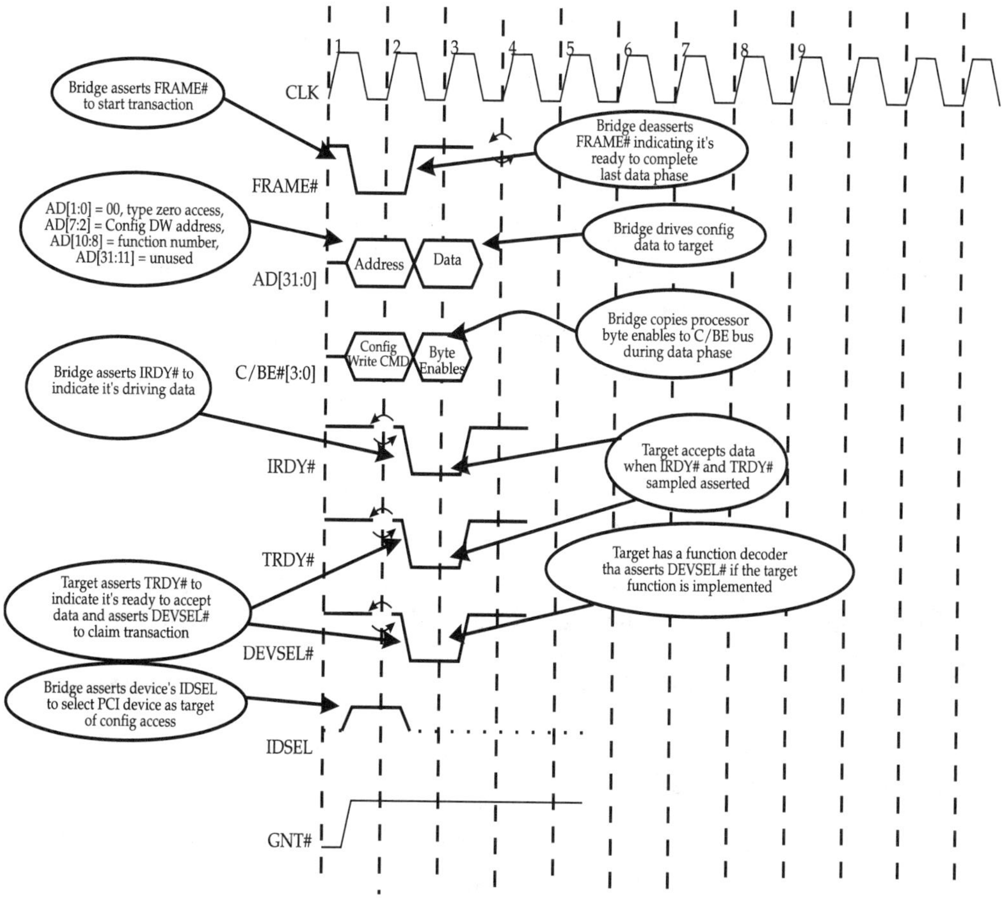

Configuration Burst Transactions

Although virtually all configuration transactions today are single data phase transactions, the specification permits burst configuration transactions. Linear addressing is implied in a multiple data phase configuration burst transaction. As each data phase completes and the next begins, the target device increments the configuration doubleword address in its address counter by four and then examines the byte enables to determine which bytes within the currently-addressed configuration doubleword are to be transferred.

CardBus Configuration Transactions

Once the CardBus bridge has been initially configured, the bridge's socket interface registers can be read by PCMCIA software to determine if a card is installed in a PC Card socket. At this point, the CardBus bridge has the ability to generate status change interrupts to notify CS that a PC Card has been inserted into a socket.

When CS detects that a CardBus card is inserted into a socket, it calls the client driver, notifying it that a card is present. The client driver, in turn, calls CS to request information about the card. These requests require CS and SS to access the card's CIS. CS must perform a configuration read transaction to obtain the contents of the CIS pointer register, which specifies the location of the CIS. Since CardBus cards do not reside on PCI bus zero, CS must use the bus number assigned to the CardBus socket in order to access the card's configuration address space.

A type one configuration access (via the PCI bus) must be used to access the configuration address space of devices that reside on the other side of a PCI-to-PCI or PCI-to-CardBus bridge. Type one configuration transactions are performed by the host/PCI bridge when it detects that the target bus number does not match its own bus number, but is within the range of buses downstream from its bus. Prior to performing a type one configuration transfer, bus numbers must be assigned to all buses on the other side of PCI and CardBus bridges.

Assigning Bus Numbers

Figure 16-5 on page 250 illustrates a system containing both a PCI-to-PCI bridge and a CardBus bridge. Notice that each bridge contains a bus number, secondary bus number, and subordinate bus number register. These register are defined as follows:

- **Primary Bus Number** — the immediate bus number "upstream" (toward the processor) from the bridge.
- **Secondary Bus Number or CardBus Number** — the immediate bus number "downstream" (away from the processor) from the bridge.
- **Subordinate Bus Number** — the highest numbered bus residing "downstream" from the bridge.

PCI configuration software is responsible for detecting all PCI-to-PCI bridges and assigning sequential (moving downstream) bus numbers to them. The algorithm software uses to assign bus numbers is not specified by the CardBus spec. PCI configuration software, if aware of CardBus bridges, could easily assign bus numbers to the CardBus sockets after numbering all PCI buses. However, if PCI configuration software is unaware of CardBus bridges, then other configuration software, either the OS or CS, could also be designed to assign the CardBus numbers. Once a bus is assigned a number, configuration read and write transactions to devices residing on the bus can be performed. The following discussion presumes that PCI software is CardBus-aware.

Figure 16-5: Example of PCI-to-PCI and CardBus Numbering

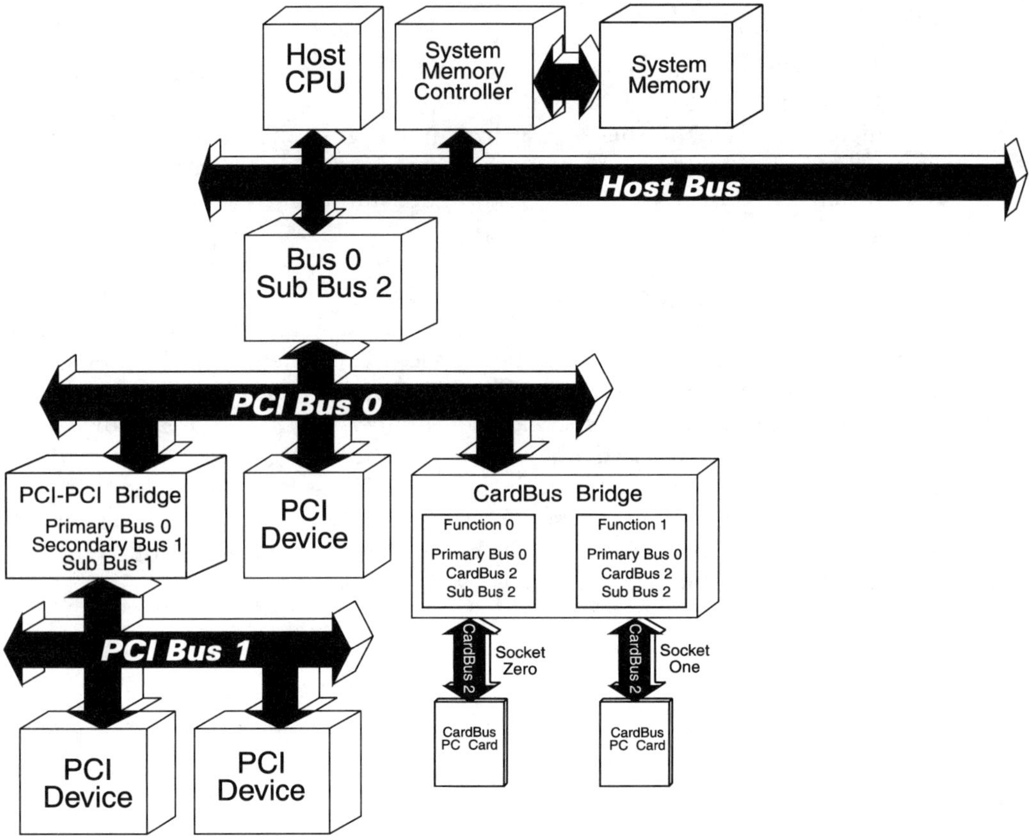

Initiating Type One Configuration Transactions

The configuration transaction is initiated by CS by writing to the configuration address port at I/O location 0CF8h. Assume that CS is attempting a configuration read from the CIS Pointer (dword 10d) of the CardBus card inserted in socket one (as illustrated in Figure 16-5 on page 250). The configuration registers are pictured in Figure 18-1 on page 299. In this example, the address consists of:

- Bits 1:0 = Reserved (00b)
- Bits 7:2 = Dword number 001010b (dword 10d, the CardBus CIS Pointer register)
- Bits 10:8 = Function number 000b
- Bits 15:11 = Device number 00001b (Socket 1)
- Bits 23:16 = Bus number 00000010b (Bus 2)
- Bit 31 = Configuration enabled

Refer to Figure 16-6 on page 252 during the following discussion. The Host/PCI bridge latches the specified address into its configuration address port. Since bit 31 is set to one and the target bus number does not match the bridge's PCI bus number the bridge will not perform a type zero configuration transaction. However, since the target bus number matches the bridge's subordinate bus number register, the bridge is enabled to convert a subsequent host access to its configuration data port into a type one PCI configuration access.

The host processor initiates an I/O read transaction from the configuration data port at 0CFCh. This is either a one, two, or four byte access (indicated by the processor's byte enable signals; or, if a PowerPC 60x processor, by A[29:31] and TSIZ[0:2]). This stimulates the bridge to arbitrate for ownership of the PCI bus and to perform a type one configuration read (since the processor is performing a read from the configuration data port). Since the target device resides on a subordinate bus, the bridge transfers the entire address from the configuration address port to the AD bus. Figure 16-6 on page 252 illustrates the configuration registers within the host bridge and the contents of the AD bus during the address space. The following sections detail the address and data phases of the type one configuration read transaction taking place on PCI bus zero.

Figure 16-6: Example of Configuration Access to CardBus Configuration Register

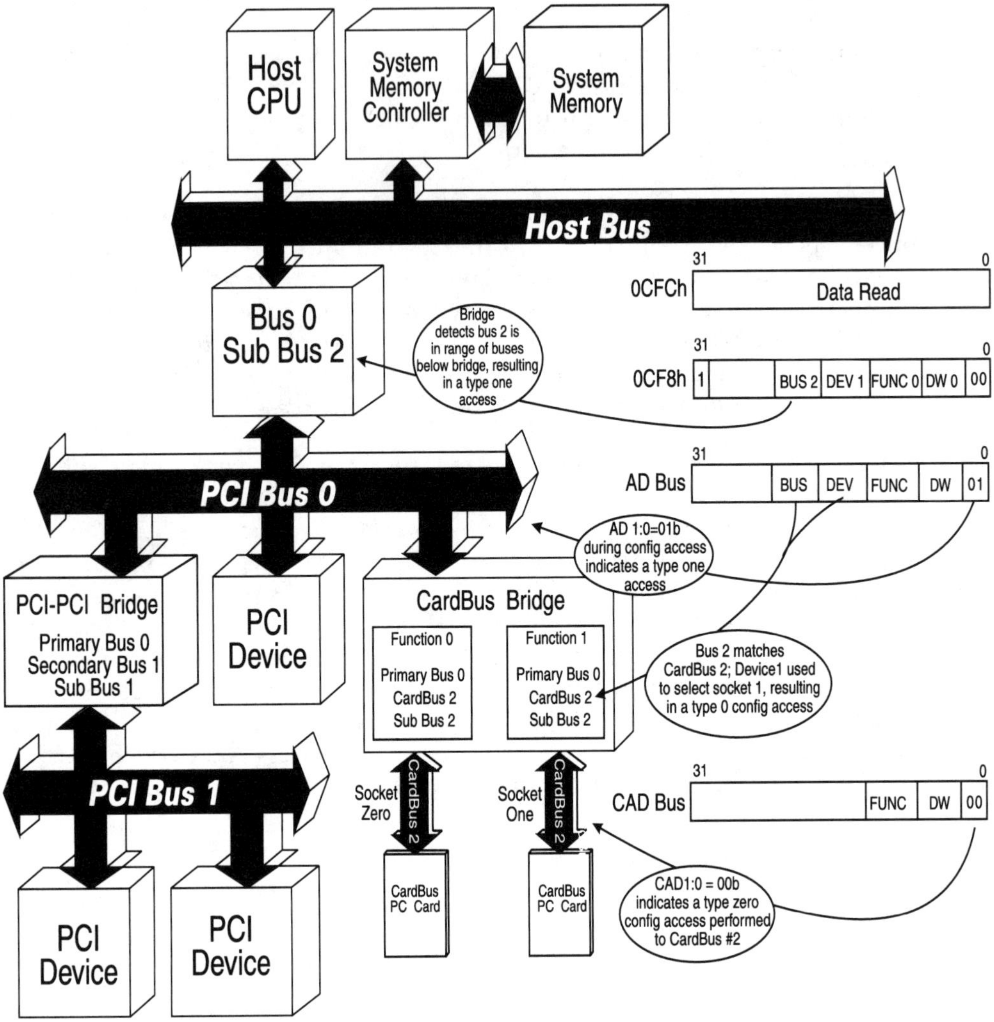

Address Phase

When the host/PCI bridge initiates a configuration access on its PCI bus, it places the configuration address information on the AD bus and the configuration command on the C/BE# bus. Figure 16-7 on page 253 illustrates the contents of the AD bus during a type one configuration transaction.

Figure 16-7: Definition of the AD Bus during a Type One Configuration Transaction

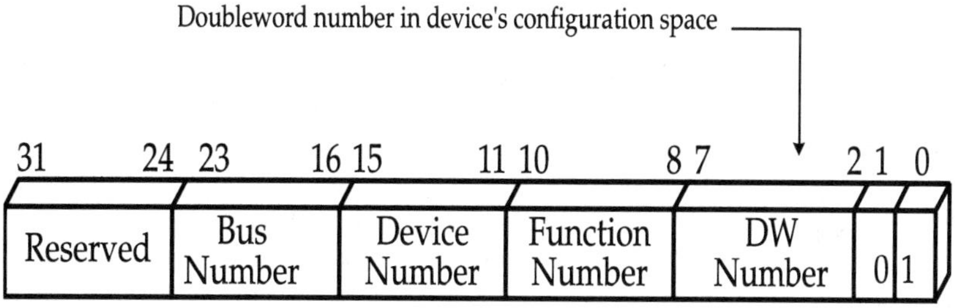

During the address phase of a type one configuration access, the information on the AD bus is formatted as follows:

- AD[1:0] contain a 01b, identifying this as a type one configuration access.
- AD[7:2] identifies one of 64 configuration doublewords within the target device's configuration space.
- AD[10:8] identifies one of eight functions within the target device.
- AD[15:11] identifies one of 32 physical devices. This field is used by a CardBus bridge to identify the target CardBus socket, whereas, PCI-to-PCI bridges use the device number to select which PCI device's IDSEL line to assert.
- AD[23:16] identifies one of 256 CardBus/PCI buses in the system.
- AD[31:24] are reserved and are cleared to zero.

The configuration read or write command is presented on the C/BE bus during the address phase. Type one accesses (defined by AD[1:0] set to 01b) are ignored by all PCI devices except PCI-to-PCI and PCI-to-CardBus bridges. Also, during a type one access, PCI devices ignore the state of their IDSEL inputs.

If the target of a configuration access resides on a CardBus or PCI bus that is subordinate to the bus upon which the configuration access is being run, the PCI-to-CardBus or PCI-to-PCI bridge connecting the two buses must pass the configuration access through to its secondary bus. The transaction must be passed to the secondary bus in one of two forms:

- If the access is for a device residing on the bridge's secondary bus (i.e., the target bus number matches the secondary bus number), the bridge must pass it through as a type zero configuration access.
- If the access is for a device residing on a CardBus or PCI bus that is subordinate to its secondary bus (i.e., the target bus number does not match the secondary bus number, but is within the range of buses defined by the secondary and subordinate bus numbers), the bridge must pass the access through as a type one configuration access.

In the example illustrated in Figure 16-6 on page 252, the PCI-to-PCI bridge recognizes that the target bus number does not match its secondary bus number, nor does the target bus reside downstream (i.e., the bus number is outside the range defined by the secondary and subordinate bus numbers), and therefore ignores the transaction. However, the CardBus bridge recognizes that the target bus number matches its secondary bus number (i.e., its CardBus number), thus one of its CardBus cards is the target device. The CardBus bridge determines the target CardBus card by decoding the device number. Since the device number is one, the CardBus card in socket one is the target of the transaction and a type zero configuration read transaction must be performed by the PCI-to-CardBus bridge on the socket one interface.

Data Phase

Since the configuration register being targeted does not reside within the CardBus bridge itself, it performs a type zero configuration access to the target CardBus card to read the configuration register. The bridge will issue a retry to the host/PCI bridge if the data will not be available within 16 PCI clocks (PCI 2.1 spec rule).

If however, the CardBus bridge recognizes that the first data item can be returned to bus zero within 16 PCI clock cycles from the assertion of FRAME# then the CardBus bridge keeps TRDY# deasserted until the contents of the target register is returned from the CardBus card's configuration register.

Figure 16-8 on page 255 and Figure 16-9 on page 256 illustrate the timing of type one configuration read and write transactions respectively.

Figure 16-8: Type One Configuration Read Transaction

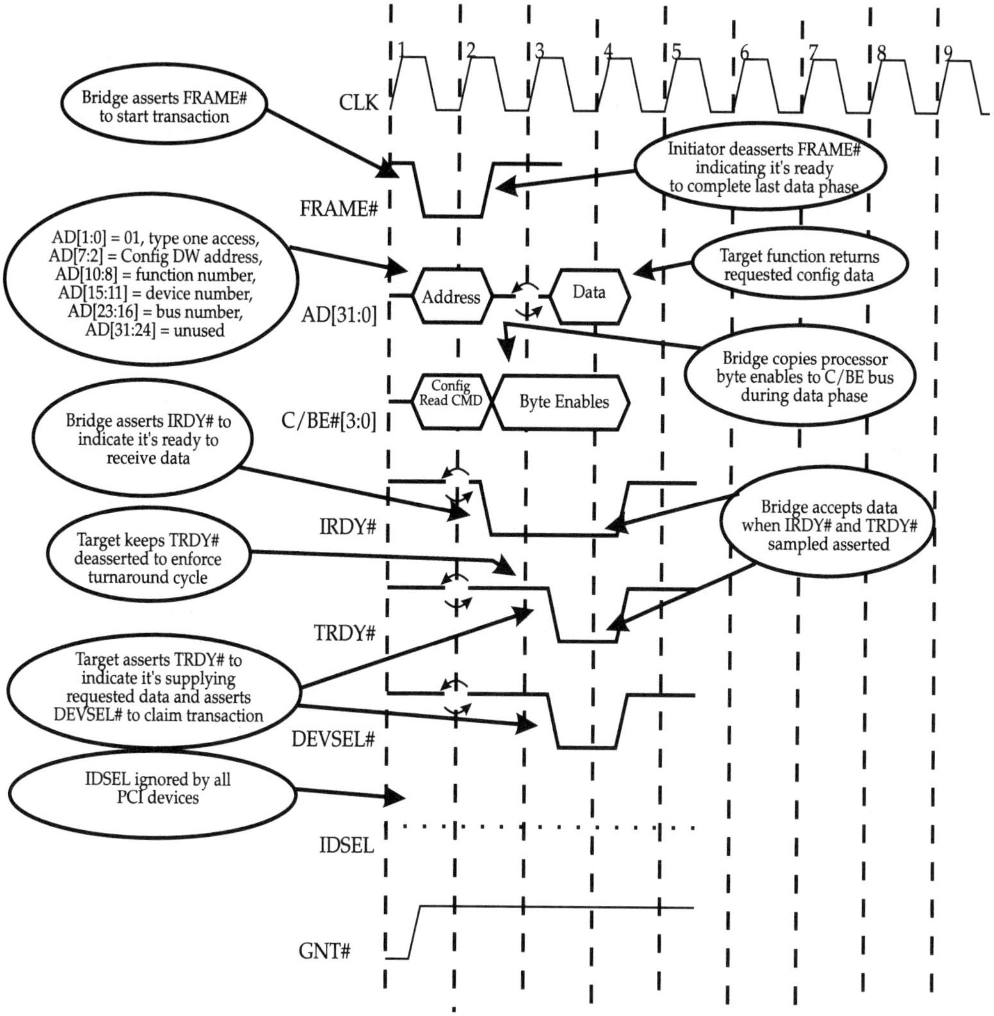

Figure 16-9: Type One Configuration Write Transaction

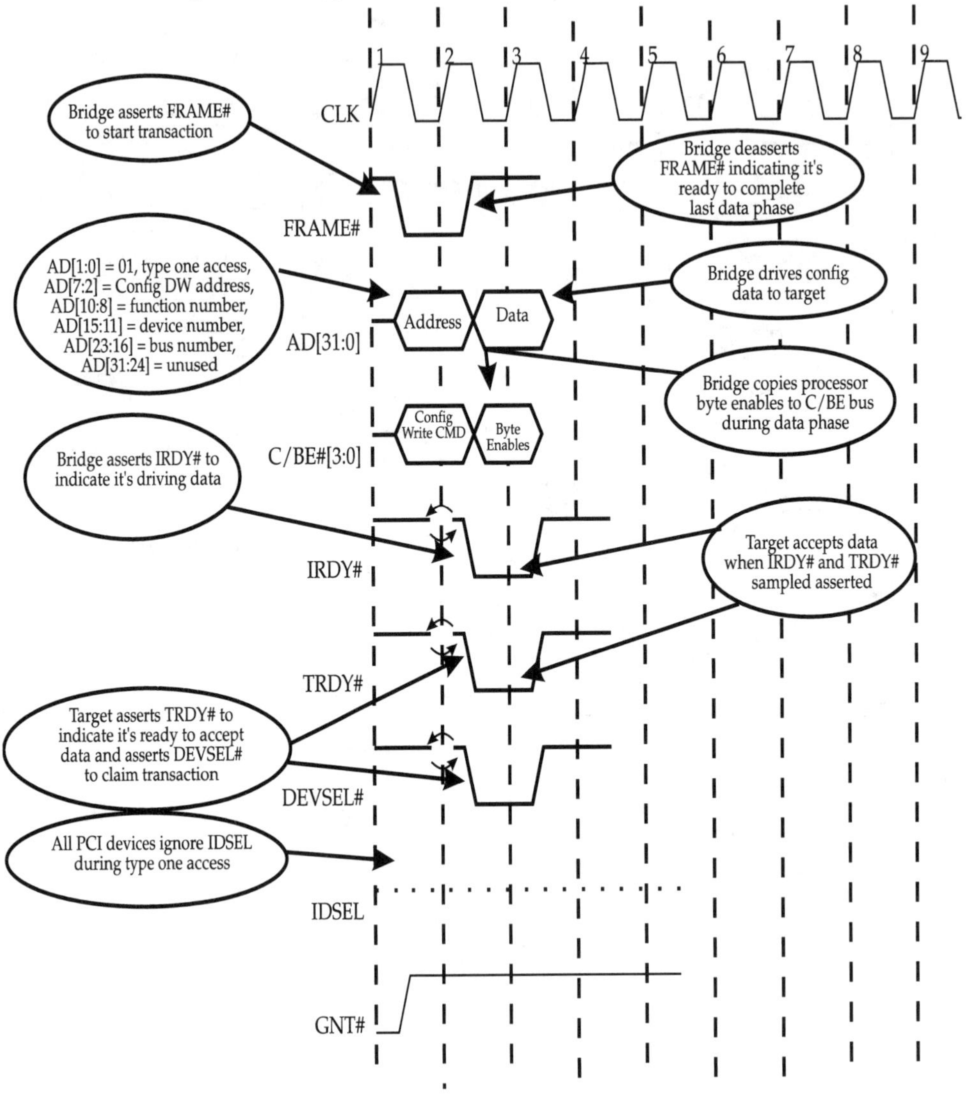

CardBus Type Zero Configuration Transaction

When the CardBus bridge detects that the configuration register being targeted resides within the CardBus card in socket 1 (i.e., the target bus number matches the CardBus bridge's secondary bus number), it begins a type zero configuration transaction via the CardBus interface to socket one. Refer to Figure 16-6 on page 252 during the following discussion.

Address Phase

The contents of the CAD bus during the CardBus type zero configuration transaction is as follows:

- CAD[1:0] contain a 00b, identifying this as a type zero configuration access.
- AD[7:2] contain 001010b, specifying the target register.
- AD[10:8] contain 000b, identifying function zero within the target device.
- AD[31:11] are reserved.

The device number field latched from the PCI AD bus is used by the CardBus bridge to select the socket interface being targeted (note that a PCI-to-PCI bridge uses the device number to generate IDSEL, which identifies the target device residing on its secondary bus. IDSEL is not needed for CardBus since only one physical device resides in a CardBus socket).

Data Phase

During the data phase the target register is accessed and passed via the CardBus bridge to PCI bus zero and on to the processor.

Figure 16-10 and Figure 16-11 on page 259 illustrate CardBus type zero configuration read and write transactions, respectively.

Figure 16-10: CardBus Type Zero Configuration Read Transaction

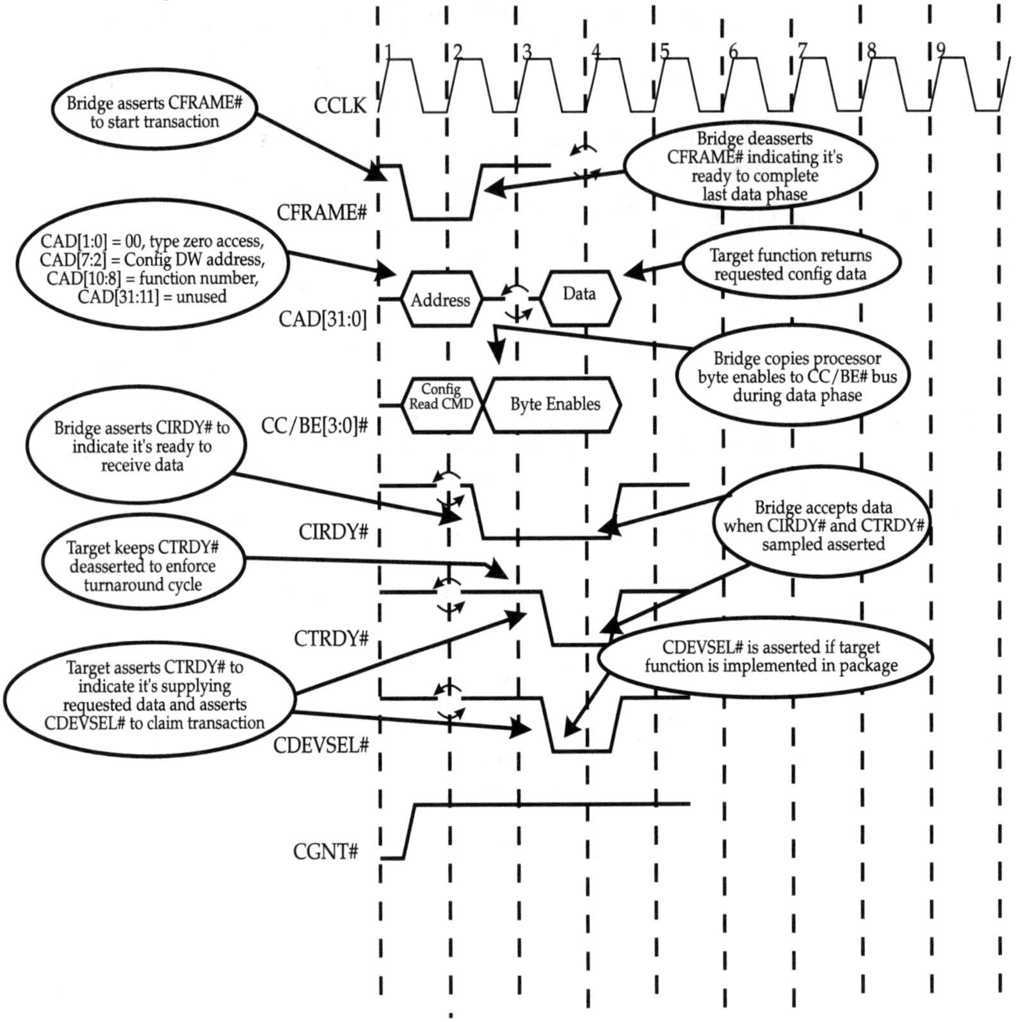

Figure 16-11: CardBus Configuration Write Transaction

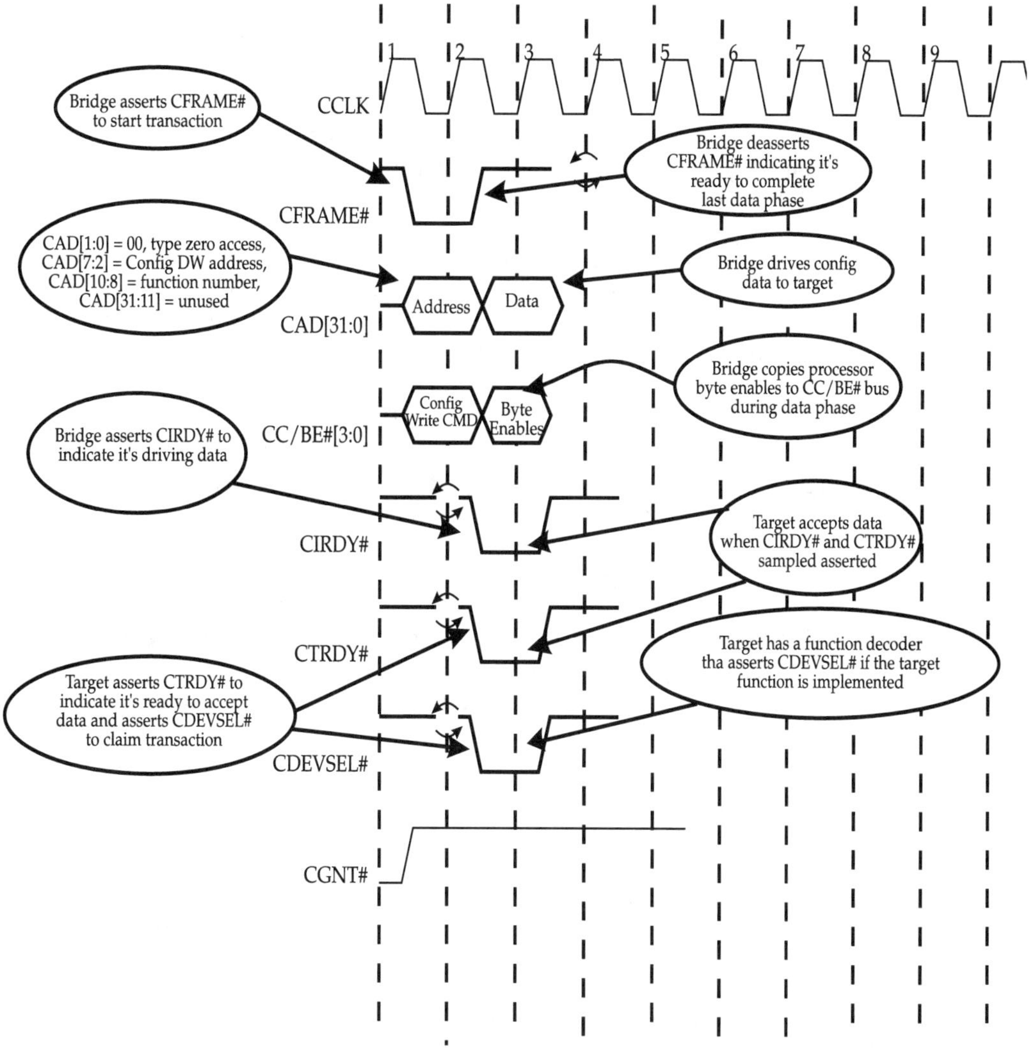

CardBus Cards Implemented as Bridges

When a CardBus card is implemented as a CardBus-to-CardBus bridge or a CardBus-to-PCI bridge, devices residing below the CardBus bridge implemented on the card must also be configured by accessing their configuration registers. This necessitates that a type one configuration transaction be performed over the CardBus interface. In such cases, the bus number field will not match the socket's CardBus number, but will be within the range of buses that are subordinate to the Cardbus interface.

During type one configuration transfers presented on the socket interface, the entire address on the socket's CAD[31:0] bus must be passed directly through to the secondary bus, CAD[31:0]. This results in the PCI type one transfer being passed to the CardBus interface as a type one transfer.

Note that in the previous discussions it was assumed that each socket was assigned the same CardBus number. This means that a configuration one transaction is targeted to both sockets and both would see the type one configuration transaction. Since type one configuration transactions are intended for bridge devices only, a CardBus card that is not a bridge device will ignore the transaction. A CardBus-to-CardBus or CardBus-to-PCI Bridge residing in the socket must determine if its CardBus number matches the target address or falls within the range of buses specified by the secondary and the subordinate bus registers. If the target bus is downstream, it performs either a type zero or type one configuration transaction over its secondary CardBus interface. If the bus numbers do not match, the bridge ignores the transaction.

Some implementations may choose to assign separate CardBus numbers to each socket. In this case, the PCI-to-CardBus bridge will direct the configuration one transaction only to the CardBus socket targeted by the bus number.

Special Cycle Generation

When a CardBus bridge detects a type one configuration access on either side, it must check the bus number, device number, function number and dword number to determine if it should pass the transaction through the bridge and whether or not to convert it into a special cycle (if the bus on the other side is the target bus). A special cycle request is encoded as a type one configuration write transaction with the following logical address:

- Target device number = 1Fh
- Function number = 7h
- Dword number = 0h

The message is received as the data during the data phase of the type one configuration write.

17 CardBus Bridge Configuration Registers

The Previous Chapter

The previous chapter defined the configuration transactions use to configure the CardBus bridge and CardBus card(s). It also described both type zero and type one configuration transfers.

This Chapter

This chapter defines the CardBus bridge's configuration registers and socket interface initialization.

The Next Chapter

The next chapter defines the configuration registers implemented in CardBus cards. It also describes the methods used by PCMCIA configuration software to configure a CardBus card.

Introduction

This chapter provides a detailed discussion of the configuration registers within a PCI-to-CardBus bridge. A bridge that implements one socket implements it as socket zero. One with two sockets implements them as functions zero and one. A bridge may implement up to eight sockets, each of which is implemented as a separate function within the bridge. Each function (i.e., socket interface) has its own set of configuration registers, adhering to the CardBus bridge header format (illustrated in Figure 17-1 on page 263).

The CardBus bridge's configuration header format was defined by an industry group known as Yenta (Yiddish for "matchmaker"). The Yenta group submitted the format to the PCI SIG for approval and inclusion in the PCI spec, but, as of this writing, it has not yet been officially approved. The authors have no doubt that it will be, however, because a number of major vendors have already completed their designs and gone to silicon.

The rev 2.1 PCI spec currently defines two configuration header types:

- Header type zero for all devices other than PCI-to-PCI bridges
- Header type one for PCI-to-PCI bridges

The CardBus bridge implements header type two (pictured in figure Figure 17-1 on page 263). The CardBus configuration header is used to set up the socket interface, and consists of the following elements:

- A configuration register that assigns an address range to the socket's interface registers (i.e., Socket Event, Socket Mask, Present State, Socket Force Event, and Socket Control).
- A configuration register used to route the status change interrupt.
- Configuration registers used to specify the range of IO addresses mapped to the PC Card installed into the socket. The PC Card Standard requires the ability to assign two separate IO ranges to each socket.
- Configuration registers used to specify the range of memory addresses mapped to the PC Card installed into the socket. The PC Card Standard requires the ability to assign two separate memory to each socket.
- Configuration registers used to route the function-specific interrupt (CINT#).
- Configuration registers used to assign space to implementation-specific registers associated with the socket.

As discussed in the preceding chapters, configuring the CardBus bridge is performed in two phases:

1. Initializing the socket interface (i.e., configuring the socket in preparation for detecting and powering a PC Card when it is installed).
2. Configuring the socket interface to pass (or block) transactions between the CardBus card and the PCI bus and to steer the function-specific interrupt.

This chapter provides a detailed description of the methods utilized by PCI configuration software to initialize the socket, as well as the methods used by the configuration software to program the socket's decoders to recognize its assigned memory and IO address ranges.

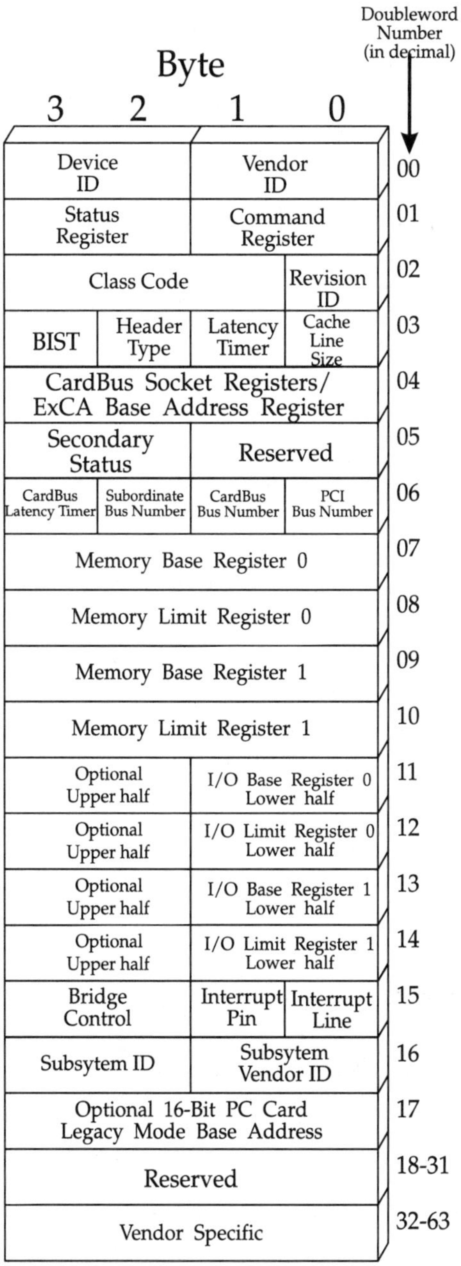

Figure 17-1: PCI-to-CardBus Bridge's Configuration Registers

Header Type Register

Required. Location in header: byte two (the least-significant byte in the doubleword is zero and the most-significant is three) within doubleword three of the bridge's configuration space. The register is illustrated in Figure 17-2. If the bridge supports more than one socket or contains other functions in addition to the bridge function, bit seven is hardwired to one; otherwise, bit seven is hardwired to zero. Yenta has defined a PCI-to-CardBus bridge header type of two. (i.e., the header type field is hardwired to 000010b, or 02h). This indicates that doublewords 4 through 16 are structured according to the header type two definition.

Figure 17-2: Header Type Register

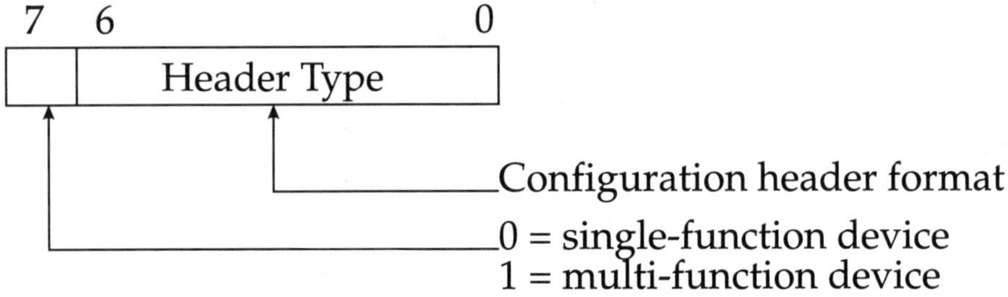

Registers Related to Device ID

There are six registers associated with device identification. They are:

- Vendor ID register
- Device ID register
- Revision ID register
- Class code register
- Subsystem Vendor ID register
- Subsystem ID registers

The sections that follow describe these registers.

Vendor ID Register

Required. Location in header: bytes zero and one in doubleword zero. This 16-bit register contains the hardwired vendor ID and is implemented exactly the same as it is for any PCI device. The vendor ID is assigned by the PCI SIG and is guaranteed to be mutually-exclusive from the IDs issued to other vendors. In combination with the device and revision ID, the vendor ID register can be used by a device driver to "discover" an instance of its associated device. The vendor ID of FFFFh is reserved and is not used. This is the value returned during a configuration read from a non-existent PCI device (returned to the host processor when the host/PCI bridge experiences a master abort due to no reply).

Device ID Register

Required. Location in header: bytes two and three in doubleword zero. The 16-bit device ID register is hardwired with a value chosen by the device vendor.

Revision ID Register

Required. Location in header: byte zero in doubleword two. The 8-bit revision ID register contains the device's hardwired revision number.

Class Code Register

Required. Location in header: bytes one, two and three in doubleword two. The class code register is pictured in Figure 17-3. It is a 24-bit, read-only register divided into three sub-registers: base class, sub-class, and programming interface. It identifies the basic function of the device (e.g., a bridge), a more specific device sub-class (e.g., CardBus), and, in some cases, a register-specific programming interface. The MindShare book entitled *PCI System Architecture* (Addison-Wesley) contains a complete listing of the class codes (note that the class codes are defined by the PCI spec).

The values specified for a PCI-to-CardBus bridge are:

- class code = 06h (bridge)
- sub-class = 07h (PCI-to-CardBus bridge)
- programmer's interface byte = 00h (no special requirements)

Figure 17-3: Class Code Register

23 16	15 8	7 0
Class Code	Sub-Class Code	Prog. I/F

Subsystem ID and Vendor ID and Registers

Optional. A CardBus bridge may be implemented on a PCI expansion card or be embedded within another subsystem. Two cards or subsystems that embed the same PCI CardBus bridge chip would have the same vendor and device IDs. These two optional registers are used to uniquely identify the add-in card or subsystem that the function resides within. Software can then distinguish the difference between cards or subsystems manufactured by different vendors that use the same bridge chip. The subsystem vendor ID is obtained from the SIG, while the vendor supplies its own subsystem ID. A value of zero in these registers indicates there is no subsystem vendor and subsystem ID associated with the device.

Bus Number Registers

Required. Each PCI-to-CardBus bridge interface must implement three bus number registers. All of them are read/writable and are cleared to zero by reset. During configuration, the configuration software initializes these three registers. They are:

- Primary bus number register.
- Secondary bus number register (aka CardBus number register).
- Subordinate bus number register.

The combination of the secondary and the subordinate bus number registers defines the range of buses that exists behind the socket interface. This information is used by the bridge to determine whether or not to pass type one configuration transactions through to the socket interface's CardBus. A type one configuration transaction on the CardBus bridge's primary side may result in one of the following transaction on the secondary (CardBus, or socket, side):

- Type zero configuration reads or write (if target bus number and secondary bus numbers match).
- Type one configuration reads or writes (if the target bus number does not match the secondary bus number, but is within the range defined by the secondary and subordinate bus numbers).
- A special cycle (i.e., a type one configuration write that is to be converted to a special cycle on the target bus).

Primary Bus Number Register

Required. Location in header: byte zero in doubleword six. The primary bus number register is initialized by PCI configuration software with the number of the bridge's bus that is closer to the host processor.

Secondary Bus Number Register

Required. Location in header: byte one in doubleword six. Also known as the CardBus number register, the secondary bus number register is initialized by PCI configuration software with the number of the bridge's bus that is further from the host processor. It could also be thought of as the socket bus number register.

Subordinate Bus Number Register

Required. Location in header: byte two in doubleword six. The subordinate bus number register is initialized by PCI configuration software with the number of the highest-numbered bus accessible via this socket. If there are no CardBus-to-PCI or CardBus-to-CardBus bridges on the secondary bus, the subordinate bus number register is initialized with the same value as the secondary bus number.

Address Decode-Related Registers

The bridge must decode the address for each transaction originating on the PCI bus or on CardBus. It must determine whether the transaction addresses a register internal to the bridge, a device residing on the other side of the bridge, or neither. The bridge must be programmed by PCMCIA software to recognize when to forward and when to block transactions.

Bridge Support for Internal Registers

Required. A PCI-to-CardBus bridge designer must implement the socket status registers and socket control register defined by the PC Card Standard. The designer may also choose to implement a set of internal, device-specific registers that are used to select operational characteristics or check status that is outside the scope of the PC Card Standard and the PCI specification. See Chapter

23, entitled "The TI PCI 1130" for examples of device-specific registers that are used within a CardBus bridge.

CardBus Socket/ExCA Base Address Register

Required. This register points to a block of PCI memory address space assigned to the socket interface registers. The registers mapped into this address space consists of:

- the five CardBus socket interface registers required by the PC Card Standard (i.e. Socket Event, Socket Mask, Present State, Socket Force Event, and Socket Control)
- the ExCA compatible registers that provide legacy support for 16-bit PC Card software.

Figure 17-4 pictures the organization of the CardBus socket/ExCA base address register. Bits 11:0 are hardwired to zero, forcing the start address of the register block to be aligned on 4KB boundaries. The value written into bit positions 31:12 points to the start memory address of the register block.

Figure 17-4: CardBus Socket Registers/ExCA Base Address Register

31 12	11 0
Specifies start address of socket interface register block (aligned on 4KB boundaries)	0 0 0 0 0 0 0 0 0 0 0 0

The location of the registers within the memory block is illustrated in Figure 17-5 on page 269. The offsets shown are specified by the Yenta bridge definition. Note that all socket status registers (CardBus and ExCA) can be accessed at their respective offsets within the memory block. Each CardBus register and the offset that it occupies within the memory block is listed in Table 17-1.

Table 17-1: CardBus Socket Interface Registers and Location

CardBus Socket Register	Offset within Register Block
Socket Event Register	00h
Socket Mask Register	04h
Socket Present State Register	08h
Socket Force Event Register	0Ch

Table 17-1: CardBus Socket Interface Registers and Location (Continued)

CardBus Socket Register	Offset within Register Block
Socket Control Register	10h
Reserved	14-20h

Figure 17-5: Socket Interface Register Mapping

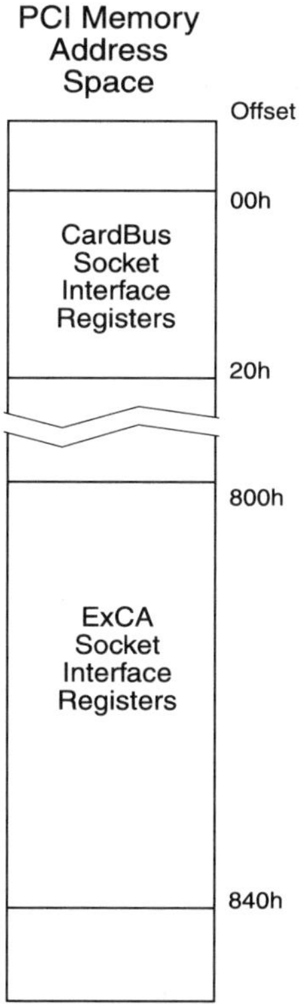

16-Bit PC Card Legacy Mode Base Address Register

Optional. Two ways are provided for accessing the ExCA-compatible registers:

- via the CardBus Socket/ExCA Base Address Register (mapped directly into memory address space); or
- via the 16-bit PC Card Legacy Mode Base Address Register.

Accessing the 16-bit ExCA socket interface registers can be accomplished via the offset from the base address in the CardBus Socket Registers/ExCA Base Address Register as discussed in the previous section. However, some applications and drivers have been designed to access the 16-bit socket interface registers using legacy methods. The legacy method for accessing 16-bit socket interface registers is based on the Intel 82365 PCMCIA host bus adapter (HBA) implementation. The 82365 uses an indexed addressing mechanism, consisting of an address register and a data register. To access a register, the programmer first writes an offset (the index associated with the register to be accessed) to the address register, to select the target register. This is followed by a read from or write to the data register.

Since some legacy software expects to be able access the socket interface registers using this indexing mechanism, Yenta defined a 16-Bit IF (interface) Legacy Mode Base Address register. This register can be programmed with the pointer to the index address register. The index data register is mapped to the location of the index address register location + 1. Figure 17-6 illustrates the socket register mapping and the two access methods for a two socket bridge.

Figure 17-6: ExCA Access Methods

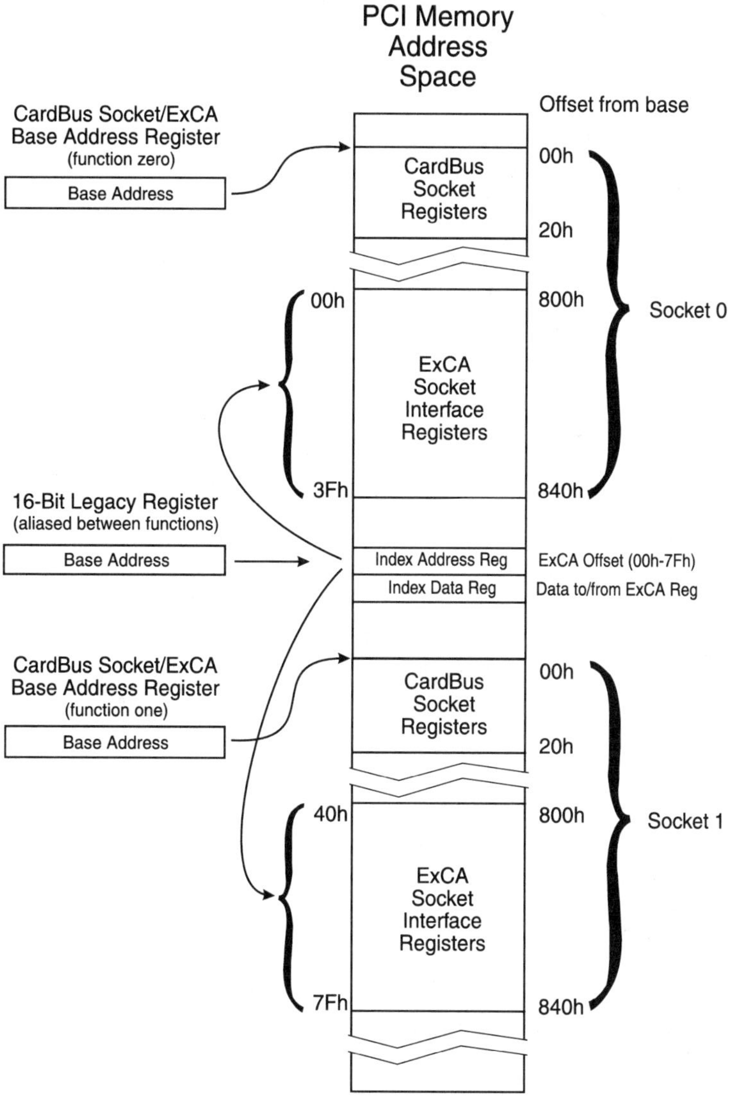

Table 17-2 provides a summary list of the ExCA registers and specifies the offsets at which they can be accessed. The ExCA offset values are the values that must be written to the index address register to access the corresponding registers.

Table 17-2: ExCA Register Summary and Access Offsets

Name	PCI Memory Address Offset	ExCA Offset (Card A)	ExCA Offset (Card B)
Identification and revision register	800	00	40
Interface status register	801	01	41
Power control register	802	02	42
Interrupt and general control register	803	03	43
Card status change register	804	04	44
Card status change interrupt configuration register	805	05	45
Address window enable register	806	06	46
IO window control register	807	07	47
IO window 0 start-address low-byte register	808	08	48
IO window 0 start-address high-byte register	809	09	49
IO window 0 end-address low-byte register	80A	0A	4A
IO window 0 end-address high-byte register	80B	0B	4B
IO window 1 start-address low-byte register	80C	0C	4C
IO window 1 start-address high-byte register	80D	0D	4D
IO window 1 end-address low-byte register	80E	0E	4E
IO window 1 end-address high-byte register	80F	0F	4F
Memory window 0 start-address low-byte register	810	10	50
Memory window 0 start-address high-byte register	811	11	51
Memory window 0 end-address low-byte register	812	12	52
Memory window 0 end-address high-byte register	813	13	53

Table 17-2: ExCA Register Summary and Access Offsets (Continued)

Name	PCI Memory Address Offset	ExCA Offset (Card A)	ExCA Offset (Card B)
Memory window 0 offset-address low-byte register	814	14	54
Memory window 0 offset-address high-byte register	815	15	55
User-defined	816	16	56
User-defined	817	17	57
Memory window 1 start-address low-byte register	818	18	58
Memory window 1 start-address high-byte register	819	19	59
Memory window 1 end-address low-byte register	81A	1A	5A
Memory window 1 end-address high-byte register	81B	1B	5B
Memory window 1 offset-address low-byte register	81C	1C	5C
Memory window 1 offset-address high-byte register	81D	1D	5D
User-defined	81E	1E	5E
Reserved	81F	1F	5F
Memory window 2 start-address low-byte register	820	20	60
Memory window 2 start-address high-byte register	821	21	61
Memory window 2 end-address low-byte register	822	22	62
Memory window 2 end-address high-byte register	823	23	63
Memory window 2 offset-address low-byte register	824	24	64
Memory window 2 offset-address high-byte register	825	25	65
User-defined	826	26	66
User-defined	827	27	67
Memory window 3 start-address low-byte register	828	28	68
Memory window 3 start-address high-byte register	829	29	69
Memory window 3 end-address low-byte register	82A	2A	6A
Memory window 3 end-address high-byte register	82B	2B	6B

Table 17-2: ExCA Register Summary and Access Offsets (Continued)

Name	PCI Memory Address Offset	ExCA Offset (Card A)	ExCA Offset (Card B)
Memory window 3 offset-address low-byte register	82C	2C	6C
Memory window 3 offset-address high-byte register	82D	2D	6D
User-defined	82E	2E	6E
User-defined	82F	2F	6F
Memory window 4 start-address low-byte register	830	30	70
Memory window 4 start-address high-byte register	831	31	71
Memory window 4 end-address low-byte register	832	32	72
Memory window 4 end-address high-byte register	833	33	73
Memory window 4 offset-address low-byte register	834	34	74
Memory window 4 offset-address high-byte register	835	35	75
User-defined	836	36	76
User-defined	837	37	77
User-defined	838	38	78
User-defined	839	39	79
User-defined	83A	3A	7A
User-defined	83B	3B	7B
User-defined	83C	-	-
User-defined	83D	3D	7D
User-defined	83E	3E	7E
User-defined	83F	3F	7F
Optional memory window 0 upper byte of start address	840	40	80
Optional memory window 1 upper byte of start address	841	41	81
Optional memory window 2 upper byte of start address	842	42	82
Optional memory window 3 upper byte of start address	843	43	83

Table 17-2: ExCA Register Summary and Access Offsets (Continued)

Name	PCI Memory Address Offset	ExCA Offset (Card A)	ExCA Offset (Card B)
Optional memory window 4 upper byte of start address	844	44	84
User-defined	845-FFF		

Transaction Filtering Mechanism

The CardBus devices that reside behind a PCI-to-CardBus bridge may consist of only memory, only IO, or a combination of memory and IO cards. Furthermore, some of the IO devices may be mapped into memory space while others are mapped into IO space. The PCMCIA configuration software automatically detects the presence, type and address space requirements of these devices and allocates space to them by programming their address decoders to recognize assigned address ranges. See Chapter 18, entitled "CardBus Card Configuration Registers" for a detailed description of the CardBus card configuration process.

The configuration program assigns an exclusive IO address range to all IO devices that reside behind a PCI-to-CardBus bridge. Actually, provision is made for two inclusive ranges. The PCI-to-CardBus bridge is programmed to pass any IO transactions detected on the primary side of the bridge to the secondary side if the target address is within the range associated with IO devices that reside behind the bridge. Conversely, any IO transactions detected on the secondary side of the bridge are passed to the primary side if the target address is outside the range associated with the IO devices that reside on the secondary side (because the target device doesn't reside on the secondary side, but may reside on the primary side).

The same inclusive range (or two ranges) is used to support memory-mapped IO devices that reside behind a PCI-to-CardBus bridge. The PCI-to-CardBus bridge is programmed to pass any memory transactions detected on the primary side of the bridge to the secondary side if the target address is within the range associated with the memory-mapped IO cards that reside behind the bridge. Conversely, any memory-mapped IO transactions detected on the secondary side of the bridge are passed to the primary side if the target address is outside the range associated with the memory-mapped IO cards residing on the secondary side (because the target device doesn't reside on the secondary side, but may reside on the primary side).

The same inclusive range (or two ranges) is used to support memory devices that reside behind a PCI-to-CardBus bridge. The PCI-to-CardBus bridge is programmed to pass any memory transactions detected on the primary side of the bridge to the secondary side if the target address is within the range associated with the memory cards that reside behind the bridge. Conversely, any memory transactions detected on the secondary side of the bridge are passed to the primary side if the target address is outside the range associated with the memory devices that reside on the secondary side (because the target device doesn't reside on the secondary side, but may reside on the primary side).

Bridge's IO Filter

When the bridge detects an IO transaction initiated on either bus, it must determine which of the following actions to take:

- Ignore the transaction because the target IO address isn't located on the other side of the bridge, nor is it targeting an IO location embedded within the bridge itself.
- Claim the transaction because the target IO address is one of the bridge's internal IO registers. The initiator is permitted to access the targeted internal register and the transaction is not passed through the bridge.
- Claim the transaction because the target IO location is located on the other side of the bridge. The transaction is passed through the bridge and is initiated on the opposite bus.

IO Base and Limit Registers

Optional. The IO base and IO limit registers provide the bridge with the ability to filter IO transactions. The IO base register defines the start address and the IO limit register defines the end address of the range to recognize and pass through. Each socket interface contains two sets of IO address registers.

The format of the IO base and IO limit registers is illustrated in Figure 17-7 and Figure 17-8 on page 277. The IO base registers have the following format:

- Bits [1:0] are encoded to specify whether 16- or 32-bit addressing is supported by the bridge. A value of 00b indicates that 16-bit IO decoding is used (e.g., if the bridge supports only 64KB of IO space, consistent with the IO addressing capability of x86 processors. In this case, the upper bits [31:16] will be set to all zeros.) A value of 01b indicates that the bridge supports 32-bit IO addressing.
- Bits [31:2] define the start address of the IO range within 4GB of IO address space.

The PC Card Standard specifies that each register must have four byte granularity and power-of-two alignment. This is satisfied by assuming that bit [1:0] are always zero.

The IO limit registers have the same format. The upper bits [31:16] are read only and always return all zeros, when only 16-bit addressing is supported, thereby limiting the IO addresses to the first 64KB of IO address space.

In summary, the socket's IO base address registers define whether 16- or 32-bit IO addressing is supported and enforces four byte granularity when programming the IO address registers. These registers are programmed by PCMCIA configuration software, with an IO base address selected from the CardBus Card's CIS. The power-of-two alignment is enforced by the configuration programmer.

Figure 17-7: IO Base Address Register

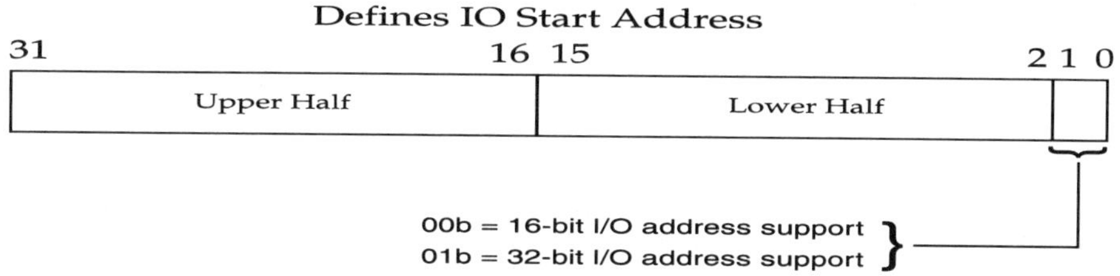

Figure 17-8: IO Limit Register

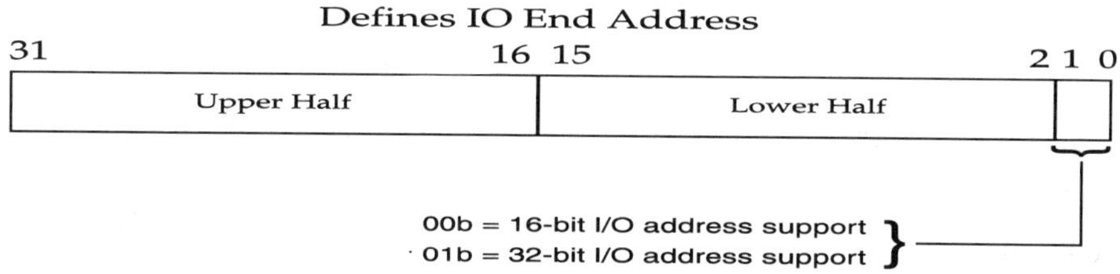

IO Filtering When ISA Expansion Bridge is Present

IO filtering is complicated by the presence of a PCI-to-ISA expansion bus bridge. The following discussions describe background information necessary to understand the problem and the solution.

The Subtractive Decode. ISA bridges typically implement subtractive decode to determine when a PCI transaction is to be claimed and forwarded to the ISA bus. A subtractive decode means that if no other PCI device claims the transaction by asserting DEVSEL# within four clocks from the assertion of FRAME#, the transaction does not target any PCI device. This is possible since all PCI devices, including PCI-to-CardBus bridges must claim transactions based on a positive decode within the first four clocks of a transaction. The ISA bridge claims the transaction and forwards it to the ISA bus in case it targets an ISA device.

ISA Aliasing Within IO Address Space. The first ISA expansion boards, and many designed since, perform a partial address decode during IO bus cycles. Of the 64KB of IO address space, only the first 1KB is occupied by legacy boards. These boards decode A[9:0] of the 16-bit IO address (A[15:0]). This creates an aliasing condition in which locations above 1KB are seen as valid addresses by the legacy boards (because they do not look at the upper address lines, A[15:10]).

Table 17-3 shows how the first IBM PCs mapped devices into the first 1KB of IO address space. As Table 17-4 on page 279 indicates, not all IO locations above 1KB alias to the ISA legacy boards. The first 256 bytes of IO space are reserved for embedded IO devices (e.g., DMA controllers, interrupt controllers, timers, keyboard controller, etc.).

Table 17-3: IBM PC AT IO Mapping

IO Address Range	Reserved For
0000h through 00FFh	256 locations set aside for IO devices integrated onto the system board.
0100h through 03FFh	768 locations set aside for IO expansion cards.
0400h through FFFFh	Reserved.

A full address decode is performed by the system board for all embedded devices, thereby eliminating aliasing to the first 256 bytes of each 1KB block of IO space. Table 17-4 lists the ranges of IO address space that alias to legacy ISA boards and those that do not (note that the "x" in the upper digit can be any hex digit). The ranges that do not alias can be used by other devices in the system without concern for aliasing problem.

Table 17-4: IO Address Ranges that Alias to Legacy IO Space

IO Address Range	Usable or Unusable
x000h - x0FFh	usable
x100h - x1FFh	Unusable. Appears to be 0100h - 01FFh
x200h - x2FFh	Unusable. Appears to be 0200h - 02FFh
x300h - x3FFh	Unusable. Appears to be 0300h - 03FFh
x400h - x4FFh	usable
x500h - x5FFh	Unusable. Appears to be 0100h - 01FFh
x600h - x6FFh	Unusable. Appears to be 0200h - 02FFh
x700h - x7FFh	Unusable. Appears to be 0300h - 03FFh
x800h - x8FFh	usable
x900h - x9FFh	Unusable. Appears to be 0100h - 01FFh
xA00h - xAFFh	Unusable. Appears to be 0200h - 02FFh
xB00h - xBFFh	Unusable. Appears to be 0300h - 03FFh
xC00h - xCFFh	usable
xD00h - xDFFh	Unusable. Appears to be 0100h - 01FFh
xE00h - xEFFh	Unusable. Appears to be 0200h - 02FFh
xF00h - xFFFh	Unusable. Appears to be 0300h - 03FFh

Some ISA Boards Use the Alias Space. On the surface, it appears that legacy ISA devices do not create a problem for mapping PCI and CardBus devices above 1KB. In other words, since PCI-to-ISA expansion bus bridges perform a subtractive decode, the CardBus bridge or any PCI device that wishes to use IO address space could safely use the ranges above 1KB (because legacy ISA cards only occupy the range from 0100h to 03FFh). However, some ISA cards perform a full 16-bit decode and use the alias space above 1KB to avoid conflicts within the crowded legacy range. For example, an ISA board designer could obtain 63 bytes of additional IO address space by selecting a single byte location within the legacy range and performing a 16-bit decode. The upper address lines (A15:10) could be decoded to provide exclusive access to the same relative location within each succeeding 1KB of address space, thereby yielding 64 bytes of total address space.

In summary, systems that provide ISA expansion slots create the possibility of an ISA board being installed that uses locations within the alias range. The vast numbers of ISA boards available make it virtually impossible to guarantee that any address locations within the alias range can be used by PCI or CardBus devices.

ISA Enable Bit. PCI-to-CardBus bridges implement an ISA ENABLE bit to provide compatibility with ISA legacy boards. (See "Bridge Control Register" on page 286.) The ISA Enable bit is set by PCI configuration software when a PCI-to-ISA expansion bus bridge is installed on the same primary bus as the PCI-to-PCI or PCI-to-CardBus bridge. This specifies to the bridge that it cannot respond to any location within an alias address range. This bit also notifies PCMCIA configuration software that the alias range cannot be safely used and must not be assigned to CardBus cards.

Bridge's Memory Filter

Required. The CardBus bridge must support memory address decoding to determine which transactions should be transferred across the bridge and which should be blocked. Yenta defines two sets of memory base and limit registers, each of which can be configured to provide either prefetchable or non-prefetchable address ranges. Figure 17-9 and Figure 17-10 illustrate the format of the memory base and limit registers, respectively.

Bits [31:12] of the Memory Base Address registers are used to specific the start address of the memory range, while the memory limit registers are used to specify the end of the memory address range. The lower bits [11:0] of both the base and limit registers are hardwired to all zeros, thereby forcing the base and limit registers to start and end on a 4KB boundary anywhere within the 4GB address space. The lower 12 bits of the assigned base address are assumed to be zero, while the lower 12 bits of the assigned end address are assumed to be all ones.

Figure 17-9: The Memory Base Address Register

31 ... 12	11 ... 0
Specifies memory base address (aligned on 4KB boundaries)	0 0 0 0 0 0 0 0 0 0 0 0

Figure 17-10: The Memory Limit Register

31 ... 12	11 ... 0
Specifies memory end address (aligned on 4KB boundaries)	0 0 0 0 0 0 0 0 0 0 0 0

Each register set can be programmed as prefetchable or not. Issues relating to prefetchable and non-prefetchable memory are discussed in the following sections.

Prefetchable Memory

A memory device that always returns the same data from a location no matter how many times the location is read from is Prefetchable. In other words, reading from a memory device doesn't in any way alter the contents of memory. Due to this operational characteristic, it is permissible for a bridge to perform a read-ahead when performing a memory read for a master on the other side of the bridge. Assume that a master initiates a memory read to read a doubleword from a memory device. The bridge could read the requested doubleword and go on to prefetch data that hasn't been requested yet (e.g., an entire line of information) into a read buffer in case the master should ask for that data as well. If the master does subsequently request that data, it can be delivered quickly, yielding better performance. If the master doesn't ask for it, no harm is done.

A bridge could incorporate a posted-write buffer that quickly absorbs data to be written to a memory device on the other side of the bridge. Since the master doesn't have to delay until the write to the memory device has actually been completed, posting yields better performance during memory write operations. The bridge would ensure that, before any subsequent memory read is permitted to propagate through the bridge, the bridge would flush its posted-write buffer to the memory device.

To summarize, it is permissible to perform prefetches from and posted-writes to regular memory devices. The PC Card Standard refers to areas of memory space occupied by regular memory as prefetchable memory areas. Yenta permits the range assigned to each set of memory base and limit registers to be designated as prefetchable or not. The Bridge Control register defines whether the memory window is prefetchable and whether write-posting is enabled. Figure 17-12 on page 286 illustrates the fields in the Bridge Control register.

Non-Prefetchable Memory

Memory-mapped IO devices present a different set of operational characteristics. Performing a memory read from a memory-mapped IO location often has the effect of altering the contents of the location. As examples, one of the following may be true:

- The location may be occupied by a memory-mapped IO status port. Reading from the location causes the IO device to clear any status bits that were set in the register (on the assumption that they've been read and will therefore be dealt with by the device driver). If the read was caused by a speculative read performed by the bridge and the prefetched data is never actually read by the device driver, then status information has been erroneously discarded.
- The location may be the front-end of a FIFO data buffer. Performing a read from the location causes the delivery of its current contents and the next data item is then automatically placed in the location by the IO device. The device assumes that the first data item has been read by the device driver and therefore sets up the next data item in the FIFO location. If the read was caused by a prefetch and the prefetched data is never actually read by the device driver, then the data was discarded.

Reads within an area of memory space occupied by memory-mapped IO devices must never cause prefetching to occur. Any writes to the memory-mapped IO ports must not be posted in the bridge. A set of registers are provided to permit the configuration software to define the start and end address of the memory-mapped IO space that is occupied by memory-mapped IO devices behind the bridge.

Detection of Prefetchable Memory

Configuration software determines that a CardBus memory target supports prefetching by reading and parsing the CIS. The Base Address Register (BAR) tuple includes a PREFETCHABLE attribute bit, indicating whether the associated memory mapped device are prefetchable. This subject is covered in the Chapter 19 on page 321.

Command Registers

The PCI-to-CardBus bridge designer must implement two required command registers in the bridge's configuration header region:

- The Primary **command register** is the standard configuration command register defined by the PCI specification for any PCI device. It is associated with the bridge's primary bus interface.
- The **bridge control register** is an extension to the standard command register and is associated with the operation of both of the bus interfaces. It is defined by the PCI-to-PCI bridge specification. However, the spec has been extended for the PCI-to-CardBus bridge.

These registers are defined in the next two sections.

Command Register

Required. The command register format is pictured in Figure 17-11 on page 284. When the PCI RESET pin is asserted, all PCI devices, including the PCI-to-CardBus bridge, clear their configuration registers, placing them in a disabled state. The only type of transactions that a PCI device responds to immediately after RESET is a configuration transaction. The command register enable bits are only set after the PCI configuration software has configured the bridge. Table 17-5 on page 284 describes each bit.

Figure 17-11: Command Register

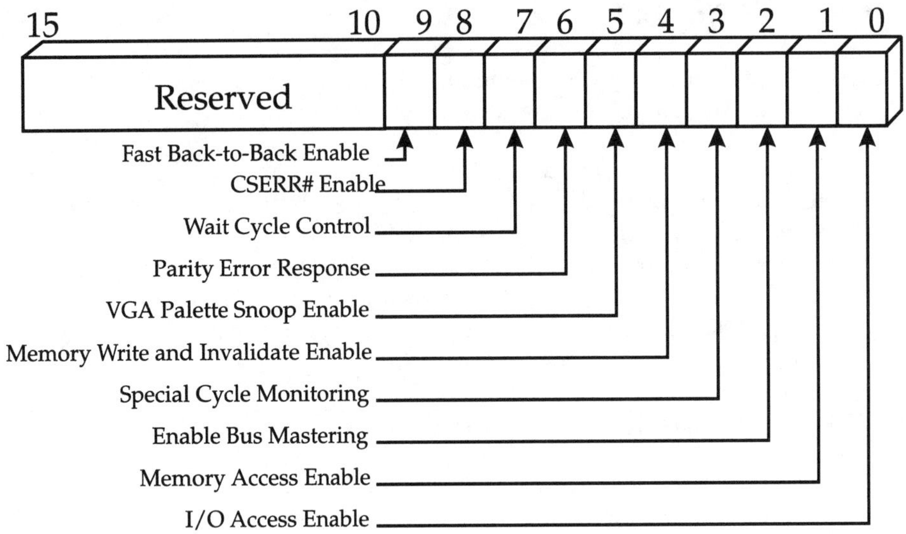

Table 17-5: Command Register Bit Assignment

Bit	Description
0	**IO Space Enable**. When set, the bridge's IO address decoders on its primary side are enabled. When cleared, they are disabled. When cleared, any IO transactions detected on the secondary side are passed through to the primary side and all IO transactions detected on the primary side are ignored. Reset clears this bit.
1	**Memory Space Enable**. When set, the bridge's memory and memory-mapped IO address decoders on its primary side are enabled. When cleared, they are disabled. When cleared, any memory transactions detected on the secondary side are passed through to the primary side and all memory transactions on the primary side are ignored. Reset clears this bit.
2	**Bus Master Enable**. Control's the bridge's ability to act as a master on the primary side. However, the bridge is always enabled to forward and convert configuration transactions. When cleared, the bridge ignores all memory and IO transactions detected on the secondary side. Reset clears this bit.

Table 17-5: Command Register Bit Assignment (Continued)

Bit	Description
3	**Special Cycle Enable**. Hardwired to zero (because PCI-to-PCI bridges don't monitor special cycles).
4	**Memory Write and Invalidate Enable**. Hardwired to zero because this bit is irrelevant to the bridge. The initiating master decides what type of memory write transaction to use. The bridge only evaluates the address to determine whether to pass the transaction through to the other side.
5	**VGA Palette Snoop Enable**. Implementation of this bit is optional. If not implemented, must be hardwired to zero. Reset clears this bit. When set, IO writes to 03C6h, 03C8h and 03C9h (including any IO addresses that alias to these addresses) are positively decoded on the primary side and are passed through to the secondary side. If IO writes to these addresses are detected on the secondary side, they are ignored. Also see description of the VGA ENABLE bit in the bridge control register.
6	**Parity Error Response**. When set, the bridge takes the normal actions defined by the specification when a parity error is detected on the primary side. When cleared, parity errors are ignored, but the bridge must generate proper parity. Reset clears this bit.
7	**Wait Cycle Control**. Bridges that never use stepping hardwire this bit to zero. Bridges that always use stepping hardwire this bit to one. Bridges that permit stepping to be turned on and off implement this as a read/writable bit. If the bit is read/writable, reset sets the bit to one.
8	**SERR# Enable**. Controls the SERR# output driver on the primary bus. When set, the bridge is enabled to generate SERR# on the primary side. When cleared it cannot generate SERR#. Reset clears this bit.
9	**Fast Back-to-Back Enable**. Controls the bridge's ability to utilize fast back-to-back transactions with different targets on the primary bus. A bridge that doesn't support this ability hardwires this bit to zero, otherwise it must be read/writable. Reset clears this bit.
15:10	**Reserved**. Read-only and must return zero when read.

Bridge Control Register

Required. The bridge control register is a required extension to the bridge's command register. Figure 17-12 illustrates this register and Table 17-6 on page 286 defines its bit assignment.

Figure 17-12: Bridge Control Register

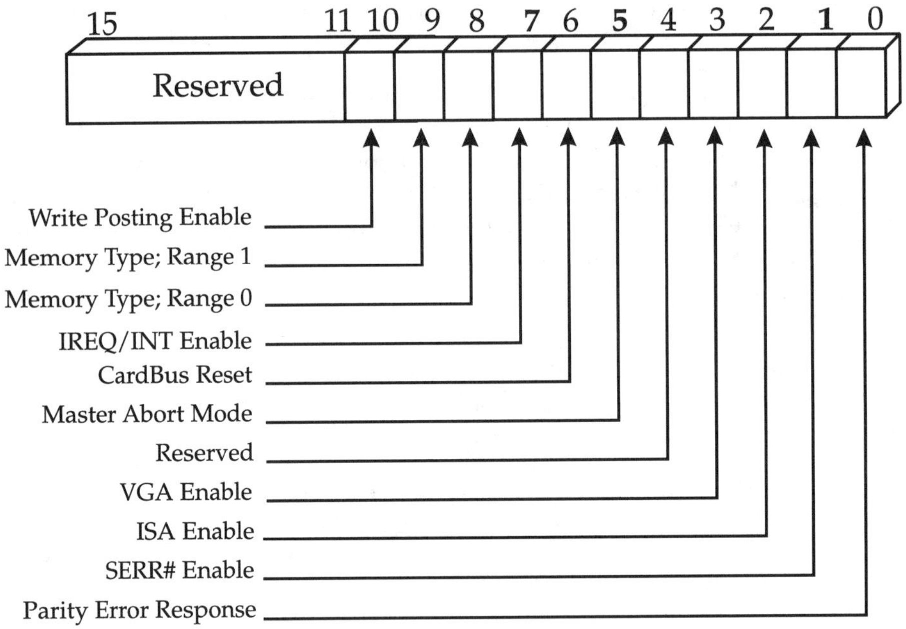

Table 17-6: Bridge Control Register Bit Assignment

Bit	Description
0	**Parity Error Response**. When set, the bridge takes the normal actions defined by the specification when a parity error is detected on the secondary side. When cleared, parity errors are ignored, but the bridge must generate proper parity. Reset clears this bit.

Table 17-6: Bridge Control Register Bit Assignment (Continued)

Bit	Description
1	**SERR# Enable**. When set, detection of SERR# asserted on the secondary side causes the bridge to assert SERR# on the primary side (but only if the SERR# ENABLE bit in the device's configuration command register is set). When cleared, bridge ignores SERR# on secondary side. Reset clears this bit.
2	**ISA Enable**. This bit is set when an ISA expansion bus is present in the system. When set, the bridge only recognizes IO addresses within the usable ranges that do not alias to an ISA range. This permits the expansion bus bridge to perform the required subtractive decode for any IO address that might be used by ISA expansion adapters.
3	**VGA Enable**. When set, bridge performs positive decode on memory accesses in the range from 000A0000h through 000BFFFFh (the address range of the video frame buffer), IO addresses from 03B0h through 03BBh, and IO addresses 03C0h through 03DFh (including addresses that alias into these two IO ranges). This bit is qualified by bits zero and one in the command register. Reset clears this bit.
4	**Reserved**. Hardwired to zero.
5	**Master Abort Mode**. Controls the manner in which the bridge responds when it is mastering a transaction on either bus and experiences a master abort. When this bit is cleared, any reads that experience a master abort return all ones; any writes complete normally and the data is thrown away. When this bit is set and the bridge experiences a master abort, it issues a target abort to the initiating master (for all reads and non-posted writes). If the bridge experiences a master abort while performing a posted-write, it signals SERR# on the primary side (if the SERR# ENABLE bit in the command register is set). Reset clears this bit.
6	**Secondary Bus Reset**. When set, the bridge asserts RST# on the secondary bus. When cleared, the secondary bus RST# is deasserted. Irrespective of the state of this bit, secondary bus RST# follows primary bus RST#. The bridge's interface to the secondary bus and all buffers between the two buses are initialized by the assertion of RST# on the secondary bus. Assertion of RST# on the secondary bus, however, does not affect the configuration registers nor the primary bus interface logic. Reset clears this bit.

Table 17-6: Bridge Control Register Bit Assignment (Continued)

Bit	Description
7	**IREQ/INT Enable**. When set, enables the IRQ routing register for 16-bit cards. When cleared, IREQ interrupts are routed to the INT pin indicated by the Interrupt Pin register. Reset clears this bit.
8	**Memory Type for Range zero**. This bit controls whether the range of memory locations specified by memory base and limit register pair zero is prefetchable (1) or non-prefetchable (0).
9	**Memory Type for Range one**. This bit controls whether the range of memory locations specified by memory base and limit register pair one is prefetchable (1) or non-prefetchable (0).
10	**Write Posting Enable**. This bit is set to enable write posting to and from the socket (i.e., CardBus card). When cleared, the bridge must flush any data within its buffers before accepting data going to or coming from the socket.
15:11	**Reserved**. Hardwire to zero.

Status Registers

The bridge contains two required status registers, one associated with the PCI bus and the other with CardBus.

Status Register (Primary Bus)

Required. This required register is completely compatible with the status register definition for a non-bridge PCI device and only reflects the status of the primary side. Figure 17-13 on page 289 illustrates the Status register and Table 17-7 on page 289 defines each bit.

Figure 17-13: The Status Register

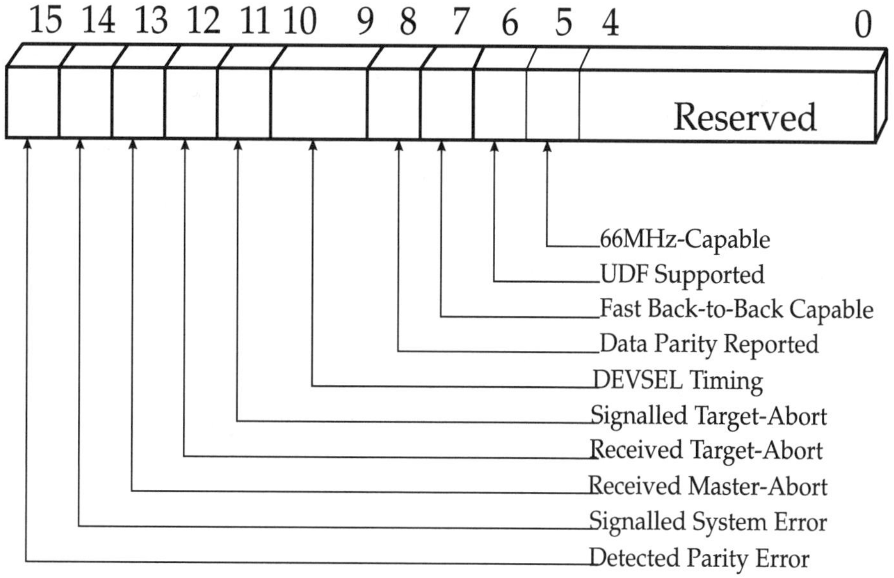

Table 17-7: Status Register Bit Assignment

Bit	Function
4:0	**Reserved**. Hardwired to zero.
5	**66MHz-Capable**. 1 = device is capable of running at 66MHz. 0 = capable of running at 33MHz. Value hardwired by designer.
6	**UDF Supported**. 1 = device supports user-definable features. 0 = device does not support UDFs. Value hardwired by designer. Refer to the MindShare book entitled *PCI System Architecture* (published by Addison-Wesley) for details.

Table 17-7: Status Register Bit Assignment (Continued)

Bit	Function
7	**Fast Back-to-Back Capable**. This read-only bit indicates whether or not the target device supports fast back-to-back transactions with different targets. It must be hardwired to zero if the device does not support this feature and to a one if it does. A complete description of fast back-to-back transactions can be found in the chapter entitled "PCI Bus Arbitration" in the MindShare book entitled *PCI System Architecture* (published by Addison-Wesley) Also refer to the description of the FAST BACK-TO-BACK ENABLE bit in the command register (in this chapter).
8	**Data Parity Reported**. This bit is only implemented by bus masters and is set only if the following conditions are met: the reporting bus master was the initiator and set PERR# itself or detected it asserted by the target (during a write); and the PARITY ERROR RESPONSE bit in the master's command configuration register is set to a one.
10:9	**Device Select** (DEVSEL#) **Timing**. These bits are read-only and define the slowest DEVSEL# timing for a target device (except configuration accesses). 00b = fast 01b = medium 10b = slow 11b = reserved
11	**Signaled Target Abort**. Set by the target device whenever it terminates a transaction with a target-abort. A device that is incapable of signaling target-abort does not need to implement this bit.
12	**Received Target Abort**. This bit is set by a bus master whenever its transaction is terminated by a target-abort from the currently-addressed target. All bus masters must implement this bit.
13	**Received Master Abort**. This bit should be set by a master whenever its transaction (except for a special cycle) is terminated due to a master-abort. All bus masters must implement this bit.
14	**Signaled System Error (SERR#)**. This bit should be set whenever a device generates a System Error on the SERR# line. If incapable of generating SERR#, it need not implement this bit.

Table 17-7: Status Register Bit Assignment (Continued)

Bit	Function
15	**Detected Parity Error**. This bit should be set by a device whenever it detects a parity error (even if parity error reporting is disabled by bit six of its command register).

Secondary Status Register

Required. With the exception of the RECEIVED SYSTEM ERROR bit and the 66MHz capable bit, this required register is completely compatible with the status register definition for a non-bridge PCI device and only reflects the status of the secondary side.

Bit 14, the SIGNALED SYSTEM ERROR bit, has been redefined as the RECEIVED SYSTEM ERROR bit for the secondary side. When set, indicates that SERR# was detected asserted on the secondary side. Writing a one to it clears the bit, while a zero doesn't affect it. Reset clears this bit.

Bit 5, the 66MHz capable bit is not defined for the secondary status register, since CardBus supports only 33MHz operation.

Cache Line Size Register

Required. This read/write configuration register specifies the system cache line size in doubleword increments (e.g., a 486-based system would store the value 04h, indicating a cache line size of four doublewords).

It defines the system cache line size for both sides of the bridge. The value in this register is used by the bridge:

- in determining when it has transferred an entire line when using the memory write and invalidate transaction.
- in determining the cache line size during performance of memory read line and memory read multiple transactions.

Latency Timer Registers

The bridge includes an independent, read/write master latency timer for each of the two buses. The contents of each of these required registers defines the minimum period of time (in bus clock cycles since the beginning of the transaction) the bridge may continue a burst transaction if it's preempted.

The latency timer defines the minimum amount of time, in bus clock cycles, that the bus master can retain ownership of the bus. The bus master decrements its latency timer by one on the rising-edge of each clock after it initiates a transaction. It may continue its transaction until either:

- it has completed the overall burst transfer, or
- it has exhausted its timeslice (LT value) and it has been preempted (lost its GNT# to another master), whichever comes first.

In a typical implementation of a programmable LT register, the low-order three bits are hardwired to zero and the programmer can program any value into the high-order five bits. This permits the programmer to specify the timeslice with a granularity of eight PCI clocks. If the register is programmable, reset clears it.

Latency Timer Register (Primary Bus)

Required. This required read/write register defines the timeslice for the primary interface when the bridge is acting as the initiator.

Secondary Latency Timer Register

Required. This required read/write register defines the timeslice for the secondary interface when the bridge is acting as the initiator.

BIST Register

Optional. This register is implemented by the bridge, if it implements a built-in self-test, or BIST. The BIST register is illustrated in Figure 17-14. Table 17-8 on page 293 describes the function of each field within the BIST register. If the device doesn't support a BIST, this register must return zeros when read. The device's BIST is invoked by setting bit six to one. The device resets bit six upon completion of the BIST. Configuration software must fail the device if it doesn't reset bit six within two seconds. At the conclusion of the BIST, the test result is indicated in the lower four bits of the register. A completion code of zero indicates successful completion. A non-zero value represents a device-specific error code.

Figure 17-14: The BIST Register

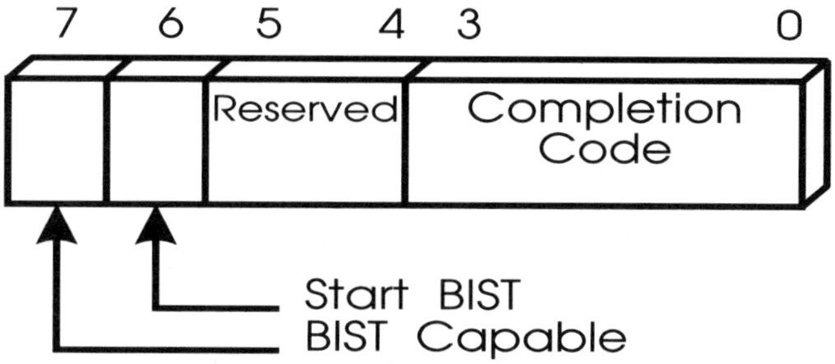

Table 17-8: BIST Register Bit Assignment

Bit	Function
3:0	**Completion Code**. A value of zero indicates successful completion, while a non-zero result indicates a device-specific error.
5:4	Reserved.
6	**Start BIST**. A one in this bit starts the device's BIST. The device resets this bit automatically upon completion. Software should fail the device if the BIST does not complete within two seconds.
7	**BIST Capable**. Should return a one if the device implements a BIST, a zero if it doesn't.

Interrupt-Related Registers

Required if the bridge generates PCI interrupts. A CardBus bridge will likely use a PCI interrupt line to report status change events that it detects via the CardBus CSTSCHG pin. The interrupt pin and interrupt line registers are implemented to support the delivery of the status change interrupt. PCI configuration software is responsible for detecting that an interrupt line is used by the bridge and must assign an IRQ line to each bridge function (i.e., socket).

Interrupt Pin Register

The read-only interrupt pin register defines which of the four PCI interrupt request pins, INTA# through INTD#, a PCI function is connected (i.e., bonded) to. The values one through four correspond to PCI interrupt request lines INTA# through INTD#. A return value of zero indicates that the device doesn't use interrupts.

Interrupt Line Register

The read/writable interrupt line register is used to identify which of the system interrupt request lines (i.e., IRQs) on the interrupt controller the device's PCI interrupt request pin (as specified in its interrupt pin register) is routed to. In a PC environment, for example, the values zero (00h) through fifteen (0Fh) in this register correspond to IRQ0 through IRQ15. The value 255, or FFh, indicates "unknown" or "not assigned." The values from 10h through FEh, inclusive, are reserved.

Configuration Process Summary

At start-up time, the configuration software must accomplish the following:

- The bus number registers in all bridges must be assigned.
- Detection of all IO and memory devices and the assignment of mutually-exclusive address ranges to each of them.
- Detection of interrupt-driven PCI devices and programming the interrupt routing information into each of their interrupt line registers.
- Initialization of the display subsystem on the PCI bus.

Bus Number Assignment

At start-up time, the configuration software is only aware of the existence of PCI bus zero. It must build a picture of the bus "tree" that represents the overall system topology (including CardBus sockets). The system start-up configuration software must walk the base PCI bus (bus zero) and search for PCI-to-PCI bridges and PCI-to-CardBus bridges. When a bridge is discovered (via its class code register), the software walks the secondary bus in an attempt to discover other bridges. The software proceeds with this process until all PCI/CardBus buses behind the first PCI or CardBus bridge have been discovered. As each bus is discovered, the software assigns it a bus number and must also go back and update the subordinate bus number registers in each bridge that resides upstream of the bridge (including the host/PCI bridge).

When a complete picture of the tree branch that extends behind the first bridge has been built, the software searches for other PCI/CardBus bridges stemming from the first PCI bus and builds a topological image of the branch behind each.

The PCI specification does not define in what order bus numbers are assigned and when they are assigned. This is system-specific. It does, however, dictate that the bus number assigned to each bus that resides behind a PCI-to-PCI bridge must be a value greater than the bridge's secondary bus number and less than or equal to the value placed in its own subordinate bus number register.

Note, however, that bus numbers should be assigned to the buses below a CardBus bridge last. This is necessary because another CardBus bridge (i.e., a CardBus card can be implemented as a bridge) may be installed at any time and must then be numbered. If the CardBus numbers are not assigned last, the sequential numbers that must be assigned by PCMCIA configuration software may conflict with PCI bus numbers.

Address Space Allocation

The Yenta-defined PCI-to-CardBus bridge contains four sets of registers that are used to define the address space allocated to each socket residing behind the bridge:

- Two sets of base and limit for IO space allocated to IO devices that reside in a socket or downstream from a socket.
- Two sets of base and limit for memory-mapped devices that reside in a socket or downstream from a socket. The space can be defined as memory-mapped IO (i.e., non-prefetchable), or as prefetchable.

IRQ Assignment

The start-up configuration software also determines which PCI devices are interrupt driven during the discovery process. Each device that indicates that is interrupt-driven (a value between 01h and 04h hardwired into the device's interrupt pin register) also implements an interrupt line register. The start-up software must write the interrupt routing information into each device's interrupt line register.

18 CardBus Card Configuration Registers

The Previous Chapter

The previous chapter defined the CardBus bridge's configuration registers and socket interface initialization.

This Chapter

This chapter discusses the configuration registers used by CardBus cards. Each configuration register is described, along with the methods used by PCMCIA configuration software to determine the values that should be loaded into these registers.

The Next Chapter

The next chapter discusses the Card Information Structure (CIS) implemented on all CardBus cards. Information contained in the CIS specifies how a given card should be configured.

Intro to Configuration Header Region

Each function within a CardBus card possesses a block of 64 configuration doublewords reserved for the implementation of its configuration registers. The format, or usage, of the first 16 doublewords is called the configuration header and is predefined by the PC Card Standard. The definition of the configuration header was derived from the PCI specification. However, several modifications have been made to tailor the header definition for CardBus use. The rev 2.1

specification currently defines two header formats with a third type pending approval. Header type one is defined for PCI-to-PCI bridges, header type two has been defined by Yenta for PCI-to-CardBus bridges, and header type zero is used for all other devices. CardBus cards use a modified version of header type zero.

Figure 18-1 illustrates the format of a CardBus function's header region. If a CardBus card implements more than one function, each has its set of configuration registers. The registers within this range are used to configure and enable a CardBus card function, and to sense its status. The remaining 48 doublewords of its configuration space is defined as device-specific. Note that a CardBus card implemented as a bridge (e.g. CardBus-to-CardBus or CardBus-to-PCI bridge) does not use header type zero.

Figure 18-1: Format of a CardBus Function's Configuration Header

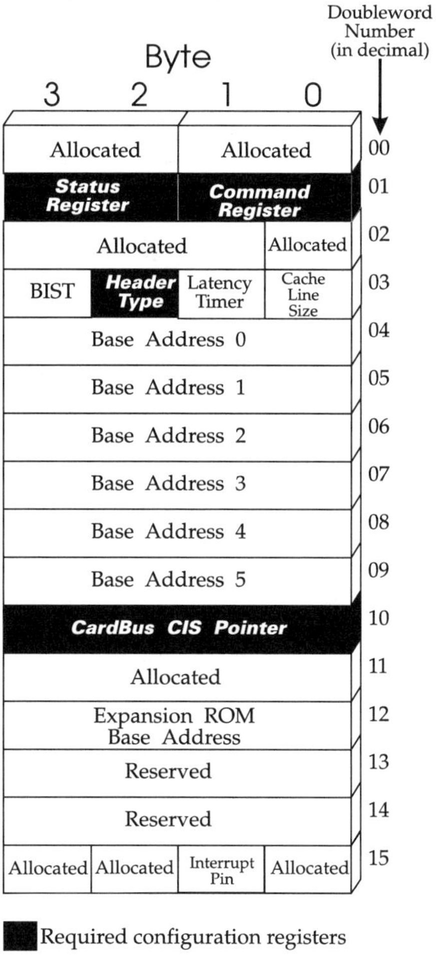

Allocated Registers

Registers that are designated as allocated are not used by CardBus devices nor PCMCIA software. These registers are referred to as allocated since they are defined by the PCI specification, but are not used by CardBus card implementations.

Due to the similarities between CardBus and PCI, some ASIC designers may choose to design their parts to operate directly on the PCI bus or as CardBus devices. PCI devices do not use a CIS for device identification nor to specify configuration requirements; rather, they use configuration header registers for function identification and for encoding configuration information. Some of the registers defined for PCI devices are not used by CardBus and are therefore defined as allocated. A device designed only for CardBus would hardwire the allocated registers to zero. See "Appendix B—PCI & CardBus Differences" on page 383 for a summary of differences between PCI and CardBus implementations.

Command Register

Required. This register provides basic control over the device's ability to respond to and/or perform CardBus accesses. The command register is a 16-bit register, but only bits [9:0] are currently defined. Bits [15:10] are reserved for future use. The bits are described in Table 18-1 on page 301 and the register is illustrated in Figure 18-2 on page 300. The designer only implements the bits that make sense for the device. As an example, an IO device with no memory requires bit zero, but not bit one.

Figure 18-2: The Command Register

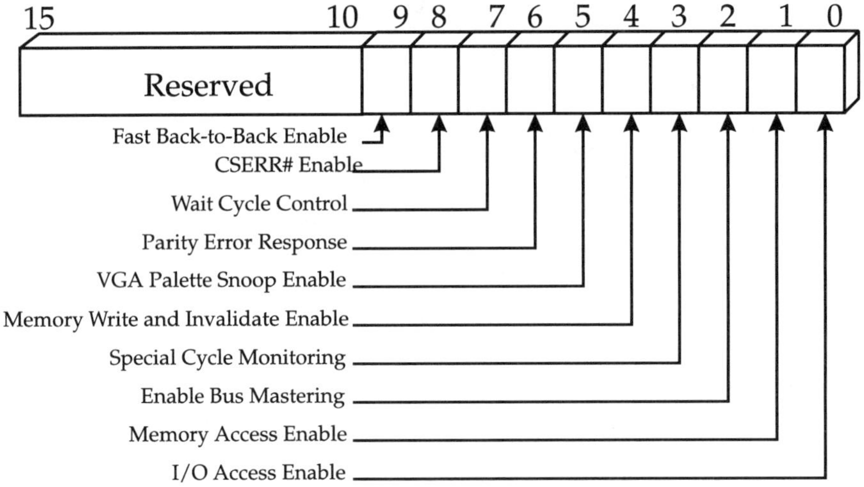

After reset, all bits in this register are cleared to zero (except possibly for the Wait Cycle Control bit and/or a device that must be enabled at start-up time because it's used during the raw boot process). This effectively disables the device (the exception being it remains responsive to configuration accesses) until it is configured and enabled by the configuration software. Devices that must be accessible at boot time through fixed addresses must provide an enable/disable bit to control the recognition of its fixed address ranges. This would permit the configuration software to turn off the recognition of the fixed ranges after boot up and to reconfigure the address range(s) the device responds to.

Table 18-1: Command Register Bit Definition

Bit	Function
0	**IO Access Enable**. When set, the device's IO address decoder(s) (if any are implemented) respond to CardBus IO accesses. Zero disables them. Default setting is zero.
1	**Memory Access Enable**. When set, the device responds to CardBus memory accesses (if it implements any memory address decoders). Zero disables them. Default setting is zero.
2	**Bus Master Enable**. When set, enables the device to act as a bus master (if it has bus master capability). Zero disables it. Default setting is zero.
3	**Special Cycle Recognition**. When set, the device is enabled to monitor CardBus special cycles (if it's designed to monitor special cycles). Zero causes it to ignore special cycles. Default setting is zero.
4	**Memory Write and Invalidate Enable**. When set, the device can generate the memory write and invalidate command. When cleared, the device uses memory write commands instead. This bit must be implemented by bus masters that are capable of generating the memory write and invalidate command. Software should not enable this bit until the device's cache line size configuration register is initialized with the system cache line size. Reset clears this bit.
5	**VGA Palette Snoop Enable**. When set, this bit instructs its VGA-compatible device to perform palette snooping. RESET clears this bit in a VGA-compatible controller. In non-VGA graphics device, RESET sets it, enabling palette snooping.
6	**Parity Error Response**. This bit is required for all devices. When set, the device can report parity errors. When cleared, the device ignores parity errors. This bit is cleared by reset.

Table 18-1: Command Register Bit Definition (Continued)

Bit	Function
7	**Wait Cycle Enable**. Controls whether the device does address/data stepping. Devices that never use stepping must hardwire this bit to a zero. Devices that always use stepping must hardwire this bit to a one. Devices that can work both ways must implement this bit as read/writable and initialize it to one after reset. Additional information regarding stepping can be found in the section "Address/Data Stepping" on page 108 and in the chapter entitled "The Read and Write Transfers" in MindShare's *PCI System Architecture* book (published by Addison-Wesley).
8	**System Error Enable**. When set, the device can drive the SERR# line. A zero disables the device's SERR# output driver. State after a reset is zero. All devices that use SERR# must implement this bit. This bit and bit six must be set to report address parity errors.
9	**Fast Back-to-Back Enable**. Optional bit for bus masters. If a bus master is capable of performing fast back-to-back transactions with different targets, this bit is used to enable or disable this functionality. If all targets have the FAST BACK-TO-BACK CAPABLE bit set in their Status registers, configuration software can use this bit to enable this master's ability to perform fast back-to-back transactions to different targets.
15:10	Reserved

VGA Color Palette Snooping

A system may have two display devices present in the system: a VGA-compatible interface and another graphics controller. In this case, both devices implement a set of color palette registers. Whenever the host processor performs an IO write to update the palette registers, the palette in both devices must be updated. This presents a problem. Both devices implement the color palette registers at the same IO addresses. If a write is performed to the palette registers, both recognize the address and assert DEVSEL# and TRDY# (resulting in a collision on the DEVSEL# and TRDY# signals). Note that the CardBus bridge would assert these signals in response to receipt of CDEVSEL# and CTRDY# from a CardBus VGA device. To prevent this, the configuration software must program one of the devices to actively participate as the target, while the other device is programmed to quietly "snarf" the write data from the bus as it is being transferred to the other device. Note that configuration software must set the PCI-to-

CardBus bridge's control register to reflect the same setting used the by the CardBus VGA-compatible device.

The CardBus VGA device always responds to reads (asserts CTRDY# and supplies the data) from its color palette registers. Either the VGA or the other graphics device is configured to respond to palette register writes (by asserting DEVSEL# and TRDY# and accepting the data), while the other one is configured to quietly accept the data into its palette register. It doesn't assert DEVSEL# or TRDY#, but it does latch the write data when the other device has asserted DEVSEL# and TRDY# (indicating that the other display adapter is ready to accept the data) and IRDY# (indicating that the master is presenting the data) are sampled asserted. The device that quietly accepts the palette register update is the device programmed to perform VGA color palette snooping.

Assuming that the CardBus display device resides in a socket downstream from a PCI-to-CardBus bridge that resides on PCI bus zero. There are two cases regarding the physical location of the other display device:

- The other device is present on PCI bus zero. The configuration software programs the bus zero display device to snoop palette writes (by setting the VGA PALETTE SNOOP bit in its configuration command register). The CardBus bridge performs a positive decode (because its VGA ENABLE bit is set), and forwards the transaction to the CardBus display device to claim the transaction.
- The other device resides in another CardBus socket. In this case, configuration software programs one to snoop and the other to respond to the write transaction.

In a system that only contains a VGA interface or where the graphics device is integrated into the VGA device, the VGA's snoop bit is turned off and it actively participates in palette register updates. For more detail regarding palette snooping refer to the PCI-to-PCI spec.

Status Register

Required. The status register tracks the status of CardBus-related events. A device must implement the bits that relate to its functionality. This register can be read from, but writes are handled differently than the norm. On a write, bits can be cleared, but not set. A bit is cleared by writing a one to it. This method was selected to simplify the programmer's job. After reading the state and ascertaining the error bits that are set, the programmer clears the bits by writing the value just read back to the register.

Table 18-2 on page 304 describes the status register bits and Figure 18-3 illustrates its bit assignment.

Figure 18-3: The CardBus Status Register

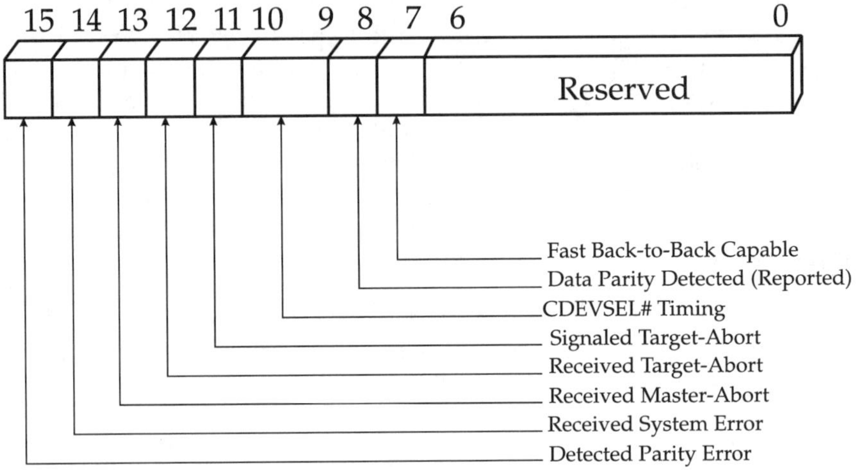

Table 18-2: Status Register Bit Definition

Bit	Function
6:0	**Reserved**. Hardwired to zero.
7	**Fast Back-to-Back Capable**. This read-only bit indicates whether or not the target device supports fast back-to-back transactions with different targets. It must be hardwired to zero if the device does not support this feature and to one if it does. A complete description of fast back-to-back transactions can be found in the section entitled "Fast Back-to-Back Transactions" on page 94. Also refer to the description of the FAST BACK-TO-BACK ENABLE bit in the command register.
8	**Data Parity Detected**. This bit is only implemented by bus masters and is set only if the following conditions are met: the bus master is the initiator and sets CPERR# itself or it detected CPERR# asserted by the target (during a write); and the PARITY ERROR RESPONSE bit in the master's command configuration register is set to a one.

Table 18-2: Status Register Bit Definition (Continued)

Bit	Function
10:9	**Device Select** (CDEVSEL#) **Timing**. These bits are read-only and define the slowest CDEVSEL# timing for a target device (except configuration accesses). • 00b = fast • 01b = medium • 10b = slow • 11b = reserved
11	**Signaled Target Abort**. Set by the target device whenever it terminates a transaction with a target-abort. A device that is incapable of signaling target-abort does not need to implement this bit.
12	**Received Target Abort**. This bit is set by a bus master whenever its transaction is terminated with target-abort by the currently-addressed target. All bus masters must implement this bit.
13	**Received Master Abort**. This bit should be set by a master whenever its transaction (except for a special cycle) is terminated due to a master-abort. All bus masters must implement this bit.
14	**Received System Error**. This bit should be set whenever a device generates a System Error on the SERR# line. If incapable of generating SERR#, it need not implement this bit.
15	**Detected Parity Error**. This bit should be set by a device whenever it detects a parity error (even if parity error reporting is disabled by bit six of its command register).

Cache Line Size Register

Required for a bus master that uses the memory write and invalidate command. Also required for executable memory targets that reside on the PCI bus. This read/write configuration register specifies the system cache line size in doubleword increments (e.g., a 486-based system would store the value 04h, indicating a cache line size of four doublewords). The register must be implemented by bus masters that implement the memory write and invalidate command. Because it must know the cache line size in order to write a line into memory, the bus master may not use the memory write and invalidate command when this register is set to zero. In this case, the master should only use memory write transactions to update memory.

When a memory target is configured into memory space that the host processor does not cache from, the configuration software must set its cache line size to zero. A memory target that is mapped into cacheable memory address space must have its cache line size register set to the proper line size by the configuration software. This permits the target to detect when a burst transfer is crossing a line boundary. The target can then issue a disconnect to the master, forcing it to terminate the current burst, re-arbitrate for the bus, and then re-initiate the transaction at the start address of the next line. This ensures that the new line address is snooped by the host/PCI bridge. The register is cleared when reset.

Latency Timer: "Timeslice" Register

Required for bus masters. The latency timer defines the minimum amount of time, in CardBus clock cycles, that the bus master can retain ownership of the bus. The bus master decrements its latency timer by one on the rising-edge of each clock after it initiates a transaction. It may continue its transaction until either:

- it has completed the overall burst transfer, or
- it has exhausted its timeslice (LT value) and it has been preempted (lost its CGNT# to another master),

whichever comes first.

Every bus master that performs burst of more than two data phases some of the time or all of the time must implement the latency timer, or LT, register as a read/write register. It may be implemented as a hardwired, read-only register by masters that can burst two or less data phases, but the hardwired value returned must not exceed sixteen. Target devices do not implement this register.

In a typical implementation of a the LT register, the low-order three bits are hardwired to zero and the programmer can program any value into the high-order five bits. This permits the programmer to specify the timeslice with a granularity of eight PCI clocks. If the register is programmable, reset clears it. More information on the latency timer can be found in the section entitled "Master Latency Timer" on page 90.

Optimally, every bus master should implement this as a read/write register. This permits the PCMCIA configuration software maximum flexibility when it divides up the available bus time between the CardBus masters.

Header Type Register

Required. Figure 18-4 on page 307 illustrates the format of the header type register. Bits [6:0] of this one byte register define the format of doublewords 4d through 15d of the device's configuration header. In addition, bit seven defines the device as a single (bit cleared) or multi-function (bit set) device. During configuration, the programmer determines if there are any other functions in this package that require configuration by testing the state of bit seven.

Currently, the only header format defined by the rev 2.1 PCI specification, other than the one pictured in Figure 18-1 on page 299 (header type 00h) is header type one (PCI-to-PCI bridge header format). However, header type two has been defined by Yenta and was pending approval by PCI at the time of this writing. A description can be found in the chapter entitled "CardBus Bridge Configuration Registers" on page 261.

Figure 18-4: Header Type Register

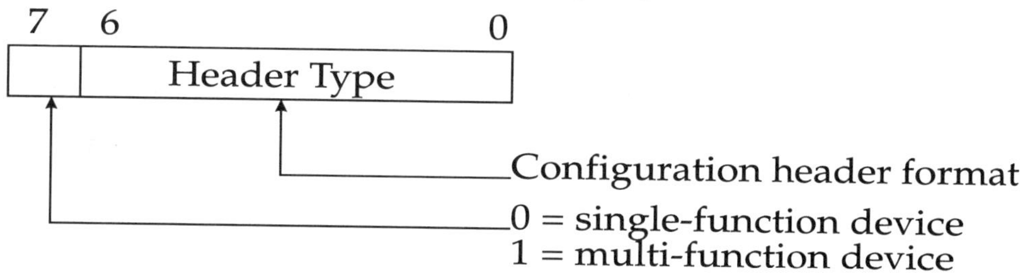

CardBus CIS Pointer

Required. This register identifies the location of the Card Information Structure (CIS). The register is read-only and contains the offset of the CIS in one of the following places:

- Offset within the device-specific configuration space (after doubleword 15 in the device's configuration space).
- Offset from the start address indicated in one of the device's memory base address registers.
- Offset within a code image in the device's expansion ROM.

The format of the CardBus CIS Pointer register is illustrated in Figure 18-5 and the fields are defined in Table 18-3 on page 308.

Figure 18-5: CIS Pointer Register

PCMCIA configuration software must read this register to determine the location of the CIS. It can then be read and parsed to determine the function type and configuration requirements of the function. The values specified by the CIS determine how the card can be configured.

Table 18-3: CIS Pointer Register Bit Assignment

Bit(s)	Definition
2:0	**Address Space Indicator**. Specifies the base address within the space indicated. The offset (defined by bits [27:3]) is added to this base address to identify the start of the CIS. The address indicators values are: 0 = CIS is in device-specific configuration space. 1 = CIS is in the memory pointed to by the base address register 0 2 = CIS is in the memory pointed to by the base address register 1 3 = CIS is in the memory pointed to by the base address register 2 4 = CIS is in the memory pointed to by the base address register 3 5 = CIS is in the memory pointed to by the base address register 4 6 = CIS is in the memory pointed to by the base address register 5 7 = CIS is in the device's expansion ROM. Bits [31:28] identify which ROM image.

Table 18-3: CIS Pointer Register Bit Assignment (Continued)

Bit(s)	Definition
27:3	**Address Space Offset**. Bits [2:0] define which space the CIS resides within. The address space offset is interpreted as follows for each type of address space: • **Configuration space** — the offset is from location 40h in device-specific region up to a maximum value of F8h (dword 63d). • **Memory space** — the offset is from the base address specified by the selected base address register (0-5). The base address value can be from 0 to FFFF FFF8h. • **Expansion ROM space** — the offset value is from the start of the ROM image identified by bits[31:28].
31:28	**ROM Image Number**. Defines the ROM image number (0-Fh) in which the CIS is located. The offset value is added to the start of the ROM image to identify the start of the CIS.

If the CIS is in configuration space, the offset must be in the range from 40h through F8h, inclusive. If the CIS is in memory space, the offset is in the range from 0000000h through FFFFFF8h. If the CIS is in the expansion ROM, the offset is located within the specified ROM image. PCMCIA configuration software must map the entire ROM into memory space and scan ROM to detect the start of the ROM image indicated.

Each function within a multi-function CardBus card must have this register implemented with a valid pointer. A detailed description of the CIS can be found in the chapter entitled "CardBus CIS" on page 321.

Note that the function's CIS contains information that specifies the size and type of resources that are assignable via the device's configuration registers. Problems arise if the address space indicators specify that the CIS is located within a memory range specified by one of the base address registers or by the expansion ROM base address register. This creates a "chicken and egg" type of paradox: the CIS must be read to determine the size of memory-mapped device or size of ROM associated with a particular base address register, but the base address register must be programmed to map the CIS into memory before it can be read.

It is the author's opinion that the PCMCIA configuration software must probe the base address register or expansion ROM base address register (in PCI fashion), to determine the size and mapping requirements. This is the mechanism used by PCI configuration software to determine the size, type, and mapping requirements of devices mapped via the base address registers. Once the size of the device is known, it can be mapped into memory address space and the CIS can be read and the requirements for mapping other resources can be obtained.

Interrupt Pin Register

Required if the device generates interrupts. The interrupt pin register must be implemented to provide a method for PCMCIA software to determine if the function requires use of a hardware interrupt. A value of 00h in the interrupt pin register indicates that this function does not use interrupts, while any other value indicates interrupts are generated by this function.

The CardBus configuration table within the CIS specifies which of the IRQ lines can satisfy the requirements of the function. The function's client driver will request each possible IRQ assignment from CS until it finds one of the specified IRQ lines available. If an IRQ line has already been allocated to another function within the card, then the interrupt sharing protocol is used. Refer to the chapter entitled, "CardBus Function Interrupts" on page 193 for details.

BIST Register

Optional. This register may be implemented by both master and target devices. If a device implements a built-in self-test, or BIST, it must implement this register as illustrated in Figure 18-6. Table 18-4 on page 311 describes each bit's function. If the device doesn't support a BIST, this register must return zeros when read. The device's BIST is invoked by setting bit six to one. The device resets bit six upon completion of the BIST. Configuration software must fail the device if it doesn't reset bit six within two seconds. At the conclusion of the BIST, the test result is indicated in the lower four bits of the register. A completion code of zero indicates successful completion. A non-zero value represents a device-specific error code.

The BIST register is intended to be accessed only by client driver software, not CS and SS. The client driver could provide an option for performing the BIST or choose to test the card before enabling it for operation.

Figure 18-6: The BIST Register

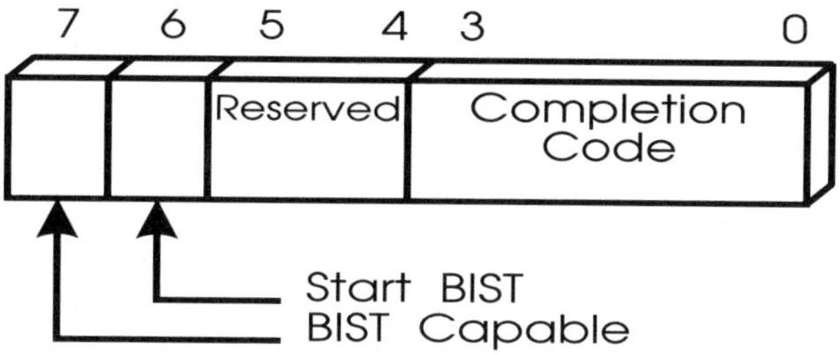

Table 18-4: BIST Register Bit Definition

Bit	Function
3:0	**Completion Code**. Read-only. A value of zero indicates successful completion, while a non-zero result indicates a device-specific error.
5:4	Reserved.
6	**Start BIST**. Read/write. A one in this bit starts the device's BIST. The device resets this bit automatically upon completion. Software should fail the device if the BIST does not complete within two seconds.
7	**BIST Capable**. Read-only. Should return a one if the device implements a BIST, a zero if it doesn't.

Base Address Registers

Virtually all devices utilize some memory address space, IO address space or both. Some examples follow:

- A serial port's status, command and data registers would typically reside in IO address space (but could be mapped into memory space as well).
- A network interface's control registers (command/status, etc.) typically reside in IO address space (but could be mapped into memory space as well). The interface may also incorporate RAM memory that must be mapped into the system's memory space. In addition, a device ROM containing the device's BIOS and interrupt service routines may be present.

When a CardBus card is inserted into a socket, it must be automatically configured so that its device's IO and memory functions occupy mutually-exclusive address ranges. In order to accomplish this, PCMCIA software detects the number and size of memory and IO address ranges a device requires. This is accomplished by parsing the function's CIS. In addition, the system must have the capability of programming a device's address decoders to assign non-conflicting IO and memory address ranges to them.

The base address registers, located in doublewords four through nine of the device's configuration header space, permit this relocatibility. Each register is 32 bits in size and is used to implement a programmable memory or IO address decoder. Figure 18-9 on page 317 and Figure 18-9 on page 317 illustrate the two possible formats of a configuration base address register. If bit zero is cleared, the register is a memory address decoder, whereas, a one indicates it's an IO address decoder.

Mapping IO Registers

In a PC environment, IO space is densely populated and will likely become more so in the future. For this reason and because some processors are only capable of performing memory transactions, the PC Card standard requires that the device designer provide a memory base address register to map a device's register set into memory space. Optionally, an IO base address register may also be included. Therefore, if IO address mapping is used to map a block of registers, the designer must also provide memory mapping for these same registers.

Figure 18-7: IO Register Mapping — Convention One

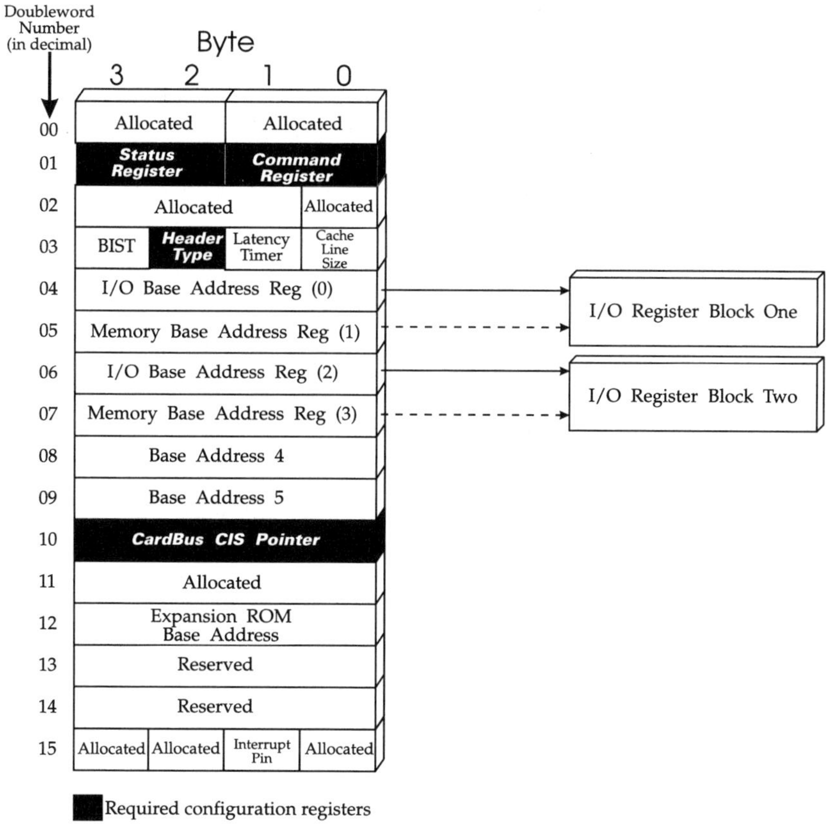

This gives the configuration software the flexibility to map the device's register set into the address space best suited for a given host environment. The client driver associated with the device can choose whether to communicate with its device's register set through memory or IO space, but is not permitted to double map the same set of registers into both IO and memory space simultaneously. To avoid this double mapping, the PC Card Standard defines two conventions for implementing base address registers that provide both IO and memory mapping for its registers. The designer may choose either convention.

1. Each IO base address register is followed by a memory base address register as illustrated in Figure 18-7 on page 313.
2. Several contiguous IO base address registers are implemented, followed by a single memory base address register that maps all registers into a single memory address space. This is illustrated in Figure 18-8 on page 314.

Note that other than these two IO register mapping conventions, there are no other restrictions regarding which base address register can be used for memory or IO device mapping. The Base Address Register (BAR) tuple within the CIS contains a bit map of the function's implemented base address registers. This tuple also defines the space associated with each base address register. The BAR tuple is discussed in the section entitled "CardBus Tuples" on page 324.

Figure 18-8: IO Register Mapping — Convention Two

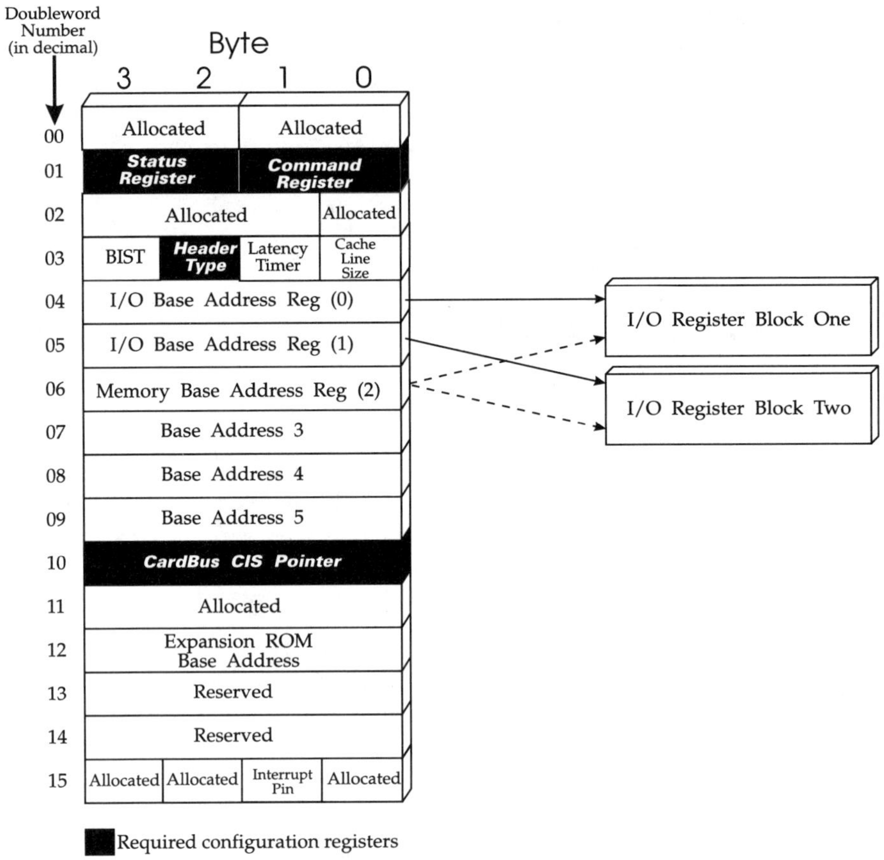

Memory Base Address Register

Required if the function implements a memory decoder. The memory base address register is comprised of four separate fields (Figure 18-9 on page 317):

- **Memory Space Indicator** bit—defines the BAR as a memory or IO decoder.
- **Type**—defines where memory should be mapped (below 1MB, or anywhere in lower 4GB).
- **Prefetchable** bit—specifies category of device being mapped in memory.
- **Base Address**—used to assign start memory address for memory.

The values for the memory space indicator, type, and Prefetchable bits must be set to the correct values by the device designer (e.g., hardwired to Vcc or Ground) and are read-only. Note that these register values can also be read from the BAR tuple within the CIS. The base address register value is determined by PCMCIA configuration software based on the device size (obtained from the BAR tuple) and the memory address space that is available for assignment to the device.

Memory Space Indicator

A zero in bit zero indicates it's a memory decoder, while a one indicates it's an IO decoder.

Type Bit

Bits [2:1] within each memory base address register (see Figure 18-9 on page 317), define where the block of memory can be located (in the first megabyte or the first 4GB of memory address space). These bits are set to the appropriate values by the device designer and are read-only.

Prefetchable Bit

Bit three defines the block of memory as prefetchable or not. A block of memory space may be marked as prefetchable only if it can guarantee that:

- there are no side effects from reads (i.e., the read doesn't alter the contents of the location).
- on a read, it always returns all bytes irrespective of the byte enable settings.
- the CardBus bridge can merge writes within this range without causing errors.
- the memory is not cacheable.

The CIS defines whether a given memory base address register is used to map a prefetchable memory array or memory-mapped IO ports, thereby specifying the value that should be written to the prefetchable bit. As an example, if a block of IO ports is being mapped into memory space, the BAR tuple within the CIS would specify that the corresponding memory base address register have the PREFETCHABLE bit cleared to zero. When PCMCIA configuration software configures the corresponding memory base address register, it must ensure that bit three is cleared to indicate that this range of memory addresses is not prefetchable. Conversely, the BAR tuple would specify that the PREFETCH-ABLE bit be set for a regular memory array.

PCMCIA configuration software uses the PREFETCHABLE bit settings to determine what memory address ranges within which the CardBus bridge can safely implement performance enhancing techniques such as speculative reads and byte merging.

Memory Base Address

Bits [31:4] make up the base address field and are used assign the start address in memory where the corresponding memory (or memory-mapped IO) device is mapped. The number of bits implemented as read/write in the base address field reflects the size of the memory array or block of registers that are mapped into memory by this register. Device size is restricted to powers-of-two, with the binary-weighted value of the least-significant read/write bit reflecting the size of the device. For example, if base address register bits 11:4 are not implemented (hardwired to zeros), the first bit implemented (bit 12) has a binary-weighted value of 4KB (2^{12}), reflecting the size of the memory array. Consequently, a device of a given size can only be assigned a start address divisible by the size of the device. Bits not implemented must be hardwired to always return zero.

A memory base address register that implements all bits within the base address field, [31:4], represents the smallest memory address decoder that can be implemented. Since the binary-weighted value of bit four is 16, 16 bytes is the smallest memory block that a CardBus memory decoder can be designed for.

Figure 18-9: Memory Base Address Register

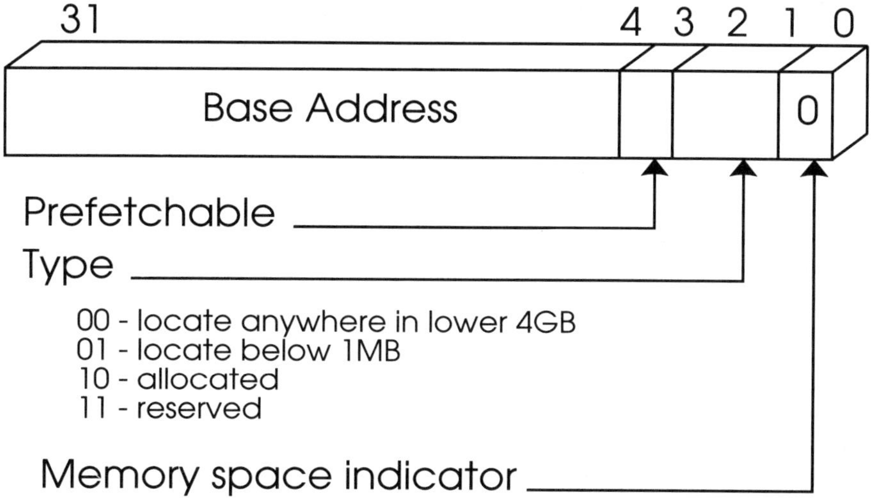

IO Base Address Register

Required if the function implements an IO decoder. A base address register must have bit zero set to a one to identify it as an IO base address register. Bit one is reserved and should be hardwired to zero. Bits 31:2 make up the base address field and are used to assign a start IO address to the device. The number of read/write bits implemented in the base address field, bits[31:2], must reflect the size of the block of registers mapped by this register. Device size is restricted to powers-of-two, with the binary-weighted value of the least-significant read/write bit reflecting the size of the device. There is a minimum four byte granularity.

Figure 18-10: IO Base Address Register

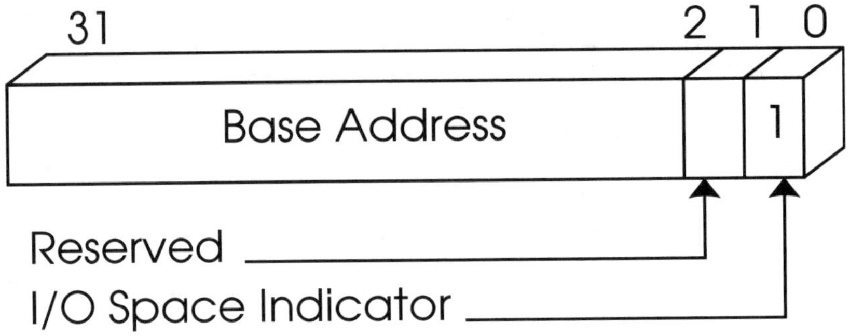

PCMCIA configuration software parses the CIS to determine the size of the register block to be mapped via each IO base address register. After discovering this information, the programmer then uses the base address register to assign a start address to the address decoder.

Expansion ROM Base Address Register

CardBus devices may also incorporate a device ROM that contains the device's power-on self-test (POST), BIOS and interrupt service routine. Typically a device ROM is included in devices that are designed to be involved in the boot process (e.g., a hard disk drive or display device). To boot using the driver within a device ROM, firmware within the system would be required to parse the CIS to determine if any CardBus card installed during powerup is a bootable device. If so, the expansion ROM is mapped into memory (using the expansion ROM base address register) and then scanned to find the desired code image. This image contains the initialization code necessary for the device to be set up to be used in the boot process.

The expansion ROM size is specified in the BAR tuple within the CIS. Once the ROM's size is determined, configuration software must determine a non-conflicting address range that the ROM can be mapped into. The ROM base address register can then be set to configure the ROM's address decoder.

The format of the expansion ROM base address register is illustrated in Figure 18-11. A one in bit zero enables the device's ROM address decoder. Bits [10:1] are reserved. Bits [31:11] are used to specify the ROM's start address (starting on an address divisible by the ROM's size). Like the memory and IO base address registers, the least significant bit implemented in the base address field reflect the size of the ROM. Using bits [31:11], the smallest ROM that can be mapped is a 2KB ROM.

Figure 18-11: The ROM Base Address Register

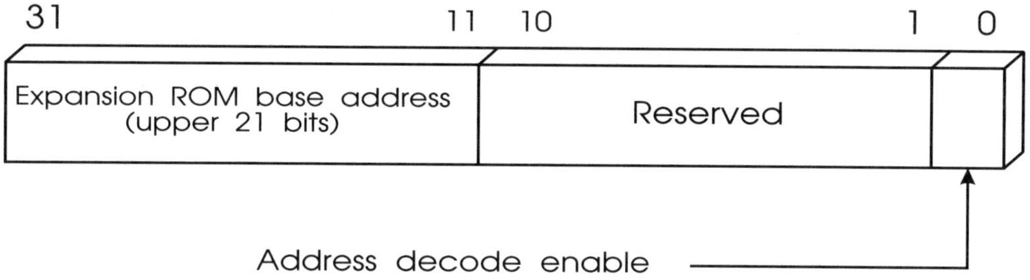

The MEMORY ENABLE bit in the command register has precedence over the EXPANSION ROM ENABLE bit. The device's expansion ROM should respond to memory accesses only if both its MEMORY ENABLE bit (in its command register) and EXPANSION ROM ENABLE bit (in its expansion ROM base address register) are both set to one.

19 CardBus CIS

The Previous Chapter

The previous chapter discussed the configuration registers used by CardBus cards. Each configuration register was described, along with the methods used by PCMCIA configuration software to determine the values that should be loaded into these registers.

This Chapter

This chapter discusses the Card Information Structure (CIS) required by all CardBus cards. Information contained in the CIS specifies how a given card should be configured. In many cases, additional detail can be found in the MindShare book entitled *PCMCIA System Architecture* (published by Addison-Wesley).

The Next Chapter

The next chapter reviews the role of socket services (SS) during the CardBus configuration process. The chapter also lists all socket service function calls that have been either added or modified to support CardBus implementations.

Overview

CardBus cards, like 16-bit PC Cards, include a data structure called the Card Information Structure (CIS) that is stored in non-volatile memory on the card. CardBus cards include a separate CIS for each function within the card. Each CIS provides a method for function-specific software (e.g., client drivers) to determine the type of function and configuration options for a given function. This information is used by the client driver to obtain system resources needed by the function for normal operation.

Figure 19-1 on page 322 illustrates the software flow involved in configuring a PC Card. The CIS is parsed by the client driver during card initialization to determine the configuration options supported by the card. The client driver accesses the CIS via CS and SS. Once the card type and resource requirements have been read from the CIS, the client driver requests that the configuration be performed by CS and SS. No further access is typically made to the CIS after the card has been initialized. The CardBus function can then be accessed using regular memory and IO transactions (just as if it resided on the PCI bus). Note that the CIS is only accessed by programs that are PCMCIA aware (e.g., client drivers). During normal operation, most application programs have no knowledge that they are accessing devices implemented in PC Card packages.

Figure 19-1: PCMCIA Software Flow

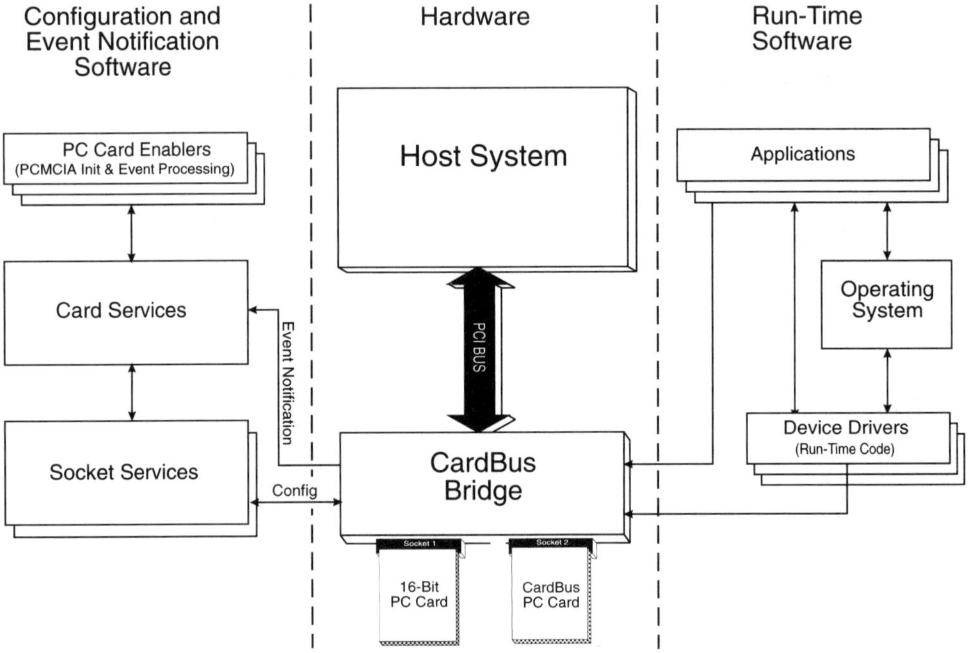

Card Information Structure (CIS)

The CIS consists of a linked list of data blocks, called tuples, that describe the function and characteristics of a CardBus function. Configuration software accesses the CIS to determine the characteristics and configuration requirements of a given CardBus function. Each function and its CIS is identified by the function number (0-7) that is used when accessing the function's configuration address space.

The CIS may consist of multiple chains in different address spaces (except IO space). The CIS start address is specified by the CIS Pointer within the function's configuration address space (see the next section for details). The CIS begins with a Link Target tuple (CISTPL_LINKTARGET) aligned on an eight-byte boundary (due to the address offset value in the CIS Pointer). A CardBus Long Link tuple (CISTPL_LONGLINK_CB) can be used to continue the CIS in another address space. This tuple has the same format as the CardBus CIS Pointer register. Each tuple chain must begin with the Link Target tuple and terminate with an End tuple.

CIS Start Address

The starting location of the CIS within a CardBus card is specified by the CIS Pointer configuration register, illustrated in Figure 19-2 on page 323. For additional information, see "CardBus CIS Pointer" on page 307. This register provides the option of mapping the CIS into one of the following address spaces:

- **Configuration address space** — located within the device-specific region of the function's configuration address space.
- **Memory address space** — located within a memory range specified by one of six memory base address registers in the function's configuration header.
- **Expansion ROM** — located within one of the code images in the expansion ROM.

Figure 19-2: The CardBus CIS Pointer Register

Traversing CIS Chain

Note that processing software should save a Longlink tuple when it is encountered and continue processing the current tuple string until it reaches the end.

Upon reaching the end of a tuple chain, the Longlink tuple can be processed and tuple processing can begin at the location specified by the Longlink tuple. A No Link (CISTPL_NO_LINK) tuple indicates that the current tuple string is the last string in the chain. When a No Link tuple is detected, it too is saved until the end of the chain is reached, at which time tuple processing has been completed.

The PC Card Standard recommends that a CardBus client driver obtain information from the CIS by calling the GetFirstTuple/GetNextTuple services. In this way, CS automatically processes the Long Link tuples, thereby simplifying client driver CIS processing.

CardBus Tuples

Tuples are identified by a unique code contained in the first byte of each tuple. The PC Card Standard defines the format of each tuple. Several new tuples have been added for CardBus card designs. The complete list of tuples supported for CardBus implementations is shown in Table 19-1. The shaded areas represent new tuples that apply to CardBus only. Each of the new tuples are detailed in the sections that follow the table. The exact set of tuples incorporated into the CardBus CIS depends primarily on the type of card and its capabilities. However, some of the tuples are mandatory and are indicated with an asterisk in the Code column of Table 19-1.

Table 19-1: Tuples Defined for Compatibility Layer One (CIS)

Code (h)	CISTPL_NAME	Description and Purpose
00	NULL	**Null Control tuple** — used as a place holder. Ignored by tuple processing software.
02	LONGLINK_CB	**CardBus Long Link tuple** — This tuple indicates to processing software that the CIS continues in another address space. This tuple has the same format as the CardBus CIS Pointer register within the CardBus card's configuration header. It specifies the address space and offset where the next tuple string begins. Each tuple string must begin with a CISTPL_LINKTARGET tuple.

Table 19-1: Tuples Defined for Compatibility Layer One (CIS) (Continued)

Code (h)	CISTPL_NAME	Description and Purpose
04*	CONFIG_CB	**CardBus Configuration tuple** — specifies the index number of the last entry within the configuration table. Also specifies the location in memory address space where the CardBus card's status registers are located. May contain subtuples containing additional information related to the card's configuration.
05*	CFTABLE_ENTRY_CB	**CardBus Configuration Table Entry tuple** — identifies a set of possible configuration options for the card's function. The configuration table may contain multiple entries, each describing possible configuration combinations.
07*	BAR	**Base Address Register tuple** — specifies the size and type of address space required by a CardBus function. This information is used by configuration software to determine how much address space is required to map a given device into either memory or IO address space. Each BAR tuple entry corresponds to a Base Address Register implemented in the card's configuration header.
10	CHECKSUM	**Checksum Control** — provides a means for verifying the contents of the CIS in memory. Multiple checksum control tuples can be implemented within a single CIS.
13*	LINKTARGET	**Link Target** — verifies the continuation of a valid tuple string. The Link Target tuple is the first tuple at the entry point specified by a Long-Link tuple.

Table 19-1: Tuples Defined for Compatibility Layer One (CIS) (Continued)

Code (h)	CISTPL_NAME	Description and Purpose
15*	VERS_1	**Level 1 (also layer 1)Version/Product Information tuple** — identifies the PCMCIA compliance level of the CIS (also called the compatibility layer or metaformat layer one). Following the Version information, production information is provided in a series of ASCII strings, ending in zeros (called ASCIIZ).
16	ALTSTR	**Alternate Language String** — includes additional languages for ASCII strings used in the product information tuple (code 15h). Also used for the Level 2 Version / Product Information tuple (code 40h).
18	JEDEC_C	**Joint Electronic Device Engineering Council's identifier tuple for memory devices** —specifies the JEDEC manufacturer and the programming algorithm required by programmable devices implemented in memory (01h) for common memory. Entries in the JEDEC identifier tuple have a one-to-one correspondence to the entries in the device information tuple.
1C*	DEVICE_OC	**Other Conditions Device Information** (common memory) — Specifies the characteristics of devices mapped in the common memory address space, when operating under conditions other than the defaults. For example, if the card is a dual-voltage card (operates at both 5 volts and 3.3 volts) the characteristics of the common memory devices may be altered depending on which voltage is applied. There must be a one-to-one correspondence between the information fields listed in the Device Information tuple and the Other Conditions Device Information tuple.

Table 19-1: Tuples Defined for Compatibility Layer One (CIS) (Continued)

Code (h)	CISTPL_NAME	Description and Purpose
1E	DEVICEGEO	**Device Geometry (common memory)** — Device geometry provides the erase, read, and write characteristics of programmable devices. This tuple consists of multiple entries for each device identified in the device information tuple.
1F	DEVICEGEO_A	**Device Geometry (attribute memory)** — Device geometry provides the erase, read, and write characteristics of programmable devices. This tuple consists of multiple entries for each device identified in the device information tuple.
20*	MANFID	**PCMCIA Manufacturers Identification** — Contains the PCMCIA manufacturer identification code and manufacturer card identifier and revision information.
21	FUNCID	**Function Identification** — Categorizes the card's functional type and specifies whether the card should be initialized during basic system initialization or when the operating system loads. A multi-function device may also be specified, in which case additional Function Identification tuples for each of the card's functions will follow.
22	FUNCE	**Function Extension** — Provides detailed information about a specific function previously identified by the function identification tuple. This tuple contains additional information useful to application programs or utility programs that are PCMCIA-aware. Function extensions, if applicable, follow each Function Identification tuple in the tuple chain. Extensions are useful for defining the capabilities of various types of devices such as modems and network interface cards.

Table 19-1: Tuples Defined for Compatibility Layer One (CIS) (Continued)

Code (h)	CISTPL_NAME	Description and Purpose
FF*	END	**End** or termination **tuple** — Indicates that this tuple is the last tuple in the string.

* Tuples that must be implemented in each CardBus CIS.

Configuration Table

All CardBus functions must have a CIS that includes a configuration table. This table consists of multiple entries, each of which describes a set of configuration options that the function needs for normal operation. Each configuration table entry reflects the possible resource combinations that the function can be configured for.

Figure 19-3 on page 329 illustrates a CIS containing a configuration table. Directly preceding the configuration table is the configuration tuple that specifies the index number of the last configuration table entry and the location of the CardBus function's status registers.

Figure 19-3: Tuples within Sample CardBus CIS

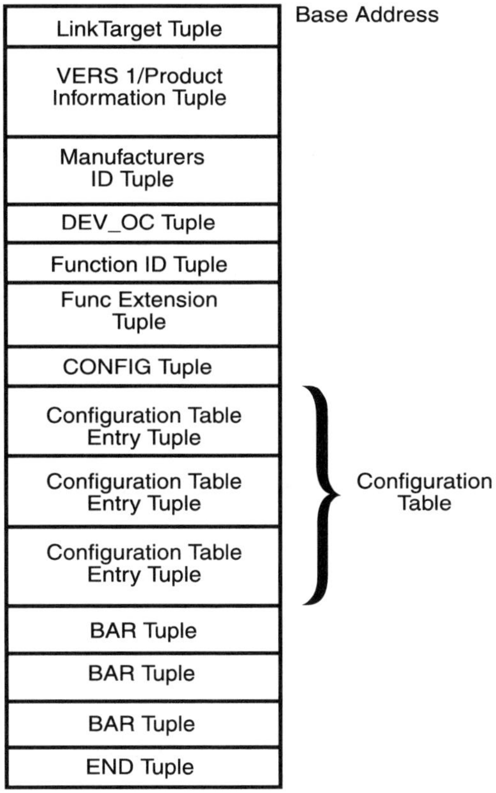

The Configuration Tuple

The items that comprise the configuration tuple and the basic tuple format are illustrated in Table 19-2. This tuple must immediately precede the configuration table.

Table 19-2: The Configuration Tuple Format

Byte	Description
0	Tuple code (04h)
1	Tuple link value

Table 19-2: The Configuration Tuple Format (Continued)

Byte	Description
2	Size of fields (must be 03h to reflect status register size 4 bytes).
3	Index number of last configuration table entry.
4..7	A 32-bit pointer that specifies where the status registers reside in memory. The format of this entry identifies a base address and offset as follows: • Bits 2:0 = memory base address register (1 - 6) containing base address • Bits 31:3 = offset from base address specified
8	Reserved area (four bytes)
C..n	Reserved for subtuples

Configuration Entry Tuple

The configuration table may consist of a series of configuration table entry tuples (CFTABLE_ENTRY_CB). Each entry contains up to six data structures that describe the operational characteristics of the PC Card. Table 19-3 shows the elements that may be contained within each CardBus configuration table entry tuple. The specific structures implemented within a given entry are specified by the feature selection byte (TPCE_CBFS).

Table 19-3: Format of the CardBus Configuration Table Entry Tuple

Byte	Name	Description of Entry
0	TPL_CODE	Configuration Entry tuple code (CISTPL_CFTABLE_ENTRY_CB, 05h)
1	TPL_LINK	Link to next tuple (n-1, {2 minimum})
2	TPCE_INDX	Configuration table index byte — this byte contains the index number of the entry and specifies whether this entry is a default entry or not.
..	TPCE_CBFS	Feature selection byte indicates the optional structures present.
..	TPCE_PD	Power description (same as 16-bit definition).

Table 19-3: Format of the CardBus Configuration Table Entry Tuple (Continued)

Byte	Name	Description of Entry
..	TPCE_CBIO	IO Base Address Register used.
..	TPCE_IR	Interrupt request description (same as 16-bit definition).
..	TPCE_MS	Memory Base Address Register used.
..	TPCE_CBMI	CardBus miscellaneous features field.
n	TPCE_ST	Additional information about the configuration in subtuple format (same as 16-bit definition).

The elements within the CardBus configuration table entry tuple are defined in the following bullet list:

- A **power description byte** — the power parameters specified within this structure may apply to Vcc only, Vcc and Vpp1 and Vpp2 (Vpp1=Vpp2), or separately to Vcc, Vpp1, and Vpp2. The specific power parameters described by the structure are also selectable as defined by the parameter selection byte within the power description structure.
- **IO address space description** — this descriptor is a bit map of the base address registers within the function's configuration header. Each bit that is set indicates that the corresponding base address register in the configuration header is used to map a block of IO registers. If all bits are cleared, then no IO base address registers are implemented (i.e., the function requires no IO address space). Table 19-4 on page 333 lists the format of the BAR tuple.
- **Interrupt request description** — specifies the system interrupt request line required for this configuration. A single IRQ can be specified or a group of IRQs can be defined, any of which will satisfy the configuration requirements. Also included in the description is information that defines: the signaling protocol (level or pulse, but CardBus functions must specify level mode only); whether the function supports interrupt sharing (required for CardBus functions); and alternative interrupt signal definitions (e.g., NMI, IO check, bus error, vendor-specific interrupt).
- **Memory address space description** — this descriptor is a bit map of the base address registers within the function's configuration header. Each bit that is set indicates that the corresponding base address register in the configuration header is used to assign memory address space. If all bits are cleared, then no memory base address registers are implemented (i.e., the function requires no memory address space).

- **Miscellaneous feature field** — contains information regarding support for special features required by this configuration. Two bytes are defined for CardBus features as shown in Table 19-5 on page 334. The first byte provides information on how the command register should be set. The bits in this field should match the corresponding bits in the command register, with one exception. The Fast Back-to-Back field specifies how the Fast Back-to-Back bit in the status register should be set. The second byte defines two bits that specify whether the function supports Binary and/or Pulse Width Modulated (PWM) audio.
- **Subtuple information** — permits definition of additional information relating to this configuration. Subtuples are included as extensions to the configuration table entry tuple and may include information such as the system for which the configuration was intended and the physical device being implemented in this configuration.

Table 19-4: Base Address Register (BAR) Tuple

Byte	Description of CISTPL_BAR
0	Tuple code (07h)
1	Tuple link value
2	**Base address register indicator and attributes**. This field identifies and describes the base address register (BAR) that this tuple applies to. The bits within the field are defined as follows: • Bits 2:0 (**address space indicator**) — identifies the BAR that this tuple describes. Values of 1-6 correspond to BARs 0-5 in the configuration header, respectively. (Note that a value of zero specifies configuration address space and is an illegal value.) • Bit 3 (reserved for future use) • Bit 4 (**address space**) — defines whether the BAR is defined for memory address space (including ROM) or IO address space. (Note that IO address space is restricted to BARs 0-4 in the configuration header.) • Bits 6:5 (**prefetchable/cacheable**) — If the corresponding BAR is used for memory, this field specifies whether the address space is prefetchable and/or cacheable. 00=neither prefetchable or cacheable 01=prefetchable only 10=both prefetchable and cacheable 11=reserved • Bit 7 (**below 1MB**) — When set, this bit specifies that the memory-mapped device should be located below 1MB. When cleared, no address mapping restrictions apply.
3	Reserved (must be zero)
7:4	**Base address register size field**. This 32-bit value specifies the size of the device(s) to be mapped into the corresponding BAR or Expansion ROM BAR. The size must be specified in powers-of-two values.

Table 19-5: Miscellaneous Features Bit Assignment

7	6	5	4	3	2	1	0
EXT	Fast Back-to-Back	SERR# Enable	Wait Cycle Control	Parity Error Response	VGA Palette Snoop	Memory Write & Invalidate	Bus
EXT	RFU	RFU	RFU	RFU	RFU	Binary Audio Enable	PWM Audio Enable

Interpreting Configuration Table

When the software responsible for parsing the CIS (usually a CardBus client driver) processes an entry within the configuration table, it must determine if the resources specified are available (refer to Chapter 22, entitled "CardBus Client Drivers," on page 359 for a discussion of resource acquisition.) If all resources that are requested are available, then the configuration is satisfied and no additional configuration table entries need be evaluated. If, however, one or more of the resources required to satisfy the configuration are not available, then parsing software must evaluate subsequent entries in an attempt to find alternative system resources that will satisfy the PC Card's configuration requirements.

The first entry within the configuration table is typically specified as a default entry. Default entries indicate that all configuration information specified within the entry should be retained even in the event that the full configuration was not satisfied. For example, consider a configuration table that has the following characteristics.

The first entry is a default entry that specifies a power structure, an IO address space structure, an interrupt request structure and a miscellaneous information structure. Assume that parsing software was able to satisfy all configuration information specified by this entry except the interrupt request line.

Since this is a default entry, all resources successfully acquired are retained. This eliminates the need to re-specify all of the parameters that apply globally to the card's configuration regardless of which IO address space and IRQ line is assigned to the card. In this example, since the entire configuration was not satisfied, parsing software proceeds to the next entry, attempting to find alternative resources that the PC Card can use.

Assume that entry two is not a default entry and contains only an IO address structure and IRQ structure. Parsing software, recognizing a non-default entry, knows it must successfully acquire all configuration options specified, and, if unable to do so must release the partial configuration by returning the resources previously acquired. Furthermore, since a pair of resources is being requested, the parsing software recognizes that the IO address space acquired when attempting to satisfy the previous default entry must be released in favor of the new IO address space and IRQ lines specified by this entry. If the new configuration options are acquired successfully, then the configuration is completed. If not, the incomplete configuration is released and parsing software proceeds to the next entry.

Assume that entry three is not a default entry and contains another set of IO addresses and another IRQ line. Once again parsing software attempts to acquire both resources, and, if not successful, must release any resource acquired and proceed to the next entry. As before, if both are acquired the configuration is complete.

Entry four is the last configuration entry and contains the final IO address space and IRQ options for configuring the PC Card. If these resources cannot both be acquired, then the parsing software must report to the user that the card cannot be configured.

Assuming that the client driver successfully obtained the required configuration resources from the system, it must then configure the CardBus bridge and CardBus card so that they respond to the resources. This is done by calling the RequestConfiguration service to request that the configuration be performed.

Part Six

CardBus Software

20 *Socket Services*

The Previous Chapter

The previous chapter discussed the Card Information Structure (CIS) required by all CardBus card functions. Information contained in the CIS specifies how a given card should be configured.

This Chapter

This chapter reviews the role of socket services (SS) during the CardBus configuration process. It lists the functions that have been either added or modified to support CardBus implementations.

The Next Chapter

The next chapter reviews the role of card services (CS) during the CardBus configuration process. It lists the services that have been either added or modified to support CardBus implementations.

Introduction

Socket services (SS) provides a set of software routines written specifically to access the registers within a given host bus adapter (in this case a PCI-to-CardBus bridge). SS eliminates the need for special knowledge of the CardBus bridge hardware programming interface. These routines or functions are comparable to the BIOS routines that are used in the PC environment. In practice, most client drivers seldom, if ever, directly access SS functions, because properly designed enablers access the bridge and CardBus card via CS. CS, in turn, makes calls to SS at the client driver's request.

Installation and Initialization

SS can be contained in system ROM, can be loaded into system memory via an installable device driver, or can be incorporated as extensions to the operating system. In the PC environment, SS are typically installed via a device driver and must be loaded into the system before CS and other client drivers (i.e., any software that requires SS). Without SS, CS and PC Card client drivers will not install.

The method used to install SS and the protocol used to call the functions is platform dependent. The PC Card Standard currently defines the SS calling interface for Intel x86-based platforms. Refer to the PC Card Standard for details.

Socket Services Functions

As discussed in previous chapters, the CardBus bridge must be programmed to allow system access to the CardBus card and to manage a variety of bridge functions including:

- Specifying the socket interface type (for CardBus or 16-bit PC Cards).
- Programming the memory base and limit address registers.
- Programming I/O base and limit address registers.
- Steering each PC Card's IREQ# signal to the selected system interrupt line.
- Steering the CardBus bridge's status change interrupt to the selected system interrupt line.
- Controlling socket power switching.
- Monitoring status change events.
- Enabling power conservation features.
- Controlling EDC (error detection and correction) generators.

SS controls these functions through a defined set of function calls, each related to objects managed by the adapter. Table 20-1 on page 341 lists the functions according to the object-based grouping defined below:

- **Adapter Functions** — Those functions that affect all sockets that are controlled by the CardBus bridge. For example, the status change interrupt applies to all sockets and reports status change events.
- **Socket Functions** — Those functions controlled individually at the socket level (e.g., setting Vcc to 3.3 volts for a given socket affects only that socket).
- **Window Functions** — Those functions that control the memory and I/O address windows (i.e. the base and limit address registers).

- **Error Detection and Correction (EDC) Functions** — Those functions used to interact with the EDC generators (if implemented).

Table 20-1: CardBus Socket Services Functions by Type

Socket Service Function Types			
Adapter	**EDC**	**Socket**	**Window**
AcknowledgeInterrupt	GetEDC	AccessConfigSpace	GetBridgeWindow
GetAdapter	InquireEDC	GetSocket	InquireBridgeWindow
GetAdapterCount	PauseEDC	GetStatus	SetBridgeWindow
GetSetPriorHandler	ReadEDC	InquireSocket	
GetSetSSAddress	ResumeEDC	ResetSocket	
GetSSInfo	SetEDC	SetSocket	
GetVendorInfo	StartEDC		
InquireAdapter	StopEDC		
SetAdapter			
VendorSpecific			

Numerous SS functions required by 16-bit PC Card implementations are not used by CardBus functions. Conversely, one new SS function, required by CardBus, is not used in 16-bit PC Card implementations. Table 20-2 lists and describes all of the SS functions that apply to the CardBus environment. Since SS is primarily called by CS, details regarding the use and implementations of these functions are not included in this text. Detailed information can be found in the MindShare book entitled *PCMCIA System Architecture* (published by Addison-Wesley). For details regarding each of the SS functions refer to the PC Card Standard.

Table 20-2: Socket Services Functions

Function	Code	Description
ACCESS_CONFIG_SPACE	A2h	Used to access a CardBus card's configuration address space.
ACK_INTERRUPT	9Eh	Returns information about the socket (or sockets) that have experienced a status change.
GET_ADAPTER	85h	Returns the current adapter setting within the CardBus bridge.
GET_ADP_CNT	80h	Returns the total number of adapters found in the system along with the compliance information about each adapter.
GET_BRIDGE_WINDOW	A4h	Returns the current settings of the memory and I/O windows within the CardBus bridge.
GET_EDC	96h	Returns the current settings associated with the EDC hardware within the CardBus bridge.
GET_SOCKET	8Dh	Return the current settings of the selected socket interface within the CardBus bridge.
GET_SS_INFO	83h	Returns information regarding the SS version and the identifies the adapters that this SS handles.
GET_STATUS	8Fh	Returns status information related to the selected socket interface and PC Card.
GET_VENDOR_INFO	9Dh	Returns information about the vendor of the SS that handles the specified adapter.
INQ_ADAPTER	84h	Returns information about the capabilities and implementation of the CardBus bridge.
INQ_BRIDGE_WINDOW	A4h	Returns the capabilities related to the bridge windows settings supported by the CardBus bridge.
INQ_EDC	95h	Returns the capabilities of the EDC hardware implemented within the CardBus bridge.
INQ_SOCKET	8Ch	Returns the capabilities of the socket interface implemented within the CardBus bridge.
PAUSE_EDC	99h	Pauses the EDC hardware within the bridge.
PRIOR_HANDLER	9Fh	Obtains or sets the entry point of a prior SS handler.
READ_EDC	9Ch	Returns the values computed by the EDC hardware.
RESET_SOCKET	90h	Resets both the CardBus bridge's socket interface and the CardBus card to their initialized states.

Table 20-2: Socket Services Functions (Continued)

Function	Code	Description
RESUME_EDC	9Ah	Re-starts the EDC generation hardware that has been paused.
SET_ADAPTER	86h	Sets the selected values within the CardBus bridge that satisfies the configuration.
SET_BRIDGE_WINDOW	A5h	Configures the bridge window within the CardBus bridge.
SET_EDC	97h	Sets the selected values within the CardBus bridge's EDC configuration registers.
SET_SOCKET	8Eh	Configures the specified CardBus bridge's socket interface.
SS_ADDR	A0h	Provides a method of specifying regions of memory that contain code and data that a given SS implementation may need to access.
START_EDC	98h	Starts the EDC generation hardware within the CardBus bridge.
STOP_EDC	9Bh	Stops the EDC generation hardware within the CardBus bridge.
VEND_SPECIFIC	AEh	Provides a method for the vendor of SS to add specific functions not defined by the PC Card Standard.

21 *Card Services*

The Previous Chapter

The previous chapter reviewed the role of socket services (SS) and summarized the functions supported by CardBus implementations. It also listed the functions that are supported for CardBus implementations.

This Chapter

This chapter reviews the role of card services (CS) during the CardBus configuration process. It also lists the services supported for CardBus implementations.

The Next Chapter

In the next chapter, the role of the CardBus function's client driver (i.e., enabler) is reviewed.

Card Services — a Review

Card services (CS) provides a central resource available to all PC Card client drivers (enablers). Specifically, CS is a collection of service routines designed for use by programmers writing enablers for PC Card functions. These services provide a software interface that permit the programmer to simplify code and that help to reduce conflicts with other client drivers and with allocating system resources for PC Cards.

Enablers that use CS are also called CS client drivers. The term client driver is used because CS and the enablers perform their functions based on the client/server model. CS exists to serve the needs of its clients (i.e., the enablers) as they attempt to configure and access their related functions.

The client/server model is employed to provide call-back services to notify the enablers that a particular event has occurred. Each enabler must register with CS and specify which events that it wishes to be notified of. When CS detects a given event (e.g., a card has been inserted or removed), it calls each enabler that had previously registered to receive notification of card insertion or removal.

The services provided to client drivers are divided into five functional groupings by the PCMCIA specification:

- **Client Services** — Provides a registration facility that permits client drivers to register and be notified by CS when specific socket events occur (such as card insertion or removal).
- **Resource Management** — Allows client drivers to request the use of system resources required by the PC Card they are enabling. If the resources are granted, addition resource management functions can be used to assign these resources by programming the HBA (via socket services, or SS) and configuring the PC Card (by writing to the PC Card's configuration registers).
- **Client Utilities** — Provides a set of functions that allow the client driver to perform common jobs with ease. For example, the functions include accessing the PC Card's CIS, thereby simplifying tuple processing code.
- **Bulk Memory Services** — Provides block memory functions to read, write, copy and erase blocks of data within memory cards (without knowledge of the specific memory technology). These functions are passed to the appropriate Memory Technology Driver (MTD) that understands the hardware protocol necessary to erase or write devices such as flash memory. See the next chapter "CardBus Client Drivers" for details regarding memory technology drivers.
- **Advanced Client Services** — Provides specialized functions that may be needed by some client drivers.

Card Services Initialization

CS is designed as an operating system-dependent extension that provides client services for the PC Card environment. CS may be included with the operation system (e.g., OS/2 and Windows 95), implemented as an installable device driver (e.g., typical MS-DOS implementations). Note that neither OS/2 version 3.0 nor Windows 95 support CardBus.

Card Recognition and Configuration

Each CardBus function must have a client driver that recognizes it, reads its CIS to determine its resource requirements, programs the CardBus bridge and configures and enables the CardBus function. As illustrated in Figure 21-1, CardBus client drivers (enablers), interface directly to CS. CS simplifies the job of configuring a PC Card and monitoring status change events.

Figure 21-1: Relationship of Card Services to Other PCMCIA Software

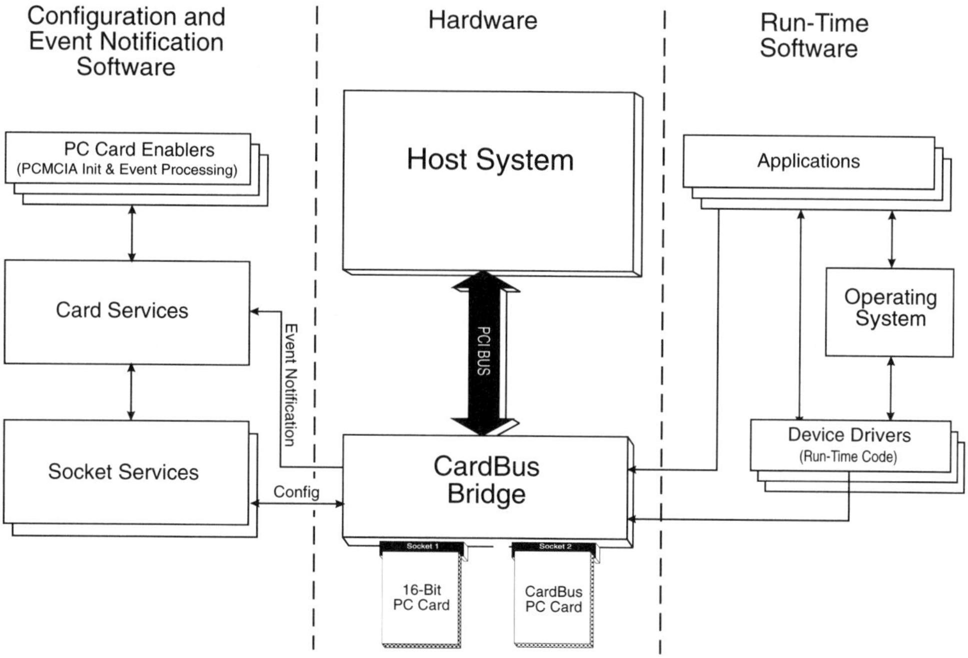

Configuration of CardBus functions may take place when the system powers up (if the CardBus card is already installed in a socket), or when a CardBus card is inserted into a socket (after the system is powered up and fully operational). In either case, each CardBus card's function must be detected and configured by its enabler (i.e., client driver). Without an enabler, CardBus functions are not recognized by the system. However, once a function is recognized and configured by the enabler, it then responds like any other device residing on the host bus.

Only one copy of CS is required (and permitted), since it controls access to all sockets (whether associated with a single adapter or multiple adapters). Once a

PC Card has been configured, it responds like any other host bus device. As a result, application programs designed to access a particular function need not even be aware of the existence of CS and SS. CS and SS are employed by enablers during:

- PC Card initialization and configuration (client driver makes calls).
- PC Card event notification (interrupt driven calls).
- Block transfers to/from memory card (memory client driver makes calls during run-time).

During other times, CS and SS remain in memory, but are not used. The following sections discuss typical uses of the CS functions. The information included in this chapter is not intended for reference purposes, as they provide only a basic description of the function's purpose. Refer to the PCMCIA CS standard for the exact calling parameters, format, field sizes, etc., of each function.

System Resources Availability

One of the major functions performed by CS is to allocate available system resources to PC Cards. Resource management services are called by a PC Card's client driver in an attempt to acquire the resources (e.g., IO address space, memory address space, or IRQ line) that will satisfy the card's configuration requirements. CS must check the available system resources to verify that the requested resources are not already used by the system.

Since CS is an extension to the operation system, in many operating environments it does not have specific knowledge of resources that are already being used by other devices installed into the system. Some method must be employed by CS (or by other platform-specific software) to determine free resources that can be assigned to PC Cards. The exact method used is operating system and hardware platform-specific.

Whether operating in the DOS or Windows 95 Plug and Play environment, the host system (firmware, PCMCIA utilities, and/or OS) must detect the presence of devices that use system resources. The system must then build a table of available system resources that are not in use and pass the table to CS. CS then manages the resources table as resources are requested and released by the client drivers when PC Cards are inserted and removed from sockets.

Power Management Support

Power management support was added to the PC Card standard (95 release). Card service defines power management (PM) support via power management call-back events. CS can be designed to detect the presence of a power management facility within the PC platform and register to receive notification of power management events. When CS receives the power management notification, it calls back all client drivers that have previously registered to receive notification of PM events.

Summary of Services

The following table lists the Card Services supported for the CardBus environment. For a more detailed review of these functions, refer to MindShare's *PCMCIA System Architecture* book (published by Addison-Wesley).

Table 21-1: Card Services Supported by CardBus Implementations

Service Name	Service Code
AccessConfigReg	36h
AddSocketServices	32h
AdjustResourceInfo	35h
CheckEraseQueue	26h
CloseMemory	00h
CopyMemory	01h
DeregisterClient	02h
DeregisterEraseQueue	25h
GetCardServicesInfo	0Bh
GetClientInfo	03h
GetConfigurationInfo	04h
GetEvenMask	2Eh
GetFirstClient	0Eh

Table 21-1: Card Services Supported by CardBus Implementations (Continued)

Service Name	Service Code
GetFirstPartition	05h
GetFirstRegion	06h
GetFirstTuple	07h
GetFirstWindow	37h
GetMemPage	39h
GetNextClient	2Ah
GetNextPartition	08h
GetNextRegion	09h
GetNextTuple	0Ah
GetNextWindow	38h
GetStatus	0Ch
GetTupleData	0Dh
MapLogSocket	12h
MapLogWindow	13h
MapMemPage	14h
MapPhySocket	15h
MapPhyWindow	16h
ModifyWindow	17h
OpenMemory	18h
ReadMemory	19h
RegisterClient	10h
RegisterEraseQueue	0Fh
RegisterMTD	1Ah
RegisterTimer	28h
ReleaseConfiguration	1Eh

Table 21-1: Card Services Supported by CardBus Implementations (Continued)

Service Name	Service Code
ReleaseDMA	3Bh
ReleaseExclusive	2Dh
ReleaseIRQ	1Ch
ReleaseSocketMask	2Fh
ReleaseWindow	1Dh
ReplaceSocket Services	33h
RequestConfiguration	30h
RequestDMA	3Ah
RequestExclusive	2Ch
RequestIO	1Fh
RequestIRQ	20h
RequestSocketMask	22h
RequestWindow	21h
ResetCard	11h
ReturnSSEntry	23h
SetEvenMask	31h
SetRegion	29h
ValidateCIS	2Bh
VendorSpecific	34h
WriteMemory	24h

Table 21-2 on page 352 provides a brief description of all the card service functions supported by CardBus, organized by functional grouping. Many of these functions have been modified to support multifunction cards and CardBus implementations. For example, the RequestWindow service has been modified to permit a BAR number specifying the register to be programmed. Note also that the RequestIO and ReleaseIO services are not used by CardBus client drivers. The RequestWindow and ReleaseWindows services have been modified to allow IO address space to be allocated, as well as memory address space.

Table 21-2: Description of Card Services

Tuple Name	Description
Client Service Services	
GetCardServicesInfo	Determines if a valid copy of CS is installed and reports information regarding this copy of CS, including its revision and compliance level.
RegisterClient	Used by the client to register with CS as either a memory, MTD or IO client. The client driver also specifies which card status events (such as card removal) it wishes to be notified of by CS. The client can also request that CS generate artificial card insertion events for all PC Cards that are currently installed, allowing the client to configure PC Cards it wishes to use.
DeregisterClient	Allows the client to notify CS that it no longer requires notification of status change events.
GetStatus	Returns the current status of the PC Card and its socket. It returns the same information obtained with the SS GetStatus function.
ResetCard	This function resets the PC Card specified in the input argument, providing that all other clients that are using the same PC Card agree. Since more that one client may use a card, the ResetCard function will not be satisfied until all other clients agree to the reset. CS generates Reset Request call-back events to all registered clients. Once all client drivers have responded to the call-back, CS calls the client that initiated the request via a Reset Complete call-back to inform the client whether the reset succeeded or failed.
SetEventMask	Used by the client to indicate the events it wishes to receive call-backs for. During registration, a client driver can specify which PC Card events that it wants to be notified of. This function can be used after registration to change the global event mask, originally set using RegisterClient. This function can also be used to change the SocketEvent mask originally set using Request-SocketMask (see table 20-8), but only if the RequestSocketMask function has been previously called by the client.
GetEventMask	Allows the client to obtain the current values of either the global or socket event mask.
Resource Management Services	

Table 21-2: Description of Card Services (Continued)

Tuple Name	Description
RequestIRQ	Used to obtain a system interrupt line for the calling client. The client specifies which interrupt line or lines will satisfy its interrupt needs. Input parameters request that an interrupt be either exclusive (not shared), time-multiplexed shared (client coordinates with other clients sharing this line, using the ModifyConfiguration function to enable and disable its connection to the interrupt line) or shared dynamically through an interrupt sharing protocol supported by the system. An input parameter also specifies whether the interrupt sent from the PC Card should be pulse or level mode. This function, if successful, assigns the specified IRQ line to the client and adjusts the CS resource table to indicate that the assigned IRQ is no longer available.
RequestWindow	Allows the client to request ownership of a block of system memory addresses. The client passes the starting (base) address and the size of the memory window along with a variety of other parameter to CS. Other parameters include: type of memory window (attribute or common), window enabled or disabled, whether window can be shared with other clients (only time-multiplexed sharing is permitted), whether paging of window is enabled, and speed of the memory devices. This function assigns the address ranges (if available) to the client and adjusts the resource table to indicate that they are no longer available. Note that this same block of addresses can be assigned to another client if the shared parameter is set. This function can be called multiple times per socket, up to the maximum number of memory windows supported by the HBA. CS passes a window handle back to the client to be used when calling other functions pertaining to this window.
RequestDMA	Requests the use of a desired DMA channel for a given PC Card. One of 16 DMA channels can be specified (numbered zero through fifteen). Also specifies whether the DMA channel is to be shared and if so by which method, which PC Card pin is used for DREQ#, and what the DMA channel size is.
ReleaseIRQ	Adjusts the resource table by releasing the IRQ acquired by a client with the RequestIRQ service.
ReleaseWindow	Adjusts the resource table by releasing the block of memory addresses acquired by a client with the Request Window function. The window handle is passed to CS to specify the window to be released.
ReleaseDMA	Adjusts the resource table by releasing the DMA channel acquired by a client with the RequestDMA service.
GetFirstWindow	This service returns the window handle and information associated with the first memory or IO window (i.e., base address, size, and related attributes) of the specified socket and function.
GetNextWindow	This service is called following the GetFirstWindow call to obtain information associated with the next window used by the specified socket.

Table 21-2: Description of Card Services (Continued)

Tuple Name	Description
GetMemPage	This service returns information for the specified page within the requested memory window. The window is specified by the window handle returned by the GetFirstWindow or GetNextWindow services.
ModifyWindow	Allows parameters assigned to a given block of memory addresses acquired with the RequestWindow function to be modified. These parameters include memory device speed, window type (attribute or memory) and window enabled or disabled. The window handle is passed to CS to specify the window to be modified.
MapMemPage	Selects a 16KB memory block within the PC Card to be mapped into a 16KB page within system memory. The 16KB memory block within the PC Card is identified by the client with an absolute offset value from the beginning of the PC Card's memory array.
RequestSocketMask	Selects the status change events that the client wishes the PC Card to generate. The client specifies which status change events it wants to be generated at the socket. A bit-map of the events masks each status change event that should not be reported by the HBA from the specified card. Note that during the RegisterClient function, the client driver indicates which status change events it wishes to be notified of, setting a global event mask.
ReleaseSocketMask	Releases the status change events mask, so that no status change events are reported by the PC Card residing in the specified socket.
ModifyConfiguration	Allows the configuration established by the Request Configuration function to be modified. Note that IRQ routing and the IO address range assigned cannot be modified with this function. These parameters can only be changed by first releasing the configuration and then performing the requests for those resources again.
RequestConfiguration	Used to establish the configuration for an IO interface. The IO address ranges and system interrupt previously acquired are established at the hardware level (HBA and PC Card). Other configurable items are also specified based on the values indicated by the selected Configuration Table Entry, including: Vcc, Vpp1, Vpp2, interface type (memory only or memory/IO) and setting for the configuration registers, if present.
ReleaseConfiguration	This function releases the configuration information set previously using the RequestConfiguration function. This function returns the interface to a memory-only interface and power is removed from the socket (if no memory client indicates its use of the PC Card). The IRQ and IO resources must be released separately to adjust the resource table.
Client Utility Services	
AccessConfigRegisters	Used to access a PC Card function's configuration registers.

Table 21-2: Description of Card Services (Continued)

Tuple Name	Description
GetConfigurationInfo	Provides the client with information about a specified socket and the PC Card installed. This information can be used to determine the configuration requirements of the PC Card installed.
GetFirstTuple	Permits the client to specify a given tuple code and find the first occurrence of that tuple within the PC Card's CIS.
GetNextTuple	Requests that CS find the next occurrence of the tuple code that was previously specified for the GetFirstTuple function.
GetTupleData	Requests the contents of the specified tuple, once it has been located using GetFirst/NextTuple.
GetFirstRegion	Used by memory technology client drivers (MTDs) to get device information for devices defined for the first region within the PC Card (as defined in the card's CIS). Information received by the client includes: location of region within the card, size of region, speed of devices within region, memory type (attribute or common), erase/write capabilities, etc.
GetNextRegion	Finds the device information for the next region within the card.
GetFirstPartition	Similar to the GetFirstRegion function, this function returns information for the first partition on the card based on information contained in the PC Card's CIS. If a PC Card has no partition information defined in its CIS, then CS may be able to determine partition information based on a given file system structure (such as the BIOS parameter block (BPB)/FAT structure used by DOS).
GetNextPartition	Finds device information for the next partition.
Bulk Memory Services	
OpenMemory	This function opens an area of common memory within a PC Card that is to be accessed some time in the future (e.g., read, write, copy or erase operation). A memory handle is returned that identifies this memory range when performing one of the operations mentioned above.
ReadMemory	This function reads data from an area of common memory specified by a given memory handle (obtained from the OpenMemory function). The calling MTD passes a pointer during the call specifying a system memory buffer to which data is to be returned.
WriteMemory	This function writes data to a common memory area identified with a memory handle obtained via the OpenMemory function. The calling MTD passes a pointer to a system memory buffer that contains the data to be written.

Table 21-2: Description of Card Services (Continued)

Tuple Name	Description
CopyMemory	This function reads data from a source location and writes it to a destination within the same common memory region that is identified by a memory handle obtained via the OpenMemory function.
CloseMemory	This function closes an area of common memory that was previously opened with the OpenMemory function. The calling MTD passes the memory handle of the memory area to be closed along with the call.
RegisterEraseQueue	Establishes an erase queue where erase entries can be made.
CheckEraseQueue	Notifies CS that one or more erase request entries have been sent to the erase queue.
DeregisterEraseQueue	Eliminates an erase queue previously registered using the Register-EraseQueue function. This function fails if erase entries within the queue are still pending completion.
Advanced Client Services	
ReturnSSEntry	Provides a means of gaining access directly to SS. Normally, access to SS is denied by CS to ensure that it maintains synchronization with the state of the HBA. If client drivers are allowed access to SS, the HBA setting can be modified without CS knowledge. If absolutely required, a client driver can request access to SS via the ReturnSSEntry call. The programmer must be certain that nothing is changed at the HBA level that will affect the operation of CS.
MapLogSocket	Determines the physical adapter and socket that is assigned to a logical socket number.
MapPhySocket	Identifies the logical socket number assigned to a physical adapter and socket.
MapLogWindow	Identifies the physical adapter and window that are mapped to a given logical window handle.
MapPhyWindow	Identifies the logical window handle assigned to a given physical adapter and window.
RegisterMTD	Assigns an MTD to a region of memory. When access to the assigned region occurs, the MTD is called to handle the memory operation.

Table 21-2: Description of Card Services (Continued)

Tuple Name	Description
RegisterTimer	Allows a client driver to register for callback at specified time intervals. A client may register multiple times to get notification at various time intervals. Timing is based on 1ms interval. The client specifies the call-back interval based on the number of 1ms ticks specified during registration. A timer handle is returned during registration and passed to the client when the call-back occurs. This permits the client to identify the specific timer that has expired when the call-back occurs.
SetRegion	Allows a client driver of a card that does not have a CIS to specify the characteristics of a given region within the card.
ValidateCIS	Scans the CIS by reading the tuple chain contained on the PC Card. The function returns the number of valid tuples found within the chain.
RequestExclusive	Permits a client driver to request exclusive access to a given PC Card. CS ensures that no other client is currently using the card before granting exclusive access to this client driver. If another client driver is currently using the card and is unwilling to release control, then function will fail.
ReleaseExclusive	Releases exclusive access to a card that was previously granted via the RequestExclusive function.
GetFirstClient	Returns the client handle of the first client to register with CS.
GetNextClient	Returns the client handle of the next client to register with CS.
GetClientInfo	Provides client driver information for the client handle specified.
AddSocketServices	Allows another SS handler to be installed to support an additional HBA.
ReplaceSocketServices	Replaces the current version of SS with a new version.
VendorSpecific	Defined by the vendor of CS to extend functionality.
AdjustResourceInfo	Adjusts the resource database maintained by CS. This data base contains the system resources that are available for use by PC Cards. This function allows system resources to either be added or removed from the database.

22 CardBus Client Drivers

The Previous Chapter

The previous chapter focused on the role of card services (CS) in the CardBus environment. It also reviewed each of the Card Service calls defined by the PC Card specification that apply to CardBus PC Cards.

This Chapter

This chapter discusses the role of client drivers, or enablers, in the configuration process. The chapter also describes the specific requirements for supporting CardBus functions.

The Next Chapter

The next chapter provides an overview of the Texas Instruments PCI1130 PCI-to-CardBus bridge. The bridge incorporates distributed DMA capability, a serialized interrupt delivery mechanism, and a ZOOM Video (ZV) Port.

Role of Client Driver (Enabler)

PC Card enablers must recognize that a PC Card has been installed and access the card's CIS to determine if it should attempt to configure the card. If the enabler recognizes a function within the PC Card, it may attempt to configure the function (whether contained within a 16-bit or a CardBus PC Card). The PC Card Standard recommends that an enabler be specifically designed to support both 16-bit and CardBus PC Cards.

Registration

In order to recognize and configure a PC Card function, enablers must first register with card services. The primary function of an enabler is to detect and configure PC Card functions that it supports. As such, the enabler must be prepared to configure its associated functions no matter when they are installed. In order to configure cards installed after power up, the enabler registers with card services to receive a call back (i.e., a card insertion call-back) each time card services detects that a PC Card has been installed or removed. During registration, the enabler can also request that card services generate a call-back for each PC Card already installed, thereby calling the enabler's configuration routine.

Card Insertion Call-Back

When card services makes a card insertion call-back, it specifies the type of call-back, along with the logical socket that the card was inserted into. The enabler's call-back routine then attempts to configure the card. The CIS may have to be accessed several times to obtain a combination of card-required resources that can be successfully allocated to the card (i.e., resources that are not already assigned to other devices).

The configuration process begins when card services makes the card insertion call-back to the enabler. The enabler detects which event caused the call-back and obtains information supplied by card services (e.g., which logical socket the card was inserted into).

The method used to configure a card varies depending on the type of card to be configured. The next two sections discuss generic memory and IO enablers.

As discussed in the previous chapter, a variety of services are available for the PC Card enablers (i.e., card services client drivers) to configure a PC Card.

PC Card Function Recognition

Enablers recognize their associated functions in a variety of ways, including but not limited to information obtained from:

- the GetConfigurationInfo service call.
- the Version One/Product Information tuple
- the Manufacturers ID tuple
- the Function ID tuple
- combinations of tuples

The PC Card Standard recommends that enablers use the GetFirstTuple, GetNextTuple, and GetTupleData services to locate and read the CIS contents. Once an enabler has detected a function that it should attempt to enable, it proceeds with determining the resource requirements by parsing the CIS.

Configuring the PC Card Function

Once a PC Card function has been recognized by an enabler that it wishes to configure it must determine the configuration requirements of the function. In a CardBus implementation, this can be accomplished by parsing the CIS. Specifically, the interrupt table can be parsed to determine the configuration options that will satisfy the function's memory address space, IO address space, and IRQ requirements.

Unlike 16-bit PC Cards, CardBus cards contain the BAR tuples that must be parsed to detect the amount and type of address space that is being requested. The enabler then requests that IO and/or memory address space be allocated using the RequestWindow service. (Note that the RequestWindows service is used for both memory and IO address space requests.) If interrupts are required by the CardBus function, the enabler uses the RequestIRQ service to obtain an IRQ line for the function. (Note that CardBus enablers must support interrupt sharing).

When all resources have been successfully acquired, the enabler makes the RequestConfiguration service call to enable the IO address range and route the CINT# signal to the selected IRQ line. (Note that the Request Window function enables the memory windows and are not included in the RequestConfiguration service definition.) If this service completes successfully, the configuration is complete and the function is enabled.

Changes Required for CardBus Support

The PC Card Standard recommends that an enabler be designed to support both 16-bit PC Cards and CardBus PC Cards. When adding CardBus support to a 16-bit PC Card enabler, the programmer must provide support for:

- new card services that have been added to support CardBus.
- card services that have been modified to support CardBus.
- new tuples defined for CardBus cards.
- interrupt sharing.

For More Information

See MindShare's *PCMCIA System Architecture* book (published by Addison-Wesley) for more details regarding client drivers and the overall software environment. Also refer to *PCMCIA Software Developer's Handbook* (published by Peer-to-Peer Communications; see Appendix C, "References," for details).

Part Seven

The TI PCI1130 CardBus Bridge Chip

23 The TI PCI 1130

The Previous Chapter

The previous chapter discussed the role of client drivers, or enablers, in the configuration process. It also described the specific requirements for supporting CardBus functions.

This Chapter

This chapter provides an overview of the Texas Instruments PCI1130 PCI-to-CardBus bridge. The bridge incorporates distributed DMA capability, a serialized interrupt delivery mechanism, and a ZOOM Video (ZV) Port.

Overview of Features

The PCI1130 PCI-to-CardBus bridge chip includes the following major features:

- 3.3vdc core logic, employing low-power CMOS technology.
- PCI 2.1 compliant 32-bit interface supporting both 3.3vdc and 5vdc bus switching.
- Support for two PC Card socket interfaces of either type.
  - PC Card Standard ('95) compliant 16-bit PC Card socket interface, supporting 5vdc and 3.3vdc Vcc.
  - PC Card Standard ('95) compliant CardBus socket interface, supporting 3.3vdc Vcc.
- Supports CardBus clock rates up to 33MHz.
- Bi-directional read/write buffering for enhanced throughput (supports burst transactions in either direction).
- Serialized interrupt routing to ISA-compatible IRQ lines.
- Direct routing to ISA-compatible IRQ lines.
- Yenta-compliant configuration space.
- 16-bit distributed DMA support.
- Zoom Video support.

Functional Block Diagram

Figure 23-1 on page 367 illustrates the major subsystems within the PCI1130. The PCI1130 PCI-to-CardBus bridge passes transactions between the PCI bus and two PC Card sockets, both of which support the 16-bit PC Card socket interface and the CardBus socket interface. The PCI1130 detects and identifies PC cards during power-up or when installed during run-time.

Socket power is controlled by an external Dual-PCMCIA Power Switch (TI TPS2202). The CardBus bridge communicates the required voltage to the TPS 2202 via a three-line serial protocol. The TPS2202 provides independent power switching to each socket via this serial protocol.

The PCI1130 also supports interrupt routing via PCI interrupt lines, ISA IRQ's, or a serialized IRQ protocol. Status change interrupts and function interrupt requests from the PC Cards (via IREQ# or CINT#) can be routed using any of these methods.

Distributed DMA is also supported to provide full support for the optional DMA capability specified for 16-bit cards by the PC Card Standard('95 release).

The following sections provide additional details regarding the functions illustrated in Figure 23-1 on page 367.

PCI Interface

The PCI interface is compliant with the 2.1 revision of the PCI specification. The PCI interface consists of two functions (one for each socket interface). Function zero is associated with socket A and function one with socket B. Each function has its own configuration address space as defined in Figure 23-2 on page 368. The configuration register definition is compliant with the Yenta-defined PCI-to-CardBus bridge header. Additionally, device-specific registers have been defined to support additional functionality. Note that the PCI interface supports both 3.3vdc and 5.0vdc signaling by connecting the two Vccp terminals to the desired switching level.

The PCI1130 supports all PCI transaction commands except: Interrupt Acknowledge, Special Cycle, and Dual Address Cycle. When responding to a transaction, the bridge always responds with a medium-speed decode. The chip is also capable of accepting and generating PCI burst cycles during transfers between CardBus and the PCI bus. Burst transfers can occur at zero wait states in either direction until the internal FIFO's are either filled or emptied.

Figure 23-1: The PCI1130 Block Diagram

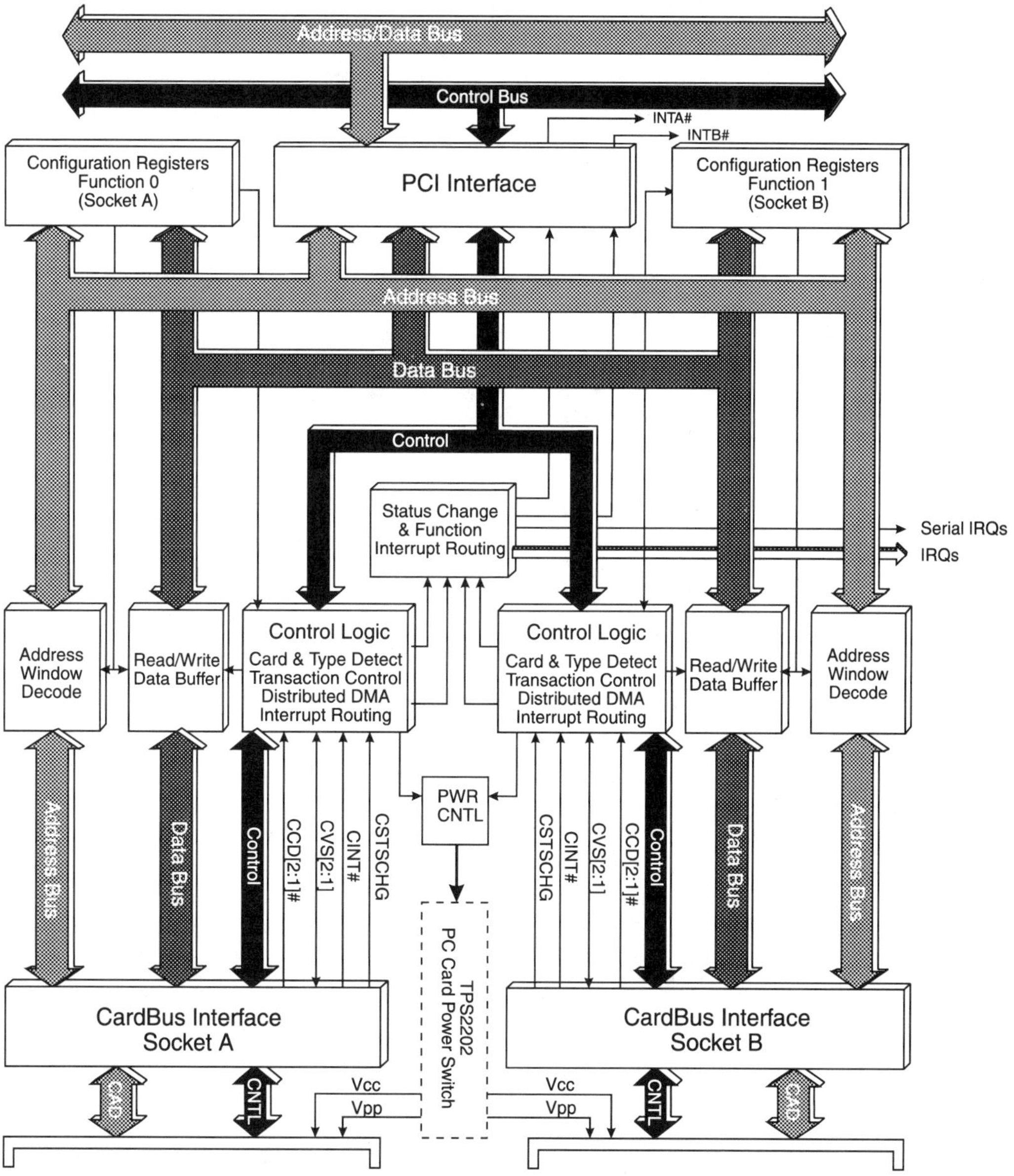

Figure 23-2: The PCI1130 Configuration Registers

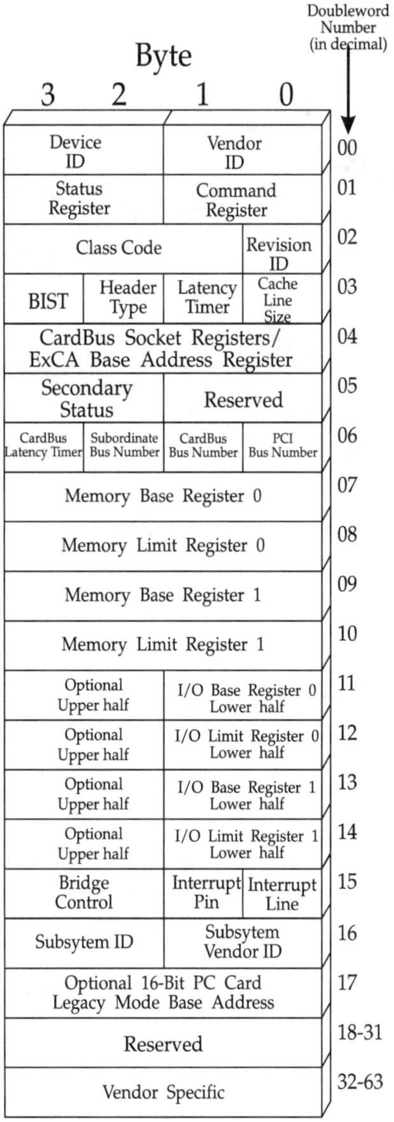

The PCI1130 supports mapping two groups of internal registers into system IO address space: the 16-Bit PC Card Legacy registers (index address and data registers); and the DMA Socket registers that support distributed DMA. The IO Base and Limit registers are programmed recognize transactions to be forwarded to the targeted socket and PC Card.

The only internal registers that are memory-mapped are the CardBus/ExCA registers. These registers are mapped into a 4KB-aligned memory address range for each socket. The Memory Base and Limit registers are positively decoded to determine if a memory transaction is intended for the PC Card installed in the socket.

Note that the PCI interface supports the 2.1 latency requirements and ordering rules. In other words, the PCI1130 performs the required delayed transactions and satisfies the transaction ordering that is specified by the PCI specification. For information related to PCI device latency requirements and ordering rules, refer to MindShare's *PCI System Architecture* book (published by Addison-Wesley).

Socket Interfaces

The PCI1130 includes two PC Card socket interfaces that are compliant with the PC Card Standard ('95 release). As required by the PC Card Standard, the bridge detects the presence of PC Cards and performs an interrogation to determine the type of card installed and the initial Vcc that should be applied (Chapter 5 on page 49 details this process). The card type and Vcc requirements are reflected in the socket status registers defined by the PC Card Standard. The bridge automatically configures the interface to provide either a 16-bit memory-only interface or a CardBus interface. The following sections provide additional information about each type of interface.

CardBus Interface

A 33MHz CardBus clock signal is supported, permitting fast transactions. The CardBus bridge also performs all of the support functions required (e.g., including pull-ups, pull-downs, arbitration, and clock control, etc.).

A major function of the bridge is to monitor transactions initiated by the CardBus card and perform an inverse decode (i.e., inverse from the decode performed on the primary side of the bridge to determine if the PC Card is targeted) to determine if the transaction is targeted to a device residing on the PCI side of the bridge. If a CardBus read transaction is for a PCI device, the bridge latches the transaction and signals a retry to the CardBus card. The bridge then requests use of the PCI bus and, when granted, initiates the read over the PCI bus. When the transaction completes from the PCI target, the FIFO will contain the information requested by the CardBus card. When the CardBus card retries the access, the data is passed from the FIFO to the card. The bridge also posts writes into the FIFO when a CardBus card attempts a write transaction targeted for the PCI side of the bridge.

The CardBus socket interface logic supports the standard socket status registers and the control register specified by the PC Card Standard and provides additional vendor-specific registers. Table 23-1 lists the Yenta registers supported. The offset specified is from the base address specified by the CardBus Socket Base Address register within the configuration header. Table 23-2 lists the vendor-specific registers and their locations within the configuration address space.

Table 23-1: CardBus Socket Interface Registers

Socket Register Name	Offset
Socket Event Register	00h
Socket Mask Register	04h
Socket Present State Register	08h
Socket Force Event Register	0Ch
Socket Control Register	10h
Reserved	14-1Fh
Socket Power Management Register	20h

Table 23-2: Vendor-Specific Socket Interface Registers

Socket Register Name	Offset
Retry Status Register	90h
Card Control Register	91h
Device Control Register	92h
Buffer Control Register	93h

16-Bit PC Card Interface

The bridge provides complete backward compatibility with the ExCA legacy programming model. The 16-bit interface is configured initially as a memory-only interface, powered to either 5.0vdc or 3.3vdc as dictated by the VS1# and VS2# interface pins. This permits the PC Card's CIS to be accessed to determine the card type and socket interface that it requires (i.e., memory, IO, or DMA).

The bridge provides compatibility with the Yenta bridge definition. The intended use of the legacy register support is to provide backward compatibility for existing CS and SS. However, legacy CS and SS are not compatible with CardBus cards.

Interrupt Routing

The PCI1130 provides a variety of PC Card interrupt routing mechanisms:

- Direct ISA IRQ routing
- PCI interrupt routing (INTA# and/or INTB#)
- Serialized IRQ routing

Each socket may have two separate interrupts that need to be routed to the host system's interrupt controller: the function interrupt and the status change interrupt. Function interrupts are reported via the socket interrupt pin (CINT# for CardBus and IREQ# for 16-bit cards). Status change interrupts are reported via the CSTSCHG pin for CardBus and STSCHG# for 16-bit cards. Either of these interrupt types can be routed to the interrupt controller via any of the three mechanisms listed above.

Figure 23-3 on page 372 illustrates the interrupt routing possibilities provided by the PCI1130. Note that some of the interrupt pins are shared with other functions. The pins that have dual functionality are:

- IRQ3/PCI INTA# output
- IRQ4/PCI INTB# output
- IRQ9/Serial IRQ output
- IRQ15/Ring Indicator output

Figure 23-3: The PCI1130 Interrupt Routing Capabilities

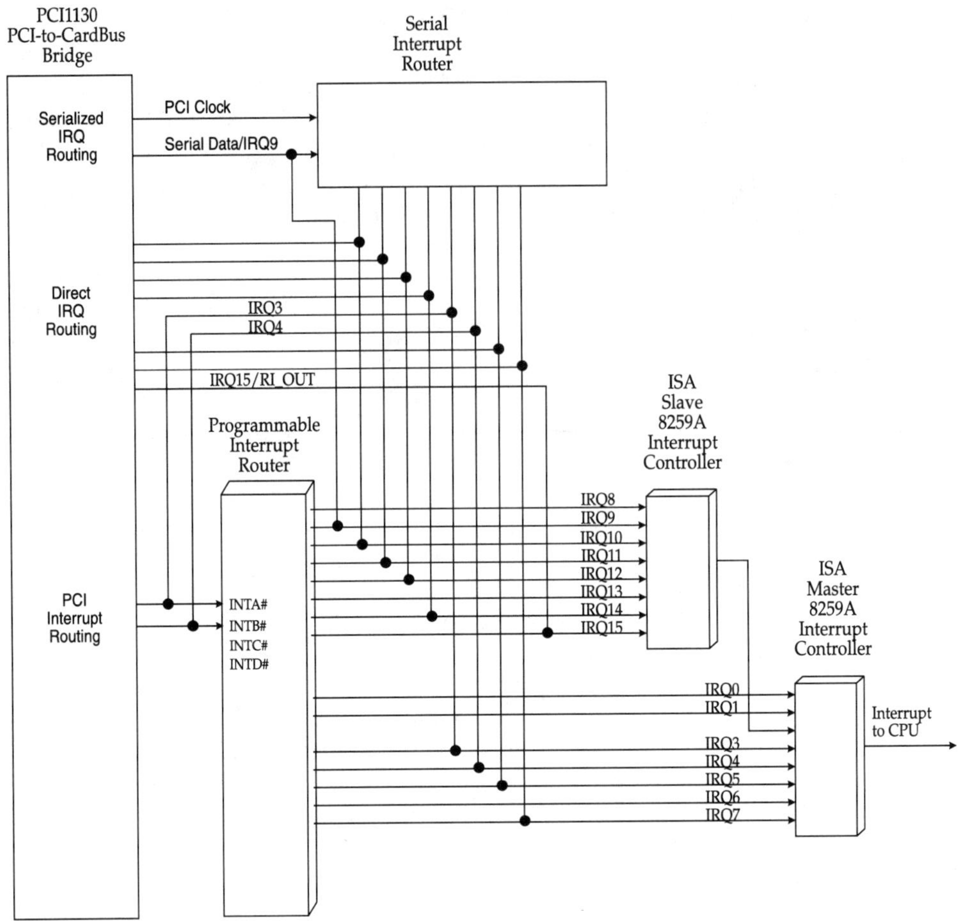

PCI Interrupt Routing

The Card Control register within the device-specific configuration address space controls PCI interrupt routing for the socket interface. Table 23-3 on page 373 lists the bits used to enable and control interrupt routing via the PCI interrupt pins.

Table 23-3: Card Control Register Bit Assignment

Bit	Description
0	**Interrupt Pending** bit. Set when a function interrupt from the PC Card has been detected. Writing a one clears the interrupt.
1	**SpeakerOut/Suspend Enable**. When set, the Audio, or SPKR#, signal from the PC Card is transferred to the SPKROUT pin of the PCI1130.
2	Reserved
3	**CSTSCHG (STSCHG#) Routing Enable**. When set, the status change pin from the PC Card is routed to the corresponding PCI interrupt pin (INTA# for socket A, or INTB# for socket B). When this bit is cleared, status change-to-PCI interrupt routing is disabled.
4	**Function Interrupt Routing Enable**. When set, the function interrupt from the PC Card is routed to the corresponding PCI interrupt pin. When cleared, function interrupt-to-PCI interrupt routing is disabled.
5	**PCI Interrupt Enable**. Enables/disables the corresponding PCI interrupt. When set, PCI interrupts are enabled.
6	**ZOOM Video Mode Enable**.
7	**Ring Indicator Output Enable**. Configures the IRQ15/RI_OUT pin for the RI_OUT function.

Direct IRQ Routing

The PCI1130 includes ten IRQ terminals for routing interrupts directly to the inputs of the interrupt controller. The IRQ lines supported include: IRQ3, IRQ4, IRQ5, IRQ7, IRQ9, IRQ10, IRQ11, IRQ12, IRQ14, and IRQ15. Direct ISA interrupt routing is enabled via the Device Control register. When ISA interrupt routing is enabled, the actual routing is controlled via the legacy mode registers. Table 23-4 on page 374 defines the bits within the Device Control register. These interrupts can be used for either status change interrupt delivery or for PC Card function interrupt delivery.

Table 23-4: Device Control Register Bit Assignment

Bit	Description
0	Reserved
2:1	**Interrupt Mode Enable.** The following bit combinations determine which interrupt routing mode will be used. Note that one of the interrupt modes below must be selected to prior to enabling PCI interrupts: • 00b = No interrupt enabled • 01b = ISA mode enabled (direct IRQ routing) • 10b = Serialized interrupt mode enabled • 11b = Reserved
3	Reserved
4	Reserved
5	3v Socket Capable Force bit.
6	5v Socket Capable Force bit
7	Reserved

Serialized IRQ Routing

The serialized interrupt delivery mechanism uses a single terminal to communicate all interrupt status information to the host interrupt controller. The protocol sends a serial packet of interrupt information that begins with a start cycle and ends with a stop cycle. The transfer is synchronous to the PCI clock and permits all IRQ lines from IRQ0 - IRQ15 to be transferred, along with SMI (transferred in the IRQ2 position), and the IOCHK interrupt for NMI delivery.

Serialized interrupt delivery, like direct IRQ delivery, is enabled via the Device Control register. Note that these two modes are mutually exclusive. Once serialized interrupt routing is enabled, the programmer must select the IRQ line that the function interrupt and/or status change interrupt is to be assigned to.

Distributed DMA

The PCI1130 complies with the PC Card Standard mechanism for supporting DMA capability for 16-bit PC Cards. The socket interface can be configured to support DMA. However, the ISA DREQn and DACKn# lines are not supported by the PCI1130. In lieu of the actual ISA signals, the bridge supports distributed DMA via the PCIway, revision 6.0 specification. At the time of this writing the Distributed DMA specification had not been publicly released.

ZOOM Video Port

The PCI1130 also supports the Zoomed Video (ZV) port. At the time of this writing, ZOOM video was a proposal pending approval by PCMCIA. The ZV Port is used in conjunction with a 16-bit PC Card interface and is enabled via bit 6 of the Card Control register (See Table 23-3 on page 373). When this bit is set, address lines A25:4 of the PC Card interface are placed into a high impedance state. These lines (19 for video and 3 for audio) can be used to transfer video and audio information directly to the video and audio controllers. Note that A3:0 remain active and can be used to access the configuration registers.

The Zoomed Video (ZV) Port is a direct connection between a PC Card and a VGA controller/audio DAC. The ZV Port allows a PC Card to write video data directly to an input port of a graphics controller such as the VGA and audio data directly to a digital-to-analog converter.

The ZV Port provides a low-cost solution that allows video data on a PC Card to be transferred directly into the VGA frame buffer. The video and audio data is transferred real-time without the need for the PC Card to buffer data. The PC Card sends audio data to the host system using Pulse Code Modulation (PCM). The audio data is transferred using the serial I2S format. The audio circuitry in the host system is primarily a pulse code modulated (PCM) D-to-A converter (DAC). Since video data is transferred via a dedicated bus, high throughput is achieved without the need to implement costly bus mastering capability and eliminates the latency problems associated with gaining control of the system bus.

Power Control

Power to the socket is controlled by software via the Socket Control register. When a legal Vcc or Vpp is requested by PCMCIA software, the PCI1130 chip uses a synchronous serial protocol to communicate with the TI TPS2202 PCMCIA socket power switch. The TPS2202 can independently control both Vcc and Vpp to two separate sockets. A three-wire bus consisting of a data line, a clock line, and a latch line comprise the transfer mechanism. Power information is encoded on the data line such that an 8-bit serial transmission can specify Vpp and Vcc settings for both sockets simultaneously.

The TPS2202 clock signal is derived from the PCI clock divided by 36. This clock runs only when sending the power information to the TPS 2022.

Appendix A—CardBus Signaling Environment

Introduction to CardBus Signaling

CardBus employs a 33MHz synchronous transfer mechanism based on the PCI bus. The primary difference between the PCI environment and CardBus is that CardBus must perform the transfer via a 68 pin connector, whereas PCI employs 108 pins (including many additional Vcc and Ground connections). Problems arise in the CardBus environment when attempting to perform high speed transfers across the 68-pin PCMCIA connector because the connector was never intended for switching 36 or more signals at a 33MHz rate.

PCI Signaling Method

The PCI bus is typically unterminated and uses wavefront reflections to its advantage. Output buffers are designed to create a fast edge rate that switches the bus half way to the required high or low voltage. As the resulting wave propagates down the bus and reflects off the unterminated end, the returning reflection doubles the amplitude of the incident wave. Each device along the bus detects Vih as the reflection returns to the source driver. The driver's low impedance absorbs the returning wavefront. Note that the driver is in the middle of its switching range during the propagation time.

CardBus Signaling Method

CardBus sockets must also support 16-Bit PC Cards, necessitating a point-to-point connection between each CardBus card and the bridge. The limited numbers of ground and Vcc pins create severe $\Delta i/\Delta t$ noise problems. As a result, CardBus cannot tolerate the switching characteristics of the PCI buffers.

To reduce these noise problems, several techniques have been employed:

- A shrouded connector has been designed to provide additional grounding.
- CardBus buffers are designed with slew rate control to obtain slower rise times, thereby eliminating transmission line characteristics (reflections).
- A 3.3vdc or lower switching voltage is required to offset the effects of slower rise times (PCI permits 5.0vdc switching).
- Universal buffers must be employed that support 5vdc and 3.3vdc for 16-bit PC Cards.
- To control skew, use of reflected-wave switching (only for the clock).

In summary, unlike PCI, the CardBus interface employs incident-wave switching for the interface signals, but uses reflected-wave switching for the CardBus clock. The following sections provide basic information on these signal characteristic.

Clock Timing

The CardBus Standard specifies that CardBus cards sample their inputs on the rising-edge of the CardBus clock signal. When a driver (the card or bridge) asserts or deasserts a signal, it is sampled on the next rising-edge of the CardBus clock. To ensure that valid signals are sampled, clock skew must be controlled.

Since CardBus uses a synchronous transfer mechanism governed by the rising edge of the CardBus clock, the slow edge rate buffers used for the interface signals would result in uncontrollable clock skew. The clock skew between the driver and receiver is specified to be no greater than 2ns. An edge rate of 0.25 v/ns could easily cause slew rates greater than 2ns. To gain control of clock skew, a fast rise time is required. CardBus uses a PCI-like reflected-wave design to deliver a crisp, monotonic clock edge on the clock. The CardBus card detects the incident wave and sees the reflection almost instantaneously, resulting in a sharp monotonic clock input to the card. The physical layout of the clock trace is very important to ensure that the skew remains within limits.

Figure A-1 on page 379 illustrates the basic timing parameters associated with CCLK. The minimum CCLK cycle time is 30ns (at 33MHz). The clock frequency can be changed as long as the clock edges remain clean and the T_cyc, T_high, and T_low minimums are not violated. The clock can also be stopped, but only in the low state. Note that compliance with the clock specification is measured at the component, not at the socket connector. The clock trace length for CCLK is 2.5 inches ±0.1 inches (63.5 ±2.54mm) and must be routed to only one load. Refer to the PC Card Electrical Specification for additional information.

Figure A-1: CCLK Timing Parameters

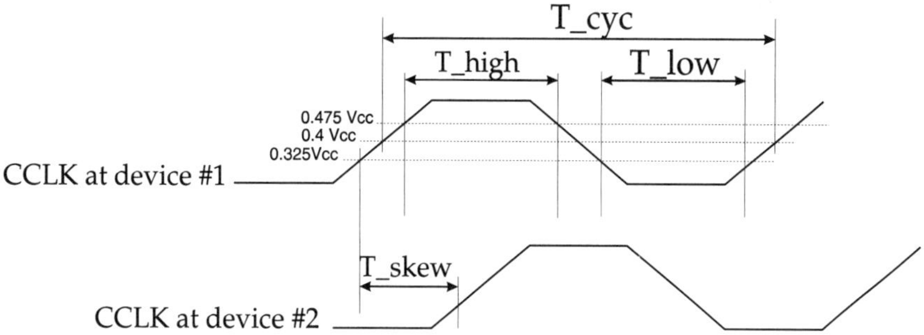

T_cyc is measured from one rising-edge to the next (when CCLK crosses the threshold).

minimum = 30ns (33MHz)
maximum = ∞

T_high is the CCLK high time

minimum = 12ns
maximum = none

T_low is CCLK low time.

minimum = 12ns
maximum = none

T_skew represents the delay from the rising-edge of the CCLK on one component to another.

minimum = none
maximum = 2ns

CCLK slew rate (rate of change in volts/ns):
minimum = 1V/ns
maximum = 4V/ns

Interface Signal Timing

The CardBus interface signals used in the synchronous signaling protocol require edge rate control to eliminate reflected waves. The rise time is specified to be between 0.25v/ns and 1.0v/ns. The rise and fall times specified provide a range that can deliver signal edge rates that meet timing requirements while keeping the Δi/Δt noise within reasonable bounds. Figure A-2 illustrates and lists the basic input timing parameters and Figure A-3 on page 381 illustrates and lists the basic output timing parameters.

Figure A-2: Input Timing Parameters

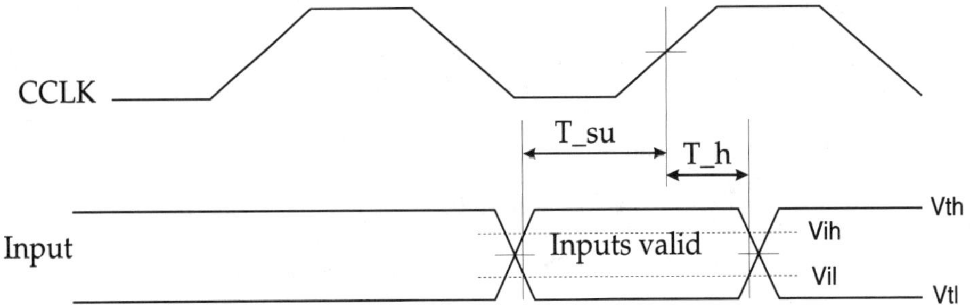

T_su is the setup time. Starts when signal crosses threshold to new state and lasts until the next rising-edge of CCLK crosses threshold.

minimum = 7ns
maximum = none.

T_h is the hold time.

minimum = 0ns
maximum = none.

Figure A-3: Output Timing Parameters

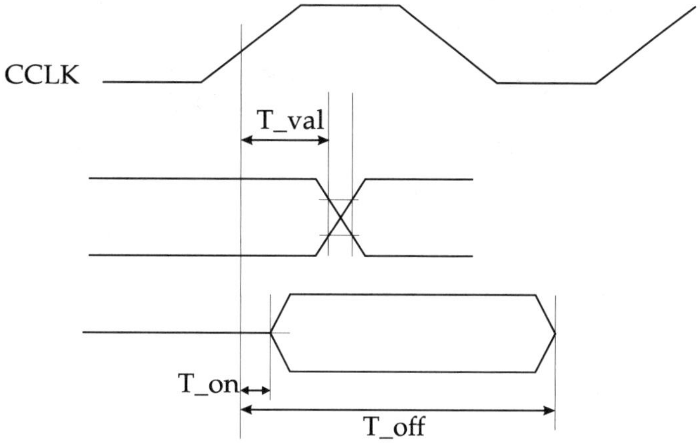

T_val, for all bussed signals, delay from point when CCLK crosses threshold (on rising-edge) to point where signal crosses threshold to new state.

minimum = 2ns
maximum = 18ns

T_on delay from float to point where signal crosses threshold to new state.

minimum = 2ns
maximum = none

T_off delay from float, plus driven period and back to float:

minimum = none
maximum = 28ns

Slew rate (rate of change in volts/ns):

minimum = 0.25v/ns
maximum = 1.0v/ns

Appendix B—PCI & CardBus Differences

Introduction

This list of differences comes from the PC Card Standard and is intended only as a guideline of issues that should be considered when designing silicon that can be used as CardBus and PCI devices.

Pin Definition Differences

The pinout differences between CardBus and PCI include the following items:

1. CardBus does not have an IDSEL signal. PCI uses IDSEL as a chip select for configuration read and configuration write cycles. Since CardBus PC Cards always operate in a point-to-point environment, they are always the intended target of configuration cycles on the interface. Therefore, a CardBus PC Card will always claim a configuration cycle.

   Common silicon components must implement IDSEL in order to meet PCI requirements. This signal should be strapped high (always asserted) when mounted on a CardBus PC Card. This will cause the component to be selected whenever a configuration cycle is executed on the CardBus interface.

2. CardBus does not have the SBO# or SDONE signals. PCI uses these optional pins to signal address snooping results to the target of a transaction. The target continues the access when CLEAN is signaled (SBO# deasserted and SDONE asserted) or terminates with retry when HITM is signaled.

   The CardBus adapter can take appropriate action on the system bus (e.g., terminate with retry) and on CardBus (e.g., discard read data, terminate write cycles) without informing the card of the snoop results. Therefore, CardBus does no implement these two signals.

Common silicon which implements SBO# and SDONE, but not CBLOCK#, must strap SBO# and SDONE high on CardBus PC Cards so the component will always see the CLEAN state. IF CBLOCL# is implemented, SBO# an SDONE must be disabled. Strapping them high causes CLEAN to be signaled during the address phase of a write to a locked resource. This causes the component to conclude the write cycle is a writeback of a dirty cache line so it would override the locked status and complete the write. If you intend to implement a function with SBO#, SDONE, and LOCK#, please contact the PCI SIG for assistance in defining this disable mechanism.

3. CardBus does not have the 64-bit bus extension pins. Because of pin constraints in the 68-pin connector, CardBus does not support AD[63:32], C/BE[7:4]#, REQ64#, ACK64#, and PAR64. If common silicon implements these signals, the REQ64# signal must be pulled up to Vcc on CardBus cards so that it is put in 32-bit mode during reset. Floating inputs on AD[63:32], C/BE[7:4]#, PAR64, and ACK64# must be dealt with during runtime. This could be done by enabling input "keepers" when REQ64# is seen high during reset.

4. CardBus does not have the JTAG pins. Because of pin constraints in the 68-pin connector, CardBus does not support IEEE 1149.1 "Standard Test Access Port and Boundary Scan Architecture" across the interface. If the capability is not needed in CardBus, common silicon must tie TRST# and TCK to ground and leave TDI, TDO, and TMS unconnected.

   If the scan chain is to be used on the CardBus card, then the common silicon component and card design must provide a means for manipulating it across the CardBus interface. In general, this will involve incorporating BIST circuitry and using the BIST register defined in configuration space.

5. CardBus has a CSTSCHG pin. CardBus uses CSTSCHG to signal battery low/dead, write protect, ready, and remote wakeup conditions. Common silicon must implement this pin if the functionality is desired for CardBus. It will be a no-connect, or available as a sideband signal when attached to the motherboard, in the PCI environment.

6. CardBus has a CAUDIO signal. Common silicon requiring access to the speaker must implement this signal. Usage of this silicon in the PCI environment requires either a local speaker, a connection to the system speaker via a cable from PCI add-in boards, or a sideband signal when mounted on the motherboard.

7. CardBus has a CCLKRUN# signal. Common silicon desiring a hardware mechanism to start the clock, or continue it for a period of time, must implement this function. CCLKRUN# should be strapped low when the PCI environment doesn't support this capability.

8. CardBus only has one interrupt (CINT#) pin. PCI allows interrupts to be signaled using up to four INTx# pins. Due to pin constraints, CardBus requires using a single interrupt signal, CINT#. If common silicon chooses to implement multiple INTx# pins, they must be wire-OR'd together (shorted) when mounted on a CardBus card.

9. CardBus does not provide exceptions to supporting CPERR# an CSERR#. Common silicon must implement the CPERR# and CSERR# pins along with the associated parity generation and checking logic.

Functional Differences

The functional differences between CardBus and PCI are:

1. CardBus doesn't support PCI's Interrupt Acknowledge command. This command is intended for the target responsible for interrupt handling duties. Such hardware cannot reside on a CardBus PC Card due to the dynamic insertion/removal nature of PC Cards. A common silicon component, which requires this capability in the PCI environment, must implement this command This will not cause problems because the command will never occur on CardBus. Also, CardBus will never assign a different meaning to the bit encoding for this command.

2. CardBus doesn't support PCI's Dual address cycle (DAC) command. CardBus does not address the issue of 64-bit addressing although the intention is to add it later. Common silicon that could benefit from this command (i.e., bus masters) should implement it. Although the command has no meaning on the CardBus interface based on the present specification, CardBus will never assign a different meaning to the bit encoding for this command.

3. CardBus doesn't address ignoring byte enables when the target determines cacheability. In PCI, targets which determine cacheability (e.g., memory controllers) must ignore the byte enables and return all bytes when the access is cacheable. An example for Intel Architecture systems is a memory controller telling the CPU that the access is cacheable via the KEN# signal. This capability does not exist across the CardBus interface.

This has no impact on common silicon. Even if a function existed, which could signal cacheability information to the CPU and had use in the CardBus environment, the CPU would never use the non-requested bytes returned from CardBus cards. This is because the cacheability indication mechanism will never exit the card.

4. CardBus imposes additional usage rules on CBLOCK#. CardBus PC Cards, like PCI add-in boards, are targeted for usage across multiple CPU architectures. These differing architectures place different constraints on which transactions can be guaranteed to be atomic. CardBus has additional usage rules for CBLOCL# to clarify how exclusive accesses can be guaranteed across differing architectures. These rules apply only to software developers. The operation of CardBus's CBLOCK# pin is identical to PCI's LOCK# pin. Therefore, there is no impact to the design of common silicon.

   PCI also requires locking a minimum of 16 bytes, naturally aligned, while CardBus only requires locking what was read. Common silicon must lock at least 16 bytes when lock is established.

5. CardBus does not support PCI's Configuration Mechanism #2. PCI requires usage of mechanism #1 for new designs, but defined a second mechanism for existing designs. The components which implemented configuration mechanism #2 do not have any use on CardBus PC Cards (e.g., host bridges for PCI). In general, functions which have applicability on PCI and CardBus will never generate configuration cycles.

   However, if common silicon ever does need to generate configuration cycles, it must be designed to use mechanism #1.

6. CardBus requires parity checking and reporting without exception. CardBus does not allow PCI's exceptions for functions which "never deal with or contain or access any data which represents permanent or residual system or application state, e.g., human interface and video/audio devices." Therefore, all common silicon must implement the CPERR# and CSERR# pins along with the associated parity checking and reporting logic for address and data.

7. CardBus's CSTSCHG capability requires registers in memory space. The implementation of CSTSCHG requires providing the Event, Mask, Force, and Present Value registers. These registers reside in memory. Common silicon which implements the CSTSCHG capabilities for CardBus must implement these registers and indicate the need for address space in the

appropriate manner (PCI = base address register in configuration space, CardBus = base address register and the CISTPL_CFTABLE_CB and CISTPL_BAR tuples). A unique base address register is not required for these registers, other memory requirements may be included as appropriate.

8. CardBus does not require cards to drive CAD[31:0], CC/BE[3:0]#, and CPAR when CGNT# is asserted but REQ# isn't. CardBus doesn't allow cards to be designated the default owners of an idle interface. However, PCI requires any bus master to assume such ownership when directed. Therefore, common silicon must be designed to drive these signals when CGNT# is asserted but CREQ# isn't. Since this condition will never occur on CardBus, there is no conflict.

Electrical Differences

The electrical differences between CardBus and PCI are:

1. CardBus requires special slew rate controlled buffers. CardBus cannot tolerate the switching characteristics of PCI buffers due to the limited number of ground pins on the connector. Further, the slew rate controlled buffers typically offered by ASIC houses do not provide enough edge rate control to meet the CardBus requirements. Therefore, common silicon must do one of the following:

   a.) Incorporate dual mode buffers (PCI + CardBus modes) and mechanism to enable the appropriate mode. Note that the primary difference between these two modes is the slew rate control. Therefore, the difference in the buffer's modes could be as simple as reducing or disabling the pre-driver for CardBus.

   b.) Series terminate each line to get acceptable $\Delta i/\Delta t$ characteristics. These resistors must be located very close to the interface component on the card so that signals being driven by the adapter are not affected.

   c.) Add inductance or resistance to the Vcc and GND paths to pull up of pull down the buffer's supply rails during transitions. This reduces the edge rate by making it a function of the RC time constant of the Vcc or GND supply. the rate can be controlled by adjusting the value of resistance/inductance and the amount of current switched through it.

   CardBus uses the same DC characteristics as PCI, but the loading is reduced. Therefore, input buffer behavior is identical between the two standards. Only in the AC characteristics do differences emerge where CardBus simply specifies a rise/fall time since it operates in a lumped load regime rather than PCI's transmission line environment.

2. CardBus does not support the 5V signaling environment. Common silicon must be designed to operate in the 3.3V signaling environment with Vcc = 3.3V. It may additionally be designed to accept Vcc = 5.0V for the PCI domain.

3. Timing differences. CardBus is a point-to-point environment so there is no need to distinguish between CREQ#, CGNT#, and the other signals with respect to timings. The timing differences are:

   a.) Tval is measured at the DC Vih and Vil values instead of PCI's 0.4(Vcc) to cleanly specify what constitutes a valid signal in the CardBus environment.

   b.) CardBus specifies the minimum time from CCLK stable to the deassertion of CRST# as 100 clocks instead of PCI's 100 microseconds. This change better defines reset requirements with any speed clock. Common silicon must be fully reset in 100 clock cycles.

4. CardBus assigned pins on the connector in a different sequence than PCI. This was done to better align CardBus signals with the PCMCIA 2.0 and 1.0/JEIDA 4.1 and 4.0 publication's cards since the adapter must configure the interface for any of the three protocols. The signals affected are CSERR#, LK, CRST#, and CREQ#. The impact is to the PC Card of PCI add-in board, since the routing of a common silicon component will require traces crossing each other. The component designer needs to choose the environment in which these crossovers will occur (CardBus vs. PCI).

5. CardBus specifies a maximum current immediately following power up or reset. The parameter Icc (CIS) gives CardBus PC Card sockets a guarantee that they can power up any CardBus PC Card and read the CIS without causing a power fault condition by putting too much load on the battery. PCI has no equivalent parameter. Since this may extend beyond the common silicon component, the designer must ensure that cards using their component will not exceed this value when reading the CIS or reading and writing configuration space.

Configuration Space Differences

The Configuration space differences between CardBus and PCI are:

1. CardBus does not define all the configuration space fields defined by PCI. Due to dynamic insertion/removal and generic configuration concerns, CardBus chose to provide all configuration information in the CIS rather than using PCI's predefined header region in configuration space. As a result, CardBus functions must provide configuration information in a different manner than PCI. This means that:

   a.) Common silicon must implement the 16-byte header required by PCI including Vendor ID, Device ID, Class code, and Revision ID.

   b.) Common silicon must implement PCI's Max_Lat, Min_GNT, and Interrupt line registers if the function requires them for PCI.

   c.) The base address registers must be encoded with size information as defined by PCI. These fields and encodings are not used by CardBus so there are no implications with respect to common silicon.

2. Certain Command register fields are not optional for CardBus. Both PCI and CardBus define a Command register in configuration space. CardBus requires common silicon to implement the following fields:

   a.) Memory Space must be implemented on all cards which support I/O space because I/O space must be mappable into memory space.

   b.) Parity Error Response must always be implemented because CardBus does not allow the exceptions provided by PCI.

   c.) SERR# Enable must always be implemented because CardBus does not allow the exceptions provided by PCI.

3. Certain Status register fields are not optional for CardBus. Both PCI and CardBus define a Status register in configuration space. CardBus requires common silicon to implement the following fields:

   a.) Signaled System Error must always be implemented because CardBus requires all functions to be able to check and report address and data parity errors.
   b.) Detected Parity Error must always be implemented because CardBus

requires all functions to be able to check and report address and data parity errors.

4. CardBus uses four bytes in the configuration space header for a CIS pointer. Common silicon must implement these bytes with a pointer to the beginning of the CIS structure (see the Metaformat and Electrical Specification for details). In addition, if the CIS cannot fit in configuration space along with PCI's driver dependent information, common silicon must locate it in memory or expansion ROM space and provide a mechanism(s) to access it (i.e., base address registers and a data path). Unique base address registers are not required.

5. CardBus requires a memory-mapped base address register whenever I/O space is used by the card.
   CardBus requires all I/O space to be mappable into memory space. This means that I/O base address registers must be accompanied with a memory base address register. Therefore, common silicon must implement this companion memory base address register.

Software Driver Differences

If a common software driver is to be developed, the following differences must be recognized:

1. CardBus imposes additional interrupt handling requirements. CardBus defined the INTR field in the Event, Mask, Force, and Present Value registers so Card Services could do end of interrupt (EOI) processing in environments which don't provide a system-level interrupt handler. This created a standard mechanism for clearing interrupts. Common silicon must implement this field in the above registers. In PCI, the function's device driver must either use this standard mechanism to clear interrupts or a means to disable it and enable the desired proprietary method must be provided.

2. CardBus requires drivers to have a Card Services interface including tuple comprehension. This means that a "common driver" must implement the Card Services interface. When implemented in a PCI system, the driver must first check for its function's existence on PCI. If it doesn't find anything, or if it can handle more than one instance, it must then register with Card Services. If Card Services doesn't exist in the system, determined with the GetCardServiceInfo call, the driver may disable its Card Services interface an proceed knowing no PC Card will show up.

Upon finding its function, the driver must proceed with completing the configuration in the appropriate manner—tuple traversal for CardBus vs. configuration space interrogation for PCI.

3. Common drivers must handle dynamic insertion and removal events. The driver must allow for the fact that its function may disappear or appear at any time and must not treat it as a catastrophic error condition.

4. PCI specifies that expansion ROM code is never executed in place. The only software usage model that PCI defines is where ROM code is always copied from the ROM device to RAM and executed out of RAM. There is nothing in the architecture which prohibits execute-in-place (XIP) operation. CardBus allows this ROM code to be executed-in-place.
   When XIP capability becomes a part of CardBus, a common software driver, which wants to take advantage of XIP, must deal with differences between the two usage models (copy to RAM for PCI vs. XIP for CardBus). Details of what these differences are cannot be determined until the capability is defined.

Appendix C—References

The following is a list of recommended reference materials:

Title	Author	Publisher	ISBN #
ISA System Architecture	MindShare	Addison-Wesley	0-201-40996-8
PCI System Architecture	MindShare	Addison-Wesley	0-201-40993-3
PCMCIA System Architecture	MindShare	Addison-Wesley	0-201-40991-7
The PCMCIA Developer's Guide	Mori and Welder	Sycard Technology	0-9640342-1-2
PCMCIA Software Developer's Handbook	Beatty, Kipisz, and Moore	Peer-to-Peer Communications	1-57398-010-2
PC Card Standard (1995 Release)	Copyright — PCMCIA/JEIDA Phone: 408 433-CARD (2273) Internet: office@pcmcia.org		

Appendix D—Glossary

Access Latency. The amount of time that expires from the moment a bus master requests the use of the PCI bus until it completes the first data transfer of the transaction.

AD Bus. The PCI address/data bus carries address information during the address phase of a transaction and data during each data phase.

Address Ordering. During PCI burst memory transfers, the initiator must indicate whether the addressing sequence will be sequential (also referred to as linear) or will use cacheline wrap ordering of addresses. The initiator uses the state of AD[1:0] to indicate the addressing order. During I/O accesses, there is no explicit or implicit address ordering. It is the responsibility of the programmer to understand the I/O addressing characteristic of the target device.

Address Phase. During the first clock period of a PCI transaction, the initiator outputs the start address and the PCI command. This period is referred to as the address phase of the transaction. When 64-bit addressing is used, there are two address phases.

Agents. Each PCI device, whether a bus master (initiator) or a target is referred to as a PCI agent.

Arbiter. The arbiter is the device that evaluates the pending requests for access to the bus and grants the bus to a bus master based on a system-specific algorithm.

Arbitration Latency. The period of time from the bus master's assertion of REQ# until the bus arbiter asserts the bus master's GNT#. This period is a function of the arbitration algorithm, the master's priority and system utilization.

Atomic Operation. A series of two or more accesses to a device by the same initiator without intervening accesses by other bus masters.

Base Address Registers. Device configuration registers that define the start address, length and type of memory space required by a device. The type of space required will be either memory or I/O. The value written to this register during device configuration will program its memory or I/O address decoder to detect accesses within the indicated range.

BIST. Some integrated devices (such as the i486 microprocessor) implement a built-in self-test that can be invoked by external logic during system start up.

Bridge. The device that provides the bridge between two independent buses. Examples would be the bridge between the host processor bus and the PCI bus, the bridge between the PCI bus and a standard expansion bus (such as the ISA bus) and the bridge between two PCI buses.

Bulk memory services. A category of card services used by memory client drivers to gain access and manage block memory transfers.

Bus Access Latency. Defined as the amount of time that expires from the moment a bus master requests the use of the PCI bus until it completes the first data transfer of the transaction. In other words, it is the sum of arbitration, bus acquisition and target latency.

Bus Acquisition Latency. Defined as the period time from the reception of GNT# by the requesting bus master until the current bus master surrenders the bus and the requesting bus master can initiate its transaction by asserting FRAME#. The duration of this period is a function of how long the current bus master's transaction-in-progress will take to complete.

Bus Idle State. A transaction is not currently in progress on the bus. On the PCI bus, this state is signalled when FRAME# and IRDY# are both deasserted.

Bus Lock. Gives a bus master sole access to the bus while it performs a series of two or more transfers. This can be implemented on the PCI bus, but the preferred method is resource locking. The EISA bus implements bus locking.

Bus Master. A device capable of initiating a data transfer with another device.

BVD1 and BVD2. Memory cards used to emulate disk drives must provide a battery to retain information, if they use volatile memory. These cards have two signals pins (BVD1 and BVD2 - battery voltage detect 1 and 2) that can be used to report a low battery warning or a dead battery indication to the system.

Call-back. The process used by card services to notify clients of events that they should respond to. The call-back calls a routine within the client driver used to handle the event notification.

Card detection. The process of recognizing that a PC Card has been inserted into a socket and notifying enabling software responsible for configuring the card.

Card information structure. Also called the CIS, this data structure is incorporated into PC Cards to characterize the function(s) contained within the card. The CIS consists of individual elements called tuples, each of which describes a given characteristic of the card. The CIS is typically mapped into attribute memory address space, but is sometimes implemented in common memory address space.

Card services. A collection of software functions based on the client server model that permits unified control to all PC Card sockets and related hardware. PC Card client drivers register with card services to obtain access to PC Cards and sockets.

CCD1# and CCD2#. The CardBus Card Detect (CD) pins signal that a card is fully inserted into a PC Card socket. When the HBA detects these pins asserted it notifies card services via an interrupts.

Central Resource Functions. Functions that are essential to operation of the PCI bus. Examples would be the PCI bus arbiter and "keeper" pullup resistors that return PCI control signals to their quiescent state or maintain them at the quiescent state once driven there by a PCI agent.

CIS. See Card information structure.

Claiming the Transaction. An initiator starts a PCI transaction by placing the target device's address on the AD bus and the command on the C/BE bus. All PCI targets latch the address on the next rising-edge of the PCI clock and begin to decode the address to determined if they are being addressed. The target that recognizes the address will "claim" the transaction by asserting DEVSEL#.

Class Code. Identifies the generic function of the device (for example, a display device) and, in some cases, a register-specific programming interface (such as the VGA register set). The upper byte defines a basic class type, the middle byte a subclass within the basic class, and the lower byte may define the programming interface.

Client driver. A client driver, also called an enabler, is responsible for configuring and enabling a PC Card when it is first inserted into a card socket. The client registers with and makes calls to card services provides the services necessary to fulfill the clients requests.

Client utility services. A category of card services used by client drivers to request that card services perform complex tasks that would otherwise require many low-level requests be made by the client driver.

Configuration process. The process involving reading and interpreting a PC Cards CIS entries to determine the type of function implemented by the PC Card and it configuration requirements.

Configuration registers. Configuration registers within a PC Card provide the ability to program it for a given configuration and obtain status information about the card.

Coherency. If the information resident in a cache accurately reflects the original information in DRAM memory, the cache is said to be coherent or consistent.

Commands. During the address phase of a PCI transaction, the initiator broadcasts a command (such as the memory read command) on the C/BE bus.

Configuration Access. A PCI transaction to read or write the contents of one of a PCI device's configuration registers.

Configuration Address Space. x86 processors possess the ability to address two distinct address spaces: I/O and memory. The PCI bus uses I/O and memory accesses to access I/O and memory devices, respectively. In addition, a third access type, the configuration access, is used to access the configuration registers that must be implemented in all PCI devices.

Configuration Header Region. Each functional PCI device possesses a block of two hundred and fifty-six configuration addresses reserved for implementation of its configuration registers. The format, or usage, of the first sixty-four locations is predefined by the PCI specification. This area is referred to as the device's configuration header region.

CVS1 and CVS2. Voltage sense pins defined for the low-voltage socket interface. These pins determine the initial Vcc level to apply to the socket.

Data Phase. After the address phase of a PCI transaction, a data item will be transferred during each data phase of the transaction. The data is transferred when both TRDY# and IRDY# are sampled asserted

Deadlock. A deadlock is a condition where two masters each require access to a target simultaneously, but the action taken by each will prevent the desired action of the other.

Digital Audio Waveform. The audio information output over a PC Card's SPEAKER# (SPKR#) pin to the host system's, used to drive the host system's speaker.

Disconnect. A very slow access target may force a disconnect between accesses to give other initiators a chance to use the bus. This is known as a disconnect. If the current access is quite long and will consume a lot of bus time, the target signals a disconnect, completes the current data phase, and the initiator terminates the transaction. The initiator then arbitrates for the bus again so that it may re-initiate the transaction, continuing the data transfer at the point of disconnection.

Enabler. The software responsible for detecting, configuring, and enabling a PC Card. Enablers are also called client drivers, because they interface to the PC Card environment via card services. Compare Point Enabler.

Event call-back. The mechanism used by card services to notify its clients (PC Card enablers) of specific events that have occurred at the PC Card and socket. The enablers are responsible for processing the events.

Event notification. Another term for a card services call-back. See Event call-back.

Event wakeup. An event that is external to the PC that stimulates a PC Card to perform some type of action (e.g. a remote call to a modem), when the system is in a power conservation state. The external event is used to "wake" the system so that it can respond.

ExCA. Exchangeable Card Architecture (or, ExCA) is a specification defined by Intel to promote interoperability of PC Cards between x86-based PCs. Note that ExCA has been renamed QuickSwap.

Exclusive Access. A series of accesses to a target by one bus master while other masters are prevented from accessing the device.

Expansion ROM. A device ROM related to a PCI function. This ROM typically contains the initialization code and possibly the BIOS and interrupt service routines for its associated device.

Functional PCI Devices. A PCI device that performs a single, self-contained function. Examples would be a video adapter or a serial port. A single, physical PCI component might actually contain from one to eight PCI functions.

Host/PCI Bridge. A device that provides the bridge between the host processor's bus and a PCI bus. The bridge provides transaction translation in both directions. It may also provide data buffering and/or a second-level cache for the host processor.

Idle State. See the definition for the Bus Idle State.

Incident-Wave Switching. See the definition of Class I Driver.

Initiator. When a bus master has arbitrated for and won access to the PCI bus, it becomes the initiator of a transaction. It then starts a transaction, asserting FRAME# and driving the address and command onto the bus.

Interrupt Acknowledge. The host ix86 processor responds to an interrupt request on its INTR input by generating two, back-to-back interrupt acknowledge bus cycles. If the interrupt controller resides on the PCI bus, the host/PCI bridge translates the two cycles into a single PCI interrupt acknowledge bus cycle. In response to an interrupt acknowledge, the interrupt controller must send the interrupt vector corresponding to the highest priority device generating a request back to the processor.

Interrupt Controller. A device requiring service from the host processor generates a request to the interrupt controller. The interrupt controller, in turn, generates a request to the host processor on its INTR signal line. When the host processor responds with an interrupt acknowledge, the interrupt controller prioritizes the pending requests and returns the interrupt vector of the highest priority device to the processor.

Interrupt request. A request to the system that indicates that the I/O card needs servicing. The interrupt request ultimately calls the PC Card's interrupt service routine (or, ISR). The interrupt request is signaled via the card's IREQ# pin.

JEDEC. Acronym for Joint Electronics Device Engineering Council.

JEIDA. Acronym for Japanese Electronics Industry Development Association.

Level mode interrupts. A method of signaling interrupts to the host system. A PC Card using level mode interrupts causes an interrupt to be registered, or triggered, by asserting the IREQ# pin and keeping it low until the interrupt is cleared by the ISR.

Linear Addressing. If a PCI master initiates a burst memory transfer and sets AD[1:0] equal to a 00b, this indicates to the addressed target that the memory address should be incremented for each subsequent data phase of the transaction.

Master Abort. If an initiator starts a PCI transaction and the transaction isn't claimed by a target (DEVSEL# asserted) within five PCI clock periods, the initiator aborts the transaction with no data transfer.

Master Latency Timer. Each bus master must incorporate a Latency Timer, or LT. The LT benefits both the current bus master and any bus master that may request access to the PCI bus while the current bus master is performing a transaction. The LT ensures that the current bus master will not hog the bus if the PCI bus arbitrator indicates that another PCI master is requesting access to the bus. Looking at it from another point of view, it guarantees the current bus master a minimum amount of time on the bus before it must surrender it to another master.

Master-Initiated Termination. The LT count may have expired and the transaction continued without preemption by the arbitrator (removal of its grant) because no other PCI master required the bus. Another bus master may then request and be granted the bus while the current master still has a transaction in progress. Upon sensing the removal of its grant by the arbitrator, the current bus master must initiate transaction termination at the end of the current data transfer with the target. This is referred to as master-initiated termination.

Memory Read Command. The PCI memory read command should be used when reading less than a cache line from memory.

Memory Read Line Command. This PCI command should be used to fetch one complete cache line from memory.

Memory Read Multiple Command. This command should be used to fetch multiple memory cache lines from memory. When this command is used, the target memory device should fetch the requested cache line from memory. When the requested line has been fetched from memory, the memory controller should start fetching the next line from memory in anticipation of a request from the initiator. The memory controller should continue to prefetch lines from memory as long as the initiator keeps FRAME# asserted.

Memory Write Command. The initiator may use the PCI memory write or the memory write and invalidate command to update data in memory.

Memory Write and Invalidate Command. The memory write and invalidate command is identical to the memory write except that it transfers a complete cache line during the current transaction. The initiator's configuration registers must allow specification of the line size during system configuration. If, when snooping, the cache/bridge's write-back cache detects a memory write and invalidate issued by the initiator and has a snoop hit on a line marked as dirty, the cache can just invalidate the line and doesn't need to perform the flush to memory. This is possible because the initiator is updating the entire memory line and all of the data in the dirty cache line is therefor invalid. This increases performance by eliminating the requirement for the line flush.

Message. An initiator may broadcast a message to one or more PCI devices by using the PCI Special Cycle command. During the address phase, the AD bus is driven to random values and must be ignored. The initiator does, however, use the C/BE lines to broadcast the special cycle command. During the data phase, the initiator broadcasts the message type on AD[15:0] and an optional message-dependent data field over AD[31:16]. The message and data are only valid during the clock after IRDY# is asserted. The data contained in, and the timing of subsequent data phases is message dependent.

Multi-Function Devices. A physical PCI component may have one or more independent PCI functions integrated within the package. A component that incorporates more than one function is referred to as a Multi-Function Device.

Peripheral Component Interconnect (or PCI). Specification that defines the PCI bus. This bus is intended to define the interconnect and bus transfer protocol between highly-integrated peripheral adapters that reside on a common local bus on the system board (or add-in expansion cards on the PCI bus).

Physical PCI Device. See the definition of Functional PCI Devices.

Point-To-Point Signals. Signals that provide a direct interconnect between two PCI agents. An example would be the REQ# and GNT# lines between a PCI bus master and the PCI bus arbiter.

Posted-Write Capability. The ability of a device to "memorize" or post a memory write transaction and signal immediate completion to the bus master. As long as there is room in the posted-write buffer, this permits the bus master to complete memory writes with no wait states. After posting the write and signalling completion to the bus master, the device will then perform the actual memory write.

Preemption. Preemption occurs when the arbitrator removes the grant from one master and gives it to another.

Prefetching. Fetching a line of information from memory before a bus master requests it. If the master should subsequently request the line, the target device can supply it immediately. This shields the master from the slow access time of the actual target memory.

Primary Bus. The bus closest to the host processor that is connected to one side of an inter-bus bridge.

READY. An output pin from a memory card that indicates that it is ready for the next transaction. If deasserted, indicates that the memory card is busy performing a command and is not ready to receive the next transaction.

Reflected-Wave Switching. The output drivers commonly implemented in highly-integrated components fall into the class II category. They take advantage of the reflected-wave switching characteristic common to high-speed transmission lines and printed circuit traces in order to achieve the input logic thresholds. When a class II output driver transitions a signal line from a logic low to a high, the low-to-high transition is rather weak and only achieves half of the voltage change required to cross the logic threshold. This transition wavefront is transmitted along the trace and is seen sequentially by the input of each device connected to the line. When the wavefront gets to the end of the transmission line, it is reflected back along the trace, effectively doubling the voltage change and thereby boosting the voltage change past the logic threshold. As the wave passes each device's input, the new valid logic level is detected.

Registration. The process used by enablers to obtain the services of card services.

Reset. A socket interface pin used to reset the PC Card.

Reserved Bus Commands. Several of the PCI bus command codes are reserved for future use. Targets should ignore reserved bus commands.

Resource allocation. The process employed by a PC Card enabler and card services to determine if system resources are available to be assigned to the PC Card.

Resource Lock. The PCI bus implements a signal, LOCK#. It allows a master (a processor) to reserve a particular target for its sole use until it completes a series of accesses to the target. The master then indicates that it no longer requires exclusive access to the target. One of the nice features of the PCI bus is that it permits other masters to use the bus to access targets other than the locked target during the period that a master has locked access to a particular target.

Resource Management Services. A category of card services that used by a client driver to acquire system resources needed for configuring their card. When a client driver requests resource for their card, card services checks to verify that the requested resource is not being used by some other device within the system. Card services performs look-ups within its resource management table that contains the resources that are available for allocation to PC Cards.

Retry. If a target cannot respond to a transaction at the current time, it will signal "retry" to the initiator and terminate the transaction. The initiator will respond by ending the transaction and then retrying it later. No data transfer takes place during this transaction. An example of the need for a retry would be if the target is currently locked for exclusive access by another initiator.

Secondary Bus. The bus further from the host processor that is connected to one side of an inter-bus bridge.

Sideband Signals. A sideband signal is defined as a signal that is not part of the PCI bus standard and interconnects two or more PCI agents. This signal only has meaning for the agents it interconnects.

Single-Function Devices. A physical PCI component may have one or more independent PCI functions integrated within the package. A component that incorporates only one function is referred to as a Single-Function Device.

Socket interface. The electrical and mechanical interface for PC Cards.

Socket services. PCMCIA specific software that provides low-level routines needed to access a given implementation of HBA. Socket services consists of a collection of functions that are typically called by card services to access HBA registers.

Soft-Encoded Messages. The first two message codes, 0000h and 0001h, are defined as SHUTDOWN and HALT. Message code 0002h is reserved for Intel device-specific messages, while codes 0003h through FFFFh are reserved. Questions regarding the allocation of the reserved message codes should be forwarded to the PCI SIG. Also see the definition of Message.

Special Cycle Command. See the definition of Message.

Special Interest Group, or SIG. The PCI SIG manages the specification.

Status change events. PC card and socket events that reflect some change in the status of the PC Card. When a status change event occurs, the HBA generates an interrupt to signal card services of the event.

STSCHG#. Status change is an output signal from an I/O card to signal that a status change has occurred.

Subordinate Bus Number. The subordinate bus number configuration register in a PCI-to-PCI bridge (or a host/PCI bridge) defines the bus number of the highest-numbered PCI bus that exists behind the bridge.

Subtractive Decode. The PCI-to-expansion bus bridge is designed to claim many transactions not claimed by other devices on the PCI bus. If the bridge doesn't see DEVSEL# asserted by a PCI target within four PCI clock periods from the start of a transaction, the bridge may assert DEVSEL# to claim the transaction and then pass the transaction onto the standard expansion bus (such as ISA, EISA or the Micro Channel).

Target. The PCI device that is the target of a PCI transaction initiated by a PCI bus master.

Target Latency. Defined as the period of time until the currently-addressed target is ready to complete the first data phase of the transaction. This period is a function of the access time for the currently-addressed target device.

Target-Abort. If the target detects a fatal error or will never be able to respond to the transaction, it must signal a target-abort (using the STOP# signal). This will cause the initiator to end the transaction with no data transfer and no retry.

Target-Initiated Termination. Under some circumstances, the target may have to end a transfer prematurely. The following are some examples. A very slow access target may force a disconnect between accesses to give other initiators a chance to use the bus. This is known as a disconnect. If the current access is quite long and will consume a lot of bus time, the target signals a disconnect, completes the current data transfer, and the initiator terminates the transaction. The initiator then arbitrates for the bus again so that it may re-initiate the transaction, continuing the data transfer at the point of disconnection. If a target cannot respond to a transaction at the current time, it will signal retry to the initiator and terminate the transaction. The initiator will respond by ending the transaction and then retrying it. No data transfer takes place during this transaction. An example of the need for a retry would be if the target is currently locked for exclusive access by another initiator. If the target detects a fatal error or will never be able to respond to the transaction, it may signal a target-abort. This will cause the initiator to end the transaction with no data transfer and no retry.

Tuples. The name given to the elements within the CIS that describe characteristics of the PC Card.

Turn-Around Cycle. A turn-around cycle is required on all signals that may be driven by more than one PCI bus agent. This period is required to avoid contention when one agent stops driving a signal and another agent begins.

Type One Configuration Access. The type one access is used to configure a device on a lower-level PCI bus (in a system with hierarchical PCI buses).

Type Zero Configuration Access. The type zero access is used to configure a device on the PCI bus the configuration access is run on.

Vendor ID. Every PCI device must have a vendor ID configuration register that identifies the vendor of the device.

Vpp1 and Vpp2. Programming voltage pins defined for the socket interface.

Index

Technical Seminars

PCI System Architecture
PCI Software Environment
PCMCIA System Architecture
486 System Architecture
EISA System Architecture
CardBus System Architecture
Pentium System Architecture
Plug and Play System Architecture
ISA System Architecture
PowerPC Hardware Architecture
PowerPC Software Architecture

MindShare courses are presented at your site and are tailored to suit the needs of the audience.

To Contact MindShare

Internet: mindshar@interserv.com
Phone: (800) 633-1440 or (214) 231-2216
Fax: (214) 783-4715

MindShare, Inc.
2202 Buttercup Drive
Richardson, TX 75082

Note: New courses are constantly under development. Please contact MindShare for the latest course offerings.